Asian Higher Education

ASIAN HIGHER EDUCATION

An International Handbook and Reference Guide

Edited by
GERARD A. POSTIGLIONE
and
GRACE C. L. MAK

Foreword by Philip G. Altbach

Susan F. Semel, Advisory Editor

GREENWOOD PRESS
Westport, Connecticut • London

Library of Congress Cataloging-in-Publication Data

Asian higher education : an international handbook and reference guide
/ edited by Gerard A. Postiglione and Grace C. L. Mak ; foreword by Philip G.
Altbach.
    p.   cm.
    Includes bibliographical references and index.
    ISBN 0–313–28901–8 (alk. paper)
    1. Education, Higher—Asia—Handbooks, manuals, etc.
I. Postiglione, Gerard A., 1951– . II. Mak, Grace C. L.
LA1058.A82   1997
378.5—dc20   96–33072

British Library Cataloguing in Publication Data is available.

Library of Congress Catalog Card Number: 96–33072
ISBN: 0–313–28901–8

First published in 1997

Greenwood Press, 88 Post Road West, Westport, CT 06881
An imprint of Greenwood Publishing Group, Inc.

Printed in the United States of America

The paper used in this book complies with the
Permanent Paper Standard issued by the National
Information Standards Organization (Z39.48–1984).

10 9 8 7 6 5 4 3 2 1

CONTENTS

CONTENTS   vii

FOREWORD

Philip G. Altbach

Asia, home to a majority of the world's population as well as most of the fastest-growing academic systems, is centrally important in higher education.

Asian Higher Education provides up-to-date information and useful analyses of Asia's academic systems. It is, I think, difficult to generalize about the universities in as vast a region as covered in this book. Yet there seem to be a few common elements. The following trends can be seen in the region.

Expansion. Asia has perhaps the world's highest rate of growth in higher education. Academic systems continue, in much of the region, to expand. The proportion of the world's students in the Asian region continues to grow. In a few countries, such as Japan, expansion has ceased, and it has slowed in a number of other countries, such as India. But, in general, growth is more of the pattern in Asia than in other parts of the world.

Asian higher education is becoming more research-oriented. Countries that just a decade ago had to send students abroad for advanced study are now able to offer doctoral study at home. Many Asian nations, especially those with rapidly expanding economies, have started to invest heavily in research and development, and universities have been a central part of this expansion of research. There is a growing amount of scientific publication in Asia, and the past two decades have seen the establishment of journals and publishers in many scientific fields. Asia, with the exception of Japan, remains a peripheral part of the world's knowledge production system, but it is growing in importance. This importance is magnified by trends in Europe and North America to "disinvest" in higher education. The world balance of research production is slowly shifting toward Asia, but in most countries research continues to be well below world standards in terms of both quality and quantity.

Asia produces a significant portion of the world's scientists and engineers.

With some exceptions, its academic systems are more focused on science and engineering than are those of most Western countries. The better-developed Asian countries, such as China, India, and Japan, as well as the "tigers" (Hong Kong, Singapore, South Korea, and Taiwan) produce a large number of graduates in these fields.

Private higher education. More than any other region in the world, Asia has relied on private initiative to build and maintain higher education and to provide access to expanding populations. A large majority of students in such countries as Japan, South Korea, Taiwan, and the Philippines attend private institutions. Private higher education is growing in Indonesia, Malaysia, and elsewhere. In China and Vietnam, private institutions are being established, and state-run universities are being privatized. Reliance on private initiative has meant that higher education has received less government funding. It has also meant that research has not been greatly emphasized. In some Asian countries, private higher education institutions operate as profit-making companies.

Export of students and highly educated personnel. Asia is the largest exporter of students. The majority of the world's foreign students are from Asian countries, and they generally study in North America or Europe. There is also a significant amount of intra-Asian flow of students, with significant numbers studying in Japan, the Philippines, and India. Related to the flow of students is the fact that there is a significant flow of highly educated personnel from many Asian countries. India and China are large exporters of talent. Significant numbers also come from the Philippines, South Korea, Hong Kong, and Taiwan. There is some flow to other Asian countries, with Japan, Singapore, Hong Kong, and Malaysia as destinations, but the majority go to North America, Europe, and Australia, with smaller numbers going to the Middle East.

The world academic system. Asian universities are increasingly part of the world academic system, participating in flows of faculty and students, producing and consuming research, and in general operating in the mainstream of world knowledge. Asian countries remain somewhat peripheral in this system, depending on knowledge, research, and intellectual trends from outside the region. English is increasingly used as the regional medium of communication, and is of growing importance in higher education. Some countries, such as Singapore, use English exclusively in teaching and research. Others, including India, the other South Asian countries, and Malaysia, have a tradition of using English in higher education. Even Japan receives more knowledge from abroad than it exports. The situation is changing, but the trend nonetheless remains.

All academic systems in Asia are based on Western models. Even in countries such as China, India, Vietnam, and Japan, which have long intellectual traditions and distinguished traditional academic histories, contemporary higher education has utilized Western models. Formerly colonized areas, such as South Asia, Malaysia, the Philippines, and others, have inherited the institutional pattern of the former colonial power, although significant changes have been made since independence. Even Japan and Thailand, which never experienced colonial rule, chose Western models. China, semicolonized, had a variety of Western institutional models prior to 1949. The communist government turned to the Russian model, which remains largely in place today. The American academic model has, especially in the past two decades, become highly influential.

There are, of course, many important variations among Asian academic systems. This is not surprising in a region that has many variations in economic and human resources, historical development, and policy frameworks. Furthermore, despite the international nature of science and scholarship, universities remain national institutions, rooted in national traditions and realities, and shaped by local political, cultural, and economic circumstances. The tremendous variations in the region are often forgotten. In several countries, political circumstances have hindered the development of higher education, or have even damaged or destroyed what existed. Cambodia, Afghanistan, and Myanmar are tragic examples. Other academic systems remain underdeveloped and cannot compete internationally. Bangladesh and Pakistan illustrate this trend. The struggle between national circumstances and the growing internationalism of science and scholarship will help shape the Asian university of the twenty-first century. *Asian Higher Education* permits us to look carefully at circumstances and trends in key Asian countries.

PREFACE

Asian higher education is expanding rapidly at a time when many Asian societies are experiencing great economic as well as sociopolitical transition. The purpose of this reference book is to provide a sense of the situation and changes taking place in twenty Asian societies. The attempt is modest in that the volume seeks to provide an introduction to the problem of how Asian higher education systems react to internal societal demands as well as the demand of participation in the global economy. Nevertheless, the volume is representative of some of the major trends in Asian higher education, especially in East and South Asia. In the case of almost all chapters, the writer is a native of that country or society, and therefore, the perspective is more indigenous than one would find in most other volumes of this type. Moreover, a balanced gender perspective is promoted in that almost half the chapters have a woman contributor. We provided this reference for students and scholars of Asian higher education in the hope that it will be useful in gaining a better understanding of the complexities facing higher education in Asia.

Producing a handbook of Asian higher education is an enormous endeavor. Many academic book editors have become dependent on electronic mail to communicate with their volume contributors. While some of our contributors had access to the Internet, most did not. In fact, given the vast gap in development among Asian societies, it is not surprising that some of our contributors did not have access to a fax machine and so communication by mail was essential. Nevertheless, we have succeeded in bringing together many indigenous Asian scholars of higher education in one volume. Therefore, we thank our contributors for their hard work and patience. The special qualities of each contributor are evident in each chapter.

We would like to acknowledge Philip Altbach, whose experience in editing volumes on higher education is unsurpassed. We thank him for his insights in this project, as well as for a few excellent suggestions regarding contributors. Susan Semel's encouragement and consultation were extremely valuable.

The Comparative and International Education Society provided a forum for a panel that contributed to this volume, and through the Comparative Education Society of Hong Kong we were able to make contact with many Asian contributors to the volume. Finally, we thank Patrick Lam for his skillful assistance in the final stages of preparing the manuscript for production.

INTRODUCTION

Gerard A. Postiglione

GROWTH, DIVERSITY, AND CHANGE

The pace of change in Asian higher education is as much a function of rapid economic development as it is of sociopolitical transition. Asian economic growth, the fastest in the world, was 8.6 percent in 1994 (International Monetary Fund, 1995). Much of the population of Asia is experiencing a transition in emphasis from marxism to markets. The preference of many Asian nations for stability has not hindered major changes in higher education. Aside from expansion of enrollments, the relationship between universities and the state is changing, with increased calls for institutional autonomy, financial diversification, and quality control in higher education. Meanwhile, more traditional concerns—demands of different social groups for access, and of the state for positioning in the world economy—have also contributed to the transformation.

Asian higher education will continue to be distinguished by its size and diversity. Four Asian countries—Japan, South Korea, China (including Taiwan and Hong Kong), and India—represent close to 45 percent of the world's population and over 77 percent of the population of the whole of Asia. Their universities produced more than twice as many natural science and engineering bachelor's degrees as the United States in 1990 (Johnson, 1993). Asia has over thirty other countries, most with expanding higher education systems.

Marked diversity makes it virtually impossible to offer a concise overview of Asian higher education. Long entrenched but differing cultural traditions interweave with colonial heritage, multiethnic and religious states, socialist regimes and divided states, as well as some genuinely democratic systems. The giants of China and India have struggled to maintain their unique intellectual traditions in the face of Western intervention. Higher education in Hong Kong, Malaysia, and Singapore has preserved aspects of its British colonial heritage, as the Philippine universities have preserved American styles. Indonesian universities have completely shed Dutch colonial influence, as Korean universities have shed the Japanese colonial influence. Thailand and Japan have never been colonized; the latter has borrowed many innovations in higher education from Germany and the United States (Altbach and Selvaratnam, 1989).

CHALLENGES WITHIN CONTEXT

Despite much diversity, growth, and change, systems of higher education in Asia face strikingly similar challenges. All have budgets to balance, standards to maintain, faculties to satisfy, and demands from the public to meet. However, the contexts within which such challenges are faced differ greatly, and inevitably influence the way in which these common problems are addressed.

There is little argument in Asia over the role that higher education must play in economic development. However, that priority is compromised to a greater or lesser extent by social, political, and cultural contexts. Malaysia seeks to balance economic development with ethnic equity in higher education. Iran is hesitant to diminish the priority given by its universities to the religious goals of the revolution. China's universities have set a high priority on promoting economic development, but are not permitted to challenge the authority of the Communist Party. The new states of Central Asia born out of the collapse of the Soviet Union view higher education as a way of strengthening national identities. Leaders of Kabul University are content to merely resume classes, and have yet to work toward aiding a war-torn Afghan economy. Transition societies such as Laos and Cambodia aspire to having a few major universities as indicators to international investors of their potential for technological progress. In the Philippines, university leaders get well-deserved credit for having achieved great progress in giving women access to higher education, yet must continue to be sensitive to issues of access by ethnic groups and social classes. Japanese universities have long been viewed as a model for supporting economic development, but the impending crisis caused by a shrinking student age group has pushed it to consider broadening access to women and older students.

As literacy rates continue to increase and basic education becomes universal, expanding populations will inflate university enrollments, inevitably making Asia the largest higher education system in the world. Participation rates of the relevant age cohort in higher education are still generally low, but will not remain so for long. With the exception of Japan, the four tigers (Korea, Taiwan, Hong Kong, and Singapore), and the Philippines, most participation rates are under 10 percent. This will change, however, as economies continue to prosper in other Asian countries. China, with its massive population, has already decided to increase the percentage of the relevant age group in higher education from 3 percent to 8 percent between 1994 and 2000.

Nevertheless, even as these rates increase, Asia will continue to depend on North America and Europe for advanced degrees for some time to come; this in turn will further global academic integration and internationalization of the academic profession. In some specializations Asia might even take the lead, as professors of Asian origin in Western universities are attracted back to Asia by high salaries (Nash, 1994; Webster, 1994).

FINANCING THE EXPANSION

This rapid and massive expansion in participation rates will not be accompanied by proportionally increased budgets. Most Asian governments will only support a small group of national universities, leaving the rest to the private sector. Even national universities are increasingly expected to raise more of their own funds. Asian governments are notorious for their conservative levels of funding for educational institutions.

The achievement of Asian education becomes all the more remarkable when levels of government spending on education are compared across regions. Expressed as a percentage of GNP, governments in Asia spend less on education than governments in all other regions. This apparent paradox—high coverage despite relatively little financial effort—gives a first indication that as a determinant of education development, public policies in the sector are at least as important as the size of public spending. (Tan and Mingat, 1992:11)

In a 1990 sample of low- and middle-income countries in six world regions (plus the OECD countries), the World Bank noted that the two Asian regions, South Asia and East Asia and the Pacific, had the lowest percentages of public recurrent expenditures on higher education (14.8 percent and 13.9 percent, respectively) compared to 18.4 percent in Latin America and the Caribbean, 19.7 percent in Sub-Saharan Africa, and 20.6 percent in the OECD countries. Between 1980 and 1990, public recurrent expenditures on higher education in the sampled low- and middle-income countries of South Asia actually dropped by over 10 percent. East Asia had only a nominal increase, and its public spending per student in higher education from 1980 to 1990 as a multiple of primary education declined from 30.8 percent to 14.1 percent.

The above figures highlight the importance of viewing the challenges facing higher education in Asia according to levels of national income. For example, the governments of Singapore and Hong Kong spent 31 percent and 25 percent, respectively, of their education budgets on higher education in 1985, while Malaysia, Thailand, and Indonesia spent only 15 percent, 12 percent, and 9 percent, respectively. This is so despite the fact that the proportion of the relevant age group in university places in 1985 in Hong Kong and Singapore was below 10 percent and private universities were prohibited from conferring degrees.

Higher education in South Korea received only 10 percent of the government education budget at that time even though it was heading toward mass higher education. The more higher education costs are financed by student fees, the greater the overall coverage of the education system (World Bank, 1995:71). East Asian countries have taken note. Taiwan and Korea have relied heavily on private higher education for their expansions.

Many Asian governments are placing more responsibility on leaders of institutions of higher education by providing policy frameworks that permit more autonomy from the state. In exchange, university leaders in Asia as in other parts of the world must begin to generate more of their own funds, justifying themselves on the basis of the quality of their programs and the quantity of the human resources they produce to support national development. However, as responsibilities shift from government to the institution, the autonomy of institutional leadership becomes more complex. Culpability for poor performance rests more with institutional leaders than before. Nevertheless, while some Asian systems are moving in this direction, others still cling to old ways despite inefficiencies.

SOCIAL PERSPECTIVES: A MARKET OF DEMANDS

Institutions of higher education in Asia are responding to a variety of demands. There are demands of individuals for high-level scientific and professional skills; demands of social groups for status and prestige, including elites, social classes, ethnic groups, and women; and demands of the state for social order as well as legitimacy in the global order. The three types of demands change often and overlap within specific contexts and operate much like a market that shapes the form and content of higher education in Asian societies.

In the functionalist view, enrollment increase is cited as evidence of development and is correlated with economic productivity and per capita GNP. In short, higher education expands to meet the increasing need for science and technology, which contributes to economic development. This view has been influential in Japan and the four tigers, where it appeared to work. However, using research that includes Asian data, Ramirez and Lee (1995:33) have cast doubt on the functionalist view: "There is apparently a considerable degree of loose coupling between both what takes place within the science sector of tertiary education and scientific and infrastructural formation and between the latter and economic development."

The conflict perspective sees access to higher education as part of a mechanism of domination and social class reproduction. While this perspective has much relevance, its focus on economic struggle causes it to pay less attention to cultural aspects. For example, despite high underemployment rates among university graduates in the Philippines, the demand of the population for university credentials has not decreased, as higher education is still a key resource for status group competition.

Without a full consideration of the role of the state, these perspectives provide an incomplete picture. Universities play an indirect role in maintaining social order through support of state ideology, preparation of civil servants, and recognition of the legitimacy of the state and the credentials it confers (Carnoy and Levin, 1985; Collins, 1979). The state in China and Singapore is still very important in this respect, and while Hong Kong is considered a laissez-faire system, it joins Singapore and China in giving the state a virtual monopoly over higher education.

The future challenges facing higher education in Asia are many and not easily generalized. On the whole, the main challenges are tied to the expansion of student enrollments, including financial viability, support for economic development, and the social integration of an increasingly diverse population (women, minorities, rural and adult students, and the expanding middle class). Moreover, there are increasing demands placed on institutional leaders by academic staff, who have a crucial role to play in a context of rapid change (Altbach, 1996). Cultural traditions will continue to play an important role within higher education as part of status group competition, but they will also be essential tools of academic staff in helping their institutions cope with rapid change. In fact, it could be argued that change is occurring faster in Asia than anywhere else, and that as a result, a crisis in Asian higher education should not be unexpected. Wang Gungwu (1992), a former vice chancellor of the University of Hong Kong, places a heavy emphasis on the role of cultural tradition as the solution to such a crisis: "Where [Asian universities] have failed most notably has been their inability to provide this area of their work with the vitality to cope with the conditions of rapid change." The next section further examines forces that are contributing to the transformation of Asian higher education and the challenges they provide for institutions of higher education.

EAST ASIA

The East Asian region is the most dynamic area both economically and sociopolitically, and this is reflected in its rates of enrollment in higher education. If we put aside reformist Mongolia and isolationist North Korea, we find that Japan, South Korea, and Taiwan (with close post–World War II ties to the United States) all have established systems of mass higher education. Singapore and Hong Kong, which have colonial ties to the United Kingdom, moved more slowly but rapidly expanded enrollments in the early 1990s. In Singapore, Hong Kong, and China, only government-sponsored institutions can award university degrees. Japan, Taiwan, and South Korea support a number of high-prestige national institutions, but most students attend private institutions. The challenges facing each also differ. Japan's mass higher education system is experiencing demographic challenges, while Taiwan and South Korea are struggling to financially support their greatly expanded systems and at the same time incorporate the sociopolitical changes into their institutions of higher education to meet the growing demands of their academic staff for more autonomy. China's major challenge is also economic; increased autonomy is viewed as a way of not only generating more financial resources but also of increasing efficiency. However, autonomy is greatly restricted by the totalitarian state. While little is known about North Korean higher education because of a lack of data, Mongolia's higher education is probably the most rapidly expanding sector of its education system (Weidman et al., 1995; chapter 11).

Major challenges await East Asian higher education. In Japan, the most serious challenge is demographic. There will be a sharp decline in the population of 18–22-year-olds, a group that makes up more than 90 percent of the college enrollment in Japan. Another challenge is to change the rigidity and uniformity that mark structure, curricula, and teaching methods, as well as to encourage a broad international outlook necessary for Japan to face an increasingly complex and competitive world. Finally, women (as well as older and foreign students) are demanding greater access to the system. Incremental change may not be enough. To Kitamura (1992:315), "What is really needed is a basic structural change which will include significant innovations for strengthening the functions of education." Fortunately, administrators in Japan have the mandate to make changes. In a recent study (Boyer et al., 1994), 58.2 percent of Japanese faculty respondents agreed that top-level administrators were providing competent leadership, the highest percentage of the fourteen other participants included in the international study, including its neighbors in South Korea and Taiwan.

In Korea and Taiwan, the dual challenge is to generate alternative sources of income for private universities, which make up the bulk of the system, and to deal with the increased calls for autonomy. Over three-quarters of all of the institutions of higher education in South Korea are private. In 1992, the national government provided 71.7 percent of the income of public institutions and only 1.7 percent of the income of private institutions. Autonomy is controversial. According to Lee (chapter 17) there is a shift occurring from "government hegemony to university autonomy, and from autocratic external governance to democratic internal governance." Still, only 10 percent of Korean faculty believe they have been influential in shaping key academic policies at the institutional level, and only one percent characterized the relationship between faculty and administration as excellent (Boyer et al., 1994). In Taiwan, the Ministry of Education still has a major influence on educational reform. The promulgation of the University Act in 1994 has laid a legal basis for decentralization and depoliticization. Government control will be loosened somewhat and universities will play a decisive role in choosing their presidents. Sociopolitical transitions in Taiwan have led to major changes in its higher education system. Political pluralism and participation are increasing. University teachers and students will become more active in the formulation of educational policy (Law, 1995). There has already been faculty struggle for autonomy in presidential selection (Chen, chapter 19).

In Singapore and Hong Kong where governments have the monopoly on higher education, it is necessary to examine the challenges in these terms. In referring to Singapore, Tan (chapter 16) notes the government's dominant interventionist role in directing major policy decisions concerning higher education. Singapore's development strategy seems to go against the international trend of moving institutions from state control to state supervision. Nevertheless, there is a certain amount of autonomy internal to the institution in such areas as student recruitment, development of courses, determining examination, and internal financial management. This self-administration, however, is conditional upon meeting the needs defined by government agencies. Meeting the needs of the market economy is not viewed as incompatible with the great extent of administrative control. The Singapore case raises fundamental questions about government control and institutional autonomy. Everything becomes subordinate to economic modernization.

Finally, there is little indication that this situation will change. Singapore has delivered the second highest living standard in Asia (tied with Hong Kong), as well as social stability, to its population.

For Hong Kong, 1997 means that it will become a Special Administrative Region of the People's Republic of China under a "one country–two systems" arrangement, in which the current education system may be maintained (Postiglione, 1991). Within the context of decolonization, higher education is confronting many challenges. Within a period of less than ten years, Hong Kong has moved from a colonial society with two universities serving a small elite to a transitional society with seven publicly funded universities and colleges serving a larger population, as well as the modernization of mainland China. The rapid expansion has not occurred without difficulty. The expansion and resulting decrease in student ability levels, especially language ability, have created a need for more effective teaching measures, as well as prompting a call for addition of a foundation year at the start of the three-year university degree program. Also, the diversity that has accompanied the expansion has led to increased demands on university administrators to operate more transparently in order to contribute to improved morale and institutional loyalty among the faculty. Channels of communication between faculty and administration have to be continually improved (Boyer et al., 1994). University leaders in Hong Kong meet informally to discuss common interests but have not formed a consortium as such. Finally, whether or not they accept the challenge, Hong Kong's universities will continue to be viewed as key institutions for the development of democratic institutions in Hong Kong's future (Postiglione, 1997).

Probably no other place in Asia has the greatest potential for a massive transformation of higher education in the coming decades than mainland China. As the central government looks more toward the localities and individual universities to raise funds for resources, it is promising more autonomy. The government has increased allocation to higher education in absolute terms and relative to government expenditure and GNP. Calls for efficiency, equity, and transparency are increasingly heard. Willingness to grant autonomy is conditional upon a guarantee of stability. Universities are called on to serve economic modernization while maintaining political control (Hayhoe, 1989). China is facing a major transition to a socialist market economy and prefers a slow pace. Private universities, self-paying students, professors supplementing their incomes, and an open labor market for graduates are quite novel for a society which, not long ago, saw capitalism and free markets as enemies of the state. Weifang Min (chapter 3) notes some of the more important changes, including how universities were given more autonomy to adjust their curricula according to the local needs. Institutional leaders are faced with a number of challenges. These include raising funds through university enterprises and tuition fees, increasing enrollments, offering specializations that will attract students, stemming the flow of academic staff leaving the university, and developing economies of scale by consolidating with other universities when necessary. On top of this, university leaders must still deal with the remnants of the socialist system, including the allocation of housing, medical coverage, and other benefits. Despite the fact that student–teacher ratios average 7:1 at best, it is virtually impossible to dismiss staff. Institutional leaders are also responsible for the moral and political development of students, a difficult task at a time when ideology has lost its appeal.

Among the internal demands facing the system as well as institutional leaders is to increase female and national minority participation; the implementation of tuition fees will also make it necessary for university leaders to see to it that those of peasant background find sufficient funds to attend their institutions, as well as finding ways for them to repay their loans to the university. There are other challenges as well, including the necessity to give time to professors to upgrade their education. In 1991–92, only 1.4 percent of the total number of faculty had a doctoral degree, 20.7 percent had a master's degree, and 42.3 percent had a bachelor's degree or equivalent. The rest had no academic degree (*China Education Statistical Yearbook*, 1993).

SOUTHEAST ASIA

The East Asian societies discussed above exhibit trends that are also reflected in Southeast Asia to some extent. Although Japan, South Korea, Singapore, Taiwan, Hong Kong, and mainland China vary in size and form of government, their development is studied with great interest by Southeast Asian societies. Indonesia, Malaysia, Thailand, and the Philippines look to Japan and the four tigers for innovations, while the regimes in Vietnam and Myanmar, which prefer a gradual departure from centrally planned communist development strategies, look to China's step-by step experiments with the market economy. While Japan, Korea, Taiwan, Hong Kong, and mainland China share a Confucian heritage and largely homogeneous population, Singapore and its Southeast Asian neighbors, including Indonesia, Malaysia, Thailand, and the Philippines, are notable for their religious (Islamic, Buddhist, and Christian) and ethnic (including their

Chinese minorities) diversity, as well as their growing economies. They share many common challenges, including a need to upgrade the qualifications of their faculties and graduate schools. The following discussion focuses on the cases of Malaysia, Indonesia, and the Philippines, and, to a lesser extent, of Cambodia, Laos, and Vietnam.

The major change in Malaysia's higher education system is the shortening of university education from 4 to 3 years (except medical schools). This is occurring due to rapid development, which has caused an acute shortage of skilled manpower. Unemployment in the first quarter of 1995 was only 2.9 percent, the lowest in 30 years. The labor market is tight and the country needs 153,000 engineers and technicians by the year 2000, though projected supply is only three-quarters that. This has intensified the debate over quality, which previously focused on the affirmative action–like policies that favor the indigenous Bumiputra (mostly Malay Muslims, but also indigenous people of the southern provinces, many of whom are Christian). Of the 90,000 students who graduated from Malaysia's 9 universities in 1995, half were Bumiputras. As in other parts of Asia, many students, including the best and brightest, are sent overseas to study. There is also concern about language standards, especially on the part of university lecturers. When the colonial period ended, Bahasa Malay replaced English as the medium of instruction in universities (*Far Eastern Economic Review*, August 31, 1995:16–17). There has been discussion about establishing a more independent governance structure in universities. Academicians have been calling for the adoption of a charter whereby universities would be run by a council of higher education instead of the Ministry of Education. This would advance the shift from state control to state supervision, a less interventionist monitoring role. Lee (chapter 10) believes that Malaysia will have to formulate policies toward greater cost recovery. This may lead to a corporatization of the local universities to increase efficiency and reduce the government's financial burden.

Indonesia has a system of over one thousand institutions that enroll over 1.8 million students (8 percent of the 19–24-year-old age cohort). The government maintains that stress is placed on access, equity, quality, relevance, and efficiency. Most policies are initiated by officials in consultation with university representatives and, sometimes, foreign donors. The public sector is the main vehicle for attaining the government's policy objectives. Public sector institutions are quite dependent on government for funds: Even the most enterprising ones receive over 80 percent of their revenues from the central government (Cummings, Malo, and Sunarto, chapter 6). Though less than 10 percent of all public funding goes to the private sector, the government defines the direction of development. As the government's share of total funding to higher education decreases in the future, its leadership role may change. A strong popular demand for higher education continues to fuel a rapid expansion. Public sector expansion has increased equity across regions, while private sector higher education is mainly located in urban areas. The public sector curriculum stresses technological fields such as agriculture, engineering, and teacher education, while the private sector has focused on fields like computer science and management, which easily attract clientele.

Though much smaller than Indonesia in population, the Philippines has about the same number (1,038) of institutions (one-quarter public and three-quarters private) of higher education (1.4 million students), giving it a much higher percentage of the age group in higher education. With most students enrolled in a 10-year system of primary and secondary education (rather than 12 years), the issue of quality as well as accreditation has been important. A major problem has been the production of graduates that are underemployed or cannot be employed. However, since the quality of many programs is low, underemployment is not quite accurate given the actual qualification. Since the Second World War a laissez-faire attitude toward higher education created a heavy reliance on market forces. In this respect, the private sector has not been able to meet the needs of society in a balanced way and the magic hand of the free market has had temporary advantages at best. Gonzalez (chapter 15) believes that there is a need for strong leadership, political will, and strong executives to implement reform to redirect the system toward heightened productivity. He points out that the permissiveness with regard to the private sector, which allowed it to operate virtually unfettered, led to an imbalance. Many schools and programs that were not financially viable were allowed to open. The result was often an overproduction of some graduates and the underproduction of needed graduates in crucial fields. Incentives are needed to make priority programs more attractive. Gonzalez believes that laissez faire must be accompanied by timely and limited interventions.

Southeast Asia's transition states, such as Cambodia, Vietnam, Laos, and Myanmar, are in a less advantaged situation than the new economic tigers (Malaysia, Indonesia, and the Philippines). Nevertheless, the former are in the midst of a rapid transformation. In Cambodia, 6 higher education institutes and 54 specialized educational institutes reopened in the early 1980s. By 1990 it graduated 977 doctors, dentists, and pharmacists, 474 technical engineers, 400 economists, and 184 agricultural engineers. Political education and the core courses in Marxism–Leninism were cancelled between 1989 and 1991. Clayton and Ngoy (chapter 2) note the rapid changes taking place and identify probable trends. These include the following: Higher educational institutions will be placed under one ministry; demands of the labor market will be surveyed and higher education will be more closely linked to the labor market; students will help defray the cost of their education; institutions will be granted more financial autonomy and responsibility for day-to-day management; and new curricula will be based on socioeconomic need.

In Laos, there are three institutes of higher education as well as technical institutes, in which only 1.3 percent of the age group are enrolled. Limited resources and a lack of a high-level trained labor force constrain growth. University graduates will be gobbled up by private enterprises, and without international donors, the future of higher education would be extremely modest. The main reform, formulated and funded by the Asian Development Bank, is the establishment of a comprehensive university that would provide first degrees in arts and sciences as well as advanced degree programs. Weidman (chapter 9) sees good prospects for the consolidation and rationalization of higher education in the Lao PDR. For Vietnam, rapid transformation is more tempered by politics. The pace is slower though no less deliberate. Like China, the ruling Communist Party has implemented a policy of openness and cooperation with other countries in the region. According to Dang Ba Lam (chapter 20), there are 102 universities, colleges, junior colleges, and institutes where 125,000 students are trained annually. The state views its participation in the global economy as directly linked to its response to internal demands for specialized technical and professional manpower. Modes of delivery have been diversified, and some consolidation of institutions has taken place. A major hurdle that must be overcome concerns the upgrading of teaching staff.

SOUTH ASIA

India is the higher education giant in Asia and of special importance in South Asia because of the British colonial heritage in higher education that it shares with other South Asian countries, including Pakistan, Bangladesh, and Sri Lanka. It was the earliest among developing countries to have established universities. With over 5 percent of its relevant age group (20–24-year-olds) in higher education, India has practically doubled its enrollment since 1975 when it had four times as many students as China. By 1990, its 4.4 million students in higher education far exceeded any other place in Asia, including Japan's stable 2.7 million and China's rapidly expanding 2.7 million. The size of its system is only exceeded by that of the United States. Nevertheless, there are fundamental differences between it and its Asian competitors. For example, while the ratio of natural science and engineering degrees to total bachelor's degrees in China was close to 55 percent in 1990, it was barely 25 percent in India (Johnson, 1993). Indian higher education is confronting challenges similar to others already discussed above, including producing relevant high-quality degrees, raising teacher qualifications, generating income for higher education, improving efficiency, increasing privatization, and reducing government control. However, Indian sociologist Jayaram (chapter 5) notes the complexities of reform in such a massive system of higher education and tempers the optimism of those who anxiously await the fate of dozens of seemingly promising proposals for improving the system. While Bangladesh and Sri Lanka are confronting some of the same challenges as India, including great ethnic diversity as an overlay to its hurdles in improving higher education, Chowdhury (chapter 1) and Jayaweera (chapter 18) place greater stress on the problems of graduate unemployment and student unrest. The impact of privatization in higher education on these problems is of much interest. Chowdhury notes that unlike public universities, the private universities in Bangladesh are not facing student activism. For Sri Lanka, Jayaweera suggests that further research is necessary to ascertain the degree to which private universities can solve the problem of graduate unemployment.

CONCLUSION

Despite the similarities across Asian higher education systems, they are far outweighed by the differences. Contrasts abound. For example, wedged narrowly between the giants of China and India, Nepal's Tribhuvan University, with over 100 campuses and 102,000 students (with great ethnic and linguistic diversity), contrasts sharply with China, where over 80 percent of its universities have under 3,000 students (Regmi, chapter 12). Likewise, one is stretched to find the similarities between the aim of self-reliance for Iranian higher education (Mehran, chapter 7) and the economic dependency of the 7 universities within 21 countries that make up Papua New Guinea and the Pacific Islands in Asia's far west (Bray, chapter 14).

There is an unmistakable trend. Throughout many parts of Asia, higher education institutions are gaining autonomy. As the state tightens its purse strings and loosens its grip, however, the locus of influence follows new sources of funding. Support from industry, enterprises, and students calls for a different type of leadership. Support from business, commerce, and industry will demand practical scientific skills and quantifiable outcomes that institutions of higher education are not always disposed or able to provide.

At the same time that the state loosens control, it also places more traditional demands on higher education. This includes the demand for social order, support for a state ideology, and continued service to the state bureaucracy, as well as the preparation of civil servants by national universities.

Until student fees and student numbers increase, their demands and those of their families will be less felt, though no less important. Moreover, as institutional leaders get more autonomy in selecting students, they may lose some of the insulation from social groups that call for more access, including women in Japan, rural students in China, workers in South Korea, and national minorities in China and Singapore. Nevertheless, the expansion of the middle class in Asia has not become a major force in most places. Higher education is still an institution mostly for a small social elite, though this situation will gradually change.

Many East Asian higher educational leaders will find their institutions with more professionalized faculty. As the level of qualification rises, faculty will demand more participation in decision making, as well as more guarantees of academic freedom and autonomy. While the Philippines, Malaysia, Indonesia, Vietnam, and most Southeast Asian nations, as well as China, face a daunting challenge to upgrade the qualifications of their faculties, other countries in East Asia have already reached an important threshold. Faculty members in Taiwan,

Hong Kong, and South Korea are demanding more transparency in institutional decision making.

REFERENCES

Altbach, Philip. 1997. *The Academic Profession in Higher Education: A Study of 14 Countries.* Princeton: The Carnegie Foundation for the Advancement of Teaching.

Altbach, Philip, and Viswanathan Selvaratnam. 1989. *From Dependence to Autonomy: The Development of Asian Universities.* Amsterdam: Kluwer Academic.

Boyer, Ernest, Philip Altbach, and Mary Jean Whitelaw. 1994. *The Academic Profession in International Perspective.* Princeton: The Carnegie Foundation for the Advancement of Teaching.

Carnoy, Martin, and Henry Levin. 1985. *Schooling and Work in the Democratic State.* Stanford: Stanford University Press.

China Education Statistical Yearbook. 1993. Beijing: People's Education Press.

Collins, Randall. 1979. *The Credential Society: An Historical Sociology of Education and Stratification.* New York: Academic.

Far Eastern Economic Review. 1995. August 31, pp. 16–17.

Hayhoe, Ruth. 1989. *China's Universities and the Open Door.* New York: M. E. Sharpe.

International Monetary Fund. 1995. *World Economic Outlook.*

Johnson, Jean M. 1993. *Human Resources for Science and Technology: The Asian Region.* Surveys of Science Resources Series, Special Report, National Science Foundation, NSF 93–303. Washington, D.C.

Kitamura, Kazuyuki. 1992. "Gakusei ni yoru jugyo hyoka" (Class Evaluation by Students). *IDE, 332,* 18–26.

Law, Wing Wah. 1995. "The Impact of Socio-Political Transition on Higher Education: Taiwan." Paper presented at the International Symposium on Education and Socio-Political Transition in Asia, May 29–31, University of Hong Kong.

Nash, Madeleine J. 1994. "Tigers in the Lab: Asian Born, U.S. Trained Researchers Are Headed Home to Challenge the Technological Supremacy of the West." *Time* (International Edition), November 21, pp. 48–49.

Postiglione, Gerard A. 1997. "Hong Kong's Academic Profession in a Period of Profound Change." In Philip Altbach, ed., *The Academic Profession in Higher Education: A Study of 14 Countries.* Princeton: The Carnegie Foundation for the Advancement of Teaching.

Postiglione, Gerard A., in collaboration with Julian Leung. 1991. *Education and Society in Hong Kong: Toward One Country and Two Systems.* New York: M. E. Sharpe.

Ramirez, Francisco O., and Molly N. N. Lee. 1995. "Education, Science and Development." In Gerard A. Postiglione and W. O. Lee, eds., *Social Change and Educational Development: Mainland China, Taiwan and Hong Kong.* Hong Kong: Center of Asian Studies, University of Hong Kong.

Tan, Jee-Peng, and Alain Mingat. 1992. *Education in Asia: A Comparative Perspective of Cost and Financing.* World Bank Regional and Sectoral Studies. Washington, D.C.: World Bank.

University Grants Committee. 1995. *University Grants Committee of Hong Kong: Facts and Figures.* Hong Kong: University Grants Committee Secretariat.

Wang, Gungwu. 1992. "Universities in Transition." *Oxford Review of Education, 24,*

17–27. Cited in Albert Yee, ed., *East Asian Higher Education: Traditions and Transformations.* London: Pergamon Press, 1995, p. 1.

Webster, Justin. 1994. ''Success in Hong Kong: Universities Attract Top International Scholars Despite Concern about Colony's Future after 1997.'' *The Chronicle of Higher Education*, October 19, pp. A60–A61.

Weidman, John C., and Regesuriin Bat-Erdene. 1995. ''Higher Education in Mongolia.'' Draft, University of Pittsburgh.

World Bank. 1995. *Priorities and Strategies for Education: A World Bank Review.* Washington, D.C.: Author.

1

BANGLADESH

Kowsar P. Chowdhury

In the 1950s and 1960s, education was viewed as a vital element in bringing about major social and economic changes in Third World nations. Economists considered the "human resources" of a country as the main "missing component" of economic development.[1] Some studies even found significant correlation between stocks of higher-level workforce (e.g., teachers, physicians, dentists, engineers, and scientists) and the measure of economic development (Harbison and Myers, 1964:13–60).[2] These assumptions had great influence on educational planners and policy makers in many developing countries, including Bangladesh.

Educational development alone, however, cannot bring about the desired social change or improve the material conditions of the people.[3] Educational strategies must accompany political and economic strategies, which are geared toward building a sound and secure future for the masses by providing them with economic and social security. Despite this realization, in many countries in Asia the role of higher education is still linked with economic development. The question is whether expansion of higher education alone can contribute to such change.

This chapter reviews the development of the higher education system in Bangladesh. It explains the forces behind the rapid expansion of higher education, and whether such expansion contributed to the socioeconomic development of the country. It also examines how higher education in Bangladesh has been shaped in response to its changing position within the world system. The following section briefly describes the historical development of the higher education system.

BACKGROUND AND SOCIAL CONTEXT

The history of the present secular structure of education can be traced back to the colonial period. The British colonizers of Bangladesh, then part of India, were mainly interested in the exploitation of its economic resources and in developing a market for British manufactured goods. To do this effectively, they established new institutions to manage affairs. A cadre of locally educated English-speaking elites was needed to serve as intermediaries between the British administrators and the local masses. A liberal arts–based higher educational system was introduced. While higher education had received some attention, primary education for the masses was further neglected, reinforcing an elitist trend.[4]

This pattern continued well after the independence of Pakistan in 1947, of which Bangladesh, then known as East Pakistan, was a part. The political ascendancy of West Pakistan began another colonial era for Bangladesh, which lasted until December 1971. The concentration of power in the hands of West Pakistanis allowed planned economic and political exploitation of Bangladesh. The economic policy of Pakistan had been concerned primarily with industrialization through redistribution of resources from Bangladesh to West Pakistan.[5] The wide social and economic gap between Bangladesh and West Pakistan, the constant political instability largely because of the suspension of democratic processes almost from the inception of Pakistan, the disproportionate balance of power and the centralization of decision making in West Pakistan all had adverse effects on overall development objectives and the education system. The resource allocation for the education sector in Bangladesh was limited compared to that for West Pakistan, and was mainly spent on the expansion of the secondary and tertiary levels of education.[6] This had an impact on the expansion of education at various levels (table 1.1).

Independence in 1971 raised expectations among Bangladeshis. The overall socioeconomic situation of the country, however, deteriorated initially and had a profound impact on the education sector. Several factors were responsible for this worsening condition, one of which was the devastating war with West Pakistan, which dislocated not only the lives of many people but also the institutional structure of the country. In addition, rapid population growth, natural calamities, and constant political instability all contributed to the deteriorating condition of the country. In recent years, although some improvements have been reported in terms of the alleviation of poverty, Bangladesh still ranks as one of the least developed countries of the world (World Bank, 1989, 1993).

Bangladesh comprises an area of about 144,000 square kilometers with a population of 110.6 million in 1991, which makes it one of the most densely populated countries of the world (World Bank, 1993). The average growth rate of population for 1980–91 was 2.2 percent. The male:female ratio was 106:100. The majority of people are Muslims (86.6 percent), while Hindus, Buddhists, and Christians comprise 12.1 percent, 0.6 percent, and 0.3 percent, respectively (BBS, 1992).

Table 1.1
Enrollment Increase in Education in Bangladesh, 1950–72

Levels of Education	Period	% Increase in Enrollment
Primary	1950-51 to 1960-61	36
	1960-61 to 1972-73	80
Secondary	1950-51 to 1960-61	6
	1960-61 to 1972-73	219
Intermediate (grades 11-12)	1950-51 to 1960-61	185
	1960-61 to 1972-73	522
College (Degree)	1950-51 to 1960-61	180
	1960-61 to 1972-73	600
University	1960-61 to 1972-73	600

Source: T. Islam, *An Analysis of Public Recurring Expenditure of Higher Education* (Dhaka: Government of Bangladesh, University Grants Commission, 1975), table 13, p. 28.

Bangladesh is predominantly rural, and agriculture is the main source of employment. In 1987–88, about 57 percent of the labor force was employed in this sector. Employment in the industrial sector has remained static, whereas a significant increase has occurred in service sector employment, including professional, technical, managerial, clerical, and sales areas.

Only 17 percent of the total population resides in urban areas. In 1991, the GNP per capita was U.S.$220.[7] The life expectancy at birth was 51. The adult illiteracy rate was 65 percent in 1990, and the female illiteracy rate was 78 percent (World Bank, 1993). About 57 percent of the rural families of Bangladesh are functionally landless and their numbers have been increasing. About 5 percent of the families having land above 7.5 acres own 26 percent of the land and 70 percent of the families having land below 2.5 acres own only 29 percent of the land (Ministry of Land, 1989, cited in Karim, 1993:3). In terms of income distribution, about 12.8 percent of households were in the high-income category, 31.7 percent in the middle-income category, and 55.5 percent in the low-income category (Ahmad, 1992:54–59).

The latest household expenditure surveys (HES) show that in 1991–92 close to half of the population was below poverty level, which was measured by direct calorie intake. The poverty indicators also show a greater incidence of poverty in rural than in urban areas. It appears that the absolute number of the poor have increased in both rural and urban areas (World Bank, 1995:17–18).

The country is greatly dependent on foreign aid for its development. The total external debt amounted to U.S.$12,245 million in 1990. Of the total fourth five-year plan public sector allocation of Tk 419,300 million, 73.9 percent is to come from external sources (Karim, 1993). The average annual growth rate for GDP was 4.3 percent for 1980–91 compared to 2.3 percent for 1970–80 (World Bank, 1993).

In 1972, the Constitution of Bangladesh proclaimed democracy, socialism, secularism, and nationalism as the guiding principles of the nation. The parliamentary form of government was introduced. In January 1975, the Constitution was amended and the presidential form, along with a one-party system, was established. The coup d'état in August 1975, the assassination of the founding father of Bangladesh, subsequent coups, and political turmoil had adverse effects on the society and economy. At present, the parliamentary form of government, along with a multiparty system, is again in place.

PROFILE OF THE HIGHER EDUCATION SYSTEM

The history of the growth of higher education (especially liberal arts and general education) shows that it has paid little attention to employability and work efficiency demanded by both the graduates and the labor market. The elitist trend is still reflected in the expansion of the higher education system, but considerable diversification in curriculum has taken place in recent years.

Broadly, education in Bangladesh comprises three levels: primary, secondary, and higher. Following one or two years of preprimary education (accessible mostly in the cities and some district headquarters), the primary level comprises grades 1–5 (age group 6–10). Secondary schooling consists of three stages: junior secondary (grades 6–8), secondary (grades 9–10), and higher secondary or intermediate (grades 11–12). At the end of grade 10, the first public examination, known as the secondary school certificate (SSC) examination, is held. There is another public examination at the end of grade 12, known as the higher secondary school certificate (HSC) examination, which is a requirement for admission to first degree courses (Karim, 1993:5–7).

Higher education consists of the following courses: (1) two-year ordinary first degree courses in arts (B.A.), science (B.Sc.), and commerce (B.Com.) are offered in the university-affiliated degree colleges; (2) a three-year specialized (honors) first degree in arts, science, law, and commerce is mainly available in the universities, but also offered in the limited number of affiliated colleges;[8] (3) a four- to five-year professional first degree in engineering, medicine, and so on is available in professional colleges or universities; (4) a master's degree (duration of one to two years depending on prequalification of two-year ordinary or three-year honors degree) is offered in the university or university-affiliated colleges; (5) M.Phil. (two-year) and Ph.D. (three-year) degrees are offered in the universities (ibid.).

Outside the mainstream of education, other significant types of education are available. Probably the most important of these is religious education offered at the *madrashas* that provide education from the elementary level up to the master's degree level. It is not possible to obtain the ratios of students in *madrashas*. Apart from this, a wide range of nonformal education programs are provided by several nongovernmental organizations.

In addition, one open university was established in 1992. A recent law passed by the Parliament allows the establishment of universities in the private sector. The first degree-awarding private university (North-South University) started its first academic session in Dhaka in 1993 with two hundred undergraduate students in the fields of business administration, computer science, and economics (Karim, 1993:30–31). The North-South University serves as a model for other similar institutions at the university level. By 1994, two additional private universities and two private medical colleges were in operation.[9]

Modeled after the British university, the first publicly funded university of Bangladesh, Dhaka University, was established in 1921 as a residential teaching university. In 1990–91, there were nine government-funded universities (BAN-BEIS, 1992).

The number of degree colleges increased from 200 in 1972–73 to 547 in 1991, a 173.5 percent growth over the period. Out of 547 degree colleges in 1991, 63 are exclusively for females; the rest, with few exceptions, are coeducational colleges. Most general degree colleges offer a two-year bachelor's program.[10] Some of these degree colleges also offer honors and master's degree courses in selected subjects. About 37 percent of the colleges are government and 63 percent are nongovernment.[11] In addition, there were one postgraduate medicine and research institute, 10 medical, one dental, 4 engineering, 3 agriculture, 32 law, 10 teachers training, and one music colleges in 1991 (BAN-BEIS, 1992; Planning Commission, 1973).

Table 1.2 shows that enrollment increased at a much faster rate at the higher level than at the primary level. While enrollment at the primary level increased from 5,283,787 to 11,939,949 (55.7 percent increase) during 1970–90, enrollment at the higher level increased from 117,603 to 434,309 (72.9 percent increase). Despite this increase, the ratio of age cohort (20–24) enrolled in the tertiary level was only 3.8 percent in 1990 compared with 77 percent in the primary level and 19 percent in the secondary level. Female students comprised only 16 percent of the student body at the higher level.

THE CHANGING FUNCTIONS AND PATTERNS OF HIGHER EDUCATION

Policy, Planning, and Reform

Most government documents, development plans, and Education Commission reports characterized the education system, especially university education, as elitist and not adequate for meeting the development needs of a growing econ-

Table 1.2
Expansion of Enrollment by Level of Education and Gender

Year	Primary Level Total Enrollment	Ratios	Percent Female	Secondary Level Total Enrollment	Ratios	Percent Female	Higher Level Total Enrollment	Ratios	Percent Female
1970	5,283,787	52	32	1,485,315*	19	15	117,603	2.1	10
1975	8,192,022	73	34	2,317,119**	23	—	158,604**	2.3	12
1980	8,240,169	58	37	2,659,208	17	24	240,181	3.5	14
1985	8,920,293	64	40	3,125,219	17	28	457,862	5.6	19
1990	11,939,949	77	45	3,592,995	19	33	434,309	3.8	16

*Figures for 1969.
**Figures for 1976.
Source: Unesco, Unesco Statistical Yearbook, 1977, 1980, 1985, 1993.

omy. The major goals of higher education, as reflected in the five-year plans, are the development of a knowledgeable and socially committed labor force for the development of the country. Almost all the five-year plans reiterated the need of relevant education, with an emphasis on expanding the science and technological fields, restricting the rapid expansion of liberal arts subjects, introducing selectivity in higher education, and improving the quality of education at all levels, especially at the higher level. Emphasis was also placed on introducing provisions for teacher evaluation, improving universities as "centers of excellence" by strengthening research activities, enhancing the functional character of technical education and vocational training through appropriate links with the employment market, and linking universities with industry and productive sectors to raise productivity of labor and capital. In addition, removing the existing imbalance in various levels of education, increasing literacy by expanding mass education, and achieving universal primary education (UPE) were the major policy goals of these development plans.

Although great emphasis was placed on educational reforms immediately after the liberation, reviews of all the development plans show that public expenditures on education were highly unequal. Higher education was expanded at the cost of primary education (see table 1.3).

The continuation of the past trend can be explained by the fact that upper- and middle-class parents wanted a certain type of education for their children that would prepare them to climb the next step of the educational ladder. So primary schools were organized to provide the type of education that would get the children to the secondary schools, which in turn were geared toward higher levels of education. Bacchus expressed the same view in the case of other developing countries when he stated that the "distorting influence which the universities exert on the whole educational system persists despite the fact that

Table 1.3

Allocation and Actual Expenditure of the First Plan and the Two-Year Plan (1973–80)

			(In Lakh Taka*)
Education Sub-sector	Allocation	Actual Expenditure	Percentage of total Actual Expenditure
Primary Education	800,383	341,138	13.17
Secondary Education	886,493	301,109	11.63
College Education	385,493	147,539	5.69
University Education	571,572	683,038	26.39
Technical Education	886.330	470,725	18.19
Teacher Education	282,354	79,214	3.06
Other Education Activities	727,427	565,787	21.73
Total:	4,540,052	2,588,550	100.00

*1 Lakh Taka = 100,000 Taka.
Source: Planning Commission, *Third Five-Year Plan* (1980–85:table 15.1, p. 285).

often not more than 1 percent of the students who initially enter primary school even end up at universities'' (Bacchus, 1981:218).

Further, higher education is viewed as the only means for upward mobility through a relatively highly rewarding modern sector job. Since the modern sector jobs required individuals with certain levels of education, the demand for tertiary education continued. A simple example can illustrate why this is the case. In 1992, the basic monthly salary for an entry-level secondary school teacher was Tk 1,200 ($31) to Tk 2,335 ($60), which was 1.75 to 3.3 times more than the GNP per capita. A recent study shows that on average an additional year of schooling increased the wage by 4 percent in Bangladesh (Khandker, Alam, and Greaney, 1995:17). Given this higher level of reward, who would not go for higher education? To reduce the demand for higher education, therefore, the gap in the reward structure should be decreased.

In addition, to achieve universal primary education (UPE) by the year 2000, as envisaged in the plans, it will require at a minimum a sustained increase in expenditure on primary education of about 7 percent per annum in real terms (Karim, 1989:26). Therefore, it is argued, to allocate larger resources to primary education, the provision for university education should remain at its present level of support. It is questionable whether such redistribution of resources can occur. But to reduce the financial constraints of opening up more universities, Bangladesh has decided to establish universities in the private sector.

The higher education bill for establishing universities in the private sector is probably the most important reform in the history of education in Bangladesh. This bill was introduced because of the pressure from a highly educated group that was frustrated by the low quality and ''session jams'' of the public universities. It is argued that although UPE and free secondary education are yet to be ensured, the policy of highly subsidized higher education must be abandoned. Cost recovery schemes including tuition fee increases in the universities should be introduced. Effective from July 1, 1987, tuition fees for government colleges have been doubled from Tk 12 ($0.39) to Tk 24 ($0.78) per month. Tuition fees for the universities, however, have remained virtually unchanged for nearly thirty years, and were about Tk 12 in 1987.[12] The user fees cover only one percent of the unit cost at the university level in Bangladesh as compared to 29 percent in India (World Bank, 1989:208). While restructuring the elitist system is of prime importance, how the introduction of increased user fees would affect the disadvantaged groups of the society needs consideration. It is suggested that need-based scholarships and stipends should be allowed for students from disadvantaged socioeconomic groups. Further, the government could assist by freezing budget allocations and enrollments at current levels, thereby encouraging the universities to address the issues of internal efficiency and cost recovery (ibid.). While there are some reform attempts to make the system more egalitarian, how far these reforms in the education sector alone would help in equalizing access to schooling and tackling the quantitative expansion of higher education and graduate unemployment and, therefore, development problems is unclear.

Governance

While colleges are established under executive order, universities are established under an act of parliament or an ordinance of the government. There is no legal framework for educational institutions, but some may register under the Society Act and they have to abide by the government orders regarding governance and fund management to become eligible for financial assistance or affiliation (Ahmad, 1992).

The president of the country acts as the chancellor of the universities. The chancellor appoints the vice chancellor, who is the executive and academic chief of the universities. The syndicate is the executive body of the university while the senate rectifies proposals of the syndicate and approves its annual reports, accounts, and budgets. Deans of the faculties are elected by the teaching staff. The students have six representatives in the senate. The academic council, the main authority for academic matters, is composed of deans, professors, and representatives of the teaching staff and affiliated colleges. All decisions of this council, however, require syndicate approval (Ahmed, 1992).

Universities maintain academic and administrative control of constituent departments, institutes, and affiliated colleges. Except for Jahangirnagar University, all other universities are affiliating universities. They are also responsible for establishing standards for physical facilities and teaching staff, for determining curricula and syllabi, and for administering common examinations for their affiliated colleges, which are managed by the government or private bodies. The departments are the basic unit of academic administration.

The University Grants Commission (UGC) is responsible for planning higher education within the framework of economic development and for allocating financial resources. The Ministry of Education (MOE) has no direct control in the administration of the universities other than the annual allocation of government funds through the UGC. The MOE has direct financial control of the government colleges, but not of academic programs. Similar control is exercised on nongovernment colleges through the governing body and financial grants (Ahmed, 1992:63–69; Ahmad, 1992:54–59).

Financing

Although universities are autonomous bodies, 95 percent of their financing comes from the government as block grants. The nongovernment degree colleges are highly subsidized by the public budget. The pressure for increased funding for the college levels, including secondary education, comes from the well-organized teachers' association, which lobbies the government for higher teacher salaries. While government colleges and secondary schools receive basic salary plus allowances for house rent, medical costs, and transportation costs, nongovernment institutions receive 70 percent of the basic salary plus a fixed house rent and medical allowances (Directorate of Inspection and Audit, 1992).

Despite the repeated pronouncement of the importance of education for human resources development, investment in education in Bangladesh is far too low, even when compared with other South Asian countries. From a base of about one percent of GNP in 1974, investment in education has increased to 1.8 percent of GNP in 1987. On average, 1.45 percent of GNP was invested in education from 1981 to 1987. Compared to this, India and Sri Lanka invested 3.2 percent and 3.0 percent of their GNP in 1982 and 1983, respectively (Khan, 1988: tables 3 and 4). As a proportion of the total government budget, the education sector's share decreased from 15 percent in the 1960s to about 10 percent in the 1980s. Actual developmental expenditure was reduced from 5.3 percent in the first plan to around 3 percent in the third one (Ahmad, 1992:54–59).

The per student recurrent cost in the universities increased from U.S.$458 (Tk 7,082) in 1980 to U.S.$537 (Tk 16,328) in 1986. In 1987, the Bangladesh University of Engineering and Technology spent U.S.$747 (Tk 23,107) per student, while the total tuition and other fees paid by a student did not exceed U.S.$12 (Tk 384) (Karim, 1989:10).[13] According to a World Bank estimate, the ratio of per student cost in the universities to per pupil cost at the primary level in Bangladesh was 54:1; the corresponding ratios for other developing countries and South Asia were 26:1 and 15:1, respectively (World Bank, 1989:200). This reflects the highly subsidized and elitist nature of the higher education system of Bangladesh. This pattern of subsidization is evident in many developing countries, where the relatively few people who gain access to higher education receive more subsidies (in absolute terms) than those at the lower educational levels. Further, evidence indicates that richer groups are overrepresented at all levels of education, especially at the university level, therefore contributing to social inequality (World Bank, 1986:13–14).

Admissions Policy

The admissions policy and strict selectivity of higher education institutions show the relative prestige and status of each institution. Although universities are the highest seats of teaching and learning, professional colleges (medical, engineering, etc.) usurp considerable prestige in the hierarchy of the educational structure. At the bottom of the hierarchy are the private nongovernment colleges in rural areas, most of which do not attract qualified teachers and operate under substandard conditions.

Admission to undergraduate programs is based on the higher secondary certificate examination. Admissions policies and selection are determined by each institution. Competition, particularly for professional and technical education and general universities, is acute; they require special entrance examinations. Compared to professional programs, admission to arts and social science programs is relatively less competitive. Most private nongovernment general colleges have the easiest entrance requirements.

Curriculum and Language of Instruction

A variety of programs are offered in medicine, engineering, technology, agriculture, commerce, journalism, teacher education, liberal arts and humanities, fine arts, home science, applied and physical sciences, and social science at the undergraduate and graduate levels. Courses in some subjects, such as computer science and business administration, are not offered in most institutions.

Although the native language, Bengali, was introduced as the medium of instruction after liberation, English is widely used at the universities. In recent years, about 70 percent of the students of the general universities answered their examination in Bengali. This creates a problem since appropriate textbooks and reference materials in many subjects are not available in Bengali. In addition, because of weak command of the English language, many students fail to make use of reference materials. To improve command of the English language, the Bangladesh National Education Commission (1988) recommended that students who planned to undertake higher studies in science should take English at the bachelor's level (Karim, 1989:22–23).

There is prestige and status attached to the English language. In the labor market, people who go through an English medium education have a better chance of obtaining a job than those who do not have such education. Since the boundaries of the job market have expanded internationally and an increasing number of graduates from Bangladesh seek postgraduate degrees and jobs abroad, the demand for English as a medium of instruction remains strong.

RESPONSES TO INTERNAL DEMANDS

Because higher education is a scarce commodity, who benefits from it? In addition, the high level of subsidization raises the question of how equitably it is distributed among competing social groups. In dealing with these questions, this section focuses on both students and faculty.

Despite the enormous growth in higher education in the past, the percentage of the students (20–24 age group) enrolling in higher education in 1990 was only 3.4; the ratios were 5.9 and 1.3 for males and females, respectively (UNESCO, 1993). There are no data available for ratios of students from urban and rural areas for 1990. According to UNESCO, in 1981, the percentage of total student population (age 20–24) who attained tertiary education[14] was 1.4; females consisted of only 0.6 percent. In urban areas 4.8 percent and in rural areas 0.7 percent had attained the tertiary level of education. Females consisted of 3.1 percent and 0.1 percent for urban and rural areas, respectively. During 1990–91, a total of 5,448 students from Bangladesh enrolled in foreign countries. The largest number of students enrolled in the United States (2,784), followed by the former Soviet Union (654). There were 240 foreign students in higher education institutions in Bangladesh (UNESCO, 1993).

The question is, Who are these select few? All higher education institutions are selective in some respect. Student selection becomes a social and political issue since certain social groups consistently have less access to higher education than others. In Bangladesh, a study on the background, attitudes, and expectations of students in the higher levels of education showed that most students come from the privileged classes—urban, male, upper-income, and educated families. This study also showed that the urban students were overrepresented in specializations such as social sciences, law, medicine, science, and engineering courses. The study revealed that parents' income, education, and status in society as well as expected earnings influenced the demand for certain types of higher education, irrespective of the labor market realities (FREPD, 1979, cited in UNESCO, 1988:29).

Once students drop out, there is a limited chance for reentry into higher education. There are virtually no provisions for part-time study at the university or college level. Therefore, it is almost impossible for older age groups, who missed the chance once, to enroll again, except in the recently established open university.

Student Activism

Higher education institutions play an important and active role on the nation's political scene. Even during the period of British rule, universities and other higher education institutions were the centers of protest against foreign domination and oppression. In most national movements, such as the language movement in 1952 and the liberation movement in 1971, the universities and colleges were the focal points of activities. Even today student organizations lead the protest against any undemocratic policies. In recent years, however, leading political parties use their student fronts to achieve their political interests. Power struggles among conflicting political parties have resulted in violence on campus.

Student activism and politics on campus create "session jams" in the universities because of unscheduled closure of universities and shifting of examination dates. The three-year honors program often requires five to six years to complete. The "session jam" has become a norm rather than an exception. On one occasion in 1988, the president of the country stated that between 1980 and 1987 the University of Dhaka remained closed for four and a half years; the Bangladesh University of Engineering and Technology remained closed for 472 days between 1981 and 1985; and Rajshahi University was closed for 242 days in 1987. As a result the government had been incurring a loss of Tk 1336.20 million annually (cited in Karim, 1989:20).

The private universities, however, are not facing student activism. If there are strikes and blockades in the country, these universities schedule their classes on the weekends to make up the lost time. The private universities are not supported by the government and are dependent on high admission and tuition fees from the students. The parents and students are aware of the high cost of their education and are not willing to pay for additional years. To maintain the quality and efficiency as well as the competition, these universities strictly follow their established guidelines.[15]

Higher Education and Unemployment

Although higher education institutions in Bangladesh produce a very small number of graduates, unemployment among the graduates is a major developmental problem. In 1983–84, the unemployment rates among tertiary-level graduates was 2.7 percent: for males, 2.3 percent, and for females, 9.4 percent (BBS, 1986:195). Further, there is mismatch between supply and demand of educated graduates in certain fields.

The total stock of selected types of educated human resources was 2.04 million at the end of 1983, and it was estimated that more than 171,000 educated job seekers would enter the labor market in 1984 (UNESCO, 1988:51). Table 1.4 suggests the employability of graduates from certain fields. During January–December 1984, the highest number of new job seekers were generalists (84.87 percent) followed by master's degree holders in social science (2.34 percent). Engineers, doctors, and fiber technologists have been the smallest groups to have joined the labor market.

The mismatch in labor supply is also obvious in table 1.4. At one extreme it

Table 1.4

Employment Opportunities for Estimated Number of Educated Job Seekers in 1984

Area	New Job-Seekers	% of New Job-Seekers	Vacancies	% of Vacancies
Generalists	145,385	84.87	8,931	20.31
M.A. Humanities	1,515	0.88	279	0.63
M.A. Soc. Science	4,016	2.34	313	0.71
M.A. Econ.	3,162	1.85	1,811	4.11
M.Sc. Natural Sci.	1,972	1.15	602	1.37
Engineering	1,108	0.65	1,060	2.41
Eng. Technicians	3,512	2.05	1,213	2.76
M.B.B.S Doctors	765	0.45	368	0.84
Paramedicals	2,909	1.70	2,546	5.79
Agricultural	2,345	1.37	677	1.54
Teaching**	3,047	1.78	19,038	43.30
Fiber Technology	469	0.27	166	0.38
Other	1,098	0.64	6,968*	15.84
Total	171,303	100.00	43,972	100.00

*Includes 4,402 skilled mechanics.
**The study does not mention what levels of teaching.
Source: UNESCO, *Higher Education and National Development in Four Countries* (1988: p. 51).

shows that 145,385 new generalist graduates were seeking jobs for only 8,931 (or 6.14 percent) positions. At the other end, for 19,038 professional teacher posts, there were only 3,047 (16 percent) graduate teachers seeking jobs. Overall 171,303 new graduates were seeking jobs against 43,972 (25.66 percent) available positions. This means about 74 percent of graduates would remain unemployed or underemployed. Further, although the new graduates from engineering and medical institutions are relatively smaller in number, the country still did not have the capacity to absorb them. The new job seekers must not only compete among themselves for the relatively few vacancies, but also with the large surplus of educated unemployed that has been created in past years. Why, then, do the Education Commission and all the development plans recommend more expansion of scientific and technical education, when there are no job opportunities for the graduates from these fields?

The expansion of these fields was recommended on the assumption that the graduates of scientific and technical education would contribute to the economic development of the country. The policy makers, however, failed to see that education alone cannot bring about desired development. Without overall socio-economic development, expansion of one education subsector may create more development problems: unemployment among graduates on the one hand and limited coverage for primary school age children on the other.

Faculty

The number of faculty members in all higher education institutions increased from 7,201 in 1970 to 22,447 (67.9 percent) in 1990. At the university and equivalent institutions the number of faculty increased from 1,138 to 2,959 (61.5 percent). In 1970, there were 581 (8 percent) female teachers in higher education; there were 2,861 (12.7 percent) by 1990. In the universities, there were only 69 (6 percent) female faculty members in 1970 compared to 357 (12 percent) in 1990 (UNESCO, 1977, 1993).

In 1990, the teacher:student ratio was 1:19, compared to 1:16 in 1970. However, variations exist among higher education institutions. In general colleges, the ratios are higher (1:20) than in universities (1:17). There were also differences among universities; the ratio in the Dhaka University was 1:17, whereas in the Jahangirnagar and the Khulna Universities they were 1:13 and 1:5, respectively (calculated from BANBEIS, 1992).

The number of teaching staff with higher academic degrees from abroad has been increasing mainly in universities and, to some extent, in government colleges. It increased from 17 percent in 1965 to 59 percent in 1985.[16] The composition of faculty members has also changed in favor of senior posts. The number of professors or associated professors increased from 16 percent of the total academic staff in 1960 to 31 percent in 1985 (Ahmad, 1992:54–59).

Teaching is a highly respected profession in Bangladesh. Moreover, only a selective and highly competent number of people are qualified for university teaching. In universities, one must obtain at least a first class degree at the bachelor's and/or master's level to be eligible for an appointment. At least three years of teaching experience and publication in recognized journals are required for the promotion from lecturer to assistant professor. For higher promotion, in addition to required publications, a minimum of five to seven years of teaching history is essential (Ahmad, 1992:54–59; Ahmed, 1992:63–69). The faculty members in Bangladesh are required and expected to engage in research work and get published in recognized journals. However, the financial support for research is very limited. There is no tenure system in Bangladesh as in the United States. Therefore, the phrase "publish or perish" does not apply. The fourth plan places strong emphasis on the research function of universities.

University teachers are often contracted by government or private external agencies as research consultants. In recent years, with the considerable interest of nongovernment organizations, donor agencies, and the government in research, university teachers are increasingly getting involved in consultant roles. This satisfies their academic and professional interests, besides paying them an honorarium (UNESCO, 1988:82–85, 89–90).

FUTURE DEVELOPMENTS

A number of forces contributed to the expansion of higher education in Bangladesh. First, there was a tremendous demand from the middle and upwardly mobile working class for higher education certificates without which one could not enter into the competition for highly rewarding, scarce modern sector jobs. Second, policy makers viewed higher education, especially technical and scientific education, as the vehicle for industrial and economic development. Therefore, the country invested more in this subsector. Third, the elite and the government, whose existence was dependent on the various pressure groups, tried to satisfy their interests at the expense of primary education. Thus, there was a discrepancy between actual allocation and expenditure for different levels of education, which always favored the tertiary level.

The new trend, however, seems to be the privatization of higher education institutions. The aim of private universities is to foster the development of a new generation of economists, computer scientists, and managers capable of leading the country in an era when global integration of markets is increasing (North-South University, n.d.). It was believed that with the recent growth in international trade and services, the demand for managerial, technical, and commercial studies will continue. Tremendous growth of the garment industry ($1 million in exports in 1981 to over $1.1 billion in 1991), the rapid privatization of the jute and textile sectors (one of the fastest rates in the world), and the emergence of a banking and transport infrastructure geared toward international trade all generated demand for managers and technocrats with specialized skills. Private universities in Bangladesh are intended to satisfy such demand.

Private universities are making collaborative arrangements with universities in the United States and other developed countries. The faculty members from the collaborative universities are often hired during their sabbaticals. This is believed to improve the standards of higher education to an international level.

There are other aspects of these private universities. First, for example, North-South University wants to reduce the drain of talented graduates by providing a flexible lateral entry for Bangladeshis wishing to return to the country for either a short or long term. This will also tap the skills and experience the graduates gained from their work and studies abroad.[17] Second, the private universities have greater institutional freedom in designing new curriculum that addresses the evolving economy. These universities not only focus on undergraduate and graduate degrees but also include programs for public and private sector managers. Third, the proponents of private universities believed that scarce foreign exchange spent to send students abroad should be tapped for investment in higher education in Bangladesh. It was believed that there was a large domestic market for quality higher education. Given the highly politicized student activism on campus, which contributed to "session jams" and inefficiency in higher education, private universities wanted to isolate their campuses from national politics.

Though these universities proclaim the principle of equal opportunity, they are targeting only a select group who are both academically highly qualified and financially well secured. This is evident in the tuition fees and selection process of these universities. These universities, however, planned to provide all talented but financially disadvantaged students an opportunity to pursue their education.

The establishment of universities in the private sector, it is argued, will increase the competition among the institutions and improve the quality of education to international standards. The question is whether the country will have the capacity to absorb these additional graduates, or whether the graduates will be produced to migrate abroad. Further research is needed to ascertain the role of private universities in the country's development endeavor. However, judging from the high admission and tuition fees, almost the entire student body of private universities and professional colleges come from an urban upper-class background. The establishment of private universities is not a solution to the inequitable distribution of resources. In fact, it may create further differentiation between public and private university graduates both in terms of educational outcomes and outcomes in society at large.

CONCLUSION

The expansion of higher education created development problems in Bangladesh, which cannot be solved by simple reforms within the education system alone. There is an oversupply of graduates from higher education to the labor market, though the majority of the population does not have access to even basic levels of education. This is a common problem in developing countries. Economists, policy makers, and planners have suggested, based on rates of returns on various levels of education, that priority should be given to the expansion of primary education. It is further argued that if students attending higher education institutions have to meet a larger percentage of the actual costs of their education by increased fees, the resulting rise in private costs would restrict the demand. The newly emerging universities in the private sector may answer some of the questions raised by the subsidized higher education system. But it is too early to analyze the impact of privatization.

It is also argued that the private share of educational costs should fall on the beneficiaries, not on their families and relatives, and that if private educational costs were financed directly out of a student's own resources or indirectly through loans repaid either by financial levies against the student's future income or by the contribution of expertise to social projects, students would be making an additional personal contribution to reduce costs to the society.

Another policy measure is that public agencies should indicate the level of qualifications required for particular jobs and select graduates with that specific level of qualification, and should not allow those who are "overqualified" to be considered. This will effectively discourage the private demand for higher education.[18] There is a clear case for reducing the public subsidy and controlling the output of the highly educated graduates—of which there is already a surplus in Bangladesh.

The question is why there is such a high demand for higher education, when it does not ensure employment. The demand continues, as mentioned earlier, because parents who understand the market economy view education as the only means of providing their children with an opportunity for upward mobility through relatively highly rewarding modern sector jobs. Since the modern sector requires individuals with certain levels of education, the demand for higher education will continue. While the government has adopted goals for changing the elitist structure, the process of implementation is vitally affected by the power of a small group of people who do enter the political arena and compete for educational goods (Dove, 1981). These pressure groups for higher education from urban centers had strong influence in the decision-making processes.

Finally, parental preference for higher education will continue although much of it remains "irrelevant" to the market demands. And the government has done little to restrict the expansion, even in the interest of the country. Therefore, what is needed is not only the introduction of reforms within the educational system itself, but also the reduction of the income gap between traditional and modern sector employment and between higher and lower levels of graduates. To overcome educational problems, fundamental changes in the economy and reward structures in Bangladesh are essential.

NOTES

1. The early proponents of these views are Harbison (1973), Harbison and Myers (1964), Schultz (1960), and Anderson and Bowman (1963), among others.

2. This study was strongly criticized on methodological grounds. For detailed discussions, see Blaug (1970:70); Bowman (1966:63); Sen (1966:67–75).

3. For alternative views, see Bacchus (1980).

4. For an extensive analysis on this subject, see Carnoy (1974).

5. For an elaborate discussion of the mechanism of resource transfer from East to West Pakistan, see Griffin and Khan (1972); Faaland and Perkinson (1976).

6. There were always discrepancies between allocation and actual expenditures. For example, while primary education received 24 percent and 20 percent of the allocation in the second and third five-year plans of Pakistan, the estimated actual expenditure at this level during the second-plan period was only 9 percent. This may be compared with an estimated actual expenditure of 17 percent for secondary and 25 percent (as against an allocation of 14 percent) for higher education in the second plan. The subsequent plans followed the same pattern. While the above allocation was for Pakistan as a whole, the budgetary allocation for different levels of education was the same for Bangladesh. For detailed discussions, see Chowdhury (1983: chapter 4).

7. In 1991 U.S.$1 = Tk 37.

8. Affiliated colleges follow the curricula and syllabi standard established by their respective affiliating universities. For more discussion, see the section on governance.

9. Professional colleges were government institutions until recently. The first private medical college located in Dhaka started its first session on July 1, 1987, with thirty-four students. Each student pays, by installment, a total sum of Tk 325,000 for the five-year course (Karim, 1989:18). The entry fee in North-South University is Tk 25,000

($625) and tuition fees are Tk 80,000 ($2,000) per year (personal communication with Junaid K. Ahmad, World Bank).

10. Most degree colleges also offer Higher Secondary School Certificate courses (grades 11–12).

11. Although colleges are nongovernment institutions, they receive large grants for teachers' salaries from the government.

12. Note that universities are autonomous bodies. Also note for the understanding of buying power, a secondary school teacher's basic monthly income in 1992 was Tk 1,200 to Tk 6,500, depending on qualification and post. However, there were differences in terms of other allowances and benefits, depending on whether the teachers were government or nongovernment employees and their residence.

13. The changes from Taka to U.S. dollars are calculated from IMF (1994).

14. In the document it is termed "postsecondary education," without any definition of what it consists of. See UNESCO (1993:table 1.4).

15. Personal communication with two private university officials, North-South University and Independent University, 1994.

16. The North-South University mostly employs young graduates from abroad and faculty members who are on sabbatical, especially from the United States.

17. In 1983, the World Bank funded a $7.3 million project to enhance the business management programs in the various national universities in Bangladesh. One important component of the program was faculty training abroad. According to the Bank, about 53 percent of the faculty sent abroad did not return; in the case of the Institute of Business Administration, the figure may have been as high as 83 percent. See North-South University, n.d.

18. Some of these suggestions are also incorporated into the fourth five-year plan (1990–95) of Bangladesh as strategies for restricting higher education. There are numerous suggestions as to how to improve the quality and restrict the exploding demand for higher education and, taken together, these can run into volumes. However, for important suggestions, see Blaug (1969, 1970), Todaro (1977), and the World Bank (1986, 1989). For elaborate analyses of all the suggestions and the question of why it is problematic to restrict the expansion of higher education in Bangladesh, see Chowdhury (1983:chapter 6).

REFERENCES

Ahmad, M. 1992. "Bangladesh." In B. R. Clark and Guy R. Neave., eds., *The Encyclopedia of Higher Education: National Systems of Higher Education.* Vol. 1. Oxford: Pergamon.

Ahmed, G. 1992. "Bangladesh." In W. Wickremasinghe, ed., *Handbook of World Education: A Comparative Guide to Higher Education and Educational Systems of the World.* Houston: American Collegiate Service.

Anderson, C. Arnold, and M. Bowman, eds. 1963. *Education and Economic Development.* Chicago: Aldine.

Bacchus, M. K. 1980. *Education for Development or Underdevelopment?* Ontario: Wilfrid Laurier University Press.

———. 1981. "Education for Development in Underdeveloped Countries." *Comparative Education, 17*(2), 215–27.

Bangladesh Bureau of Educational Information and Statistics (BANBEIS), Ministry of Education. 1992. *Bangladesh Educational Statistics 1991*. Dhaka: Author.

Bangladesh Bureau of Statistics (BBS), Ministry of Planning, Government of the People's Republic of Bangladesh. 1992. *Bangladesh Education in Statistics 1991*. Dhaka: Author.

————. 1993. *1992 Statistical Yearbook of Bangladesh*. 13th ed. Dhaka: Author.

————. 1970. *An Introduction to the Economics of Education*. Harmondsworth: Penguin.

Blaug, M., ed. 1969. *Economics of Education*. Vol. 2. Harmondsworth: Penguin.

Blaug, M., et al. 1969. *The Causes of Graduate Unemployment in India*. London: Penguin.

Bowman, M. H. 1966. "Review of F. Harbison and C. A. Myers, *Education, Manpower, and Economic Growth*." *Journal of Political Economy 73*(3). Reprinted in *Economics of Education*, ed. M. Blaug.

Carnoy, M. 1974. *Education as Cultural Imperialism*. New York: David Mckay.

Chowdhury, Kowsar P. 1983. "Educational Development in Bangladesh with Special Emphasis on Universalization of Primary Education." Unpublished M.Ed. thesis, the Faculty of Graduate Studies and Research, The University of Alberta.

Directorate of Inspection and Audit. 1992. "The Government Circular on New Salary Scale of July 1, 1992." Dhaka, handwritten circular in Bengali.

Dove, Linda. 1981. "Political Context of Education in Bangladesh 1971–80." In P. Broadfoot et al., eds. *Politics and Educational Change: An International Survey*. London: Croom Helm.

Faaland, J., and J. R. Perkinson. 1976. *Bangladesh: The Test Case of Development*. London: C. Hurst.

Griffin, K., and A. R. Khan, eds. 1972. *Growth and Inequality in Pakistan*. London: Macmillan.

Harbison, G. H. 1973. *Human Resources as the Wealth of Nations*. London: Oxford University Press.

Harbison, G. H., and C. A. Myers, 1964. *Education, Manpower, and Economic Growth*. New York: McGraw-Hill.

————. 1969. "Strategies of Human Resource Development." In M. Blaug, ed., *Economics of Education*. Vol. 2. Harmondsworth: Penguin.

Huq, M. S., et al. 1980. *Higher Education and Employment in Bangladesh*. Paris: IIEP (International Institute for Educational Planning).

International Monetary Fund. 1994. *International Financial Statistics Yearbook*. Washington, D.C.: Author.

Islam, T. 1975. *An Analysis of Public Recurring Expenditure of Higher Education*. Dhaka: Government of Bangladesh, University Grants Commission.

Karim, A. H. M. 1989. "Some Thoughts on Higher Education Today and Tomorrow." Dhaka.

————. 1993. *Education in Bangladesh: A Status Report, March 1993*. Dhaka: World Bank, General Education Project.

Khan, Tajul Islam. 1988. "Financing Higher Education in Bangladesh." Paper presented at the regional seminar on "Mobilization of Additional Funding for Higher Education," August 22–27, Bangkok.

Khandker, Shahidur R., Mahmudul Alam, and Vincent Greaney. 1995. *The Determinants and Impact of Basic Skill Attainment: The Role of School and Targeted Credit*

Programs in Bangladesh. Education and Social Policy Department, World Bank, and Bangladesh Institute of Development Studies.

North-South University. N.d. Unpublished document of objectives, rationale, and budget.

Planning Commission, Government of the People's Republic of Bangladesh, Ministry of Planning. 1973. *The First Five Year Plan 1973–78.* Dhaka: Author.

———. 1983. *The Second Five Year Plan 1980–85.* Dhaka: Author.

———. 1985. *The Third Five Year Plan 1985–90.* Dhaka: Author.

———. 1990. *The Fourth Five Year Plan 1990–95.* Dhaka: Author.

Schultz, T. W. 1960. "Capital Formation by Education." *Journal of Political Economy,* June.

———. 1963. *The Economic Value of Education.* New York: Columbia University Press.

Sen, A. K. 1966. "Economic Approaches to Education and Manpower Planning." *Indian Economic Review,* Vol. 1. Reprinted in *Economics of Education,* ed. M. Blaug.

Todaro, M. P. 1977. *Economic Development in the Third World.* London: Longman.

UNESCO. Various dates. *The Statistical Yearbook.* Paris: Author.

———. 1988. *Higher Education and National Development in Four Countries: India, Bangladesh, Thailand and the Philippines.* Bangkok: UNESCO Principal Regional Office for Asia and the Pacific.

World Bank. 1986. *Financing Education in Developing Countries: An Exploration of Policy Options.* Washington, D.C.: Author.

———. 1989. *Bangladesh Public Expenditure Review: Public Resources Management During the Fourth Five-Year Plan.* Washington, D.C.: Author.

———. 1993. *The World Development Report.* Washington, D.C.: Author.

———. 1995. *Bangladesh: Recent Economic Development and Priority Reform Agenda for Rapid Growth.* Washington, D.C.: Author.

2

CAMBODIA

Thomas Clayton and Yuok Ngoy

While some young men in traditional Cambodia matriculated from temple schools to "higher" education and apprenticeship-like studies in law, accounting, medicine, and several other fields (Népote, 1979), institutionalized higher education in Cambodia is a phenomenon of the colonial and postcolonial periods. Thus, following an introduction to Cambodia's geography and demography, in this chapter we discuss the development of higher education in Cambodia across four eras: French colonization (1863–1953), postcolonial independence (1953–79), Vietnamese occupation (1979–89), and postoccupation or contemporary independence (1989 to the present). In each historical discussion, we consider what Epstein (1992:413) terms the "school-society nexus": the symbiotic relationship between schools and the political, economic, and cultural/ideological milieu in which they are established. As this "nexus" is less clear in the still-evolving present, the final discussion will of necessity be more speculative than others.

CONTEXT

Cambodia is a small Southeast Asian country with a land area of 181,040 square kilometers (Vickery, 1986:1). With Vietnam and Laos, Cambodia is part of what is sometimes referred to as "Indo-china"; Cambodia borders Vietnam on the southeast and east, Laos on the northeast, Thailand on the northwest and west, and the Gulf of Thailand on the southwest. "The Kingdom of Cambodia" is the official name of the current state, a constitutional monarchy, though the country has been known as Kampuchea (before 1863), le Cambodge (1863–1953), the Kingdom of Cambodia (1953–70), the Khmer Republic (1970–75), Democratic Kampuchea (1975–79), the People's Republic of Kampuchea

(1979–89), and the State of Cambodia (1989–93) (Curtis, 1989:1). Except in reference to a specific regime, in this chapter we refer simply to "Cambodia."

The central three-quarters of Cambodia comprise the flood plains of the Upper and Lower Mekong Rivers, the Tonle Sap River, and the Bassac River. This "tilted saucer" (World Bank, 1992:3) contains most of the county's rice-growing areas. The four great rivers join at the capital, Phnom Penh, where the confluence is known as les Quatre Bras, or "the Four Arms." During the summer monsoons, the overflow from the Mekong causes the Tonle Sap River to reverse itself and flow back into the great inland lake, the Tonle Sap, filling it to many times its dry-season area. At the end of the monsoon season, in November, the river resumes its normal course, and the Tonle Sap shrinks, filled with rich alluvial silt and fish (Curtis, 1989).

Cambodia's population was estimated to be 10.5 million in 1995; 90 percent of this population live in rural areas, and 80 percent work in agriculture (Central Intelligence Agency, 1995). Approximately 95 percent of Cambodians are ethnic Khmers who speak the Khmer language (Curtis, 1989:8). In addition to Khmers, Cambodia's population includes ethnic Vietnamese, Chinese, Chams, and Khmer Loeu, a generic term for more than thirty ethnic groups living in the mountains of the north and northeast. A revolutionary literacy campaign mounted by the People's Republic of Kampuchea between 1980 and 1983 claims to have made 93.22 percent of all Cambodian citizens literate in Khmer (Ministry of Education, 1987:4), though external estimates of literacy range from 35 percent (United States Agency for International Development, 1995) to 70 percent (UNICEF, 1989:91).

FRENCH COLONIZATION, 1863–1953

Cambodia became a French protectorate in 1863. Cambodia's King Norodom agreed to French protection as a means of escaping a subordinate relationship with Thailand, though he soon found himself locked in a similar struggle with France. Throughout the nineteenth century, Norodom parried with the French, slowing but not stopping their inroads to his power and to Cambodia's traditional administrative structures (Osborne, 1969; Thomson, 1945). Following Norodom's death in 1904 and the ascent to the throne of his brother Sisowath, a "fawning collaborator" (Chandler, 1993:149), the French assumed control over all but ceremonial aspects of Cambodia's administration.

Under French protection, Cambodia was remade as a producer of raw materials for the French industrial economy (for discussion, see Whitaker et al., 1973). The French relied heavily on indigenous civil servants in administering the protectorate and accomplishing this transformation (Bilodeau, 1955; Nguyen-vo, 1992; Quinlan, 1992). In that it was designed specifically to train colonial civil servants, the French educational system in Cambodia was an integral component of this exploitative process.

The educational system established by the French served as a sorting machine, "select[ing] the better students [from basic education] for advanced education in order to equip the country with a large number of modern and competent civil servants" (Népote, 1979:775; all Népote quotes are our translation). Until 1949 and the establishment of the National Institute of Juridical, Political, and Economic Sciences (Hayden, 1967:197), "higher" education was offered exclusively at the Lycée Sisowath, the country's only secondary school. At these institutions, selected Cambodians followed such courses as law, accounting, administration, and engineering. All higher education and much basic education was offered exclusively in French (Bilodeau, 1955; Delvert, 1956; Forest, 1980; Morizon, 1931; Népote, 1979).

Scholars frequently refer to graduates of French colonial higher education as "new men" (Vickery, 1986:5; also see Osborne, 1969; Vickery, 1991), suggesting that through their educational interactions with the French, these Cambodians were fundamentally changed, discarding traditional values and ideologies for those things French. One scholar, for instance, comments that graduates were prepared to "assist . . . the French authorities [in] their work of colonization" (Bilodeau, 1955:16). Another describes the new French men as "Westernized Cambodians" dedicated to the French colonial mission (Morizon, 1931:178; all Morizon quotes are our translation).

Of central importance and value to the French was the ability of the new men to speak French. Most French administrators in Cambodia could not speak Khmer, and as a result "it [was] as if a great deal of Cambodian life . . . was carried out behind a screen, invisible and inaudible to the French" (Chandler, 1993:158). In that they were able to act as bilingual intermediaries in French-Cambodian interactions, the new men allowed the European administrators to pierce that screen and to function in the colonial setting. It would not be overstating the case to suggest that French-Khmer bilingual ability, learned in schools, was among the most important skills the new French men brought to the colonial administration (for a detailed discussion of French colonial education in Cambodia, see Clayton, in press).

POSTCOLONIAL INDEPENDENCE, 1953–79

Prince Norodom Sihanouk achieved Cambodia's independence from France on November 9, 1953. Under Sihanouk, Cambodia became a "one-party state" (Kiljunen, 1984:3) in which the prince jealously held power and ruthlessly suppressed opposition. One scholar compares Sihanouk to Louis XIV, suggesting the appropriateness for both leaders of the proclamation, "I am the state" (Chandler, 1993:195).

In spite of his dictatorial excesses, Sihanouk was at heart a nationalist driven by a sense of responsibility for achieving and preserving Cambodia's independence. While skillfully negotiating Cambodia's neutrality in relation to the escalating war in neighboring South Vietnam (Chandler, 1993; Smith, 1965), Sihanouk embarked on an agenda intended to break patterns of subordination inherited from the colonial era. Among other things, the prince developed infrastructure in order to reduce dependence on Vietnam and Thailand for international trade, and he nationalized key elements of the country's economy in an effort to wrest control from French interests (Whitaker et al., 1973).

The massive educational expansion engineered by the prince in the 1950s and 1960s was similarly linked to the nationalist enterprise. Devoting nearly 20 percent of Cambodia's budget annually to education, Sihanouk built schools and enrolled students at a staggering rate. Whereas there were fewer than eight hundred elementary and secondary schools in Cambodia at independence (Bilodeau, 1955:23–24), by 1970, nearly 5,400 such schools had been established (Whitaker et al. 1973:114; Duvieusart and Ughetto, 1973:19). The number of students in Cambodian schools increased from perhaps ninety thousand to well over one million during this same period (Népote, 1979:777–78).

Perhaps even more dramatic was the expansion of higher education. Several higher education institutions were founded in the 1950s to augment the National Institute of Juridical, Political, and Economic Sciences (Hayden, 1967:197); these institutes were subsumed as faculties within the Royal Khmer University, established in 1960 (ibid.). Eight additional institutes were opened after the university: the Royal Technical Institute (1964), the Buddhist University (1965), the Royal University of Agronomic Science (1965), the Royal University of Kompong Cham (1965), the University of Fine Arts (1965), the Popular University (1966), the Royal University of Battambang (1966), and the Royal University of Takeo/Kampot (1967) (Watts et al., 1989:153). Estimates of enrollment in higher education at the end of the 1960s range from 5,300 (Le, 1991:175), to 9,162 (Whitaker et al., 1973:119), to 14,560 (Gyallay-Pap, 1989: 260).

Education as developed during the Sihanouk regime helped Cambodia move away from French influence in two ways. First, as a result of educational expansion, greater numbers of students were able to enroll in higher education, to receive training, and to gain skills necessary to assume economic, political, and technical posts, many of which had until independence been held by French nationals (Népote, 1979; Whitaker et al., 1973). Educational expansion, then, was an important step away from colonial dependency toward national self-sufficiency and, by extension, away from French toward Cambodian control over national development.

While building educational infrastructure, the Sihanouk government additionally undertook reforms to seize ideological control of the educational system, to eradicate from it the "spirit of the colonial period" (Torhorst, 1966:166), and to install in its place a Cambodian character or identity (Whitaker et al., 1973). Accordingly, aspects of Cambodian education that were seen as serving the French colonial enterprise were replaced by policies dedicated to a nationalist vision. Perhaps the most significant reforms during this period related to language of instruction. Between 1953 and 1971, Khmer superseded French as the medium of instruction at all levels of education (Center for Applied Linguistics,

1978; Hayden, 1967; Whitaker et al., 1973), and one mechanism of French colonialism in Cambodian education was eliminated.

Unfortunately for the people of Cambodia, the educational gains realized during the Sihanouk regime were dramatically reversed following the prince's ouster in 1970 and the ascent to power of the communist Khmer Rouge in 1975 (for discussions, see Chandler, 1993; Kiernan, 1985). Compared with the radical transformation envisioned for Cambodia by Pol Pot and the Khmer Rouge, Sihanouk's efforts to assert Cambodian independence might be termed "incrementalist." Informed by the economic theorizing of French-educated Khieu Samphan, whose doctoral dissertation proposed Cambodia's escape from exploitative international structures and advocated agricultural isolationism (Burgler, 1990), the Khmer Rouge cut Cambodia off from nearly all communication with the outside world, evacuated Phnom Penh and all other cities and towns, and sent the urban population to the countryside where they were forced to work under brutal supervision in agricultural collectives (for firsthand accounts, see Haing Ngor, 1987; Pin Yathay, 1987).

Pol Pot perceived Sihanouk's educational system as a "feudal" institution supportive of social structures at odds with the Khmer Rouge's communist aspirations, and he set out systematically to destroy it. Between 1975 and 1979, the Khmer Rouge demolished 90 percent of all school buildings, libraries, and equipment (Barron and Paul, 1977; Ek Sam Ol, 1991; Hirschhorn, Haviland, and Salvo, 1991). Seven of the nine institutes of higher education in the country were destroyed, and the remaining two were badly damaged (Ek Sam Ol, 1991). Individuals associated with Sihanouk's educational system were similarly targeted by the Khmer Rouge. Among the one to three million Cambodians who died during the Khmer Rouge regime (Curtis, 1989) were 75 percent of the primary and secondary teaching force, 91 percent of university faculty, 67 percent of primary and secondary students, and 96 percent of tertiary students (Ministry of Education, 1990; UNESCO, 1991).

Though reprehensible, it is important to note that the purposeful destruction of education by Pol Pot was similar but for degree to Sihanouk's campaign against French influence in the previous decades. Both postcolonial leaders recognized dangers in the inherited educational systems for society as they visualized it, and, though their responses differed dramatically, both moved against the threatening aspects of those systems.

VIETNAMESE OCCUPATION, 1979–89

In response to repeated attacks by the Khmer Rouge, Vietnam invaded Cambodia in 1979, drove the Khmer Rouge into Thailand, and established a government of Cambodian Communists sympathetic to Vietnamese interests. As more than one hundred thousand Vietnamese troops settled in for the ten-year occupation (Vickery, 1984), Cambodia was transformed into a site of struggle in the Cold War. The Vietnamese were aligned with the Soviet Union; the

Khmer Rouge, established in camps on the Thai border, were provisioned directly and indirectly by the People's Republic of China, the United States, and the Association of South East Asian Nations. All actors were interested in either supporting or hindering both the Vietnamese presence in Cambodia and the Cambodian communist government, struggling to its feet under Vietnamese patronage (for discussions, see Chanda, 1986; Vickery, 1986).

Though the occupation is rightly described by many scholars in terms of regional and global geopolitics (Haas, 1991; Pike, 1987; Zagoria, 1988), it is important as well to acknowledge its humanitarian aspects. The Khmer Rouge had attempted to return Cambodia to the "Year Zero" (Mysliwiec, 1988; Ponchaud, 1978), and they succeeded to the extent that they destroyed most of the country's infrastructure and educated citizens. As a result, Cambodia in 1979 faced severe constraints in relation to development. Without diminishing the negative aspects of the occupation for Cambodians, it is clear that those few educated and experienced individuals who survived the Khmer Rouge would not have been able to rebuild the country without the assistance of Vietnam and its allies (for a discussion of the occupation-assistance dynamic, see Clayton, 1995). As one Cambodian educator commented in 1994, "When we came back to Phnom Penh in 1979, it was as if we had to wait for someone to come and help us govern the country because, at that time, we had no intellectuals. They had all been killed by Pol Pot" (cited in Clayton, 1995:251).

While Cambodia was embargoed by the West throughout the 1980s, Vietnam, the Soviet Union, and other Eastern bloc countries provided the country with billions of dollars in aid (Haas, 1991; World Bank, 1992), a significant amount of which was directed toward education. Dozens of Vietnamese advisors worked with the Ministry of Education in building schools, training teachers, and writing texts for primary and secondary education (Clayton, 1995). Whereas there was no formal education during the Khmer Rouge regime, nearly one million students enrolled in schools in 1979; this number increased to 1.6 million by the end of the decade (Ministére de l'Education, 1990:2–4; Ministry of Education, 1990:7–9).

In addition to fifty-four specialized educational institutes, including the primary and junior secondary teacher training colleges and the educational administration institute (Ek Sam Ol, 1991; Ministry of Education, 1990), six higher education institutes were reopened in the early 1980s (Council of Ministers, 1984). In the case of each institute, one or several Eastern bloc countries provided textbooks, laboratory equipment, facilities renovation, and opportunities for overseas study; as nearly all Cambodian professors had been killed by the Khmer Rouge, donor countries also supplied full contingents of faculty.

The Faculty of Medicine was opened in 1979 with assistance from Vietnam. In 1980, the senior secondary Teachers' Training College began offering classes with Vietnamese assistance. With assistance from Vietnam, the Soviet Union, East Germany, and Cuba, the School of Languages opened its doors in 1981. Also in 1981, the Khmer-Soviet Friendship Higher Technical Institute was opened with Soviet assistance. The Economics Institute began providing instruction with Vietnamese assistance in 1984. Finally, in 1985, the Agricultural Institute opened its doors with Soviet assistance. The Teachers' Training College and the School of Languages merged in 1988, becoming the University of Phnom Penh (Ministry of Education, 1990). By 1990, Cambodia's institutes of higher education had graduated 977 doctors, dentists, or pharmacists, 2,196 senior secondary teachers, 1,481 foreign language specialists, 474 technical engineers, 400 economists, and 184 agricultural engineers (Ek Sam Ol, 1991:17–18). The University of Fine Arts, opened in 1989 without Eastern bloc assistance, graduated no students in the 1980s (UNESCO, 1994).

Throughout the 1980s, language decisions for higher education were governed by what one Cambodian from the Ministry of Education described in 1994 as the "flexible language policy" (cited in Clayton, 1995:317): The language of instruction in each higher education institute was determined by the donor. Accordingly, nearly all institutes supported by Vietnam offered instruction in Vietnamese, and those institutes with support from the Soviet Union gave courses in Russian. Typically, students devoted their first year of higher education to intensive language study under the supervision of Vietnamese and Soviet language teachers (Clayton, 1995). Such language courses additionally prepared several thousand Cambodians for advanced study in Eastern bloc countries (Ministére de l'Education, 1990).

The use of external languages in higher education led some observers in the 1980s to conclude that Vietnam in particular intended to manufacture bilingual Cambodians and, much as the French had done, to use those individuals in establishing and maintaining colonial-like structures (Becker, 1986; Luciolli, 1988). A recent study based in part on the analysis of educational policy documents written for Cambodia by the Vietnamese, however, cautions against this conclusion (Clayton, 1995). In fact, Cambodian, Vietnamese, and Soviet educators worked together throughout the decade to "Khmerize" the higher education curriculum, and, as Cambodian students graduated from higher education and assumed teaching positions in Cambodia, they lectured in Khmer. Vietnamese and Russian language policies were therefore temporary, intended to remain in place only until Cambodian lecturers could be trained to replace those killed by the Khmer Rouge.

Certain other aspects of higher education, however, were specifically dedicated to Vietnamese and Soviet geopolitical goals in Cambodia. Vietnam and the Soviet Union were allies in the international socialist revolution and, as such, were committed to the worldwide spread of Marxist-Leninist, Soviet-style communism (Pike, 1987; Vickery, 1986). As in most countries in the former Eastern bloc (for several discussions, see Mauch and Sabloff, 1995), higher education as it was developed by the Vietnamese and Soviets in Cambodia served as one mechanism of support for this socialist agenda.

According to an educational policy document written by the Vietnamese for Cambodia, an important goal of higher education was training in various academic and technical fields, but "the most important thing pertain[ed] to the political training and ideology of students" (Central Committee of the Party, 1983; cited in Clayton, 1995:339). Such political training was achieved through required courses in Marxist-Leninist theories, world revolutionary history and the history of the Cambodian revolution, the situation and the role of the revolution and the policy of the party, moral education and the revolutionary way of life, and attitude to the common people (Central Committee of the Party, 1984). One Cambodian educator in 1994 described the goal of these courses as "forming the 'new man' [who] would be willing to fight against imperialism and capitalism and be willing to defend Cambodian culture against imperialism" (cited in Clayton, 1995:343).

Thus, while the Vietnamese and Soviets were less interested in promoting their languages in Cambodia than the French had been, they were no less aware of the power of education to advance an external agenda. Much as "new men" emerged from French schools willing to work for the colonial enterprise, the new men and women who graduated from higher education during the Vietnamese occupation had been conditioned to join with the Eastern bloc in combating capitalism, its structures, and its agents at the international and regional levels.

POSTOCCUPATION INDEPENDENCE, 1989–PRESENT

In 1989, as a result both of pressure from the West and of diminishing support from the Soviet Union, Vietnam withdrew its occupation force from Cambodia, leaving a fragile but functioning government and system of social services. Recognizing in Soviet perestroika and the similar *dôi mu'o'i* in Vietnam the inevitable demise of international communism, the newly independent Cambodian government embraced a multiparty political system and a free market economy. Following the UN-supervised election of 1993, the former communist government entered into a power-sharing arrangement with a royalist party led by Prince Sihanouk's son, and the current Kingdom of Cambodia was established. (Much of the information in this section was provided to the authors by Cambodian educators and government personnel in 1992, 1994, and 1995.)

The period between the Vietnamese withdrawal and the election was particularly difficult for Cambodian higher education. Along with troops, most Vietnamese educational advisors and professors were rotated home in 1989; Soviet professors were withdrawn shortly after when the Soviet Union collapsed. In some cases, higher education institutes were able to fill teaching vacancies with recently graduated Cambodians. In other cases, however, students sent overseas for advanced study had not yet finished their courses, and institutes faced overwhelming constraints. The Agricultural Institute, for instance, was forced to close briefly in 1990, and the Khmer-Soviet Friendship Higher Technical Institute might have closed had the United Nations Development Program and UNESCO not collaborated to bring twenty-eight Soviet teachers back to the institute in 1991.

Even while engaged in these struggles to maintain viability, the institutes of higher education initiated reforms associated with the new ways of thinking of the postoccupation era. Most significantly, between 1989 and 1991, the system of political education in place during the occupation was eliminated, and the core courses in Marxism-Leninism were cancelled. As one Cambodian educator explained in 1994, after the Vietnamese withdrawal and the turn away from communist political and economic structures, "we did not want to continue with communist dogma [that] was not important for our students." Much like Cambodian leaders in the postcolonial period, then, Cambodians in the postoccupation era moved quickly to eradicate aspects of education associated with the departed external enterprise.

At around the time of the election in 1993, Western governments began providing assistance to Cambodia, first through nongovernmental organizations and then directly. With foreign aid flowing and higher education in a vulnerable position, several institutes came perilously close to becoming subordinated to external interests once again. In 1992, for instance, the Khmer-Soviet Friendship Higher Technical Institute, renamed the Institute of Technology of Cambodia, agreed to accept a full array of educational resources from the government of France; as a condition of the agreement, French was made the language of instruction. Shortly after, the French made a similar proposal to the University of Phnom Penh. Though the university ultimately agreed only to join l'Association des Universités Partiellement ou Entiérement de Langue Française (the Association of Universities Partially or Entirely in the French Language) and to offer French as a foreign language, one Cambodian official commented in 1994 that "France has helped us and given us French teachers and materials in order to 'France-isize' the university." France also supported the Faculty of Law, opened in 1992 (UNESCO, 1994), and French was established for a time as the language of instruction at that institute.

Weinstein (1976, 1980, 1985) argues that France's contemporary promotion of French in education in Africa is designed to hold countries like Mali, Senegal, and Côte d'Ivoire within "francophonie," a supranational political, economic, and cultural organization controlled by France and ultimately beneficial to that country and its economic interests (for more on francophonie, see Bourhis, 1982; Djité, 1993; Treffgarne, 1986). One Cambodian educator argued that precisely this neocolonial motivation lay behind France's conditional assistance to Cambodia. "The French are trying to reassert their language in Cambodia," he stated in 1994, "for the purpose of holding us in francophonie." Rather than allowing Cambodian higher education to once again be turned toward external purposes, however, the Cambodian government reaffirmed control with the National Seminar on Higher Education in Cambodia, held in Phnom Penh, October 17–19, 1995 (Royal Government of Cambodia, 1995).

At the seminar, six themes were identified as "the major issues that confront higher education in Cambodia today" (ibid.:1). A working group assigned to each theme was charged with preparing a set of recommendations that will contribute to a ten-year national action plan for higher education, anticipated in early 1997. Concerning the sixth theme, language, the working group wrote, "Khmer should be the medium of instruction in Higher Education[;] two foreign languages, English and French, are also necessary in order to provide the teaching staff and students with the opportunity to have access to knowledge and information which are available in those two languages" (ibid.:12). Though French remains in selective use in higher education today, the Cambodian government made clear with this statement that French language policies, and whatever benefits they may provide to France, will be short-lived.

The remaining themes identified at the National Seminar on Higher Education and selected initial recommendations of working groups illustrate the problems facing higher education today and contemporary Cambodian thinking about educational reform:

1. *Legislation and Structure*. Cambodia's higher education institutes are currently under the control of several ministries, including the Ministries of Education, Agriculture, Culture, and Health. The working group recommended that "all Higher Education should be placed under one single ministry which could be the Ministry of Education or a new ministry to be created to deal exclusively with Higher Education" (ibid.:4).

2. *Access and Output*. The Constitution of the Kingdom of Cambodia endorses education for all. Accordingly, the working group stated, "all Cambodian people have the right to education regardless of gender or socio-economic condition" (ibid.:6). Additionally, since as of 1995 higher education graduates were no longer guaranteed government jobs, as during the communist regime, higher education "must be linked to . . . the labour market[, and a] survey of demand in the labour market should be conducted in order to know the need and type of professions required" (ibid.:6).

3. *Resources*. There was no tuition for higher education during the communist regime, and even today tuition is an extremely low 5,000 riels (U.S.$2) per semester. The working group recommended that in the future, students "should contribute [more] to the cost of their education [and that] cooperation between higher education and the private sector should be encouraged" (ibid.:8).

4. *Institutional Management*. During the communist regime, most aspects of higher education administration were controlled at the central level. Today, however, a "modified system of financial autonomy for the institutions is required which will allow full responsibility for the day-to-day management of the institutions" (ibid.:9).

5. *Academic Programs*. Reflecting the political, economic, and ideological changes that led in the early 1990s to the abandonment of Marxist-Leninist political education courses, the working group recommended the "formulation of new curricula based on the socio-economic needs in Cambodia [rather than on] import[ed,] ready-made curriculum" (ibid.:10).

As the six working groups began work in October 1995 on the ten-year national action plan for higher education, the focus of their attention was on the eight contemporary institutes of higher education:

1. University of Phnom Penh. The university consists of the faculties of science, letters and human sciences, pedagogy, foreign languages, and social sciences. As of 1993, 15,051 students were enrolled at the university; 4,775 of these students followed a preuniversity, preparatory course that was abandoned across the higher education system in 1995. Nine hundred new students entered in each of the 1994 and 1995 classes. In 1993, 198 faculty members offered classes at the university. Instruction in content courses at the university is in Khmer, and French and English are offered as foreign languages.

2. Institute of Technology of Cambodia, formerly the Khmer-Soviet Friendship Higher Technical Institute, in Phnom Penh. Courses are offered in industrial chemistry, construction, electrical technology, hydrology, and geology. As of 1993, 190 teachers were attached to the institute, and 2,415 students were enrolled, including 700 in the preparatory year. One hundred and eighty new students enrolled in both 1994 and 1995. Most instruction is offered in French.

3. Institute of Business, formerly the Business Faculty of the Institute of Economics, in Phnom Penh. As of 1993, the institute enrolled 4,290 matriculated students and 2,706 preparatory students, at which time courses were offered by 43 teachers. One hundred new students enrolled in 1994, and 300 students entered the institute in 1995. Khmer is the language of instruction.

4. Faculty of Law and Economic Sciences, formerly the Faculty of Law, and the Economic Sciences Faculty of the Institute of Economics, in Phnom Penh. In 1993, 7,756 students were enrolled at the faculty, including 3,646 in the preparatory course. At that time, 27 faculty members were attached to the faculty. In 1994 and 1995, 250 and 375 new students enrolled, respectively. Most courses at the faculty are in Khmer, though a bachelor of business administration course is given in French. French and English are additionally offered as foreign languages.

5. Maharashi Vedic University, established in 1991, in Prey Veng Province. This university, the first to be situated outside Phnom Penh since the 1970s, offers courses in agriculture, medicine, and management. As of 1993, 757 matriculated and 227 preparatory students were enrolled, at which time 54 teachers offered courses. One hundred and fifty new students entered the university in 1994; 130 additional students enrolled in 1995. The language of instruction is Khmer.

6. Royal University of Agriculture, formerly the Agricultural Institute, in Phnom Penh. Offering courses in agriculture, forestry, veterinary medicine, fisheries, and agricultural mechanics, the university enrolled 2,382 students in 1993, including 800 in the preparatory year. One hundred and twenty students entered the university in each of the 1994 and 1995 classes. Instruction at the university is in Khmer, offered by 76 faculty members as of 1993.

7. University of Fine Arts, in Phnom Penh. Faculties at the university include archeology, architecture, modeling, music, and theater. In 1993, 430 matriculated students and 648 preparatory students were enrolled; 60 and 130 new students entered the university in 1994 and 1995, respectively. Instruction is offered in Khmer. As of 1993, 258 teachers were attached to the university.

8. Faculty of Medicine, Phnom Penh. The faculty offers courses in medicine, dentistry, and pharmacy. As of 1993, 4,258 students studied at the faculty, 2,169 of them in

the preparatory course. One hundred and fifty new students enrolled in both 1994 and 1995. Courses are offered by 62 faculty members. Khmer is the language of instruction, though French medical terminology is used where equivalent words do not exist in Khmer (Kingdom of Cambodia, 1993; Locard, 1993; Ministry of Education, 1993; UNESCO, 1994).

FUTURE DEVELOPMENTS

In its relatively short history, the system of higher education in Cambodia has gone through fantastic changes reflecting the equally fantastic shifts in the country's position vis-à-vis powerful external and internal interests and the political, economic, and cultural/ideological systems promoted by those interests. Originally dedicated to the production of willing and able administrators for the French colonial civil service, in the years following independence, higher education was expanded as part of one national enterprise and then destroyed as part of another. Though the system was rebuilt during the Vietnamese occupation, Cambodian tertiary students were subjected to political training predicated on the imperatives of the international socialist revolution.

Cambodia's system of higher education entered the postoccupation period susceptible to French neocolonial aspirations, and those aspirations remain a threat today. However, as educators associated with the National Seminar on Higher Education and the ten-year action plan for higher education grapple with issues of governance, access, financing, autonomy, curricular reform, and language, there is strong indication that Cambodians have taken control of the system of higher education and are in the process of realigning that system to Cambodian goals and purposes.

REFERENCES

Barron, P., and A. Paul. 1977. *Peace with Horror*. London: Hodder & Stoughton.

Becker, E. 1986. *When the War Was Over: Cambodia's Revolution and the Voices of Its People*. New York: Simon and Schuster.

Bilodeau, C. 1955. "Compulsory Education in Cambodia." In C. Bilodeau, S. Pathammavong, and Q. H. Lê, eds., *Compulsory Education in Cambodia, Laos and Viet-Nam*. Paris: UNESCO.

Bourhis, R. Y. 1982. "Language Policies and Language Attitudes: Le monde de la francophonie." In E. B. Ryan and H. Giles, eds., *Attitudes Towards Language Variation: Social and Applied Contexts*. London: Edward Arnold.

Burgler, R. A. 1990. *The Eyes of the Pineapple: Revolutionary Intellectuals and Terror in Democratic Kampuchea*. Saarbrücken, Germany: Verlag Breitenbach.

Center for Applied Linguistics. 1978. *Teaching English to Cambodian Students*. Arlington, Va.: Author.

Central Committee of the Party. 1983. Decision #129 of the Central Committee of the Party about problems of higher and technical education. Phnom Penh: Author.

————. 1984. Circular #128 of the Central Committee of the Party about ideological and political training in higher education. Phnom Penh: Author.

Central Intelligence Agency. 1995. Cambodia. World Wide Web document: http://www.odci.gov/cia/publications/95fact/cb.html.

Chanda, N. 1986. *Brother Enemy: The War after the War*. San Diego: Harcourt Brace Jovanovich.

Chandler, D. P. 1993. *A History of Cambodia*. 2nd ed. Boulder, Colo.: Westview.

Clayton, T. 1995. *Education and Language-in-Education in Relation to External Intervention in Cambodia, 1620–1989*. Ann Arbor, Mich.: University Microfilms.

————. In press. *Restriction or Resistance? Educational Development in French Colonial Cambodia*. Educational Policy Analysis Archives.

Council of Ministers. 1984. Decree #24 of the Council of Ministers concerning the creation and management of higher and technical education establishments. Phnom Penh: Author.

Curtis, G. 1989. *Cambodia: A Country Profile*. Stockholm: Swedish International Development Authority.

Delvert, J. 1956. ''L'æuvre française d'enseignement au Cambodge.'' *France-Asie*, 125–27, 309–20.

Djité, P. G. 1993. ''Francophonie: Gain d'humanité ou perte d'identité?'' *Language Problems and Language Planning, 17*, 254–64.

Duvieusart, B., and R. Ughetto. 1973. *République Khmère: Project de Restructuration du système d'éducation*. Paris: UNESCO.

Ek Sam Ol. 1991. ''The Situation of Higher and Technical Education in the State of Cambodia since January 7th 1979.'' Paper presented at the Cambodian Workshop on Reconstruction and Development, Penang, Malaysia.

Epstein, E. H. 1992. Editorial. *Comparative Education Review, 36*, 409–16.

Forest, A. 1980. *Le Cambodge et la colonisation française: Histoire d'une colonisation sans heurts (1897–1920)*. Paris: Editions L'Harmattan.

Gyallay-Pap, P. 1989. ''Reclaiming a Shattered Past: Education for the Displaced Khmer in Thailand.'' *Journal of Refugee Studies, 2*, 257–75.

Haas, M. 1991. *Genocide by Proxy: Cambodian Pawn on a Superpower Chessboard*. New York: Praeger.

Haing Ngor. 1987. *A Cambodian Odyssey*. New York: Macmillan.

Hayden, H. 1967. *Higher Education and Development in South-East Asia: Country Profiles*. Paris: UNESCO.

Hirschhorn, N., L. Haviland, and J. Salvo. 1991. *Critical Needs Assessment in Cambodia: The Humanitarian Issues*. Washington, D.C.: United States Agency for International Development (USAID).

Kiernan, B. 1985. *How Pol Pot Came to Power: A History of Communism in Kampuchea, 1930–1975*. London: Verso.

Kiljunen, K., ed. 1984. *Kampuchea: Decade of the Genocide*. London: Zed.

Kingdom of Cambodia. 1993. *Phnom Penh University*. Phnom Penh: Author.

Le, T. C. 1991. ''Higher Education Reform in Vietnam, Laos, and Cambodia.'' *Comparative Education Review, 35*, 170–76.

Locard, H. 1993. *Social Sciences at the University of Phnom Penh*. Phnom Penh: Author.

Luciolli, E. 1988. *Le mur de bambou*. Paris: Médecins Sans Frontieres.

Mauch, J. E., and P. L. W. Sabloff, eds. 1995. *Reform and Change in Higher Education: International Perspectives*. New York: Garland.

Ministére de l'Education. 1990. *Bulletin de Statistiques de l'education de l'Etat du Cambodge*. Phnom Penh: Author.

Ministry of Education. 1987. "Some Aspects of the Literacy Movement and Complementary Education from the Great Victory of January 7, 1979 to the End of 1987." Phnom Penh: Author.

————. 1990. *Education: State of Cambodia*. Phnom Penh: Author.

————. 1993. *Education Statistics and Training*. Phnom Penh: Author.

Morizon, R. 1931. *Monographie du Cambodge*. Hanoi: Imprimerie d'Extrême-Orient.

Mysliwiec, E. 1988. *Punishing the Poor: The International Isolation of Kampuchea*. Oxford: Oxfam.

Népote, J. 1979. "Education et développement dans le Cambodge moderne." *Mondes en Développement, 28*, 767–92.

Nguyen-vo, T. H. 1992. *Khmer-Viet Relations and the Third Indochina Conflict*. Jefferson, N.C.: McFarland.

Osborne, M. E. 1969. *The French Presence in Cochinchina and Cambodia: Rule and Response (1859–1905)*. Ithaca, N.Y.: Cornell University Press.

Pike, D. 1987. *Vietnam and the Soviet Union: Anatomy of an Alliance*. Boulder, Colo.: Westview.

Pin Yathay. 1987. *Stay Alive, My Son*. New York: Touchstone.

Ponchaud, F. 1978. *Cambodia Year Zero*. New York: Holt, Rinehart and Winston.

Quinlan, A. 1992. *Education Reform in Cambodia*. Master's thesis, University of London.

Royal Government of Cambodia. 1995. *National Higher Education Action Plan Project*. Phnom Penh: Author.

Smith, R. M. 1965. *Cambodia's Foreign Policy*. Ithaca, N.Y.: Cornell University Press.

Thomson, R. S. 1945. "The Establishment of the French Protectorate over Cambodia." *Far Eastern Quarterly, 4*, 313–40.

Torhorst, M. 1966. "The Development of the Educational System in the Kingdom of Cambodia." In *Educational Systems of Some Developing Countries in Africa and Asia*. Dresden: Verlag Zeit Im Bild.

Treffgarne, C. 1986. "Language Policy in Francophone Africa: Scapegoat or Panacea?" In *Language in Education in Africa: Proceedings of a Seminar Held in the Centre of African Studies*. Edinburgh: Centre of African Studies.

UNESCO. 1991. *Inter-sectoral Basic Needs Assessment Mission to Cambodia*. Bangkok: Author.

————. 1994. *Rebuilding Quality Education and Training in Cambodia*. Phnom Penh: Author.

UNICEF. 1989. *Cambodia: The Situation of Women and Children*. Phnom Penh: Author.

United States Agency for International Development. 1995. "Cambodia." Gopher document: United States Agency for International Development/Regional-Country Focus/Asia and the Near East/Cambodia/Congressional Presentation FY96/Cambodia.

Vickery, M. 1984. *Cambodia: 1975–1982*. Boston: South End.

————. 1986. *Kampuchea: Politics, Economics and Society*. London: Pinter.

————. 1991. "Cambodia." In D. Allen and N. V. Long, eds., *Coming to Terms: Indochina, the United States, and the War*. Boulder, Colo.: Westview.

Watts, K., C. Draper, D. Elder, J. Harrison, Y. Higaki, and J.C. Salle. 1989. *Kampuchea Needs Assessment Study*. United Nations Development Program.

Weinstein, B. 1976. "Francophonie: A Language-Based Movement in World Politics." *International Organization, 30*, 485–507.

———. 1980. "Language Planning in Francophone Africa." *Language Problems and Language Planning, 4*, 56–75.

———. 1985. "Francophonie: Purism at the International Level." Paper presented at the conference, "The Politics of Language Purism: A Rhetoric of Authentication," East-West Center, University of Hawaii, Honolulu.

Whitaker, D. P., J. M. Heimann, J. E. MacDonald, K. W. Martindale, R.S. Shinn, and C. Townsend. 1973. *Area Handbook for the Khmer Republic (Cambodia)*. Washington, D.C.: U.S. Government Printing Office.

World Bank. 1992. *Cambodia: Agenda for Rehabilitation and Reconstruction*. Washington, D.C.: Author.

Zagoria, D. S. 1988. "The Soviet-Vietnamese Alliance." In J. J. Zasloff, ed., *Postwar Indochina: Old Enemies and New Allies*. Washington, D.C.: Foreign Service Institute, U.S. Department of State.

3

CHINA

Weifang Min

China is situated in East Asia. It covers an area of about 9.6 million square kilometers and had a total population of 1.2 billion in 1992. The earliest Chinese state was established during the Xia Dynasty (about 2200 B.C.). From the beginning of its development, Chinese culture attached great importance to education. Many elaborations can be found from ancient Chinese classics such as "To establish a nation state, education comes first"; and "A man without education cannot be a knowledgeable and moral man." Ancient Chinese higher education originated as early as the eleventh century B.C. during the Zhou Dynasty. After many years of evolution and interaction with the outside world, China started its modern higher education in the late nineteenth century. Since then, modern higher education in China has undergone dramatic social, political, and economic changes.

In 1949, the People's Republic of China was founded. The country entered a new stage of development. The socialist system has become the basic system of the state. A centralized, state-planned economic system was established and functioned until the late 1970s, which had a profound impact on the Chinese higher education system. From 1966 to 1976, China endured the "Cultural Revolution" period, which set China's socioeconomic and scientific development back about twenty years. In 1978, new national policies for modernization, reform, and opening up to the outside world were formulated and nationwide reform was launched, aimed at speeding up economic development. The government set the target of quadrupling the total output value of industries and agriculture between 1980 and 2000 in constant price. The centrally planned economy has been gradually transformed into a more dynamic, socialist market economy. The open-door policy and the rapid growth of foreign investment have remarkably increased the interactions between China and the outside world, gradually integrating the country into the world economy. The new policies have resulted in an average growth rate of 9.4 percent over the past fifteen years. Meanwhile, fundamental changes have taken place in every sector of the society, including higher education. To understand the changes in Chinese higher education, one has to first examine the institutional context within which it is situated, as well as the international arena.

PROFILE OF THE HIGHER EDUCATION SYSTEM

Historical Development

Higher education development in Old China. Constrained by feudalism, ancient Chinese higher education evolved slowly. The ancient curriculum consisted mainly of Chinese classics aimed at producing civil servants for the feudal society. After the Opium War in 1840, Western higher education began to have an influence on China. In 1898, the Chinese government officially established the Metropolitan University in Beijing (predecessor of Peking University), symbolizing the start of modern Chinese higher education. However, since Old China suffered from continuous foreign invasions and civil wars, the economy was extremely backward, people were very poor, and higher education developed very slowly. By 1949, China had only 204 higher education institutions (including short-cycle colleges) with a total enrollment of 155,036 students.

Soviet influences and the reorganization of higher education in the early 1950s. After the founding of the People's Republic of China in 1949, the state nationalized all higher education institutions, including all private and missionary universities and colleges in 1952. Influenced by the Soviet higher education model, the new system was organized on the basis of a centrally planned economy, and was characterized by excessive specialization of colleges and universities. Unitary instructional plans, course syllabi, and textbooks were developed for colleges and universities throughout the country. The influences of the 1952 reform still exist today.

The "Great Leap Forward" of 1958 and the Cultural Revolution of 1966–76. After the completion of the first five-year plan (1953–58) for socioeconomic development, the Chinese government launched, in 1958, a nationwide mass movement for development—the "Great Leap Forward" for Socialist Construction. Thus the Chinese higher education system was faced with many new demands, which triggered the Great Leap Forward in higher education development (also called "Educational Revolution"). Higher education expanded dramatically. The number of higher education institutions increased from 229 in 1957 to 1,289 in 1960. More than 1,000 new universities and colleges were established within 3 years. The total enrollment increased from 441,181 in 1957 to 961,623 in 1960. Such a dramatic expansion caused severe problems related to low efficiency and poor quality. Also, universities experienced serious financial difficulties due to the country's economic austerity. Therefore, in 1961

Table 3.1
The Composition of the Higher Education System in China, 1993

Type of Institution	Number of Institutions
Regular Higher Education Institutions:	
Comprehensive Universities	62
Specialized Colleges	571
Short-cycle Specialized Colleges	356
Short-cycle Vocational Universities	83
Sub-Total	1065
Adult Higher Education Institutions:	
Workers' Colleges	714
Peasants' Universities	5
Management Training Colleges	166
Educational Colleges	249
Independent Correspondence Colleges	4
TV Universities	45
Sub-Total	1183
Grand Total:	2248

Source: Department of Planning, State Education Commission of China, 1994.

the Ministry of Education reduced the number of higher education institutions and consolidated small universities and colleges. After 3 years of adjustment, the total number of institutions decreased from 1,289 in 1960 to 407 in 1963. From 1963 to 1965, Chinese higher education emerged from the hectic expansion and difficult reorganization, and both quality of instruction and institutional efficiency were improved. However, this was reversed by the Cultural Revolution, which began in 1966. Universities and colleges were attacked as places disseminating bourgeois ideologies, and were not allowed to enroll students for more than 4 years. The national examinations for college entrance were abolished, and many universities were shut down. After the Cultural Revolution, China implemented new modernization policies for speeding up economic development. Since the late 1970s, Chinese higher education has been operating within a new period of vigorous development.

The Composition of Higher Education in China

The current Chinese higher education system consists of two major components: regular higher education and adult higher education (see table 3.1). Regular higher education institutions include universities with both undergraduate and graduate degree programs; independent specialized colleges with undergraduate and graduate degree programs; short-cycle (2- or 3-year) specialized colleges without degree programs; and short-cycle vocational universities without degree programs. Adult higher education institutions include workers' universities for training and upgrading enterprise employees; peasants' universities for training and upgrading peasants; management training colleges for training and upgrading managers and cadres; educational colleges for training and upgrading secondary school teachers and school administrators; independent correspondence colleges; and TV universities offering a variety of programs. Adult higher education programs offer both part-time and full-time programs, though only some of them award bachelor's degrees. They do not usually grant advanced degree programs. The rest of this chapter mainly discusses regular higher education in China.

Types of Regular Higher Education Institutions in China

The current structure of the Chinese higher education system by types of institutions was developed based on the reorganization of 1952, which was based on the principle of a centrally planned economy. Many highly specialized institutions were established, such as the Beijing Chemical Engineering College, the Beijing Institute of Posts and Telecommunications, and the Beijing Geology College. The existing universities remained, but some of their engineering departments were transferred to other specialized institutions. Currently, among the 1,065 higher education institutions in China, 62 are comprehensive universities; the rest are specialized colleges as shown in table 3.2.

Enrollment Rates of Higher Education in China

The enrollment in regular higher education since 1949 has fluctuated with the social, political, and economic situation of the country. It increased from 117,133 in 1949 to 444,359 in 1957, jumped to 965,258 in 1960 because of the "Great Leap Forward," and dropped to 47,800 in 1970 because of the "Cultural Revolution." It then increased to 2,535,517 in 1993 because of the new policies for modernization and economic development. The proportion of relevant age group of the population attending higher education has been very low in China. In 1993, the higher education enrollment rate was about 3 percent, while it was 97.2 percent for primary education, about 63.7 percent for lower secondary education, and about 23.1 percent for upper secondary education.

THE CHANGING FUNCTIONS AND PATTERNS OF HIGHER EDUCATION

Since the late 1970s, new policies for modernization, reform, and opening up to the outside world were formulated and implemented to speed economic de-

Table 3.2

Types of Regular Higher Education Institutions in China, 1993*

Type	number of institutions	number of students	number of teachers
comprehensive universities	62	303,945	47,923
engineering colleges	292	928,552	142,331
agriculture colleges	59	134,802	23,355
forestry colleges	11	21,024	4,085
medicine colleges	126	224,936	42,310
teacher training colleges	251	566,553	74,965
language colleges	14	17,760	4,689
economics and finance colleges	82	167,071	20,163
political science and law colleges	27	33,341	4,900
physical culture colleges	15	15,572	3,332
art colleges	31	15,271	5,535
ethnic minority colleges	11	26,782	4,606
short cycle vocational universities	83	79,909	9,614
Total	**1,065**	**2,535,517**	**387,808**

*The enrollment includes only undergraduate students. The total enrollment for graduate students is 106,771.

Source: Department of Planning, State Education Commission of China (1994).

velopment. Education was considered the strategic foundation for economic success because there was a growing recognition of the importance of the availability of well-educated manpower, especially high-level specialized personnel. Priority was given to higher education. Both social and private demands for higher education have been soaring. Higher education enrollment has expanded rapidly. The functions and patterns of Chinese higher education have dramatically changed.

Policy and Planning

Since the late 1970s, the fundamental national policies for Chinese higher education have been aimed at serving modernization, reform, and economic development. Many government documents stated that education must serve socialist construction, which in turn must rely on education. Thus the mission of higher education came to include the training of millions of high-level specialized personnel equipped with up-to-date knowledge of science, technology, and management, imbued with pioneering spirit, and able to keep abreast of developments in scientific, cultural, and technological fields of study. According to the *Decision on the Reform of China's Education Structure* (CPC Central Committee, 1985):

China's strategic goal in developing higher education is: by the end of this century, China will have built a well-proportioned, rationally tiered higher education system embracing a complete range of disciplines and areas of studies, on a comprehensive scale conforming to its economic strength; senior specialists will be trained basically at home and higher education institutions will contribute substantially to the country's scientific and technological development and to solving major theoretical and practical problems that crop up in the modernization process.

A more recent document, *China Education Reform and Development Outline* (CPC Central Committee and State Council, 1993), reemphasized that "in order to achieve the country's modernization goals, it is essential to place education in a strategic position and give education high priority in national development in order to raise the moral, cultural, and scientific level of the whole nation." Again, it was announced that in the 1990s higher education enrollment would be expanded; the higher education structure would be further rationalized; and the instructional quality and institutional efficiency and effectiveness would be remarkably improved.

Since the late 1970s, many policy decisions were made to promote higher education development, including: (1) expansion of regular higher education enrollment by enlarging existing institutions and setting up new higher education institutions (about three hundred new higher education institutions were established during 1982–85); (2) diversifying higher education by developing new types of institutions, including polytechnics and short-cycle vocational colleges (among the four hundred new colleges and universities established in the late 1970s and early 1980s, more than 70 percent were short-cycle institutions); (3) establishment of distance/open higher education institutions, such as TV universities and correspondence programs; (4) sending students abroad and encouraging international exchanges; (5) establishment of *minban* (non-state-run or private) universities and colleges in order to mobilize more resources for acceleration of higher education development. Regulations on *minban* higher education were formulated and published (State Education Commission, 1993). All these policy decisions had a common objective: enlarging the provision of higher education to meet the increasing need for well-educated manpower stimulated by the modernization process.

Finance and Governance

Outline of regular higher education finance and governance. Chinese universities and colleges are divided into three groups in terms of finance and governance. Table 3.3 shows that 36 universities are directly administered and financed by the State Education Commission, which is also responsible for the

Table 3.3
Affiliation of Regular Higher Education Institutions in China, 1993

Affiliation	Number of Institutions	Enrollment	Average Size	Number of Teachers
State Education Commission	36	255,699		47,485
Other Central Ministries	325	853,217		141,009
Provinces	704	1,426,601		199,314
Total	1,065	2,535,517		387,808

Source: Department of Planning, State Education Commission of China (1994).

overall guidance and coordination of the higher education system through formulation of national higher education policies, decrees, and plans. Another 325 universities and colleges are administered and financed by line Ministries of the central government, such as the Ministry of Agriculture, the Ministry of Electronic Industries, and the Ministry of Public Health. Each of these Ministries has a department of education in charge of managing its own education institutions. There are 704 local universities and colleges administered and financed by Provincial Education Commissions, including a few administered by local governments with provincial supervision.

As a result of the nationalization of higher education institutions in 1952, all 1,065 universities and colleges in China are state-run institutions. However, it should be mentioned that *minban* (private) colleges and universities, which were established by local communities, associations, and individuals, are increasing in number. Some *minban* institutions have been accredited by the state agencies concerned. Though these institutions are very active, very flexible, and adaptive to the labor market needs, serving as a complement to the public higher education, they are also small and unstable, and there are no official statistics available about them. Thus, it is very difficult to analyze them systematically, though they will grow stronger and play a more important role in Chinese higher education in the future.

Sources of funding for higher education. There are two major sources of funding: state appropriation, which has been the major source accounting for more than 80 percent of the total; and income generated by higher education institutions themselves, which has been increasing in recent years. Government allocation to higher education comes mainly from the central and provincial levels. The allocation for the 36 national universities administered by the State Education Commission and the 325 universities and colleges by the central line Ministries comes from the budget of the Ministry of Finance, which allocates funds to the State Education Commission and other Ministries, which in turn allocate the funds to the universities and colleges under their jurisdiction. The

Table 3.4
Higher Education Financing in China (in billion yuan)

Year	GNP	Total government revenue	Total national budget	Total expenditure on education	Total expenditure on higher education	Revenue generated by higher education institutions
1952	NA	18.37	17.60	1.16	0.27	NA
1965	NA	47.33	46.63	3.59	0.74	NA
1978	358.81	112.11	111.10	7.62	1.50	0.06
1979	399.81	110.33	127.39	8.81	2.32	0.09
1980	447.60	108.52	121.27	11.32	2.81	0.07
1981	477.30	108.95	111.50	12.25	3.21	NA
1982	519.30	112.40	115.33	13.66	3.44	0.08
1983	580.90	124.90	129.25	15.29	4.30	0.10
1984	696.20	150.19	154.64	17.90	5.22	0.14
1985	855.76	186.64	184.48	22.44	6.08	0.55
1986	969.63	226.03	233.08	26.49	7.51	NA
1987	1130.10	236.89	244.85	27.70	7.54	0.69
1988	1406.82	262.80	270.66	32.36	8.17	0.92
1989	1599.33	294.79	304.03	49.00	8.75	0.97
1990	1769.53	331.26	345.22	53.30	8.94	1.26
1991	2023.63	361.09	381.36	58.06	9.91	1.49
1992	2403.36	415.31	438.97	68,19	11.04	2.16
1993	3134.23	508.82	528.74	86.77	15.04	3.46

Source: State Education Commission, State Statistics Bureau of China (1994).

704 local universities and colleges receive funds mainly from the provincial finance departments. A very small proportion of them receive funds from prefectural or county-level governments. Table 3.4 provides the statistics on state allocation and revenue generated by higher education institutions.

Since the late 1970s, China has increased allocation to higher education both in absolute terms and relative to government expenditure and GNP. The annual rate of increase of expenditure on higher education is higher than the annual rate of increase in the total government revenue. For example, total public expenditure increased 3.93 times from 111.10 billion yuan in 1978 to 438.97 billion yuan in 1992, while expenditure on higher education increased 7.33 times from 1.50 billion yuan to 11.04 billion yuan during the same period. This reflects the high priority given to higher education in the country's modernization process. It also can be seen that since 1985, when universities were given greater · autonomy to generate revenue, they have increased the proportion of self-generated funds. Table 3.4 shows that higher education institutions generated

Table 3.5
Curriculum Streams in Chinese Higher Education, 1991–92

Fields of Studies	Number of Specialties	Number of Programs	Number of students*
Sciences	123	879	88,885
Humanities	69	1,031	101,375
Engineering	366	4,830	802,366
agriculture	53	679	88,193
Forestry	17	152	21,001
Medicine & Pharmacy	25	583	214,285
Teacher Training	42	3,079	547,199
Finance & Economics	45	1,597	244,414
Political Science & Law	12	200	42,849
Physical Culture	13	60	13,834
Art	67	464	19,975
Total	**832**	**13,556**	**2,184,376**

*Only includes undergraduate students.
Source: Department of Planning, State Education Commission of China (1992).

only 0.06 billion yuan in 1978, but it increased by 34.9 times to 2.16 billion in 1992.

Curriculum

Chinese higher education has 11 major fields of study; within each, detailed curricula are developed for each specialty (see table 3.5). There used to be two distinguishing characteristics in the curriculum of Chinese higher education: overspecialization and centralization of curriculum development. In the early 1980s, there were 1,419 different types of specialties for undergraduate studies, which were designed according to planned manpower needs. Graduates were trained as elements of the planning economy. They were locked into very narrow fields of specialization. When the centrally planned economy was transformed into a more dynamic market economy, these graduates were less flexible and less adaptive to the rapidly changing labor market needs and technologically induced changes in the workplace. Thus since the mid-1980s, the State Education Commission has broadened each field of study and reduced the number of specialties. Some narrow specialties were combined with others. By the end of the 1980s, the total number of specialties were reduced from 1,419 to 832. Universities have been given more autonomy to adjust their curricula according to the local needs.

Stratification within the System

The Chinese higher education system is stratified in three ways. First, it is stratified by types of institution. There are 4 types: (1) 59 comprehensive universities, (2) 571 specialized colleges or universities, (3) 338 short-cycle specialized institutes, and (4) 85 short-cycle vocational colleges and universities. In some cases, the status of specialized colleges is similar to comprehensive universities, though in general comprehensive universities are more prestigious from a traditional perspective. Among the 2 categories of short-cycle institutions, the specialized colleges have a somewhat higher status. Second, status is stratified by administrative affiliations. The 36 universities directly under the leadership of the State Education Commission have a national influence and are more prestigious, followed by 325 institutions under the central Ministries, and the local universities and colleges. Third, stratification is also based on the designation of "key" or "non-key" institutions. Key universities are usually those leading institutions that served as model institutions in higher education, have higher quality in teaching and research, and enjoy priority in resource allocation. Among the 1,065 higher education institutions, there are 98 national key universities and colleges, 36 of which are under the State Education Commission; the remainder are under line Ministries. These key universities play a leading role in raising the quality of Chinese higher education. In each region there are also provincial-level "key" universities.

Internationalization since the Late 1970s

The international links of Chinese higher education institutions were limited to the Soviet Union and the East European countries in the 1950s, and limited to the Third World countries in the 1960s and early to mid-1970s. Since the late 1970s, when China started to implement policies of modernization, reform, and opening up to the outside world, a strong tendency of internationalization of Chinese higher education has been observed. This is demonstrated in several ways, including the following: (1) Sending students and scholars for study abroad to more than 70 countries, including the United States, Japan, the United Kingdom, Germany, France, Canada, and Australia. It is estimated that about 150,000 Chinese students and scholars went abroad since 1978, and about 50,000 returned to China. (2) Accepting foreign students to study in China. According to incomplete statistics from 1978 to 1988, more than 12,880 foreign students studied in China at different levels of study, including bachelor's, master's, and doctoral programs, as well as short-cycle programs. (3) Inviting foreign experts and scholars to teach and work in China. Currently about 3,000 of these experts and scholars work in 500 higher education institutions. Similarly, many Chinese experts and scholars work in foreign countries. (4) Organizing and participating in international seminars and study tours. From 1979 to 1989, the 36 universities under the State Education Commission sent 7,791 faculty members abroad to attend 4,185 international conferences and held 275 international academic conferences to which more than 6,000 foreign scholars were invited. (5) Developing institutional links between Chinese and foreign universities. (6) Implementing international projects with the World Bank, UNESCO, and UNDP (United Nations Development Program), as well as many types of bilateral projects. The increase of international contacts had a significant impact on Chinese higher education in curriculum, instruction, and faculty development, in improving Chinese scholarship, in student behavior, and in institutional management and finance, resulting in a tendency toward internationalization.

Scientific Research in Higher Education Institutions

In the 1950s and 1960s, scientific research was conducted largely outside universities. The Chinese Academy of Sciences (CAS) and the Chinese Academy of Social Sciences (CASS), line Ministries such as the Ministry of Electronic Industries and the Ministry of Public Health, and large enterprises operated many research institutes. The separation of teaching and research was partly due to Soviet influence. Since the late 1970s, there has been a growing recognition of the importance of combining teaching and research at universities, especially at the national leading universities with postgraduate programs. Universities were called on to be both "centers of teaching" and "centers of research." The integration of teaching and research has been considered a major strategy to update curricula, improve instructional quality, and raise the scientific level of research work. Scientific research at universities has been greatly enhanced. In 1992, China had a total of 20,425 research institutions, among which 7,976 were run by CAS, CASS, and other organizations. Another 9,432 research institutes were run by enterprises, and 3,017 by universities, including 1,191 in the humanities and social sciences (53,530 researchers with a budget of 80,35 million yuan) and 1,826 in sciences, engineering, medicine, agriculture, and the like (226,087 researchers with a budget of 248,807 million yuan). Besides these university research institutes officially recognized by the government agencies, higher education institutions also established many of their own research units to enhance their research capacity.

Continuing Reform

Along with the further opening up to the outside world and the deepening of economic and social reforms characterized by the transformation from a centrally planned economy to a socialist market economy, Chinese higher education has undergone a dramatic reform process. The key to restructuring higher education lies in eliminating excessive government control over higher education institutions, extending the decision-making power of universities, and giving them more autonomy in the management of programs and resources (CPC, Central Committee, 1985). Thus, the most distinguishing characteristic of current higher education reform is the trend toward decentralization. The major reform areas include, but are not limited to, the following: (1) giving more autonomy and decision-making power to universities and colleges so as to encourage more initiative, creativity, and responsiveness to the development process; (2) increasing and diversifying the sources for financing higher education instead of only depending on government allocation; (3) adjusting the structure of the higher education system by levels and fields of learning to better serve manpower needs; (4) broadening and updating curricula so as to make universities and their graduates more flexible and adaptive to the rapidly changing labor market; (5) changing the rigid graduate job assignment system into a graduate-employer "two-way selection" system to allow more individual choices; (6) developing a more flexible staff appointment and salary system; (7) allowing for the establishment of private universities so as to expand the provision of higher education; and (8) establishing a legal infrastructure and accreditation system for universities and colleges. The basic objective of these reforms is to expand enrollment and to improve the quality and efficiency of the higher education system.

RESPONSES TO INTERNAL DEMANDS

Along with rapid socioeconomic development, the demands of different sectors of the population for higher education have been increasing, to which universities and colleges have to respond. Since the higher education enrollment rate is still very low, the distribution of higher education among different social groups in terms of students and faculty is a critical issue.

Students

Percentage of age group attending higher education. Though Chinese higher education has expanded very quickly, the enrollment at regular higher education institutions as a percentage of the relevant age group has remained low. In 1993, the regular higher education enrollment rate was about 3 percent of the eighteen to twenty-two age group. It is estimated that the enrollment rate will reach 7 percent by the year 2000.

Participation in higher education by females. In 1950, less than one-fifth of all college students in China were female. Since then, great efforts have been made to promote female participation in higher education. The number of female students has increased steadily along with the improvement of the socioeconomic status of women in China. By 1960, female enrollment accounted for about one-quarter of the total enrollment and further increased to 34 percent of the student population in 1992. Generally speaking, in education, medicine, languages, arts, and humanities, women are relatively better represented, while in engineering, science, and business administration, women are usually less well represented.

Participation in higher education by ethnic minorities. China has 55 ethnic minority groups, which accounted for about 5 percent of the total population in the early 1950s. The enrollment of minority students in 1950 was 1,285, less than one percent of the students in tertiary education. Since then, participation of ethnic minorities in higher education has been promoted in three ways. First, ethnic minorities are given enrollment priority, and the admission standards in terms of scores on the national college entrance examinations have been adjusted. Second, starting in 1980, the Ministry of Education of China required some national universities to establish special classes for minority groups. These are mainly preparatory classes enrolling ethnic minority students at scores lower than the minimum for admission. After one or two years of preparatory studies, these minority students will be integrated into the mainstream of the student population in different fields of study. Third, special colleges and universities have been established for ethnic minorities. Since this effort was initiated in the 1950s, 12 nationality institutes have been established, enrolling 22,839 students in 1992. The total minority enrollment reached 153,000, accounting for 7 percent of the total higher education population in 1992. In the same year, the minority population of China accounted for 8 percent of the total population; therefore, minorities are reasonably well represented in higher education.

Disparities among different regions. China is a geographically large country, characterized by uneven socioeconomic development, including differing financial capacity and labor market needs, which has led to disparities among different regions in higher education. For example, the recurrent expenditure per student in 1992 in China was 3,875 yuan on average. However, it varied from region to region, showing a higher expenditure per student in the metropolitan and coastal areas (e.g., 5,309 yuan in Beijing; 4,707 yuan in Shanghai; 5,157 yuan in Guangdong) and a lower expenditure in the remote and rural areas (e.g., 3,613 yuan in Anhui; 2,625 yuan in Jiangxi). Even more significant disparities arise in the number of college students per 10,000 population. In 1992, the average number of college students per 10,000 population was 18.7. It was much higher in the metropolitan and coastal areas (e.g., 121.5 in Beijing; 88.8 in Shanghai; 56.5 in Tianjin; 33.4 in Liaoning; 30 in Jilin) and much lower in remote or rural areas (e.g., 7.9 in Guizhou; 9.5 in Guangxi; and 11.3 in Anhui). The increasing regional disparities have drawn the attention of the state. Central interventions have been made, such as intergovernment grants allocated to underdeveloped areas to narrow down the regional disparities.

Differences between social groups in higher education participation rates. There are no systematic data on the participation in higher education by different socioeconomic groups in China. However, the shift in emphasis on admission policies in higher education over four decades has had socioeconomic implications. In the 1950s, preferential admission policies were adopted for those with worker and peasant backgrounds. Some of them who failed the entrance examinations were admitted provisionally and offered special tutoring. If their academic performance turned out to be acceptable after one or two years of special treatment, they could remain in universities. Thus the representation of students from worker and peasant family backgrounds increased from 19.1 percent in 1951 to 36.3 percent in 1957 (Klitgaard, 1986). In the early 1960s, accompanying the policies of readjustment and consolidation with emphasis on higher education quality, admissions were based mainly on selection according to applicants' scores on the entrance examinations. Relatively less special consideration was given to student family background. During the Cultural Revolution (1966–76), this new admission policy was criticized as bourgeois intellectual elitism and meritocracy, which was considered against proletarian and socialist ideology. The national entrance examinations were abolished and students from worker and peasant family backgrounds were again given priority in universities and colleges. After the Cultural Revolution, the national entrance examinations were reinstituted in 1977 and admission policy was once again based mainly on grades on the entrance examinations. Again, the rationale for this change was to raise the quality and efficiency of the Chinese higher education system. All these policy changes certainly had a very strong impact on the participation of different social groups in higher education.

The changing occupational prospect of graduates. Before the 1980s, university and college graduates were trained as elements of the planned economy. They were both enrolled and assigned jobs upon graduation according to the state plan, which determined where they should go and what they should do. In those years, if one was enrolled in a teacher training institute, a teaching job would be assigned upon graduation. Similarly, an engineering major would be assigned to a certain enterprise and a medicine major would be assigned to a certain hospital. Comprehensive university graduates had a wider range of assignments, including jobs in research institutions, universities and colleges, government agencies, and public services. In general, it was a one-way, top-down process. Since the mid-1980s, this rigid graduate job-assignment system has been gradually changed into a graduate-employer "two-way selection" to allow for more individual choices. Graduates have been allowed to find jobs on their own. Tuition-paying students have full autonomy to determine what they are going to do upon graduation. This new system has changed the occupational prospect of graduates through labor market mechanisms. Though graduates are still basically selected for occupations by type of institution and academic disciplines, they have to be responsive to rapidly changing labor market needs. Higher education institutions are trying hard to broaden the specialties in order to make their graduates more flexible and adaptive to the rapidly changing labor market.

Faculty

Ranks, gender, ethnicity, and age structure. The ranks of faculty members in the Chinese higher education system include full professors, accounting for 6.3 percent of the total faculty, associate professors (24.6 percent), lecturers (41.9

Table 3.6

Age Structure of Teachers in Chinese Higher Education, 1992–93

Rank	Below 30	31-40	41-50	51-60	above 60	Total
professors	47	443	1,406	15,178	7,311	24,385
associate professors	752	8,575	19,901	64,485	1,647	95,360
lecturers	40,824	75,995	30,209	15,441	74	162,543
assistants	69,709	13,138	823	120	11	83,801
instructors	16,905	2,363	1,128	1,259	64	21,719
Total	128,237	100,514	53,467	96,483	9,107	387,808
female teachers	50,503	31,213	15,919	21,057	991	119,683

Source: Department of Planning, State Education Commission of China (1993).

percent), assistants (21.6 percent), and instructors (5.6 percent). In some research-oriented, national leading universities, senior faculty members account for a much larger proportion of the total. For example, at Peking University, professors and associate professors account for about 59 percent of the total faculty (see table 3.6).

Among the faculty members, 33.1 percent are thirty or under and were trained after the Cultural Revolution; 27.2 percent are over fifty and were trained before the Cultural Revolution; and only about 13.8 percent are aged forty-one to fifty and were trained during the Cultural Revolution. This latter group is relatively small because of the intellectual loss during the political turmoil of that time. About 25.9 percent of faculty are between thirty-one and forty. This age group is also relatively small because many young faculty of this age group went abroad when the open-door policy was implemented. Since the proportion of middle-aged faculty is relatively small, the current strategies in faculty development include senior faculty members playing a leading role in teaching, research, and training of a new generation of faculty; upgrading the existing middle-aged teaching force; attracting scholars who are currently studying abroad to join the faculty; and speeding up the cultivation and upgrading of young faculty members. Female participation in higher education faculty has also improved. In 1950, about 10 percent of the faculty members were female, which was increased to 20 percent in 1960 and 30 percent in 1992. Among the faculty members under thirty, females accounted for 37.3 percent, showing a continuous increase in participation. Teachers from ethnic minority backgrounds account for about 4.9 percent of the total faculty, slightly underrepresented in terms of the total minority population; thus efforts are being made to promote the participation of ethnic minorities in the teaching force.

Training. Faculty members are mainly trained at domestic higher education

Table 3.7
Teachers by Training and Rank in Chinese Higher Education, 1992–93

Ranks degree	Doctoral degree*	Master degree*	Bachelor degree	no degree	Total
professor	1,239	4,277	5,073	13,796	24,385
associate professor	2,587	12,077	22,923	57,773	95,360
lecturer	2,334	48,736	67,434	44,019	162,543
assistant	207	15,301	60,644	7,648	83,801
instructor	216	3,742	13,418	4,343	21,719
Total	6,583	84,134	169,512	127,579	387,808

*Or equivalent.
Source: Department of Planning, State Education Commission of China (1994).

institutions, especially at the national universities with graduate programs. Since China did not have an academic degree system until 1981, a relatively small proportion of faculty members hold postgraduate degrees. As illustrated in table 3.7, only 1.7 percent of the total faculty members have a doctoral degree, 21.7 percent have a master's degree or equivalent, 43.7 percent have a bachelor's degree or equivalent, and the rest have no academic degree. Along with the growth of the number of advanced degree-holders trained domestically and returned from abroad, the training background of the faculty in terms of academic degrees will be improved. Besides the improvement of preservice training, efforts also are being made in in-service training aimed at upgrading the existing faculty, especially the young and middle-aged faculty members without advanced degrees, including sending them abroad or to the national leading universities for advanced studies in their fields, through which some of them can pursue an advanced degree.

Teaching versus research. Since the late 1970s, higher education institutions have attached more importance to research. Faculty members are expected to do research and integrate research with teaching. Currently among the 387,585 faculty members, 279,617 are involved in major research activities. One of the criteria for faculty promotion is research accomplishment and academic publications, especially at national universities. Higher education institutions have also established thousands of research institutes on campuses across the country. These institutes are staffed by research faculty who are financed by the scientific research budget instead of general education funds. In general, teaching faculty members are expected to do research one-third of their working time, while research faculty members are expected to use two-thirds of their time to do research and one-third for teaching. However, at some small local teaching institutions, relatively less research is conducted, while at national research universities more research activities are going on. Some faculty members even use their research budget to "buy" more time for research.

Service within the university and the society. Along with the deepening of the reforms, faculty members have been given more autonomy in their work and have become more active in the operation of the universities, as well as in the economic and social development of Chinese society. Besides regular teaching and research responsibilities, they also provide administrative services on campus, serving as department chairpersons, deans, and university executives. Many university presidents and vice presidents are well known professors. Representatives of faculty members also serve on the university councils, university academic committees, and faculty appointment committees. Faculty members also provide more services off campus. Many of them get involved in the research and development activities of enterprises and the development of "science parks," which are science and technology-based developmental areas. They provide a wide range of consultation services to both domestic and joint venture companies, as well as to communities on science and technology, environmental problems, medical services, legal issues, and social work. Thousands of faculty members are involved in "supporting the poor" programs, for which they go to the remote, poor, or rural areas to help the local people overcome poverty and backwardness.

Salaries and status within the society. In general, university faculty positions are well respected in Chinese culture. However, the income of faculty members is relatively low. The basic starting salary for a full professor is about 390 yuan; for an associate professor, 275 yuan; for a lecturer, 205 yuan. Salary increases gradually with teaching experience and is supplemented with other benefits such as free medical care and subsidized housing. Even though the basic salaries of university faculty members are comparable to those of other professionals with similar educational qualifications, total remuneration is lower for faculty members because of the much larger bonuses given to employees in industries. Great effort has been made by universities to raise faculty income with revenue generated by the universities themselves. A survey conducted in Beijing, Shanghai, and Anhui Province shows that the average total monthly income of university faculty members ranged from about 400 yuan to 500 yuan, which is about 100 yuan below the average of those in other professions with similar educational qualifications. The low faculty income has led to a higher turnover rate in the university teaching force, which has drawn the attention of the State Education Commission. Measures have been or will be taken to raise the income of university faculty.

International links. Since the implementation of policies of reform and opening up to the outside world, many faculty members have been sent aboard for advanced studies. Many of those who earned advanced degrees from foreign universities and returned to China have joined the faculty in China. Other links include regular academic exchange programs, international conferences, study tours and cooperation with foreign professors working in China, joint research projects by the Chinese professors and their international counterparts, and memberships of Chinese scholars in international academic and professional organizations. These international links have been gradually institutionalized and have become part of the university life, playing an important role in improving Chinese scholarship. It is also a way for Chinese scholars to contribute to the academic development of the international community.

FUTURE DEVELOPMENTS

Higher education has expanded rapidly since the late 1970s along with the implementation of policies of modernization, reform, and opening up to the outside world. This development will continue with several irreversible trends. First, given the increasing social and private demand for higher education, the enrollment levels will continue to climb. It is estimated that by the year 2000, total enrollment will reach 6 million, among which about 3.6 million will be in regular higher education institutions and 2.4 million will be in adult higher education institutions. Second, the government's role in higher education will be further changed from administrative control to macropolicy formulation, overall guidance and coordination, monitoring, and supervision. Higher education institutions will be given more autonomy in enrolling students according to labor market needs, in adjusting curriculum orientation, in financial management and revenue generation, in personnel administration and faculty development, in developing bilateral and multilateral relations, in cooperation with industries in research and development, and in academic exchanges with foreign countries. Third, greater effort will be made by Chinese universities to rationalize the structure of higher education and to improve institutional efficiency and instructional quality. Fourth, Chinese higher education will be further internationalized and academic exchanges will become more frequent. Scientific and cultural gaps between China and the rest of the world will be further narrowed, and Chinese higher education will become an integral part of the international higher education community.

REFERENCES

CPC (Communist Party of China) Central Committee. 1985. *Decision on Educational Reform*. Beijing: Foreign Language Press.

CPC (Communist Party of China) Central Committee and State Council. 1993. *China Education Reform and Development Outline*. Beijing.

Department of Planning and Construction, State Education Commission. 1986. *Achievement of Education in China*. Beijing: People's Education Press.

———. 1992. *Educational Statistics Yearbook of China*. Beijing: People's Education Press.

Klitgaard, Robert. 1986. *Elitism and Meritocracy in Developing Countries: Selection Policies for Higher Education*. Baltimore: Johns Hopkins University Press.

State Council, China. 1981. *Regulation on Academic Degrees of the People's Republic of China*. Beijing.

State Education Commission, China. 1990. *The Development and Reform of Education in China (1989–90)*. Beijing.

————. 1993. *Provisional Stipulations for the Establishment of Minban Higher Education Institutions*. Beijing.

State Statistics Bureau, China. 1993. *Statistical Yearbook of China 1992*. Beijing.

4

HONG KONG

Grace C. L. Mak
and Gerard A. Postiglione

The development of higher education in Hong Kong has been shaped to a large extent by three factors: its status as a colony, its reliance on international trade, and social demand for higher education. British considerations were reflected in the establishment of the first university in Hong Kong in 1911 and in the governance of higher education as more tertiary institutions were set up later. However, Hong Kong has also been under the influence of China in many ways. The varying weight of the China factor in the development of higher education in Hong Kong reflects the changing relationships among Britain, China, and Hong Kong. With scarce natural resources, Hong Kong cannot but rely on its human resources and its geographical asset as a port. Thus, education is of crucial importance to its outward-looking economy. Internally, the demand for higher education has always exceeded the supply, resulting in a highly selective system with entrance to university as a goal and in large numbers of students seeking alternative opportunities abroad.

CONTEXT

Though it ranks ninetieth by population, Hong Kong is the world's eighth largest trading economy. Its 6 million inhabitants (98 percent Chinese) enjoy the second highest living standard in Asia, freedom of speech, the rule of law, and a fully elected legislature since 1995. Other features of Hong Kong include its large banking sector, efficient civil service, textile and electronics industries (robust until the recent economic restructuring), a highly skilled and educated populace, and a unique blend of internationalism and neo-Confucianism.

The effect of politics and the economy on higher education were notable from the beginning. In the first decade of the 1900s, Lugard, then governor of Hong

Kong, advocated a university in Hong Kong on various grounds: "It would help to serve the higher educational needs of an awakening China; it would be a lighthouse of learning, a symbol of the Western cultural tradition in the Far East and a meeting place for Chinese and Western cultures; it would help to maintain British prestige in Eastern Asia; and, through its dissemination of modern knowledge and of the English language, it would indirectly benefit British business" (Harrison, 1962:xiii). The university was to serve the needs of China. It was only when it failed to attract students from China that the University of Hong Kong redefined itself as a university of and for Hong Kong itself. The social and economic transformation of Hong Kong, especially after the change of government to communist rule in China in 1949, had a decisive influence on this redefinition (ibid.).

Subsequent development of higher education continued to reflect changing political and economic needs. Social demand for education was high, as shown in the three private colleges founded by scholars who fled China. In 1963 these colleges merged to form the Chinese University of Hong Kong, which became publicly funded. These two are comprehensive universities. Presently the University of Hong Kong offers courses in nine faculties: arts, education, social sciences, science, medicine, dentistry, law, architecture, and engineering; the Chinese University, in seven faculties: arts, education, social sciences, science, medicine, engineering, and business administration. The Baptist College first appeared as a private college in 1956 and became public in 1983. It has five faculties and schools: arts, business, communications, science, and social sciences. It was elevated to degree-awarding status in 1986. Lingnan College was established in 1967, again as a private college, but became publicly funded in 1991. It has three faculties: arts, business, and social sciences; it acquired degree-awarding status in 1992. As the economy shifted from relying on entrepôt trade in the 1950s to manufacturing in the 1960s and 1970s, skilled and semiskilled labor of more diverse sorts were in demand. The Hong Kong Polytechnic, established in 1972, tried to answer these needs with courses in six faculties: applied science and textiles, business and information systems, communications, construction and land use, engineering, and health and social studies. It introduced its first degree courses in 1983–84. In 1984, the City Polytechnic of Hong Kong was established and charged with a similar role. It has four faculties: business, humanities and social sciences, law, and science and technology. It started to offer degree courses in 1986–87. With competition from neighboring newly industrialized countries, Hong Kong had to shift from labor-intensive to technology-intensive industries, and the supply of intermediate-level technicians no longer sufficed. The Hong Kong University of Science and Technology began to admit students in 1991 and now has four schools: science, engineering, business and management, and humanities and social science.

These institutions are diverse in character and differ in the contributions they make to Hong Kong. In general, "the universities concentrate on first and higher degree work, emphasizing scholarship and research; the polytechnics offer a range of programs including diplomas and postgraduate courses, with a strong emphasis on professional and vocational education; and the colleges are developing as predominantly degree-awarding institutions, aiming at providing a broad general education rather than a specialized professional training" (UPGC, 1993: annex C). Until 1994, only three of the above institutions enjoyed university status, as their names indicate. In 1994, Hong Kong Baptist College was upgraded into Hong Kong Baptist University, and the two polytechnics became the Hong Kong Polytechnic University and the City University of Hong Kong, respectively. Lingnan College is expected to move in the same direction. These seven institutions constitute the bulk of higher education institutions in Hong Kong. They are all publicly funded through the University and Polytechnics Grants Committee (UPGC), which was renamed the University Grants Committee (UGC) after the upgrading of polytechnics and colleges.

On the periphery of the UGC aegis are four other institutions. Shu Yan College, founded in 1976, remains a private postsecondary college. Its faculties of arts, social sciences, and commerce offer four-year diploma courses. The Hong Kong Academy of Performing Arts, established in 1984, is funded by the Recreation and Culture Branch of the government. The Open Learning Institute of Hong Kong was established in 1989 to provide a second opportunity in degree studies to adults in the distance learning mode. It enrolls students in four schools: education, science and technology, arts and social sciences, and business and administration. With start-up funds from the government in the beginning, the institute is now financially self-supporting. The latest addition to the list is the Hong Kong Institute of Education, a conglomerate of what used to be four colleges of education that prepared teachers for primary and lower secondary schools. As primary teaching moves toward a partially graduate entry occupation, the Hong Kong Institute of Education is planning to introduce its first bachelor of education course in 1998. It joined the UGC network in September 1996.

In recent years, there has been a proliferation of offshore programs offered by overseas universities. Some of them are joint programs with local colleges; others operate on their own. According to a report, "there are about 120 non-local institutions advertising and conducting about 74 collaborative courses and close to 300 independent institutions operating in Hong Kong" (*South China Morning Post*, February 15, 1996:14). The mode of delivery varies. Some are distance programs; others are a mixed mode of distance learning and meeting with local tutors or tutors who fly in at regular intervals. Their quality has become a concern, and a bill was introduced in early 1996 to regulate the quality and operation of such courses (ibid.). The press is awash with advertisements of such educational imports, predominantly from English-speaking countries like the United Kingdom, the United States, and Australia. It is a dramatic phenomenon in a society that until recent years allowed few routes to higher education.

In Hong Kong, "higher education" typically covers the above institutions,

Table 4.1
School Attendance Rates by Age and Sex, 1971–91

Age group	1971			1981			1991		
	M	F	All	M	F	All	M	F	All
6-11	95.5	94.4	94.9	98.5	98.5	98.5	99.8	99.8	99.8
12-16	80.0	69.2	74.8	83.4	84.6	84.0	91.8	95.6	93.6
17-18	42.4	35.2	38.8	44.9	45.0	45.0	54.3	62.7	58.3

Source: Census and Statistics (1993:204).

while "postsecondary education" extends downward to include nondegree courses such as those in teacher training and nursing.

Higher education has rapidly expanded in the context of mass expansion of primary and secondary education. As table 4.1 shows, by 1991 most youth aged twelve to sixteen had access to a secondary education and more than half of those aged seventeen to eighteen to a matriculation education, hence a large base of those aspiring for tertiary education. However, the supply of university places continued to be limited. In the mid-1970s, the proportion of those in the 17–20 age group who had access to first-year first degree places never exceeded 2.5 percent. The UPGC guarded against fast expansion, which it perceived to be "impractical and damaging to the institutions" (UPGC, 1976:15–19). Until 1984, the proportion never exceeded 3 percent. The second half of the 1980s saw a steady growth and by 1989 it was close to 9 percent (UPGC, 1993:3). The major spurt came from Hong Kong's relationship with China. As 1997 approached, especially in the aftermath of the prodemocracy movement in China in June 1989, the number of emigrants soared. The attrition of the skilled labor force had reached a worrisome scale. In November 1989 the governor announced plans to nearly double the number of students admitted to university degree studies by 1994–95 to boost confidence and replenish the emigration of talent. The target was to increase the participation rate of the relevant cohort in first-year first degree studies to 18 percent, and that of those in postsecondary education in general to 25 percent.

In absolute terms, higher education has also witnessed phenomenal expansion. In 1971, the full-time enrollment at UPGC-funded institutions was 5,528 (Census and Statistics Department, 1981:167) and by 1991, 45,509. Table 4.2 shows the upsurge from 1991 to 1994, and a period of more gentle growth since then.

The expansion has accelerated the elevation of subdegree courses to degree level, and some transfer of subdegree places from the polytechnics to technical institutions at a lower level, resulting in a decline in the proportion of enrollment in subdegree courses from 28 percent in 1991–92 to the target of 15.1 percent in 1997–98. Conversely there has been a relative rise of postgraduate places,

Table 4.2
Planned Expansion of Higher Education, 1991–97

Level of programs	1991-92	%	1994-95	%	1997-98	%
Undergraduate	28,289	(62.2)	39,552	(70.9)	44,446	(71.0)
Graduate						
Taught prog.	2,815	(6.2)	4,219	(7.6)	5,110	(8.2)
Research prog.	1,285	(2.8)	2,746	(4.9)	3,595	(5.7)
Sub-degree	13,120	(28.8)	9,278	(16.6)	9,450	(15.1)
Total	**45,509**	**(100)**	**55,795**	**(100)**	**62,601**	**(100)**

Source: UPGC (1993:annexes B and D).

from 4.5 percent in 1971 (Wu 1992:91) to 9.0 percent in 1991–92, and the target of 13.9 percent in 1997–98 (table 4.2).

Higher education in Hong Kong has to be studied together with that outside Hong Kong. The limited places available locally made overseas education vital to Hong Kong students. The flow outward has been increasing. In 1972–73, 5,982 students left the territory to study abroad when the combined enrollment in the two universities and the polytechnic in Hong Kong in the same year was 7,526 (Census and Statistics Department, 1981:167). Comparable figures for overseas education are 16,267 for 1992 and 13,673 for 1994 (Hong Kong Government, 1995:504). The relative popularity of the host countries has changed somewhat. Traditionally the United Kingdom received the most students from Hong Kong. In recent years the United States has taken over, with the United Kingdom as second, and Australia and Canada in the third and fourth places.

In 1997, the territory will become a Special Administrative Region of the People's Republic of China under a "one country-two systems" arrangement, in which the current education system may be maintained. Embodied in its future Constitution, the Basic Law, is a high degree of autonomy and the provision that the people of Hong Kong will rule Hong Kong. Confidence in its future waxes and wanes, depending on events in China and the state of relations between China and the United Kingdom.

The decolonization of higher education has come to mean more frequent contacts with universities in China alongside closer economic and political ties, declining legitimacy of colonial educational policy, localization of the highest administrative positions, more attention to Chinese heritage, possible attrition of institutional autonomy, increased emigration of faculty with return migration of those who have acquired foreign passports, and expanding cultural and human resource linkages with adjacent South China—especially the Pearl River Delta (Postiglione and Leung, 1991).

Currently, higher education is confronting at least four issues. First, rapid expansion means increased competition among the seven UGC institutions of higher education for funding, students, and faculty. This has led to the introduction of increased accountability measures, as well as the pressure to establish academic centers of excellence (UPGC, 1993). Second, academic freedom and institutional autonomy have become less certain as the tendency toward self-censorship becomes more pronounced. Third, Hong Kong's research in science and technology is not keeping pace with that of its regional rivals in Singapore, Taiwan, and South Korea (Wu, 1992). The final issue concerns the large number of overseas appointees and the fact that about 90 percent of all doctorates of Hong Kong faculty were earned overseas, usually in Australia, Canada, the United Kingdom, or the United States. These factors are embedded within the problem of balancing localization of administration, nationalization of the university mission, localization of academic leadership, and an internationalization of university curriculum (Postiglione and Tang, forthcoming).

GOVERNANCE OF HIGHER EDUCATION

The most influential body in higher education is the University Grants Committee. It had a strong British orientation from the beginning. In 1964, the Hong Kong government invited Sir Edward Hale, who served as Secretary to the British University Grants Committee from 1951 to 1957, to report on the possibility of setting up a University Grants Committee in Hong Kong. The Hale report of 1965 recommended that "the Government of Hong Kong should be advised by an expert and impartial committee on the financial needs of university education in Hong Kong and its development, and the resources made available for meeting those needs should be allocated between the universities by such a committee" (Hale, 1965:27). The recommendation was accepted and a committee appointed. After the founding of the Hong Kong Polytechnic, it was renamed the University and Polytechnic Grants Committee. With the upgrading of Baptist College and polytechnics to university status in 1994, it struck the word "Polytechnic" off its name again. The UGC is an administrative device to ensure that institutions of higher education can be adequately financed without misuse of large sums of money while maintaining autonomy (UPGC, 1976:8). Its membership includes academics, businessmen, and administrators. The nationalities of its members reflect the sources of influence from abroad. In 1993, the committee included eight local Hong Kong Chinese, five British, three Americans (including a professor of Hong Kong Chinese origin), and one Australian. It is expected that the future UGC will include members from mainland China, especially since the governor of Hong Kong, who is the chancellor of the universities and who appoints the members of the UGC, will be appointed by Beijing after 1997.

Hong Kong people's anxiety about the future is also reflected in the role of the UGC after 1997. While the UGC hopes to continue its functions in spite of a possible change in name (*Hong Kong Financial Times*, July 20, 1994:21), whether institutional autonomy—a tradition of higher education imported from the United Kingdom—will be compatible with China's system is a concern of many in Hong Kong.

The governor of Hong Kong, as chancellor, is nominal head of all UGC-funded institutions. The executive head of each is its vice chancellor, who is assisted by pro-vice chancellors. The senate oversees the academic affairs of a university. Each university is subdivided into faculties, departments, and, where relevant, schools.

The length of studies used to vary, reflecting again different sources of influence. The University of Hong Kong, modeled after British universities, admits students who have completed Form 7 for three-year degree studies (5-year for medicine), whereas the Chinese University of Hong Kong used to admit students who had completed Form 6 for four-year studies. A report of the Education Commission, an advisory body, in 1988 recommended that the various admissions systems be unified (Education Commission, 1988). In spite of the strong plea for the four-year model from many members of both universities, the government insisted on the three-year model. Some people explain the government's stance with the "conspiracy theory"—that the British fortified the three-year model to continue their influence after 1997. Whether this is the case cannot be supported by documentation. Suffice it to say that the Chinese University has now adopted a credit system in which students are to complete their credit units in three years. The pattern of higher education has therefore converged in this aspect.

Accreditation

As in Britain, the universities in Hong Kong are self-accrediting institutions scrutinized by external examiners. Nonuniversities rely on external validation. The Hong Kong Polytechnic was the first nonuniversity that offered degree courses in 1983–84, which were validated by the then UPGC on the advice of the United Kingdom's Council for National Academic Accreditation to ensure academic standards and international recognition. From 1985 on the UPGC took up the responsibility of reviewing the capability of nonuniversity institutions in offering degree programs (UPGC, 1987:12). In 1990 the Hong Kong Council for Academic Accreditation was established, largely on the model of the United Kingdom's CNAA. Thus higher education institutions operate as a binary system, with universities perceived by many as the top tier and other institutions as a lower tier. The move of the Baptist College and the polytechnics toward degree programs will gradually narrow the gap between the two groups.

RESPONSE TO ECONOMIC DEMAND

Whereas the governance of higher education in Hong Kong has strong British influence, the development in terms of enrollment and content has more diverse links with the international market. And yet precisely because of the erratic nature of international trade, it is extremely difficult to forecast Hong Kong's manpower needs with a high degree of accuracy. In 1964 the government appointed a committee to consider Hong Kong's needs for higher education and to recommend ways to meet them. The committee adopted a manpower forecast approach. Based on the percentage of the 1961 labor force that should possess higher education qualifications, it projected the need in 1971 in general and conducted a survey to find out the need in the manufacturing industry in particular (Special Committee on Higher Education, 1966, 1968). The UPGC admitted the difficulty in doing long-term planning except for medicine and teaching and that student numbers could be planned only on an ad hoc basis (UPGC, 1976:10, 16). The introduction of new courses over the years nevertheless illustrates higher education's response to labor market needs. In 1993 the total enrollment at all levels of study in all UPGC-funded institutions was 70,122. Its percentage distribution by academic program is as follows: business and management (22 percent), engineering and technology (20 percent), social sciences (12 percent), information technology and computing science (7 percent), built environment (6 percent), physical sciences (5 percent), languages (5 percent), mathematical sciences (4 percent), humanities (excluding languages) (4 percent), education (4 percent), biological sciences (3 percent), art, design, and performing arts (2 percent), clinical medicine (2 percent), preclinical studies (one percent), subjects and professions allied to medicine (3 percent), clinical dentistry (0.4 percent) (Census and Statistics Department, 1994:218–19).[1] The response to the economy is, however, reactive rather than proactive; because of a lack of long-term planning, Hong Kong is losing out in its competitiveness compared with neighboring newly industrialized countries.

The economic and political factors in recent years have made it imperative for Hong Kong to respond more consciously. The UGC's planning for the next few years demonstrates a strategic repositioning of Hong Kong higher education. On the one hand, Hong Kong's imminent return to Chinese rule has broadened the context from a self-contained city to a gateway to the hinterland in China. On the other hand, as production costs rise Hong Kong manufacturing has to move to places that allow cost-cutting. The liberalization policy in China appeared in time to accelerate the economic restructuring in Hong Kong from manufacturing to service industry as a mainstay. The emphasis on the training of bilingual manpower, particularly in business and social studies and in innovative science and technology, precisely captures the planned new role of higher education in economic development (UPGC, 1993:7). This background explains the establishment of the Hong Kong University of Science and Technology and the introduction of new courses in other institutions, such as information and electronic engineering at the Chinese University of Hong Kong. When the University of Hong Kong was founded, chairs were to be in practical fields: medicine and engineering, and arts and law to prepare those for official careers (Harrison, 1962:25). This pragmatism has continued. Hong Kong excels in using the results of basic research rather than in producing them. The recent increase in attention to research and postgraduate programs has also been triggered by application, for "evaluation of the usefulness of others' research may not be possible unless one has research experience oneself" (UPGC, 1993:4). Not surprisingly, research in Hong Kong leans heavily on the applied side. In 1994–95 the UPGC awarded HK$193 million to research projects. The percentage distribution of the research grant is an indicator of how it prioritizes fields of research: biological sciences (18 percent); physical sciences (16 percent); administrative, business, and social studies (13 percent); electrical and electronic engineering (12 percent); computing science, information technology, and mathematics (10 percent); medicine, dentistry, and health (10 percent); civil engineering, surveying, building, and construction (7 percent); mechanical, production, and industrial engineering and chemical engineering (6 percent); arts and languages (4 percent); education (2 percent); law, architecture, town planning, and other professional and vocational studies (one percent) (CUHK, internal document).

Apart from looking northward to China, Hong Kong's economic restructuring has linked it to other neighboring countries in innovative ways. The expertise in training manpower for manufacturing, though in decline in importance, may benefit other countries that are blazing the trails of Hong Kong. The collaboration of the Hong Kong Polytechnic and the Malaysia Textile and Apparel Centre is a case in point. Most of Hong Kong's textile and clothing industries have moved to China, but the experience acquired in Hong Kong is transferred to Malaysia through a distance learning course. Students in Malaysia are enrolled in the Hong Kong Polytechnic programs. They use course materials developed by the Hong Kong Polytechnic staff and are supervised by Malaysian tutors who have been trained by the Hong Kong Polytechnic. The knowledge transfer between different levels of development promotes the sharing of expertise in the region (Yeung, 1994).

The career development of graduates from tertiary institutions in Hong Kong reflects a similar change in the economy. A survey of those who graduated from the University of Hong Kong in 1959–64 and from the Chinese University of Hong Kong in 1960–64 found that 71 percent of them went into education or public services (Special Committee on Higher Education, 1966:46–47), whereas a survey of first degree graduates of 1988–90 from the Baptist College, the Chinese University of Hong Kong, the City Polytechnic of Hong Kong, the Hong Kong Polytechnic, and the University of Hong Kong found that 36 percent went into these same two fields and 62 percent into the private sector (Hong Kong Baptist College et al., 1994:15). However, gender stratification persists in some aspects. Proportionately more women in the 1988–90 sample (43 percent) than men (31 percent) were in government service or education, and they earned less than men by 5 percent (1990) to 13 percent (1989) (ibid.:15, 24).

Until recently, a university education has been a passport to a good job. The rapid expansion has, however, decreased its market value. According to a Hong

Kong government study, in 2001 the supply of first degree–holders will almost meet the demand, but that of graduate degree–holders will far exceed the demand, possibly resulting in educated underemployment (*Ming Pao*, July 20, 1994:A2)

INTERNAL DISTRIBUTION OF EDUCATIONAL OPPORTUNITIES

When access to education was the privilege of a few, the University of Hong Kong was dubbed a university for the rich. However, it appeared that from the 1960s on, both universities admitted children from families of modest means, who made do by teaching part-time at evening schools or providing private tuition.[2] Prior to 1969, the government for a long time awarded scholarships based on academic performance regardless of financial situation. In 1954 a scheme of bursaries for needy students was introduced. But both systems operated on a small scale. In 1969 a new system was introduced to replace the earlier scheme of scholarships and bursaries. "Financial aid, given by a mixture of grants and interest free loans, was to ensure that no student at either University had to turn down a place offered because of financial need" (UPGC, 1976:62). A university education was no longer the preserve of the rich. By the mid-1970s, about 60 percent of university students in Hong Kong came from poor or very poor families, and those from the Polytechnic were likely to be the same (ibid.:37). The student finance scheme was extended to other institutions that came under the aegis of the UPGC later. In 1979–80, 40 percent of all full-time students received grants and 64 percent received loans (UPGC, 1983:22, 24).[3] In 1985–86 comparable figures were 39 percent and 46 percent (UPGC, 1987:22–23). The finance scheme has opened up higher education in terms of social class while remaining elitist in academic selection until the recent bulge.

However, pessimism has started to loom. A cost-recovery policy was introduced in 1994 to gradually increase tuition fees until they reach 18 percent of the total cost of education. The target year for attaining this objective is the end of the 1997–98 academic year (*Wah Kiu Daily*, December 10, 1994:6). Although poor students can apply for some financial assistance, they will still be hard hit by the policy.

Higher education also became more open to women. As in most other systems, higher education in Hong Kong started as heavily male-dominated. In 1941, of 600 students in the University of Hong Kong, about 120 were women (Harrison, 1962:51). In 1995–96, women made up 50 percent of full-time undergraduate enrollment in the UGC-funded institutions. Comparable figures for individual institutions vary: Hong Kong University of Science and Technology (37 percent), Hong Kong Polytechnic University (46 percent), City University of Hong Kong (47 percent), University of Hong Kong (52 percent), Chinese University of Hong Kong (53 percent), Lingnan College (57 percent), and Hong Kong Baptist University (62 percent) (UGC, 1996, unpublished). The statistics

Table 4.3
Women as a Percentage of Full-Time First-Year Students in CUHK and UHK, 1965–95 (in %)

Faculty \ Year	1965-66		1975-76		1995-96	
	CUHK	HKU	CUHK	HKU	CUHK	HKU
Arts	53	60	54	55	78	86
Commerce & Soc Sc (CU) Soc Studies & Law (HKU)	42	–	30	45	69	63 / 69
Science	25	22	14	15	53	46
Engineering & Technl.	–	0	–	0.5	19	15
Architecture	–	21	–	21	*	38
Medicine	–	15	–	11	54	54
Education	–	–	–	–	77	86
Total	39	35	31	29	57	55

*In CUHK architecture is organized as part of the Social Sciences.
Sources: UPGC (1976:79–80); CUHK, internal document (1995).

reveal that comprehensive and liberal arts institutions are more open to women than technological ones. While the trend is toward equality in numbers, the nature of the courses reveals the persistence of gender stratification. The non-degree courses comprise mainly teacher preparation for primary schools, a traditionally "feminine" area. At degree level, traditional stratification by field of study persists, as table 4.3 shows. Women continue to concentrate their studies in arts, education, and social sciences. A faculty that normally is heavily male, such as the faculty of medicine at CUHK, may appear more balanced with the introduction of a "feminine" department, such as nursing. Also, women's share of higher education in Hong Kong has to be examined together with that of overseas education. Available figures suggest that in the mid- to late 1980s, women constituted about a third of Hong Kong students in the United Kingdom, Canada, and Australia (Mak, 1991:174). In 1992–93 they made up 38 percent of all Hong Kong students enrolled in full-time higher and further education in the United Kingdom (Central Statistical Office, 1995:90). If the U.K. figure is an indicator, increase in female access to overseas education has been slower than that to local higher education.

THE ACADEMIC PROFESSION

The academic qualifications of the faculty have been rising. The move is toward doctoral degree entry to tertiary teaching. International influence in higher education continues, as is shown in the country of origin of faculty. For example, in 1993–94, 33 percent of all faculty in nine tertiary institutions were registered as nonlocals. Comparable figures by institution show different degrees of internationalization: Hong Kong University of Science and Technology (55 percent), University of Hong Kong (51 percent), the Academy of Performing Arts (51 percent), Chinese University of Hong Kong (37 percent), Lingnan College (30 percent), City Polytechnic of Hong Kong (28 percent), Baptist College (22 percent), Open Learning Institute (22 percent), and Hong Kong Polytechnic (18 percent) (*Ming Pao*, October 14, 1993:C8). The meaning of "international" has changed somewhat. While it still refers mostly to expatriates from English-speaking countries like Britain, the United States, and Australia, it has registered an increase in Chinese from Taiwan and mainland China and Hong Kong people with passports to those countries. Expatriates enjoyed home leave passages every two years and had priority in access to staff quarters. In the move toward localization—another preparation for the return to Chinese rule—such privileges have increasingly been challenged, and expatriate terms are now the same as local terms.

Many members of the local faculty have received advanced training abroad. While international influences enrich our higher education, they sometimes put us in the dilemma of a hybrid. Theories acquired abroad originated there and do not always fit the local context. This is especially the case in social science. We often find ourselves in the straitjacket of Western theories. By implication, we acquire rather than develop the theories. We tend to explain our society from Western perspectives. Also, there is always a time lag in our use of them. There has been concern about this mismatch and hence the effort to localize social science theories. This is not a new awareness. Already in the first half of the century, Western-trained social scientists in China started the pursuit, which is likely to continue for many more years.

The profession is hierarchical in ranks. At the Chinese University of Hong Kong, for example, about 35 percent of the faculty is ranked senior (senior lecturers, readers, and professors), 54 percent in the middle (lecturers), and 11 percent junior (assistant lecturers and instructors) (Chinese University of Hong Kong, 1994:41). The faculty is also stratified by sex. Women made up 15 percent of full-time faculty at lecturer rank or above at CUHK and HKU in 1992–93, but 17 percent of those at lecturer rank, 13 percent at senior lecturer rank, and 7 percent at reader or professorial ranks. They were unevenly represented in academic fields: 28 percent of the faculty in education, 24 percent in law, 18

Table 4.4
Academic Staff Turnover Rate, 1991–95 (in %)

Institution	1991-92	1992-93	1993-94	1994-95
Baptist Univ	4	7	5	5
Chinese Univ	14	9	11	14
City Univ	9	8	10	14
Hong Kong Univ	1	3	2	5
Lingnan Coll	6	8	10	11
Polytechnic Univ	7	10	8	11
Univ of Sci & Tech	1	2	2	5

Source: South China Morning Post, October 30, 1995, p. 6.

percent in business administration, 17 percent in arts, 2 percent in engineering, and 0.6 percent in science (Choi, 1995:118).

Until recently, tertiary teaching almost guaranteed job security. Starting in 1998, university funding will shrink by 3 percent a year, until it reaches 20 percent in 2001. This means that, apart from a higher faculty:student ratio, there will be a larger proportion of contract faculty and a more vulnerable faculty in general.

Hong Kong's academic profession has much to gain or lose in the coming years as sovereignty is returned to China. It is more closely bound to Western university traditions and practices than is the case elsewhere in Asia. This gives Hong Kong the potential to influence the academic profession in China by offering a unique model of successful East–West academic integration. In addition, given the status of intellectuals in China, Hong Kong's reincorporation into the People's Republic of China in 1997 could have major implications for its academic freedom and autonomy (Goldman, Cheek, and Hamrin, 1987; Madsen, 1990; Goldman, 1992). The academic profession has the capacity to act as a catalyst for a smooth transition or as a vehicle of resistance.

Over 40 percent of faculty respondents to a 1993 survey indicated they were likely to leave within five years. The academic staff turnover rate has registered a rising trend (table 4.4). While the reasons for leaving varied, political uncertainty was a significant one. In order to minimize the brain drain, a number of measures are being implemented, including introducing parity in all aspects of salaries and benefits and across terms of appointment (local and overseas). In addition, mobility of staff between institutions, in both directions, could be encouraged by supporting a broader distribution of internationally recognized centers of academic excellence across all institutions in a variety of fields. The expansion of higher education also necessitates casting a wider net for recruitment of faculty. That net will surely include China, which will contribute more to the staffing of the universities. At present, however, mainland China has its own shortage of doctorates and doctoral programs. This has created a large market for doctoral programs overseas, something that universities in Hong Kong are also tapping into by increasing the proportion of their doctoral students from mainland China. Hong Kong institutions of higher education have also begun to take advantage of the talent of people from mainland China who have earned doctorates in other countries but have not returned to China.

It is clear that the character of the academic profession in Hong Kong is changing in other ways as well. More doctorates are now earned in the United States than in the United Kingdom or other countries. Rather than following the changing patterns in British higher education, Hong Kong has begun to draw more on innovations from other countries as well. Of relevance in this context is the finding that those with higher degrees from the United States rate their training significantly higher than do those who earned higher degrees in the United Kingdom. The same holds true for the perception of faculty about the quality of the training they received for research.

Despite a recognition of declining academic standards, the academic profession supports the expansion of higher education provided that there are minimum standards of admission. At the same time more than two-thirds think that higher education should not be provided free to students, and more than 80 percent say that business should make a contribution.

Hong Kong higher education faculty were asked to rank in importance for Hong Kong eight aims of higher education. The ranking, based on the relative percentage of faculty selecting each stated aim, is as follows: promoting free intellectual inquiry; strengthening the society's capacity to compete internationally; promoting scholarship and research; preparing students for work; lifelong learning for adults; educating students for leadership; helping resolve basic social problems; and preserving the cultural heritage.

The state of the Hong Kong economy in the coming years may also determine whether Hong Kong decides to increase, decrease, or maintain the degree of internationalization within the profession, especially as it finds a growing pool of talent in China and the surrounding region, where economic links are growing stronger. Other factors will be equally important in the effort to maintain an international profession—factors such as working conditions, the intellectual environment, and the degree of academic freedom.

Until recent years, teaching was the primary function of higher education in Hong Kong. In the 1985–88 triennium, the UPGC allocated a small fund for research (UPGC, 1987:12). It was agreed that the research capacity in Hong Kong should be increased. This was all the more important as Hong Kong's competitive edge in industry was diminishing and a research base had to be developed in order that Hong Kong remain competitive (UPGC, 1990:16). In

1993 the UPGC underscored its emphasis on research by announcing plans to link an academic department's research output to 20 percent of its funding. Research output is measured on a scheme that ranks different types of publications (refereed journal articles, book chapters, etc.). One of the controversies surrounding the calculation is that international journal articles are ranked higher than local ones. This has created a dilemma for those who have been committed to developing a local discourse. To survive the funding and subsequently status-ranking exercise, one has to write for an international readership, which soon was made clear to mean Western. To contribute directly to the local readership, one has to withstand the pressure from perceived inferiority. Another controversy has been how to assess quality. Academics in Hong Kong are often preoccupied with publication pressure. This has led to a less than critical sieve of one's own work. Ironically, the buzz phrase of the current era is to strive to be "academic centers of excellence in the region" (UPGC, 1993). While recognizing the need to be accountable to the public, many in academe question the appropriateness of the industrial metaphor of quality assurance in assessment in higher education. Academics in Hong Kong are kept busy producing documentation of what they have been doing—the latest initiative is on teaching and learning quality. What has emerged so far seems to be an involuntary move away from genuine quality concerns. What happens in the United Kingdom should caution Hong Kong.

Under the Conservative plans, funding will be likely linked to quality. It seems inevitable that, in consequence, a compliance culture will develop, the aim of which will be to meet, or appear to meet, the criteria and standards laid down by the assessment units, irrespective of whether those are appropriate or desirable in the context of specific institutions. That the resulting quality of provision will be as high as before is not clear: if standards are to be common to the whole spectrum of higher education institutions, they may well end up as lowest common denominator threshold standards. Some institutions, pressed financially, and wishing to increase their student numbers significantly, may consciously decide to level their quality down, while still staying above the threshold. Paradoxically, under the politicians' externally controlled quality assurance models, there may well be little incentive or opportunity actually to improve quality. (Williams, 1992:158)

Sadly, the above scenario appears to be taking place in Hong Kong as well. Quality is being stifled in the proclaimed move toward quality assurance.

NOTES

1. The total exceeds 100 percent due to rounding.
2. Interviews with university graduates in the 1960s from the University of Hong Kong and the Chinese University of Hong Kong.
3. Some students received both grants and loans, while others received one form of aid only.

REFERENCES

Census and Statistics Department, Hong Kong. 1981. *Hong Kong Annual Digest of Statistics 1981*. Hong Kong: Hong Kong Government.

——. 1994. *Hong Kong Annual Digest of Statistics 1994*. Hong Kong: Hong Kong Government.

Central Statistical Office, United Kingdom. 1995. *Annual Abstract of Statistics 1995 (No. 131)*. London: HMSO.

Chinese University of Hong Kong. 1994. *Annual Report 1993–94*. Hong Kong.

Choi, P. K. 1995. "Women and Education in Hong Kong." In V. Pearson and B. K. P. Leung, eds., *Women in Hong Kong*. Hong Kong: Oxford University Press.

Craft, A., ed. 1992. *Quality Assurance in Higher Education*. London: Falmer.

Davis, D., and E. Vogel, eds. 1990. *Chinese Society on the Eve of Tiananmen: The Impact of Reform*. Cambridge, Mass.: Harvard University Press.

Education Commission, Hong Kong. 1988. *Education Commission Report No. 3*. Hong Kong.

Goldman, M. 1992. "The Intellectuals in the Deng Xiaoping Era." In A. L. Rosenbaum, ed., *State and Society in China: The Consequences of Reform*. Boulder, Colo.: Westview.

Goldman, M., T. Cheek, and C. L. Hamrin, eds. 1987. *China's Intellectuals and the State: In Search of a New Relationship*. Cambridge, Mass.: Harvard University Press.

Hale, E. 1965. *The Financing of Universities in Hong Kong*. Hong Kong: Government Printer.

Harrison, B. 1962. *University of Hong Kong: The First 50 Years*. Hong Kong: Hong Kong University Press.

Hong Kong Baptist College, the Chinese University of Hong Kong, City Polytechnic of Hong Kong, Hong Kong Polytechnic, the University of Hong Kong. 1994. *A Summary Report on the Career Development of First-Degree Graduates in Hong Kong*. Hong Kong.

Hong Kong Financial Times. 1994. July 20, p. 21.

Hong Kong Government. 1993. *Green Paper on Equal Opportunities for Women and Men*. Hong Kong.

——. 1995. *Hong Kong 1995*. Hong Kong.

Madsen, R. 1990. "The Spiritual Crisis of China's Intellectuals." In D. Davis and E. Vogel, eds., *Chinese Society on the Eve of Tiananmen: The Impact of Reform*. Cambridge, Mass.: Harvard University Press.

Mak, G. C. L. 1991. "The Schooling of Girls in Hong Kong: Progress and Contradictions in the Transition." In G. A. Postiglione and J. Y. M. Leung, eds., *Education and Society in Hong Kong*. Armonk, N.Y.: M. E. Sharpe.

Postiglione, G. A., and J. Y. M. Leung, eds. 1991. *Education and Society in Hong Kong: Toward One Country and Two Systems*. Armonk, N.Y.: M. E. Sharpe.

Postiglione, G. A., and T. H. Tang, eds. Forthcoming. *Global Dimensions of Hong Kong's Reunion with China*. Armonk, N.Y.: M. E. Sharpe.

Rosenbaum, A. L., ed. 1992. *State and Society in China: The Consequences of Reform*. Boulder, Colo.: Westview.

South China Morning Post. 1996. February 15, p. 14.

Special Committee on Higher Education. 1966. *Interim Report 1966*. Hong Kong: Hong Kong Government.

————. 1968. *Second Interim Report 1968*. Hong Kong: Hong Kong Government. University and Polytechnic Grants Committee of Hong Kong. 1976. *Special Report October 1965 to June 1976*. Hong Kong: Hong Kong Government.

University and Polytechnic Grants Committee of Hong Kong. 1976. *Special Report October 1965 to June 1976*. Hong Kong: Hong Kong Government.

————. 1983. *Bi-Annual Summary July 1980 to June 1982*. Hong Kong: Hong Kong Government.

————. 1987. *Interim Report for the 1985–1988 Triennium. January 1985 to December 1986*. Hong Kong: Hong Kong Government.

————. 1987. *Biennial Summary on Student Finance. July 1984 to June 1986*. Hong Kong: Hong Kong Government.

————. 1993. *Higher Education 1991–2001. An Interim Report*. Hong Kong: Hong Kong Government.

Wah Kiu Daily. 1994. December 10, p. 6.

Williams, P. 1992. "The UK Academic Audit Unit." In A. Craft, ed., *Quality Assurance in Higher Education*. London: Falmer.

Wu, K. B. 1992. *Higher Education in Hong Kong*. Washington, D.C.: World Bank.

Yeung, K. W. 1994. "The Need for International Cooperation in Vocational Training." Paper presented at the 21st general meeting and ASAIHL (Association of Southeast Asian Institutions of Higher Learning) Seminar, December 2–4, Hong Kong.

5

INDIA

N. Jayaram

The disjunction between the normative expectations of education and the existent constraints on its structure and functioning has led social scientists to postulate that "education seldom rises above the socio-economic and socio-political situation in which it is embedded" (Kamat, 1985:v). Nowhere is the validity of this postulate better substantiated than in the realm of higher education in India.

India was one of the earliest among the developing countries to have established universities and colleges, and it now has the second largest academic system in the world. The phenomenal expansion of the system of higher education, inherited as part of the colonial legacy, took place in a largely unplanned and haphazard fashion since 1960. While this system has no doubt undergone change, both planned and unplanned, the deliberate efforts to implement reforms have been only partially successful (Altbach, 1993). Nevertheless, the rich and variegated experience of India in policy formulation and program implementation in the area of higher education can offer useful lessons to other developing countries.

HISTORICAL BACKGROUND

The foundation for India's present system of higher education was laid by the British colonial regime in the mid-nineteenth century. The protracted controversy that had been generated by the initial efforts of the Christian missionaries and the officials of the East India Company was finally resolved by William Bentinck, barely a month after Thomas Babington Macaulay had penned his (in)famous *Minute* (on February 2, 1835). His policy was reaffirmed by Charles Wood's *Despatch* (of July 19, 1854). The first three universities were established at Bombay, Calcutta, and Madras in 1857.

Modeled after the University of London, these pioneer universities were largely affiliating and examining bodies with very little intellectual life of their own. All the universities that were subsequently established developed in an isomorphic fashion set on the pattern of the original universities. The British educational implantation in India was conceived to serve the economic, political, and administrative interests of the British, and in particular, to consolidate and maintain their dominance in the country. It grossly emphasized English, which not only was taught as a language, but also was made the exclusive medium of instruction in higher education. The content was biased in favor of languages and the humanities, and against science and technology (Jayaram, 1990:45–59).

It is not as if the British rulers did not realize the problems associated with such an educational implantation or its adverse consequences for the colonized society. But it was only during the early years of this century, thanks to the initiative of Lord Curzon, the then viceroy of India (1898–1905), that efforts were made to "rescue the original concept of the university from its corrosive narrowness." Several enquiries were instituted during the last three decades of the colonial rule, but "hardly any of their major recommendations were translated into university policy or practice" (Tickoo, 1980:34).

Thus, the legacy of higher education inherited by India at the time of her independence in 1947 was already crisis-ridden. As an integral element of colonial underdevelopment, higher education was "anaemic, distorted and dysfunctional." Low level of enrollment, "liberal" nature of education, "enclavization" of the institutes of higher learning, and spurious modernization were its festering features (see Raza et al., 1985:100–109).

While the obsolescence of the inherited system of higher education, by and large, persisted, the system itself underwent a phenomenal expansion never before seen in the world.[1] Between 1950–51 and 1991–92, the number of university-level institutions increased from 28 to 196, the number of colleges from 695 to 8,111 (besides 887 polytechnics), the number of teachers from 24,300 to 276,000, and the number of students enrolled from 174,000 to 4,611,000. The outlay on university and technical education increased from Rs 340 million in the first five-year plan (1951–56) to Rs 19,600 million in the eighth five-year plan (1992–97).[2]

What is particularly noteworthy about this "era of higher education" in Indian educational history, as Naik (1982:159) appropriately describes it, is that the expansion of higher education is taking place in a largely illiterate (about 48 percent of the +7-year-old population, according to the 1991 Census) society despite the low rating of education per se in the order of national priorities (the percentage of expenditure on education in the total plan outlay had declined steeply from 7.9 percent in the first plan [1951–56] to 3.6 percent in the seventh plan [1986–90]).

Behind the facade of impressive statistics on the expansion of higher education lies its continuing crisis. Naik (1982:163) has succinctly summarized the nature of this crisis as follows: "over-production of 'educated' persons; increasing educated unemployment; weakening of student motivation; increasing unrest on the campuses; frequent collapse of administration; deterioration of standards; and above all, the demoralizing effect of the irrelevance and purposelessness of most of what is being done.''

DEFINITION AND SCOPE

Broadly defined, the label "higher education" in India includes the entire spectrum of education beginning with higher secondary school. Candidates who are successful at the secondary school leaving certificate (SSLC) examination (conducted at the end of ten years of formal schooling) have the choice of two tracks of postsecondary education. The first track consists of several vocational, technical, and paraprofessional courses leading to a variety of certificates and diplomas. The duration of these courses varies from one year, as in industrial training or teacher training institutes, to three years as in polytechnics. Of these, only the three-year polytechnic course leading to a diploma is regarded as "higher educational."

The second track, generally described as the "plus two" stage, is a prerequisite for collegiate education, and is therefore called the Pre University Course.[3] This course, which is of two years' duration, is offered in three types of educational settings: undergraduate colleges offering first degree courses, junior colleges offering this course exclusively, and some schools, as Standards XI and XII. It is organized and controlled by a special state-level body called the Pre University Education Board.

Candidates who successfully complete the "plus two" stage can take up either a general degree course (such as bachelor of arts, bachelor of science, or bachelor of commerce) of three years' duration or a professional degree course (such as bachelor of medicine and surgery [5 years and 6 months], bachelor of dental surgery [4 years], bachelor of engineering [4 years],[4] bachelor of nursing [3 years], etc.). In both these types of courses postgraduation (master's degree) would entail two to three years of further education.

After the successful completion of any first degree course (general or professional), a graduate can pursue a second degree course such as bachelor of education, bachelor of library science, or bachelor of law. Since the mid-1980s, a five-year "integrated" degree course in law has been introduced in many universities, and the minimum qualification for admission to this course is a pass in the SSLC examination. One more year of postgraduate education would earn the graduate a master of education, master of library science, or master of law degree. In all courses, further higher education leading to master of philosophy (one to 2 years) and doctor of philosophy (3 to 5 years) is possible.

The post- "plus two" level of education is imparted in colleges and/or university departments. Based on the nature of their management, we can broadly identify four types of collegiate-level educational institutions: private unaided institutions, private grant-in-aid institutions, institutions managed by the state government (through the directorates of collegiate education, technical education, or medical education), and institutions managed by the universities. While there are internal variations in the principles and practices of management among these institutions, as far as their academic organization is concerned, they are all regulated by the university to which they are affiliated.

These institutions offer a variety of courses. If the level of instruction imparted is a function of the structural type of the institution (i.e., junior college, polytechnic, college, or university department), the quality of teaching often is a function of the basic facilities available in a given institution. This again is determined both by the extent and nature of the resources the administration is able to mobilize and their motivation.

TYPOLOGY OF INSTITUTIONS

In terms of their structure, the largest number of Indian universities belong to the *affiliating* type. They have university departments that impart instruction at the postgraduate level and undertake research. Besides, a large number of colleges generally imparting first degree–level education are affiliated to them. A major task of such universities is to oversee the academic standards of such affiliated colleges.

The *unitary* type of universities, on the other hand, are self-contained, and have no colleges. Most of them offer both undergraduate and postgraduate courses and undertake research. There are a few universities that are in some sense a mixture of these two types. The territorial jurisdiction of the *mixed* type of university (e.g., Delhi University) is usually confined to the city in which it is located. In addition to affiliated colleges, this type of university manages its own colleges.

Of the 196 university-level institutions, 138 are conventional *multidisciplinary* universities. The remaining 58 are *specialist* universities oriented to studies in a few related disciplines like agriculture, fisheries, and veterinary science (31), medical sciences (9), engineering (17), and law (1).

The central government has conferred on ten university-level institutions the status of "institutions of national importance." These include the five Indian institutes of technology, three institutions specializing in medical sciences, and one each specializing in statistical techniques and Hindi language. These institutions are empowered to award degrees, which according to the University Grants Commission (UGC) Act of 1956, can be granted only by a university. But the four Indian institutes of management, which are also national-level institutions, are not vested with the power to award degrees though their "fellowships" are treated on par with university degrees.

By 1991–92, thirty-one institutions had been recognized by the central government as "institutions deemed to be universities" under the UGC Act. These institutions either specialize in some area of knowledge or are heir to a tradition. They are not expected to grow to be multifaculty universities of the general type.

Outside the university orbit are research institutes funded by the Indian Council for Social Science Research and research laboratories established under the auspices of the Council of Scientific and Industrial Research or those maintained by the Ministries of the government of India. These institutions are not oriented toward granting of degrees, though they are recognized as centers for doctoral research work and quite a number of scholars working in them are recognized as guides for doctoral students registered with universities.

The concept of open university to impart distance education constitutes yet another landmark in higher education in India. The open university seeks to cater to the educational needs of those who for whatever reasons have not been able to obtain higher education or those who want to pursue their studies at their own pace and time. Introduced in 1962, this channel for higher learning was initially under the control of the conventional universities. But now there are five open universities specifically devoted to this. In all there are forty-one institutes or directorates of distance education functioning under some traditional universities and the five open universities, and these cater to about five hundred thousand students.

ENROLLMENT RATES

The bulk of the expansion in enrollment at the postsecondary level took place in the 1950s and 1960s when the rate of expansion was as high as 13 percent to 14 percent per annum. During the past decade or so the rate of expansion has dropped markedly. It was 5.9 percent in 1985–86, and has declined further and remained stable at 4 percent since then. While this rate of expansion is apparently of a manageable magnitude, the university system has never gotten tuned to the effects of the earlier expansion of enrollment. The shortages in infrastructure then have only become magnified now.

The overwhelming majority of the students (88.1 percent in 1991–92) are enrolled in the undergraduate courses in affiliated colleges. While those enrolled in postgraduate courses constituted 9.5 percent in 1991–92, those enrolled in research (1.1) and diploma/certificate courses (1.3) formed only minuscule percentages.

Concerning course specializations, those enrolled in arts (40.4 percent), science (19.7 percent), and commerce (21.9 percent) together accounted for 82 percent of the students in higher education. The enrollment in other courses was as follows: agriculture, 1.1 percent; education, 2.3 percent; engineering and technology, 4.9 percent; law, 5.3 percent; medicine, 3.4 percent; and veterinary science, 0.3 percent.

POLICY, PLANNING, AND IMPLEMENTATION

Policy

After independence the government of India appointed the University Education Commission (1948–49) (the Radhakrishnan Commission) to examine the development of higher education and make proposals for its future expansion and improvement. The Education Commission (1964–66) (the Kothari Commission) was the first commission in India's educational history to look comprehensively at almost all aspects of education, and to evolve a blueprint for a "national system of education."

Having influenced the two statements on the National Policy on Education (1968 and 1979) and, through them, the policies and programs adopted in the fourth, fifth, and sixth five-year plans (1968–83), the Report of the Kothari Commission (see Ministry of Education, 1971) was on the anvil for nearly two decades. However, the educational developments in the country since the report was first published "show marked variations with those postulated by the Commission" (Naik, 1982:6). This is partly attributable to the deliberately normative path chosen by the commission.

In 1985, the new Congress government proposed to embark on the complex task of "restructuring the system of education." Toward the end of August that year the Ministry of Education (since reorganized as the Ministry of Human Resources Development) presented to Parliament a 119-page document entitled *Challenge of Education: A Policy Perspective.* This document placed the utmost emphasis on higher education, since it "can provide ideas and men to give shape to the future and also sustain all other levels of education" (Ministry of Education, 1985:6). Among the key policy measures it contemplated include the delinking of degrees from jobs; the diversification of courses; placing a moratorium on the expansion of the conventional pattern of colleges and universities; selective admission to higher education based on "scholastic interest and aptitude"; establishment of new centers of excellence; decentralization of educational planning, administration, and monitoring; and depoliticizing academia.

The Program of Action of the National Policy on Education (1986) was reviewed during 1990–92. The recommendations of the Central Advisory Board on Education that considered the review report were adopted by Parliament in May 1992. But considering the nature of the constraints to be encountered (see Jayaram, 1991), one cannot be too optimistic about the outcome of this policy. If past experience is any guide, what we can expect is ad hoc, piecemeal tinkering with the system rather than its overhaul with grit and determination.

Planning

One of the main constraints on the formulation and implementation of education policy for higher education is built into the very process of planning. In a quasi-federal polity like India, educational planning becomes part of the overall national planning. Besides assuming an active participation of the constituent states, the national planning tends to be expenditure-oriented and overwhelmingly macro in perspective. Moreover, since higher education is the concern of more than one government department, the educational plan does not present a coordinated picture. Inevitably, all this has an adverse effect on the implementation of the plan.

Under the Constitution of India, education was largely the responsibility of the states, the central government being concerned only with certain areas like coordination and determination of standards in technical and higher education. In January 1977, through the 42nd Amendment, the central government was empowered to legislate on education concurrently with the states. Though the central government thereby established supremacy over education, the hopes of reform that this amendment aroused failed to materialize. With the gradual deterioration of the relationship between the center and some of these states during the past three decades, no government at the center can confidently take any bold steps in the realm of education.

The absence of a single machinery to look after higher education planning has often been commented on. The responsibility of higher education is divided among various departments, with the state governments' involvement being only peripheral. The state governments pass the buck to the universities which, being totally dependent on state funding, plead inability to take on this responsibility. Presuming that the state governments can chalk out an excellent plan for higher education, they can hardly be assured of its implementation as they are humiliatingly dependent on the central government for funds. Thus, the restructuring of center-state relations on the lines of "cooperative federalism" is a sine qua non for the planning and management of higher education (Pinto, 1984:185).

Implementation

The University Grants Commission (UGC), established by an act of Parliament in 1956, is a unique educational authority vested with the powers to provide funds and to determine as well as coordinate standards of higher education. Though it is expected to play a lead role in higher education, it is endowed with very little power (i.e., it can only withhold grants). But in view of the diarchy in higher education, with the UGC trying to oversee higher education and the state governments regulating it in practice, even this power can hardly be exercised (Pinto, 1984:63–107).

GOVERNANCE AND FINANCE

Governance

Universities in India are established by an act either of Parliament ("central universities") or of the state legislature ("state universities"). In some states all the universities are covered by a common "State Universities Act." While the "institutions of national importance" are established by an act of Parliament, those "deemed to be universities" are given that status under the UGC act. Generally, the president of India, in his capacity as the visitor, acts as the chancellor of the central universities, and the governor of a state acts as the chancellor of all the universities established by the state legislature.

Both in central and state universities, the vice chancellor is the administrative and academic head of the university. Universities are governed by such statutory bodies as the academic council (which exercises general control over all academic matters), the senate or court (which exercises general control over statutes and budget), and the syndicate or executive council (which supervises the executive actions of the university and is responsible for the general management of the university). The size and composition of these bodies vary from university to university. But nominees of central government or state government, as the case may be, represent the respective governments in these statutory bodies. The institutions of national importance and the institutes deemed to be universities are also governed by similar statutory bodies.

Finance

The universities and allied institutions of higher learning in India are mostly financed by the government, and higher education is thus highly subsidized by the state. The financial grants received by the universities are of two types: development (plan) grants and maintenance (nonplan) grants. The central universities are funded by the UGC. The institutions of national importance are funded directly by the Ministry of Human Resources Development. The state universities are funded by the state governments, but they can receive development grants from the UGC if the state government provides a matching component.

The universities and allied institutions of higher education also collect fees from the students, but fees account for under 10 percent of the total cost of higher education. Though insignificant, a few of them receive some financial support from charitable trusts, philanthropists, and industries. Government colleges and grant-in-aid private colleges are funded by the state government. They also collect nominal fees from the students. The unaided private colleges collect hefty fees, besides refundable deposits and nonrefundable donations.

An important factor behind the rising social demand for higher education is the high subsidization by the state (approximately 85 percent), which makes it very inexpensive for the beneficiaries. Tuition fees are ludicrously low throughout the country; they have been only marginally revised upwards, though the cost of living has risen considerably. In fact, the state-subsidized higher education is cheaper than primary education in the private sector! The greatest lapse in the educational policy has been the failure to evolve a rational fee structure.

Of course, the subsidization of higher education is often defended on grounds of equalizing educational opportunities. The open-door policy allowed access to tens of thousands of people from sections that had thus far remained excluded from the portals of higher education. To the extent that many of these happened to be first-generation entrants to institutions of higher learning, there was a partial substitution of "sponsored mobility" by "contest mobility." But in view of the operation sponsored by private schools of a mobility into elite institutions, and the legitimization of the system by "early selection" and "mass examination," this "contest mobility" was an illusion (Kumar, 1987). That is, in reality the high subsidization of higher education benefits the better-off sections of the society. Thus, higher education in India, contrary to expectations, has not been contributing to upward social mobility; instead it has been functioning as an instrument for status retention or as a status stabilizer.

Private Enterprise

Closely associated with the high subsidization of higher education is the steep decline in the proportion of the outlay for education at all levels to the total plan outlay, from 7.9 percent in the first five-year plan (1951–56) to 3.7 percent in the seventh five-year plan (1986–90). Though the allocation for university and technical education remained stable in terms of the percentage of total outlay on education (22.2 in 1951–56 and 22.4 in 1986–90), as a proportion to total plan outlay it declined sharply (from 1.8 percent to 0.8 percent). Even so, the per pupil expenditure is the highest for the institutions of higher education and has been increasing. This is more so in professional courses.

The inadequacy of resources for higher education at the government's disposal and the profitable proposition of the investment on higher education in general, and professional education in particular, have placed private enterprise in a commanding position in the realm of higher and professional education. Nearly 75 percent of the colleges for general education and over 50 percent of the colleges for professional education are privately managed. Private control over education is far more pervasive than what either its domain or legal authority would suggest.

MEDIUM OF INSTRUCTION

The striking feature of the colonial educational transplantation in India was English, which was not only taught as a language but also became the medium of instruction. While the secondary school certificate examination was conducted only in English until 1937, English was almost exclusively used at the university stage right through the colonial period. Immediately after independence, the University Education Commission (1948–49) recommended that higher education be imparted through the regional language with the option of using other Indian languages as media of instruction. The National Integration Council as well as the Emotional Integration Committee endorsed this recommendation in 1962. The Education Commission (1964–66) emphasized the need "to move energetically in the direction of adopting the regional languages as media of education at the university stage" (Ministry of Education, 1971:527).

A review of the trends in the medium of instruction in higher education (see

Jayaram, 1993b:112) reveals that English has not only persisted but is still the predominant medium of instruction.[5] This is especially so at the postgraduate level, in science and professional courses, and in the agricultural universities, the institutions of national importance, and the institutions deemed to be universities. The progress in the switchover from English as the medium of instruction, though still insignificant, is relatively better in the Hindi-speaking states than in the non-Hindi-speaking states. Even so, such a switchover is, by and large, confined to arts, education, and to some extent basic science courses at the undergraduate level. The review (Jayaram, 1993b:112) concluded that a complete switchover to the regional languages as media of instruction at all levels and in all courses is not a possibility in the foreseeable future. The only option that seems to be open is selective bilingualism. The introduction of the regional language as the medium of instruction in one or two subjects/papers, with the option given to the students to answer the examination either in English or in the regional language, could be an element of such a policy.

CURRENT REFORMS

In order to strengthen teaching and research activities in the universities, the UGC has undertaken different schemes to provide substantial support to selected university departments for development of training and research programs in certain selected fields. The assistance is provided at three different levels, depending on the stage of development of the department: centers of advanced studies, departments of special assistance, and departmental research support. By the end of 1991, 295 departments had received special assistance under these schemes. Among other schemes supported by the UGC, the Committee for Strengthening Infrastructure in Science and Technology, the College Science Improvement Program, and the College Humanities and Social Science Improvement Program deserve special mention. These schemes have no doubt "injected a degree of vitality in a system which was becoming moribund and breaking down under the increasing weight of its own size and the consequent thinning spread of limited resources" (Raza and Aggarwal, 1991:41).

Another important reform measure contemplated and implemented by the UGC is the decentralization of the system of higher education by granting academic autonomy to well-established colleges. This scheme spares the "autonomous colleges" from the inhibiting restrictions of the existing affiliating universities, and gives them freedom to attempt innovations in curriculum, methods of instruction, and examination. The Program of Action 1986 based on the National Educational Policy proposed granting autonomous status to about 5,500 colleges. By December 1991, only 106 colleges had been granted this status.

The growing demands of specialization and flexibility in the combination of courses as well as the need for integrating work/practical experience with theoretical study have necessitated the redesigning of curriculum in higher education. Toward this end the UGC has set up twenty-seven curriculum development centers. Moreover, to support educational broadcasts, the UGC has set up ten audiovisual research centers and four educational media research centers for production of software. As many as 2,332 programs, popularly known as "country-wide classroom programs," have been produced. A new organization called the Inter-University Consortium of Educational Communication is being established.

STUDENTS

Socioeconomic Background

In absolute terms, enrollment in higher education increased from 2.59 million in 1961–62 to 4.61 million in 1991–92—an increase of 78 percent over three decades. Even so, as a percentage of the population covered in the relevant age group (17–23-year-olds), those enrolled in institutions of higher education constituted less than 7 percent. Despite repeated emphasis in policy on equality for women, women constituted only 32.5 percent of the enrollment.

A substantial number of places in institutions of higher education are by statutes reserved for the scheduled castes, scheduled tribes, and other educationally backward classes. The latter is a flexible category, and in many states quite a large number of people are covered under it. The number of students belonging to these groups has increased over the years, and in 1991–92, they constituted about 10 percent of the enrollment. However, their participation in some faculties (like medicine and engineering) is insignificant. While the policy of protective discrimination in favor of these caste groups has created some academic problems, it has without doubt helped these traditionally disadvantaged sections of the population in a substantial way.

In terms of socioeconomic class, the main beneficiaries of the present system of top-heavy education (secondary and tertiary sectors appropriate about 60 percent of the educational expenditure) belong to the top 30 percent of the income groups, who occupy about 70 percent to 80 percent of the places in secondary and university levels. Moreover, there is a pronounced urban bias in higher education: About 60 percent to 75 percent of the students in different courses hail from urban areas.

In 1989–90, 12,613 foreign students were on the rolls of Indian universities and colleges pursuing a variety of courses of study. A majority of these students were from Africa (42.4 percent) and the Arab world (18.3 percent); 12.6 percent of the students belonged to India's neighboring countries; 16.6 percent came from other Asian countries. Those from other countries formed 10.1 percent. The foreign students are being charged the same fees as their Indian counterparts.

Occupational Prospects of Graduates

Studies on the employment prospects of the educated people show a mismatch between education and employment (see Jayaram, 1993a). More than 50 percent of the job seekers in India are found to be educated, including many with a university degree. Over the years the share in unemployment of beneficiaries of the successive higher levels of education has risen. This shows that unemployment has penetrated into hitherto protected sectors of the educational system.

While an increasing percentage of university products are likely to remain unemployed, the incidence of graduate unemployment is the highest among the graduates belonging to arts, followed by science and commerce faculties. They together constituted over 80 percent of the unemployed graduates in early 1985. If unemployed graduates from the education faculty are included, the figure rises to 93 percent. Engineering and medical graduates have formed only 2.58 percent and 1.79 percent of the unemployed graduates during this period.

Presenting the unemployed as a percentage of the graduates and postgraduates in a particular faculty, we get a slightly different but revealing insight. According to the seventh five-year plan, in 1985 the incidence of unemployment among arts/humanities, science, and commerce degree-holders was 22.00 percent, 21.98 percent, and 21.98 percent, respectively. The incidence of unemployment among technical (engineering) and technical (vocational) degree- and diploma-holders was 13.14 percent and 12.94 percent, respectively. The incidence of graduate unemployment was high for agriculture (21.8 percent), but low for medicine (13.13 percent) and veterinary science (10.71 percent). If, as noted earlier, arts graduates and postgraduates form the largest proportion of the unemployed graduates (46.21 percent) in 1985, it is because there are more students in the arts faculty than in other faculties.

The increasing availability of people with educational credentials in relation to the availability of jobs has resulted in a constant escalation of educational qualification for jobs without any necessary relation to more effective job performance or sophistication demanded by the economy. Agarwal (1985:68) quotes Panchmukhi's estimation of the devaluation of education[6] to be 5.8 percent between 1954 and 1974 and 6.9 percent between 1964 and 1974. If the experience requisite for jobs is also taken into consideration, the devaluation for the latter period rises to 11 percent. Such a devaluation is noticed in twenty-two out of twenty-eight job categories examined. "Maximum" (10 percent or more) devaluation is observed in the case of the educational categories of arts, science, commerce degrees, and engineering diplomas, "medium" (5 percent to 10 percent) with reference to engineering degrees, and "minimum" (below 5 percent) in the case of medical degrees.

An important measure of educational policy contemplated by the government recently (though the idea is nearly four decades old) is the delinking of degrees from jobs. It is inter alia expected, along with a national merit examination scheme, to reduce the scramble for university seats, raise the standards of higher education, match jobs and skills, cut down "educated unemployment," and avoid wastage of scarce resources.

Another educational reform stressed by various committees and commissions is the diversification of secondary education by introducing knowledge and skills that may prepare students for remunerative work without necessarily having to go in for higher education. Up to 1991–92, 12,543 vocational sections have been approved by the central government, creating facilities for diversion of 627,000 students to vocational streams at the "plus two" level.

Student Activism

An important consequence of the rapid expansion of postsecondary enrollment, especially in the liberal science courses, has been student activism. The wave of student agitation has not always been directly political, but has often been concerned largely with local and nonideological issues. Generally, the authorities and the lay public alike have tended to view the restlessness among students as "indiscipline." It has, therefore, been described often, even by academics, as merely a problem for the educational and political authorities. However, occasionally there have been instances of a limited transformation of student activism into articulated movements with far-reaching sociopolitical consequences (see Jayaram, 1990:177–90).

FACULTY

Ranks and Salaries

A logical corollary of the expansion of higher education has been the growth in the number of teachers—from about 24,300 in 1950–51 to 263,125 in 1990–91, with more than 80 percent teaching exclusively at the undergraduate level. Of these, 7,509 were professors, 43,790 readers (including principals of colleges and senior lecturers), 200,484 lecturers (including assistant professors), and 11,342 tutors/demonstrators. As a matter of policy the various ranks and nomenclatures in universities and colleges (both professional and nonprofessional) are now reduced to three: professor, reader (associate professor), and lecturer (assistant professor).

In addition to the basic pay, teachers are entitled to dearness allowance (cost of living allowance), city compensatory allowance (in the case of those working in cities), leave travel concession, medical aid, subsidized housing or house rent allowance, and a few other benefits. Schemes such as contributory provident fund and pension are in vogue, and retiring teachers get gratuity. While the UGC scales of pay have been accepted in principle all over the country, there are variations among states in their implementation. Thus, the gross salary of different categories of teachers in terms of their institutional affiliation is not the same across the country.

Teachers' Unions

Considering the immense variation in the organization and management of higher education institutions, it is hardly surprising that teachers are a heterogeneous lot. Their economic, institutional, and academic problems are diverse. Obviously teachers in India have not developed a single, all-purpose, effective union or movement (see Jayaram, 1992). Teachers in higher education in every state are organized at state and local levels, as postgraduate and undergraduate instructors or both, as employees of government or private or university-managed colleges, and based on the faculty of study. Such a proliferation of teachers' unions, through a process of fragmentation and segmentation, weakens the teachers' movement and hinders the professionalization of the field. The All India Federation of University and College Teachers' Organizations is the only organization of university and college teachers at the national level. This federation has existed for over twenty-five years and claims a membership of nearly a quarter million teachers through affiliated organizations.

Quality of Teachers

The spectacular expansion of higher education has meant the entry into the profession of people who happened, by and large, to be the first college-going generation in their kin circle. Studies on college teachers have invariably stressed the deficiency of academic preparation for and declining commitment to the profession. In 1985 the National Commission on Teachers also bemoaned the fact that most of the teachers are simply making a living rather than following a vocation.

Part of the explanation for the decline in the quality of teachers lies in the equally deplorable standards at the postgraduate level. But more serious is the fact that "higher education today has started feeding upon itself." A substantial number of postgraduates find employment within the sector of higher education. "As the demand for higher education grows and is met, this means more and more jobs for those who might otherwise have been unable to find jobs" (Singh, 1988:7). Thus, a vicious cycle of mediocrity has come to prevail in higher education.

In order to arrest this trend the National Educational Policy (1986) has proposed the recruitment of teachers on the basis of a common qualifying test (for universities at the national level; for colleges at the state level). The UGC has established forty-eight academic staff colleges that offer two courses: an "orientation course" to train the new entrants to the teaching profession, and a "refresher course" to update the knowledge of teachers in their areas of teaching. By the end of 1991 these colleges had organized 464 orientation and refresher courses covering 12,970 teachers.

Furthermore, under the UGC-sponsored Faculty Improvement Program, teachers are granted leave to pursue higher studies (M.Phil. and Ph.D.). Several universities have introduced sabbatical leave. The UGC has also been giving financial assistance to teachers who engage in approved schemes of research.

At the undergraduate level, however, there has always been a greater emphasis on teaching for examination, and undergraduate college teachers seldom engage in research. Over the years, even in postgraduate institutions, the emphasis has been shifting toward teaching. The New Educational Policy (1985–86) and the Ramamurthy Committee report of 1991 have emphasized the need to strengthen as well as diversify scientific research in the universities. During the past few years the UGC has also taken important initiatives in this regard. It has established two well-equipped interuniversity centers in nuclear science and astronomy and astrophysics. An interuniversity consortium for utilization of the facilities of the Department of Atomic Energy is being established.

PROSPECTIVE SCENARIO

The conclusion from a review of the literature on the crisis in higher education and the fate of a dozen proposals for reform is not particularly cheering. The system of higher education will continue to produce a small quantity of high-quality products from a small number of excellent centers of learning. These products will have currency in the national as well as the international community of scholars. The very large quantity of poor-quality products from the "academic slums" will join the swelling ranks of the unemployed and the underemployed.

That the challenge of reform in higher education is complex and onerous is hardly gainsaid. Nevertheless, scholars have from time to time made suggestions for a more effective and efficient functioning of higher education. The latest of such suggestions are derived from a World Bank-sponsored project on "Higher Education Reform in India" (see Altbach and Chitnis, 1993). These are summarized in the words of Chitnis (1993:426), the co-director of the project, as follows:

the development of a new general degree course for the mass of students who are presently shunted off into the traditional arts, science and commerce courses; the creation of resources; privatization; the reduction of government control; reconsideration of the practice of establishing universities by statute, and acceptance of private universities, and the granting of autonomy for colleges.

However, the directors of the project are hardly optimistic about these suggestions for reform materializing in a program of action. As they aver (Altbach and Chitnis, 1993:12), "the 'system,' having grown over almost a half century to an immense size, leads a life of its own. To basically alter its direction or configuration would require unprecedented political will and the exercise of considerable power."

NOTES

1. The statistical data cited in this chapter are drawn from Ministry of Education and Culture (1983), Tata Services Limited (1988), Association of Indian Universities (1992), Planning Commission (1992), Association of Commonwealth Universities (1993), and Ministry of Information and Broadcasting (1993).

2. In March 1995, Rs 1 = U.S.$0.03 and U.S.$1 = Rs 32.

3. The 1986 Program of Action of the National Education Policy has suggested that this stage should be brought within the school system gradually. But after nearly a decade, the progress in this regard has been limited: The existing school system is unable to take on the additional stage, and there is the problem of reallocation of teachers.

4. Those who have successfully completed a diploma course in the first track can enter the engineering course midway.

5. Many universities, however, give the option to students to write the examination in the language(s) of the state.

6. Approximately defined in terms of "a lower wage obtained by an educated person in relation to what he would be expected to get in ideal conditions."

REFERENCES

Aggarwal, B. L. 1985. "Nexus between Jobs and Degrees." In J. V. Raghavan, ed., *Higher Education in the Eighties*. New Delhi: Lancer International.

Altbach, Philip G. 1993. "The Dilemma of Change in Indian Higher Education." In Suma Chitnis and Philip G. Altbach, eds., *Higher Education Reform in India: Experience and Perspectives*. New Delhi: Sage.

Altbach, Philip G., and Suma Chitnis, eds. 1993. *Higher Education Reform in India: Experience and Perspectives*. New Delhi: Sage.

Association of Commonwealth Universities. 1993. *Commonwealth Universities Yearbook*. Vol. 2. 69th ed. London: Author.

Association of Indian Universities. 1992. *Universities Handbook*. 25th ed. New Delhi: Author.

Chitnis, Suma. 1993. "Gearing a Colonial System of Education to Take Independent India Towards Development." In Suma Chitnis and Philip G. Altbach, eds., *Higher Education Reform in India: Experience and Perspectives*. New Delhi: Sage.

Jayaram, N. 1990. *Sociology of Education in India*. Jaipur: Rawat.

———. 1991. "Higher Education in India: State Policy and Social Constraints." *Higher Education Policy*, 4(2):36–40.

———. 1992. "India." In Bruce S. Cooper, ed., *Labor Relations in Education: An International Perspective*. Westport, Conn.: Greenwood.

———. 1993a. "The Education-Employment Mismatch: A Sociological Appraisal of the Indian Experience." *International Perspectives on Education and Society, 3*, 123–43.

———. 1993b. "The Language Question in Higher Education: Trends and Issues." In Suma Chitnis and Philip G. Altbach, eds., *Higher Education Reform in India: Experience and Perspectives*. New Delhi: Sage.

Kamat, A. R. 1985. *Education and Social Change*. Bombay: Somaiya.

Kumar, Krishna. 1987. "Reproduction or Change? Education and Elites in India." In Ratna Ghosh and Matthew Zachariah, eds., *Education and the Process of Change*. New Delhi: Sage.

Ministry of Education, Government of India. 1971. *Education and National Development (Report of the Education Commission, 1964–66)*. Repr. ed. New Delhi: National Council of Educational Research and Training.

————. 1985. *Challenge of Education: A Policy Perspective*. Delhi: Controller of Publications.

Ministry of Education and Culture, Government of India. 1983. *A Handbook of Education and Allied Statistics*. Delhi: Controller of Publications.

Ministry of Information and Broadcasting, Government of India. 1993. *India 1993: A Reference Annual*. New Delhi: Publications Division.

Naik, J. P. 1982. *The Education Commission and After*. New Delhi: Allied.

Pinto, Marina. 1984. *Federalism and Higher Education: The Indian Experience*. Bombay: Orient Longman.

Planning Commission, Government of India. 1992. *Eighth Five Year Plan, 1992–97*. Delhi: Controller of Publications.

Raza, Moonis, and Y. Aggarwal. 1991. "Higher Education in Contemporary India." In Moonis Raza, ed., *Higher Education in India*. New Delhi: Association of Indian Universities.

Raza, Moonis, et al. 1985. "Higher Education in India: An Assessment." In J. V. Raghavan, ed., *Higher Education in the Eighties*. New Delhi: Lancer International.

Singh, Amrik. 1988. "Introduction." In Amrik Singh and G. D. Sharma, eds., *Higher Education in India: The Social Context*. Delhi: Konark.

Tata Services Limited. 1988. *Statistical Outline of India, 1988–89*. Bombay: Author.

Tickoo, Champa. 1980. *Indian Universities*. Madras: Orient Longman.

6

INDONESIA

William K. Cummings, Manasse Malo, and Kamanto Sunarto

Regulation No. 30 of the Year 1990 Concerning Higher Education, issued by the government of the Republic of Indonesia, states:

The Goal of Higher Education is:
1. To prepare the recipient of education to become a member of society with academic and/or professional ability that can apply, develop and/or create science, technology and/or arts.
2. Develop and disseminate science, technology and/or arts thereby attempting to utilize these to raise the standard of living of society and enrich the national culture.

This regulation represents the first comprehensive effort by the Indonesian government to establish a framework for a system of over one thousand institutions enrolling over 1.8 million students (8 percent of the 19–24-year-old cohort)— in short, one of the largest and most diverse higher education systems in the world.

Indonesia's population of nearly 200 million places it sixth in the world in terms of total population. Its more than one thousand islands extend over a distance of three thousand miles. Java, the central island, is among the most densely populated areas of the world, while in certain of the outer islands, there is less than one inhabitant per square kilometer. Indonesia is blessed with a rich ethnic, linguistic, and cultural heritage, and while no other country has as many followers of Islam as Indonesia, there are also numerous followers of Buddhism, Hinduism, Christianity, and Animism. Formed from volcanic eruptions, certain regions are rich in mineral resources including precious stones and oil; moreover, in many areas the soil is exceptionally fertile. Particularly for these latter reasons, Indonesia, known as the "spice islands," was viewed as highly desirable by the European imperial powers, and thus first was claimed by the Portuguese, then the British, and finally by the Dutch. The Dutch were primarily interested in exploiting the rich natural resources, and sought to co-opt local leaders for their mission. Among colonial powers, the Dutch had perhaps the least laudable record in terms of promoting indigenous development, particularly in the area of human resources.

During the Dutch colonial era, higher education for Indonesian nationals was sharply restricted; at the time of independence in 1945, less than one hundred citizens possessed a first degree. The struggle for independence, in which university graduates played a leading role, resulted in radical reforms in the purpose and content of higher education: henceforth, education was expected to foster development, and Bahasa Indonesia, rather than Dutch or some other foreign language (English was briefly considered), was to be the language of instruction. These reforms laid the foundation for the emergence of a mass higher education system. However, through the mid-1960s, expansion was restrained by the weakness of basic education and the difficulties the government encountered in steering an independent path of development.

With the emergence of the New Order government in 1966, political order was restored, and due both to sound policy and improved linkages with the world economy (notably the sharp increase in oil exports), the financial position of the Indonesian government and of the national economy has remarkably improved. Cultural, regional, and private interests have steadily fanned the demand for higher education.

PROFILE OF THE HIGHER EDUCATION SYSTEM

Historical Development

Colonial Era (up to 1945). During the period of Dutch colonial rule, when several higher education institutions were established, attendance by Indonesian nationals was not encouraged: In 1938, no more than two hundred of the over one thousand students registered in these institutions were children of Indonesian parents, and only one-third of the faculty were Indonesian by birth. Beginning with the period of Japanese occupation, when the Dutch faculty and students left these institutions, and continuing through the war of independence, these institutions were progressively "Indonesianized." Moreover, many of the students and faculty of these institutions periodically set aside their academic pursuits to participate actively in the independence struggle—by means of both pen and sword.

The colonial university sector was an extension of the Dutch-language Western educational system favored by the Dutch and by many Indonesian intellectuals. But parallel to the Western system was, on the one hand, a traditional Islamic system based in *madrasah* and *pesantren*, and on the other, a reformist indigenous sector consisting of a variety of institutions (Islamic [e.g., the Muhammadiyah group], secular, or Christian). During the colonial period, these sponsors did not establish higher education institutions, but at the preuniversity level they were quite prominent, accounting for well over half the educational opportunities available in Indonesia.

Independence (1945–50). The Republic of Indonesia was proclaimed by Sukarno and Hatta, speaking as the leaders of the independence movement on August 17, 1945, following Japan's unconditional surrender to the Allied Forces. But the Republic's sovereignty was contested by the Dutch who had, prior to World War II, maintained Indonesia as a lucrative colony. Thus followed a five-year war of independence before the Dutch officially recognized the Republic on December 27, 1949.

Toward the end of the independence struggle, two higher education institutions were founded: Gadjah Madah University in Yogyakarta and the University of Indonesia in Jakarta. While the University of Indonesia was formed from the elements of former Dutch institutions, it managed to shed most of the vestiges of the colonial heritage with the exception of some buildings and facilities. In contrast with certain other Asian higher education systems that can only be understood through examining the influence of Western models, it is important to appreciate the indigenous Indonesian drive for distinctiveness. Five themes stand out.

The first theme is nationalism over internationalism. From their inception, the Indonesian institutions were determined to carry out their education and prepare their research in the newly recognized national language of Bahasa Indonesia and to subordinate contributions at the level of international science to those essential for the development of their newly created nation.

Professor Soepomo, the third rector of Universitas Indonesia, in a commencement speech stressed the search for a new Indonesian orientation:

The National Indonesian University, the task of which is to create a new culture, must be free from the standards and valuations which, up until now, have been applied on the Indonesian society by the Western, in particular the Dutch science. . . . In all sciences we have to apply the national standards which we are studying. . . . The conception is quite wrong that all Western trained Indonesian intellectuals are alienated from the people's objectives. The Indonesian intellectuals who come from Western universities can apply Western technical knowledge and can think in Western terms, but internally they still possess their own ways which are certainly not Western. We are an Eastern people, we want to become a modern nation but we don't want to imitate the Western world.

Thus a major element in the new goal formulation was to reorient the university to Indonesian culture.

The second theme is local over foreign staff. Due to the worsening relations between Indonesia and the Netherlands as a result of the continued Dutch occupation of West Irian claimed by Indonesia as its territory, most of the Dutch staff of the colonial institutions were within a decade replaced by Indonesian nationals. As academic leaders made decisions concerning the training of new staff, aspirants desiring to study overseas were not sent to the Netherlands but to the United States and various European, Australian, and Middle Eastern countries. Today Japan is also considered an attractive destination for overseas study. But far more important than overseas study, in strict numerical terms, is the reliance on local institutions to train future academics.

The third theme is quantity over quality. The colonial system, though relying on Dutch as the accepted medium of instruction, provided opportunities to a remarkably small number. With the conversion to Bahasa Indonesia and with Indonesian control of the system, expansion proceeded at breakneck speed. During the first several years, enrollments at least doubled each successive year. And expansion has continued down to the present time. Necessarily, given the shortage of both human and financial resources, quality has suffered in the process.

The fourth theme is practice over academics. The orientation of the Indonesian system has been toward solving the problems of the here and now with relatively less interest in creating fundamentally new knowledge or focusing on problems of no practical value. This concern was clearly expressed by President Sukarno in his address on the University of Indonesia's third anniversary:

Are you conscious that you are expected to "serve mankind" to the best of your ability? That your studies in this Alma Mater of yours are not for you to collect knowledge for yourselves, nor even to enable you to become technically and mechanically trained leaders of the state? That what is also expected of you is the spirit of service? And to serve not your own interest, but "mankind," and particularly your own people.

The fifth theme is harmony with the state. Compared to many Third World situations, most academics in Indonesia strongly identify with the indigenous vision of higher education and believe that the nation's leaders should be looked to for indications of the preferable course of work for themselves and their institutions. Just as universities played a critical role in the founding of the Indonesian republic, it is expected they will play a role in its future development.

While public policy in the early years focused on the state sector, the independent sector also played an extremely prominent role in the revolution, and partly for that reason was given generous accommodation when the independent government was established. A new Ministry of Religious Affairs was established, among other things, to look after the interests of the traditional Islamic schools, and the reformist Islamic schools as well as the other independent schools were placed under a special directorate for private schools within the Ministry of Education. After independence, universities came to be established by all of these private groups: For example, the Ministry of Religious Affairs established a system of state Islamic institutes (institut agama Islam Negeri or IAIN) both to develop Islamic knowledge and to train teachers for the rapidly expanding *madrasah* system of education. Similarly the Muhammadiyah established a chain of universities to serve its need for teachers. And several of the private and Christian groups began to set up their respective institutions of higher education.

Austerity/Development (1952–67). The foundations of modern Indonesian higher education were set in the course of establishing the first two universities, Universitas Gadjah Mada and Universitas Indonesia. Most of the other top universities, including the Institute of Technology in Bandung, the Agriculture Institute in Bogor, Airlangga University in Surabaya, and Hasanuddin University in Sulawesi, were later established through breaking off pieces of the University of Indonesia.

From 1955 on, foreign donors began to provide technical assistance to Indonesian higher education. First Western donors were prominent in such fields as engineering, agriculture, and teaching. From the early 1960s, the socialist countries made major contributions, especially toward the development of buildings and of the science and engineering faculties.

But by the mid-1960s, most development efforts were grinding to a halt as the Indonesia polity came to be threatened by domestic violence and the economy went into sharp decline. Threats from the Left were finally met by the establishment of a "New Order" government, under the firm leadership of the military. Following a late-1960s hiatus in foreign assistance, donors have again become prominent, extending their assistance beyond the agricultural and technical fields to encourage the social and natural sciences.

The political turmoil of the mid-1960s was, in Nakamura and Nishino's view, conducive to the growth of the state Islamic institutions (IAIN); after all, vigorous religion was a strong bulwark against the threat of communism. Thus from 1966 to 1973 IAINs proliferated; by the latter date there were fourteen— seven in Sumatera, five in Java, and one each in Kalimantan and Sulawesi. In the years since, various policies have been launched to improve the quality of facilities and staff. Particularly of note from the late 1970s has been the effort "to rejuvenate Islamic studies with the infusion of Western scholarship" (Nakamura and Nishino, 1993:53). Initially this was realized through local training courses and library acquisitions. In recent years increasing numbers of IAIN faculty have taken up study in the West; for example, seventy-five IAIN staff members were in doctoral programs in Western universities in 1993.

Foreign assistance has facilitated the continuous expansion of Indonesian higher education to the point where, despite the overall moderate development level of Indonesian society, it can be said that opportunities for higher education are relatively generous: Over 5 percent of the college-level age cohort attends some form of tertiary education. Foreign assistance has also facilitated many interesting innovations in Indonesian higher education: For example, a nation-wide entrance exam is utilized to screen applicants for admission to the top institutions; the first-level degree program has increased from three to four years and the coursework leading to it is more rigorous; individuals aspiring to join the academic profession are expected to undergo training in both research and teaching methods; and programs of voluntary service have been created in order to enable students to become better acquainted with the actual conditions of development in the more deprived areas of their society. But while all this change has been facilitated through Western assistance, it still remains the case that the essential goals and spirit of Indonesian higher education derive from the heroic period of revolutionary struggle and survival when the two lead institutions—Universitas Gadjah Mada and Universitas Indonesia—acquired their unique indigenous character.

Equity/Privatization (1968–92). The national slogan, "Unity and Diversity," signifies several of the most important dilemmas facing Indonesian higher education. While the thrust of early development policies was toward a small number of "centers of excellence" largely on the island of Java, these institutions could effectively serve only a small proportion of Indonesia's vast territory.

In the early 1960s, increasing political support emerged for the extension of higher educational opportunities throughout the archipelago, and in 1962 the government committed itself to establishing an institution of higher education in each of Indonesia's twenty-seven provinces. This policy has proved especially difficult to realize in the far-flung eastern islands, where perhaps only Universitas Hasunuddin in Ujung Padang, Sulawesi Selatan, had an adequate foundation in terms of staff and infrastructure. It proved relatively easier to realize in Sumatra, where there already were three relatively strong public institutions (Universitas Sumatera Utara in Medan, Universitas Andalas in Padang, and Universitas Sriwijaya in Palembang). Despite the difficulties, by 1980 a multi-faculty public institution had been launched in each of the twenty-seven provinces, and much of the public sector effort in subsequent years has been devoted to raising the standard of these regional universities.

In the face of the public sector's steady expansion, leaders of the Islamic public institutions (IAIN) have sought more generous support from the government. From the early 1980s, the government responded by allowing the IAIN to establish new faculties in areas other than teacher training. Throughout the 1980s, this enabled the IAIN to double the size of their staff and to quadruple enrollments.

Meanwhile, the government loosened its enforcement of regulations on standards for the private sector. Since the mid-1970s, the private sector has also rapidly expanded. In 1991 the public sector consisted of 49 universities, institutes, and teacher training colleges, enrolling a half million students. The private sector consisted of 952 institutions—296 academies, 424 colleges and institutes, and 232 universities. The private institutions enrolled 1.3 million students or over two-thirds of the total enrollment in Indonesian higher education.

Types of Institutions

One objective of Regulation 30 of the year 1990 Concerning Universities is to clarify the types of institutions that make up the higher education system, the types of programs they can offer, and their responsibilities and privileges.

Chapter 12 of this regulation identifies the sponsoring bodies for higher education. Government is identified as one sponsor; in addition to the Ministry of Education, which sponsors some thirty-five national universities, several other government Ministries sponsor institutions to train elite cadre for their branch of service; the Ministry of Religious Affairs sponsors fourteen IAIN (Islamic universities). The regulation also recognizes private institutions as "units of education founded by the society."

Higher education institutions are classified into those providing nondegree professional training (the diploma programs) and those providing academic degrees (the *sarjana*, the magister, and the doctorate).[1] The academic degrees are largely provided by the universities. Nondegree professional education is primarily provided by academies, polytechnic institutes, higher schools, and institutes, though some of these institutions also grant academic degrees while some universities also offer professional training and diploma courses.

Considering the origins of Indonesian higher education, a useful distinction can be made between those institutions that emphasize secular as contrasted to Islamic education. Table 6.1 classifies the institutions in the two streams.[2]

Enrollment Rates and Finance

The national government in 1982 committed itself to provide universal primary education and in 1987 extended this commitment to the lower secondary level. These commitments have tied up much of the government revenues directed to education; thus government schools provide less than half of all places at the upper secondary level and only about 30 percent at the tertiary level.[3]

Figure 6.1 indicates the enrollment pattern for 1991–92 at all levels. The tertiary-level enrollment rate is 8.7 percent, which compares favorably with that of other nations at a similar development stage. This rate has been steadily increasing in response to a strong private demand for higher education.

THE CHANGING FUNCTIONS AND PATTERNS OF HIGHER EDUCATION

Recent Policy Emphases and Mechanisms

As stipulated in the People's Consultative Assembly's 1993 broad outline of the policy of the state (GBHN), the education sector stresses four major strategies: access/equity, quality, relevance, and managerial efficiency.

The Ministry of Education and Culture is the core shaper of educational policy in Indonesia, and most educational institutions, including the universities, are technically subordinate. For example, the minister of education has the final authority in the appointment of rectors and making the appointments from ranked lists of candidates supplied by the respective institutions. Moreover, the minister can even ignore the recommended candidates. While the minister is technically in charge, universities command considerable independent authority.

Table 6.1
Types of Institution by Educational Stream

Average age	Year of Schooling	Secular	Level degree	Islamic	
27 26 25	21 20	Universities Institutes	Tertiary S3 (Dr)	IAINs Universities	Pondok Presantren
24 23 22	19 18 17	Universities Institutes Schools of HE	S2 (MA, MSc)	IAINs Universities	
21 20 19 18	16 15 14 13	Universities Institutes Schools of HE Academics Polytechnics	S1 (BA, BSc) S0 (Diplomas)	IAINs Universities	
17 16 15 14	12 11 10	Senior High School (General, Teacher Training and Vocational)	Secondary	Madrasah Aliyah	
13 12 11	9 8 7	General Junior High		Madrasah Tsanawiyah	
10 9 8 7 6	6 5 4 3 2 1	Basic Schools	Elementary	Madrasah Ibtidaiyah	
5 4		Kindergartens		Rudhatul Atfal	

Notes: HE = higher education. Not all tertiary institutions are authorized to offer S2 and S3 degrees.
Source: Adapted from Gillet (1990:26).

Top professors and university presidents tend to be well-known and respected members of Indonesian society, and it is a brave minister indeed who overtly rejects the counsel of these key people.

Most university-related decision making evolves through a process of negotiation and compromise between top university leaders and government officials. The Directorate-General for Higher Education (DGHE) represents the government in these negotiations, and most of its key members have a university affiliation of their own. For example, the current director-general is a professor at Gadjah Mada, and returns to his home university nearly every week to give a Saturday lecture. The pattern of heavy university and teacher training insti-

Figure 6.1
Indonesian Enrollment Pattern, 1991–92

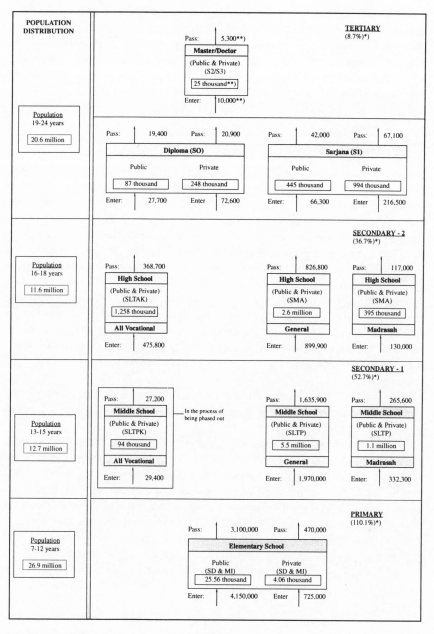

*Number enrolled as a percentage of the age group.
**Estimates.

tution (IKIP) representation in the Ministry of Education has prevailed since independence.

While the major focus of the DGHE is on the public universities, it also is responsible for the private sector, which includes many prestigious and well-connected institutions. For example, the president's family is associated with Trisakti University and certain of the other universities have close relations with major industrial groups and other key people. All of these institutions can make significant claims on the resources commanded by the Ministry.

Recent Reforms

Indonesian education, from the early 1970s through the late 1980s, has been blessed with steady increases in government revenues, including large amounts of development funds, typically associated with external assistance. The major policy emphasis until recently was on basic education, including an increasing concern with lower secondary education. While higher education has been assigned lower priority in the development plans, nevertheless the public allocations have rapidly increased. Moreover, external assistance to higher education has steadily increased: In 1982 the World Bank negotiated the First Indonesian University Development Project for nearly $100 million and followed it with the Second Project in 1987 for nearly $200 million. The Asian Development Bank has focused extensive funds on universities in the Eastern Isles as well as on polytechnics. The U.S. and Japanese governments are cooperating in an innovative project to improve the quality of university education in Sumatra. And the Australian government continues to provide extensive funds for overseas training.

The influx of funds has been accompanied by impressive creativity in the generation of new policies for higher education. The following are a few examples.

Access. Recent rapid expansion in access to higher education has occurred primarily because of rapid increases in access to low-cost schooling at lower levels of the educational system: From 1982, primary education was made "obligatory" and from 1987 this policy was extended through the lower secondary level. Increasing numbers of young people have the qualifications for higher education and think that an advanced degree will enhance their employability. While the private demand has expanded, new places have largely been supplied by the private sector. Some scholarships are now available for students from low-income families, but these are typically available only after the completion of one year of study at the tertiary level and usually are loans rather than grants.

Quality. Instructional quality is perhaps the greatest challenge to Indonesian higher education. The shift of the language to Bahasa Indonesia and rapid expansion were accompanied by the recruitment of large numbers of new university teachers who had little advanced training. A recent survey of faculty on the island of Sumatra indicates that no more than one-third have completed a second degree. Not only are professors poorly trained but they often lack access to adequate libraries or other facilities.

Various policies have emerged to enhance quality. One of the most unusual measures was a requirement that all university faculty take an official course on techniques of curriculum development and instruction; this was in place for three years before being abandoned. A second mandatory requirement (still in force) is that all university teachers complete a course on *Pancasila* (the five principles of the nation).

Distinct from these universal programs focusing on basic pedagogical skills and ideological orthodoxy are a variety of programs to enhance particular academic areas.[4] National consortia have been established in most disciplinary areas to formulate policy recommendations in the fields of teaching, research, and service, to define undergraduate as well as graduate degree programs, and to identify the universities most capable of providing these programs as well as related short-term training courses. In this manner, selected universities have been identified to specialize in particular fields, thus minimizing duplication of advanced degree offerings. Government and donor funds are channeled to the designated institutions.

Considerable funds have been made available to enable lecturers to pursue master's and doctoral programs both in-country and abroad. For example, the World Bank Second University Project supported sixteen national interuniversity centers to spearhead training efforts in their respective fields. The Third University Project is expected to continue in this vein, though placing greater emphasis on academic research. These training programs are helping establish national networks of scholars who cooperate in joint research projects. One outcome of this networking has been the increasing frequency with which academic societies are established and hold national meetings; similarly, increasing numbers of university-level textbooks are being marketed across the nation.

Relevance. Indonesian higher education has, from its conception, been committed to promoting national development. Yet universities devote little systematic thought to the specific mechanisms they should deploy toward this end; rather, it has been assumed that the knowledge and energy of individual faculty will inevitably contribute to that end. At the national level, the government has consistently relied on relevance as its standard in judging the merits of creating new programs. Thus the academic programs of public universities are slanted toward the relevant fields of medicine, engineering, agriculture, and education while the humanities and social sciences are less prominent (see table 6.2).

While university offerings may be slanted toward relevant areas, students often have difficulty moving efficiently into the labor force. Thus in 1993 the Ministry of Education announced a match-and-link policy, intended to affect all educational levels. According to this policy, concerted attention will be devoted to defining academic programs that match the needs of the various local econ-

Table 6.2
Enrollment and Graduation from Public Institutions of Higher Education, by
Field, 1984

Specialization	Enrollment[a]	Percent	Graduation[b]	Percent
Agriculture	32,800	11.00	3,400	15.5
Arts and Culture	9,900	3.3	300	1.4
Behavioral Sciences	1,700	0.6	200	0.9
Economics	35,900	12.0	1,800	8.2
Education	89,000	29.7	5,450	24.8
Engineering	33,300	11.1	3,500	15.9
Fine Arts	4,100	1.4	300	1.4
Health	16,300	5.4	2,100	9.5
Law	35,700	11.9	2,150	9.8
Natural Sciences	16,000	5.3	1,000	4.5
Social Sciences	22,400	7.5	1,750	7.9
Others	2,400	0.8	50	0.2
TOTAL	**229,500**	**100.0**	**22,000**	**100.0**

[a]Rounded to '00.
[b]Rounded to '50.
Source: Compiled from various DGHE sources.

omies; educational institutions and local employers will be encouraged to establish formal links to smooth the transition from education to work.

Related to the match-and-link policy has been the establishment of job placement/economic development centers at several universities. These centers are expected to compile systematic information about student profiles and about job opportunities in both the local and national labor markets.

Another relevant thrust has been the substantial increase in the availability of public funds for applied research, both conducted at universities and by government and corporate laboratories. New peer review committees are comprised not only of officials and professors but also of corporate sector representatives, so as to ensure the practical nature of research.

Efficiency. Efficiency in the narrow sense refers to the speed with which institutes of higher education graduate students. In the traditional university system, each faculty offered a rigid curriculum that students were required to move through in lock-step fashion; if a student failed even a single course in a particular academic year, it was necessary to repeat and pass all of the courses for that year before moving on to the next year. At the conclusion of first degree studies, a student was expected to complete a thesis (*skripsi*) acceptable to a committee of professors.

The traditional system, highly formal in nature, placed a number of obstacles in the way of graduation. A recent survey reported that students at the most efficient faculties took an average of 5.1 years to complete a "four-year" program while those at the least efficient faculties took 8.9 years; student SES background had no relation to rate of completion, and female students seemed to finish a little faster than males. While 8.9 years seems a long time, the good news from the survey was that graduation in recent years seems to be taking less time. This may be because various reforms such as the introduction of the credit system and the increasing availability of electives and course options have somewhat eased the way for students, thus enhancing efficiency.

Distinct from student efficiency in graduation are issues of administrative and financial efficiency. Until recently, public universities have had to submit line-item budgets to the Ministry of Education, and have been strictly accountable in terms of these budgets. Out of a conviction that universities would benefit from greater discretion over the deployment of funds and a policy determination that universities should take greater responsibility for the generation of their own funds, from 1992 a new policy of self-governance (swardana) was announced. The essence of this policy is that university funding will gradually be shifted to block grants, with universities enjoying full discretion over deployment. However, the block grants will only be sufficient to support a minimal level of activities; universities that seek to achieve major new initiatives, such as scholarships for deserving students, salary increases for faculty, or the construction of new facilities, will have to generate their own funds. This new policy is being implemented in stages. For example, currently most public universities collect and self-manage the proceeds from student tuition and fees, parking fees, cafeteria services, and bookstore sales.

Distinct from the public sector are the large number of private institutions of higher education that depend almost exclusively on nongovernment sources for their funding. The private institutions are known to be more efficient than the public institutions in their use and payment of faculty, staff, and buildings. On the other hand, many private institutions, in order to minimize costs, are totally devoid of a research program and do not offer courses in fields thought to be essential for development in areas such as agriculture, forestry, and public health. In other words, recent experience suggests major trade-offs between efficiency and other priorities.

Policy Implementation

Most policies are generated by government officials, in consultation with leading university representatives and, when appropriate, foreign donors. The government looks to the public sector as the main vehicle for realizing its policy objectives, and of course has a major influence on public sector institutions by virtue of its key role as chief funder; even the most enterprising public institutions receive over 80 percent of their revenues from the central government. In contrast, private institutions receive most of their funds from nongovernment sources, primarily student tuition and fees. However, the government does offer some resources to the private sector: for example, the government pays the salaries of certain lecturers it "loans" to the private sector; this includes lecturers from private institutions in its domestic faculty upgrading initiatives; it sometimes provides fellowships to enable lecturers from private institutions to pursue overseas study; and it has various programs to support faculty upgrading by private institutions in such crucial fields as mathematics and science.

In sum, the government shares extensive benefits with the private sector, which enhances its ability to obtain cooperation. Thus it can be said that Indonesia has developed a system where the government, while only a partial funder, sets the direction of development. Looking to the future, it is likely that the government share of total funding will progressively decrease, and it has thus to be asked whether the government will continue to play a leadership role.

Persisting Hierarchy

The government's funding policies tend to reinforce the longstanding hierarchy of higher education institutions. Perhaps no more than 10 percent of all public funding goes to the private sector, and within the public sector the leading national universities command comparatively large shares of public funds. During the 1970s, the lead universities were designated as "centers of excellence" and were officially favored with disproportionate funding. Subsequently, the official designation was dropped but the practice continues. For example, over the past decade Universitas Indonesia has been provided with an entirely new campus on the outskirts of Jakarta with world-class buildings and facilities. Similarly, Gadjah Mada University is currently the beneficiary of a major construction project. Other leading universities are the foci of large international loans.

According to the University of Indonesia's 1993 catalogue, it has 10 faculties, 11 libraries, 21 research centers, a university press that publishes 10 journals, a central computer center and a hospital, 19,000 enrolled students, 2,700 academic staff, and 2,040 administrative staff. Gadjah Mada University has even larger enrollments, while the universities at Bogor, Bandung, and Surabaya are somewhat smaller. In contrast with these leading public universities are upwards of 300 private institutions of higher education that enroll fewer than 200 students, and have no more than 5 full-time instructors.

RESPONSES TO INTERNAL DEMANDS

The strong popular demand for higher education has led to rapid expansion. Public sector expansion has enabled more equitable regional coverage. In contrast, private sector higher education is located mainly in the cities. Whereas the public sector tends to stress technological fields such as agriculture, engineering, and teacher education, the private sector has focused on both the cheaper fields and those that are "hot," such as computer science and management. Parallel to expanding enrollments have been associated changes in such areas as student characteristics and retention, student employability, faculty recruitment and remuneration, faculty development, research activities, and curricular emphasis. We turn to review several of these responses.

Curricular Change: Teacher Education

The fate of higher education is intimately tied up with developments in lower levels of the system. The main thrust of recent five-year plans has been to expand and strengthen primary and lower secondary education; by 1997, both are to be obligatory. Upper secondary education is also receiving new emphasis. The development of the lower levels provides higher education with increasing numbers of applicants, and to the extent these applicants are well prepared, the educational task of higher education is eased.

Teacher education is the critical link. From 1987, all primary-level teachers have been expected to obtain a diploma (D2 involving two years of postsecondary education whereas previous graduation from an educational high school was sufficient), and secondary-level teachers have been expected to obtain a bachelor's in education (S1). In the mid-1980s, Indonesia established a new Open University to provide tertiary opportunities for those youth who have difficulty attending a standard daytime university. In response to the upgrading of requirements for primary-level teaching, the Open University has developed a new modular course to provide the primary education diploma (D2). Other reforms are underway to accommodate the large numbers of upgraded and new teachers that will be required at the secondary level. As a result, education has become the second largest field of study for higher education students.

Higher education now has the responsibility for both upgrading current teachers and preparing new entrants. Effective performance of this new mission will significantly enhance both the quantity and quality of new entrants to higher education.

Curricular Change: Business Management

Recent economic growth in Indonesia has triggered a rapid increase in the number of management schools that offer programs leading to a master's in business administration (MBA). From eight schools in 1987, the number grew to twenty by 1991. While donor agencies had recommended business education for several decades and had supported various initiatives, it was not until the early 1980s that they began to take off. Habir (1991) indicates their growth in two phases.

1. The first, in the early to mid-1980s, was the establishment of programs that attended to the need for managers trained in a more practical-oriented fash-

ion. Among the most notable was the Institut Manajemen Prasetya Mulya (IMPM) (1982), the Institut Pengemgan Manajemen Indonesia (IPMI) (1984), and the Institut Pendidikan dan Pembinaan Manajemen (IPPM) (1985). Each introduced innovations such as modular curriculum, instruction in the international language of business, and night and weekend classes to accommodate the work schedules of young executives. IPMI is said, by adopting the prestigious Harvard case method, to have done the most to establish the credibility of these programs. The programs had a slow start for, almost as soon as they were founded, the Indonesian economy went into a tailspin associated with the global drop in oil prices. But by the mid-1980s, growth had returned and these new schools began to receive large numbers of applicants.

2. Some in government circles criticized these independent management schools, arguing that they did not conform to official curricular and other regulations. But the government, rather than oppose the schools, decided to imitate them by establishing management schools in the state-run universities. The first such government program began at Gadjah Mada University in 1986. Official acceptance of the management schools was followed, in the late 1980s, by a second phase in the founding of new schools, so that by 1991, twenty had been set up. Many of the new schools model themselves on the first group, while others have taken new steps. For example, PT Astra International (one of the largest business combines in Indonesia) has set up its own in-country school. Similarly, Pusri (a state fertilizer enterprise) and PT Telekomunikasi Indonesia have set up their own ventures.

Other initiatives, however, smack of pure commercialism; for example, one of the recent schools offers an MBA even though it holds classes only once a week, and others are reported to even admit high school graduates. Following the passage of Regulation No. 30, certain government officials indicated their desire to introduce new constraints on the establishment and operation of management schools; however, to date no major regulations have been imposed from above. What may eventually emerge is a form of self-regulation as the various management schools are currently in the process of establishing a national association that will have, as one of its objectives, a pledge to deliver quality education.

Student Characteristics and Employability

The rapid expansion of higher education has resulted in increasing diversity in the social backgrounds of students.[5] Higher education institutions seem to have adapted relatively effectively to these changes. As indicated above, various reforms appear to have actually resulted in an overall improvement in internal efficiency, though possibly at the price of quality. A recent survey of Sumatran students (Strudwick, 1991), while indicating that the average time required to graduate appears to have decreased, also reports that students express a high level of dissatisfaction with the way in which they are taught. Yet concerning relevance, the same students reported a high degree of ''fit'' between the tertiary education they received and the skills required by their job. Other findings from this study include the following:

1. The overall employment rate was 84 percent; half of the remainder were in a job search, and half inactive.

2. Over 75 percent of all full-time employment was in the public sector, but the public share appears to be decreasing over time.

3. The effects of fathers' education and fathers' occupational status on eventual employment were, at best, minimal; mainly those from more humble backgrounds took longer to find a job.

4. Broadly speaking, the graduates from the IKIP faculties fared well in the labor market. The graduates from the universities' Ekonomi faculties were slightly more successful in gaining employment than were the graduates of the MIPA and Teknik faculties.

5. A large disparity in earnings is evident between the public and private sectors. Mean incomes were Rp 150,600 (U.S.$68.45) and Rp 353,500 (U.S.$160.22), respectively— a 131 percent differential.

Faculty Status and Development

The long-term development of Indonesian higher education depends on the quality of the professoriate, on the incentives deployed to motivate performance, and on the facilities available for teaching and research.

Concerning facilities, current conditions are far from adequate but steady progress is being made, particularly at the lead institutions and in the high-priority areas of science, technology, and agriculture. In contrast, a recent national report of the condition of the social sciences concludes that

An important factor that limits academic activity at most of the campuses is the shortage of equipment and facilities. Most professors lack individual rooms to carry out their studies, laboratories appropriate to their speciality such as a communications laboratory, and access to appropriate academic literature. There is a scarcity of computers, and even when computers are available they are often used for administrative tasks rather than for data analysis and other research activities. (Sunarto, 1992:84)

This report goes on to document the shortage of research funds, lack of information, bureaucratic obstacles, and lack of motivation.

Concerning other factors, the academic staff in most fields are vastly undertrained, with less than one-third having an advanced degree. Various in-country, out-of-country, and sandwich programs have been devised to close the training gap, and most have achieved impressive success (Sunarto et al., 1990; Daroesman and Daroesman, 1992). However, the total number of trainees included in these programs has been small relative to the overall demand, and thus progress in upgrading academic staff has not been sufficient. Moreover, while the programs provide recipients with degrees and enhance their professional skills, it often turns out that this skill atrophy is either due to lack of follow up (Daroesman and Daroesman, 1992) or because the supporting agencies do not provide refresher opportunities (Sunarto et al., 1990).

Indonesian university faculty in the public sector are responsible for teaching between eight and sixteen hours a week, and those in the private sector slightly more. But holding responsibility for conducting courses is not the same as actually teaching; many professors provide the overall framework for courses with first day lectures and notes for the remaining lectures (*diktat*), and then lean on assistants for the actual teaching. They find opportunities for making greater sums of money outside the university; and university administrators readily accede to their requests to deploy assistants to take over the major part of the instructional task.

The system of incentives for academic staff includes low base salaries and modest compensation for merit and performance. This inevitably places pressure on professors to moonlight; most do, and many make two or more times as much outside the university as in. In the public sector, a national system of academic evaluation has been instituted that gives different amounts of points for various forms of academic work and service—locally published papers, international papers, consulting, teaching of courses, work with community groups, contribution to government commissions, and so on. While the evaluative system is impressive, its administration is felt to be tainted with favoritism, thus depriving it of major value as a motivator. Thus in this as in many other areas, Indonesian higher education is characterized by many interesting theoretical possibilities, but with perhaps too many examples of inadequate implementation.

It has been suggested that the private sector does better in holding professors accountable for performing their duties (USAID, 1993:10). But the private sector is less generous with job security, using part-time appointment to draw faculty from public universities. Perhaps 70 percent of the courses taught in private institutions are by part-timers. Those part-timers who do not attract students are dropped. The pragmatic accountability of the private sector needs to be joined with the relatively generous resources and security characteristic of the public sector.

Lessons for Other Developing Countries

The genius of Indonesia has been to develop a university system that supports "unity in diversity," a system that is responsive to the local needs of a vast and highly diverse society while at the same time promoting integration of the national scientific and intellectual culture and motivating academic staff to work for national development. Some practices associated with this achievement are as follows.

1. At the time of independence Indonesia declared a clean break with the

colonial past and its supporting educational system by stating a clear intention to develop a truly new indigenous system, while at the same time welcoming outside support so long as it was consistent with internal needs.

2. Indonesia declared achievement as the sole official (and the principal unofficial) criterion for admission and promotion in the system for both students and faculty yet at the same time quietly allowed affirmative action to enable off-Java students to gain access to higher education.

3. In support of the above practices, higher education from the first days of independence was conducted in a transregional language, Bahasa Indonesia, which was not the native language of any particular ethnic group; concurrent with the development of higher education, intellectuals became involved in developing and disseminating this transregional language through the creation of school and university texts, the support of a nationwide radio and television service, and the insistence that this language be the sole means of communication in public places.

4. To strengthen the use of the national language and its adaptation for instruction, and more generally to strengthen the quality of intellectual discourse and discovery, university leaders devised various consortia and networks to promote transregional communication. The various consortia of the central Ministry of Education and Culture are one example, which have been fortified by the establishment of university centers and national academic societies.

5. Parallel with the principle of rewarding individual achievement, institutional achievement has similarly been supported. The government has been responsive to promising initiatives from local institutions, both through continually revising regulations and, where possible, providing support.

6. A possible factor behind this responsiveness has been the principle of staffing the top jobs in the Ministry of Education and Culture (especially the top positions of the DGHE) with distinguished leaders from the university sectors, individuals who know higher education and the importance of flexible practice if academic achievement is to be encouraged.

7. Nevertheless, the administration of higher education has always operated within a framework of modest funding, with the great bulk of public educational funding going to basic education, and with the understanding that innovative higher education leaders ought to be able to find much of their funding on their own through the assessment of tuition and the charge of fees for contract research and other marketable services.

FUTURE DEVELOPMENTS

As Indonesia's New Order government approached the end of its first twenty-five years in office, it began to tidy up its various development programs. In the field of education, one important outcome was the law on education promulgated in 1989 and Regulation No. 30 of the Year 1990 Concerning Higher Education. These regulations remove many of the inconsistencies that characterized the prevailing system that had been developed in an ad hoc manner, thus providing a solid framework for the second twenty-five-year development plan.

Following the presidential elections of 1992, a new cabinet was formed that is generally regarded as having a more technological as contrasted with an economic approach to development. For example, the minister of education, Wardiman Djojonegoro, is an engineer. In an important speech to the business community on November 14, 1993, Professor Wardiman summarized his approach:

The challenges that we must face in Indonesia in developing our education system can be summarized as: (1) raising the intellectual level of all Indonesians as required by our Constitution; (2) preparing for the "world of work" in an increasingly industrialized society with stringent requirements for skilled workers; and (3) preparing for entering the "era of technology" where Indonesia needs to master and subsequently develop science and technology.

In order to meet these challenges we are pursuing three specific policy themes. Briefly summarized these themes are: (1) increasing participation in school-based education at all levels; (2) improving the skills of our graduates at all levels and establishing a closer relationship with the "world of work"; and (3) promoting and improving the use of science and technology as a necessary ingredient to continue our economic development.

The implications of this approach are presently being worked out, but they seem to imply increasing funds for higher education, particularly in the technical fields, as well as increasing support for research and development.

NOTES

1. The sarjana or S1 is roughly equivalent to a bachelor's degree in the U.S. system; the magister or S2, a master's; the S3, a doctorate. The D1 and D2 are two levels of diploma for certain specialized courses.

2. This distinction has some drawbacks. For example, while the Ministry of Religious Affairs has responsibility for most Islamic institutions, some institutions with an Islamic orientation, such as those maintained by the Muhammadyah and NU religious organizations, are classified as private institutions and are responsible to the Ministry of Education. Also while the curricula of the secular and Islamic streams were once quite distinct, in recent years various agreements have been reached, resulting in considerable similarity in the respective instructional programs.

3. However, the government provides subsidies to selected private schools in the form of salary support, the provision of materials, and the construction of facilities.

4. The *Baseline Overview Report of Mathematics and Basic Sciences in the (Higher Education Development Support) Level One Universities* prepared in October 1993 by the Mathematics and Basic Sciences Baseline Study Team provides a number of insightful recommendations, including easing student learning conditions through instituting a more flexible curriculum, allowing students to choose courses suited to their mastery level, shortening the time of normal instruction to fifty minutes per subject per day,

reviewing library capabilities, setting up procedures to systematically evaluate the subject matter knowledge and teaching skills of faculty, strengthening remedial instruction and other career development opportunities, and improving equipment and textbooks while at the same time familiarizing teachers with the improvements.

5. This generalization is based on reports from selected faculty. The government discourages research that explicitly focuses on such aspects of diversity as ethnicity or social class, reasoning that an excessive focus on these classifications might lead to misunderstanding and possibly even to discontent.

REFERENCES

Centre for Informatics, Office of Educational and Cultural Research and Development, Ministry of Education and Culture. 1990. *Educational Indicators: Indonesia*. Jakarta: Ministry of Education and Culture.

Cummings, William K. 1981. "Notes on Higher Education and Indonesian Society." *Prisma: The Indonesian Indicator 21*. The Institute for Economic and Social Research, Education and Information, Jakarta, Indonesia.

Cummings, William K., and Salman Kasenda. 1989. "The Origin of Modern Indonesian Higher Education." In P. G. Altbach and V. Selvaratnam, eds., *From Dependence to Autonomy*. Dordrecht, The Netherlands: Kluwer Academic.

Daroesman, I. P., and Ruth Daroesman. 1992. *Degrees of Success: A Tracer Study of Australian Government Sponsored Indonesian Fellowships 1970–1989*. Australian International Development Assistance Bureau and The International Development Program of Australian Universities and Colleges.

Departemen Pendidikan Dan Kebudayaan. 1990a. *Data Perguruan Tinggi Negeri Tahun 1989/1990*.

———. 1990b. *Data Perguruan Tinggi Swasta Tahun 1989/1990*.

———. 1993a. *Data Perguruan Tinggi Negeri Tahun 1991/1992*.

———. 1993b. *Data Perguruan Tinggi Swasta Tahun 1991/1992*.

Directorate General of Higher Education, Ministry of Education and Culture, and the Midwest Universities Consortium for International Activities, Inc. 1990. *Indonesia Second University Development Project: Overview of the Academic Development Program, 1987–1989*.

Djojonegoro-Ing, Wardiman. 1993. "Human Resources and Education Policy." Paper presented at the Second Economist Conferences' Roundtable with the Government of the Republic of Indonesia, Jakarta, Ministry of Education and Culture, Republic of Indonesia.

Doeriat, Winoto. 1990. *Does Management Education Make a Difference? A Case Study of IPPM 10-Month Management Training Program Graduate's Career Progress Five Years after Graduation*. Unpublished Ph.D. diss., Harvard University.

Habir, Ahmad D. 1991. "The Development of Business Education in Indonesia." In Hill, Hall, ed., *Indonesian Assessment 1991*. Canberra: Australian National University, 1991.

Keyfitz, Nathan, and Mayling Oey Gardiner. 1988. *Autonomy for Indonesian Universities*. Mimeo.

Ministry of Education and Culture. 1990. *Government of the Republic of Indonesia Regulation Number 30 of the Year 1990 Concerning Higher Education*. Translated by Sumito Corporation.

Nakamura, Mitsuo, and Setsou Nishino. 1993. "Islamic Higher Education in Indonesia." *Higher Education Policy, 6* (2), 92–101.

National Science Board. 1989. *Science and Engineering Indicators.* Washington, D.C.: U.S. Government Printing Office.

Neilsen, Dean. 1990. *A Review of Teacher Education Issues in Indonesia.* Improving the Efficiency of Educational Systems Project.

Pautler, Albert J., ed. 1994. *High School to Employment Transition: Contemporary Issues.* Ann Arbor, Mich.: Prakken.

Selvaratnam, V., and S. Gopinathan. 1984. "Higher Education in ASEAN Towards the Year 2000." *Higher Education, 13,* 67–83.

Snodgrass, Donald. 1991. "Indonesia." Mimeo. Harvard Institute of International Development.

Strudwick, Jerry. 1991. *A Reverse Tracer Study of Graduates from the Faculties of Economics, Engineering, and Mathematics and Basic Sciences from the HEDS Project Institutions.* Vol. 1: *Tracer Study Report.* Arlington, Va.: Institution for International Research.

Sunarto, Kamanto. 1992. *Penyusunan Strategi Program Hibah Bersaing: Bidang Ilmu-Ilmu Sosial.* Jakarta: Universitas Indonesia.

Sunarto, Kamanto, et al. 1990. *Final Report: Study on the Impact Evaluation Study in Indonesia.* University of Indonesia Inter-University Center for Social Science.

Thomas, Murray. 1988. "The Islamic Revival and Indonesian Education." *Asian Survey, 28* (9).

United States Agency of International Development (USAID). 1993. *Executive Summary; Baseline Overview Report of Mathematics and Basic Sciences in the HEDS Level One Universities. Higher Education Development Support.* Jakarta, Indonesia.

University of Indonesia. 1993. *Universitas Indonesia.* Jakarta: Author.

Van Den Berg, Ewe, ed. 1991. *Science and Mathematics Education in Indonesia: An Introduction with Specific Recommendations for a Project to Support Science and Mathematics Programs at Selected Universities in Sumatra.* Washington, D.C.: Academy for Educational Development.

7

IRAN

Golnar Mehran

The study of higher education in any country may focus on domestic as opposed to international challenges or emphasize internal versus external factors that shape postsecondary education. The choice depends not only on the theoretical framework used, but is also determined by the uniqueness of each nation. To analyze the development of higher education in Iran, one should present an "internalist" as well as "externalist" view of its role and function (Clark, 1992: 205–6), and explore the domestic realities that have shaped the direction of higher education in this country. Unlike other Asian countries whose changing position in the world economy and technology challenged the traditional function of their universities, higher education in Iran has been inward-looking, responding to the urgent needs of a society in rapid transition.

The present chapter focuses on the domestic factors that have shaped higher education in Iran with due attention to international challenges whenever necessary. Within the domestic framework, it offers an externalist view to illustrate the university-society links and analyze the historical, social, political, economic, and cultural factors that have led to the formation of the present system of higher education. It also uses an internalist approach to shed light on the structure, administration, curricular content, instructional methodology, admissions policy, student enrollment, and faculty recruitment at universities.

An in-depth examination of the sociopolitical factors shaping higher education in Iran illustrates how institutions of higher learning have been utilized by different ruling groups to serve their political and ideological purposes. Thus universities have been used for elite formation, status perpetuation, nation building, creating a new class of technocrats, and bringing about a cultural revolution. Higher education has, with few exceptions, basically reflected the status quo throughout time, as illustrated by the following historical review.

HISTORICAL DEVELOPMENT OF HIGHER EDUCATION

Pre-Islamic Period

The history of higher education in Iran dates back to A.D. 260 and the rule of the Sassanid Dynasty over the Persian Empire. The importance of knowledge and learning in pre-Islamic Iran is evident in an early Zoroastrian prayer that states "O, Ahuramazda, endow me with an educated child" (Arasteh, 1962:2). Yet education in the highly stratified Iranian society of the time was geared toward preparing religious leaders and educating the sons of the nobility. In addition to training elites, however, pre-Islamic Iranian educational centers acted as intellectual reservoirs in the ancient world. Such was the case of the Academy of Jundishapur, founded in 260 and located in the city of Jundishapur in what is today the province of Khuzestan.

Jundishapur was not only a prominent institute of higher learning in the Persian Empire, but was also a refuge for scholars and philosophers who were persecuted by the Christian church at the time. An influential intellectual center of the ancient world, Jundishapur attracted Persian, Greek, Syrian, and Alexandrian scholars who taught astronomy, mathematics, philosophy, and medicine. In fact, its medical center, hospital, and library became a model for generations to come. The academy reached its peak from 531 to 579, bringing together Hindu, Greek, Judaic, Syriac, Alexandrian, Christian, and Persian learning and translating significant Greek classics in science and philosophy into the Pahlavi (Middle Persian) language.

Jundishapur became one of the largest and best equipped institutions of higher education in the world at the time when Christian domination of the Western world led to the closing of the most influential centers of learning, including the academy of Athens in 529, and the flight of Western scholars to the East. Nestorian, Alexandrian, Syrian, and Jewish scholars found refuge in Jundishapur—by then a cosmopolitan center of learning—upon being driven away from their academies by early Christians.

The academy remained undisturbed even after the military surrender of Jundishapur to Arabs in 636. It remained a scientific center throughout the Umayyad period (661–750). It was not until the late 880s that Baghdad in the east and Sicily and Cordova in the west replaced Jundishapur as the intellectual centers of the vast Islamic Empire.

From the advent of Islam in Iran in 642 to the fading of the academy as an influential center almost two hundred years later, Jundishapur remained the "central clearing house of ancient learning, transferring it to the Muslim world and the West" (Nakosteen, 1964:15). The academy, upon assimilating, translating, and improving ancient knowledge, transmitted it to the Islamic civilization. Muslims during the golden age of their intellectual activities (750–1150) in turn preserved and improved the existing knowledge of the time when Europe was undergoing its dark ages in the medieval period. The sum of human knowledge, including Hindu, Greek, and Persian science and philosophy, was then passed to Western scholars during the Renaissance. The preservation and transmission of classical knowledge by the Persian and Islamic civilizations is the outstanding contribution of the East to Western education in particular and human intellect in general.

Islamic Education

Iran has witnessed thirty-five invasions throughout its history (Ayman, 1974), yet none has had the lasting impact of the seventh-century Muslim conquest that led to fundamental transformation in the national culture and religious identity of Iranians. The advent of Islam in Iran radically changed the society and the system of education. Iran was ruled by the Arab caliphate and Islam became the state religion. Arabic became the official language of the Islamic Empire and many Iranian scholars wrote in that language. Zoroastrian teaching was replaced by Islamic education, and Muslim *ulama* (learned religious scholars) rather than Zoroastrian priests determined the content of formal schooling. Being entirely in the hands of religious leaders, education became exclusively religious and the curriculum was composed mainly of religious studies. Pre-Islamic Iranian belief in the importance of education was strengthened by the teachings of Islam.

Muslims respected learning as illustrated in the wide range of educational activities taking place throughout the Islamic Empire. The formation of *halga* (circle school), *maktab* (writing school), *masjid* (mosque school), *madrasa* (public school), bookshop school, palace school, and the literary salon are examples of Islamic commitment to learning.

Seeking knowledge was further encouraged by a spirit of free inquiry, research, and scholarship along with provision of food and lodging for students and faculty, opening of public and private universities, and the introduction of the concept of the traveling scholar in pursuit of knowledge gained in the company of a learned teacher living far away. In fact, Islamic civilization flourished exactly when Muslims, free from the limitations of dogma, explored every branch of human knowledge, including philosophy, logic, history, law, theology, medicine, mathematics, jurisprudence, and art (Nakosteen, 1964:37). Iran also acted as a contributor to the Islamic civilization, and Iranian scholars such as Ibn Sina (Avicenna) and Razi have left a lasting imprint on human knowledge. In fact, in tenth-century Baghdad the *Shu'ubiyyeh* society (partisan of the gentiles) was formed, claiming Persian superiority and crying "back to Persia."

Although Iran was part of the Islamic Empire, higher education in this country took a different route from the rest of the Muslim world. Advanced learning in the Islamic countries took place in the *madrasa*, which offered both secondary and college disciplines. The year 1066 marks the beginning of the *madrasa* system, the date when Nezam al-Molk, the Iranian prime minister of the Seljuq Dynasty, founded the Nezamiyyeh College in Baghdad, named in his honor.

This was the first of a series of *nezamiyyeh* throughout the Islamic lands. They were originally founded to strengthen Sunni Islam, as opposed to the Shi'i teachings of Al-Azhar in Cairo, founded in 970 by the Fatimids.

Nezamiyyehs were state institutions that provided standardized, universal education throughout the empire with the exception of Sicily and Spain. Fifty-nine *madrasas* existed in eastern Islam, including Iran and Iraq, between 1066 and 1250. *Nezamiyyehs* provided generous salaries and stipends for teachers and students. Among the most well-known teachers of these institutions one can name al-Ghazali, while Sa'di, the great Persian poet, received a fellowship to study at the Nezamiyyeh College at Baghdad (Fischer, 1980:38–39).

Muslim higher education in the Abbasid period (750–1258) included both *naqli* (transmitted) as well as *'aqli* (rational) subjects. The curriculum at the *madrasas* of the time was comprised of legal, religious, and literary studies (such as law, jurisprudence, exegesis, tradition, rhetoric, and syntax) as well as rational, scientific, and mathematical subjects (such as logic, dialectic, natural science, chemistry, medicine, geometry, astronomy, and algebra). Various authors (Nasr, 1987) have pointed to academic freedom and the spirit of inquiry and debate during the golden age of Islam, and regarded the decline of the Muslim civilization as a result of exclusive focus on religious and literary studies at the expense of philosophy and science as well as growing intolerance of innovation and creativity leading to intellectual stagnation.

Discussion about the merits and disadvantages of the *nezamiyyeh* system of higher education, the most famous of the chair of *madrasas*, leads to an important debate on academic freedom versus state control at higher levels of education. State financial support for the *nezamiyyehs* increased learning opportunities by providing stipends, food, and lodging for students as well as salaries and well-equipped libraries for faculty members. They spread universal, public education for all throughout the vast Islamic lands. Yet *nezamiyyehs* also marked the "culmination of the first five centuries of Islamic education" and the beginning of the end of creativity and diversity of opinion (Fisher, 1980: 38). They were government institutions established to disseminate state-determined religious and political information. *Nezamiyyehs* reflected the status quo and fulfilled the aims of the ruling groups. This is, in fact, the role played by state-controlled higher education in Iran throughout time with rare historical exceptions.

Madrasas in Iran were also built by rulers, especially during the reign of the Safavids in the sixteenth century, when Shi'ism became the state religion of the country. The most famous *madrasa* named Feyziyyeh, where Ayatollah Khomeini and many other leaders at the Islamic Republic have taught and/or studied, was built by the Safavid King Tahmasb J in 1527. Yet unlike higher education in the Ottoman Empire where Sunni religious leaders/teachers worked closely with the caliphate, Iranian Shi'i scholars attempted to maintain their independence both financially and in the administration of the *madrasa* system. Funded by private endowments and being the direct recipients of *khums* tax (one-fifth religious tax), Shi'i leaders and their higher educational institutes remained financially independent.

So far one can clearly see that higher education in Iran responded to both internal demands (the need for elite formation and perpetuation of status) and international changes at the time when the Persian Empire became the intellectual sanctuary of scholar-refugees from the West and during the period in which the accumulated knowledge of the Persian civilization was assimilated in the golden age of Islam. Later, the Islamic conquest and the struggle for survival among Iranians led to their choice of assimilation and adoption of Muslim education, to which they later contributed extensively.

Higher education in the nineteenth century also responded to international challenges that threatened national sovereignty—namely, the threat of Western domination and the superiority of the European model. The "torch" of innovative thinking and creative scholarship that once passed from the Muslim world to Europe was to change direction in the nineteenth century. By then Europe, armed with science and technology, presented a serious threat to the integrity of Muslim nations in decline. The challenge was not only military but also intellectual, and the Iranian response was educational.

The inability of the *madrasa* to train much needed specialists in engineering, medicine, military, and political affairs, and the costly endeavor of sending students abroad to study (a process that began in 1811) led to the establishment of the first institutes of higher learning along modern lines in nineteenth-century Iran. The most well-known institute of modern education was Dar al-Fonun (House of Sciences), established by the reformist prime minister Amir Kabir in 1851 during the reign of the Qajor Dynasty (1785–1925). Financed by the government, it was an elitist college that admitted sixteen-year-old sons of prominent landowners and top government officials.

Using foreign, mostly Austrian, instructors and textbooks that were later translated into Persian (Arasteh, 1963), the core curriculum included mathematics, natural sciences, history, geography, and foreign languages. Students could then specialize in engineering, medicine, pharmacy, or military sciences.

Although it broke away from the traditional mold of religious instruction, serving as a model for other institutes of higher learning, Dar al-Fonrun was, in fact, an instrument of the ruling group to train political elites. Other elitist higher education institutions included a school of languages (1873), military colleges in Isfahan and Tehran (1883, 1886), a school of agriculture (1900), and a school of political science within the Ministry of Foreign Affairs (1901) (Fischer, 1980:58).

The establishment of Dar al-Fonun is important not only because it was the first modern school that attempted to heed the call for modernization and industrialization, but also because it lay the foundation of a dual system of education in Iran. The parallel coexistence of traditional/religious education in the *madrasa* and modern/secular teaching at the universities lasted a century before an attempt was made to desecularize and Islamize the universities in the post-

1979 revolution period. In fact, no study of higher education in Iran would be complete unless one studies the division of intellectual labor and the difference in the elite formation of the *madrasa* and the university.

DUAL SYSTEM OF HIGHER EDUCATION IN TWENTIETH-CENTURY IRAN

The twentieth-century history of Iran is the account of struggle for power among the secular and religious elite of the country. Although at times the liberal, Westernized members of society cooperated with the religious leaders and the *bazaaris* to fight against domestic despotism and foreign intervention (for example, during the 1905–11 constitutional revolution and the 1963 uprising), such alliance was merely a response to the exigencies of the time. One can firmly state that there has never been lasting peace between the *ulama* and the secular elite. In their competition for power, both have used the system of higher education to train their potential leaders and indoctrinate the young. A look at the formation of modern universities and the struggle for the survival and independence of the *madrasa* system bears witness to the above statement.

Traditional/Religious Education

As has been mentioned before, the *madrasa* system of higher learning has survived the most vehement attacks of the secular ruling elite throughout time, the strongest of which occurred during the reign of Reza Pahlavi (1925–41), founder of the Pahlavi Dynasty.

Reza Shah, like the Turkish leader Ataturk, aimed at the modernization, Westernization, secularization, and de-Islamization of the society and used the system of education to achieve these goals. He banned religious education such that religious studies were eliminated from the school curriculum. He dissolved *maktabs* (Islamic elementary schools) and restricted the educational activities of the *madrasa* and the *howzeh 'elmiyyeh* (theological center). Such drastic charges were clearly antireligious (Szyliowicz, 1973) and the *ulama* were faced with a real internal challenge. This was where their historical financial independence and freedom from state control prevented their collapse. *Madrasas* survived on private endowments and religious tax and their instruction never halted. In 1975, a total of 10,350 *talabeh* (students of theology) were studying in various *madrasas* throughout Iran, the highest concentration of which was in Qom. Foreign students from Pakistan, Afghanistan, India, Lebanon, Tanzania, Turkey, Nigeria, and Indonesia were also studying religion in Iran. Iranian students were usually aged sixteen to twenty-five, mostly coming from rural and clerical families (Fischer, 1980:77–80).

A comparative look at the curriculum and teaching method of the *madrasa* and the modern university will shed light on the differences between the two. The traditional *madrasa* course of study has three levels and a series of electives.

Level 1 or *moqaddamat* is composed of the "preliminaries," including ety-
mology and derivation, syntax, and rhetoric using classical texts accompanied
by commentaries on them. Level 2 or *sath* is the "subject proper" and includes
logic, principles of jurisprudence, and law. Written texts as well as notes are
used at this level. There are no texts at the third level or *dars-e Kharej*, also
known as "outside lesson" or "external studies." Here the practical use and
application of law and principles at jurisprudence are examined. Upon completion of the course at jurisprudence, the student has to compile a report on its
principles. Once accepted, "a permission to follow one's own reasoning skills"
is granted, allowing the student to become a *mojtahed* and act independently.
Finally, it is interesting to note that philosophy, moral philosophy, and com-
mentary or the Qur'an are solely electives in the *madrasa*.

The curricular content of a few traditional schools was updated in the 1960s
to meet the needs of a rapidly modernizing society. The more modern *madrasas*
not only recruited students and teachers who had received some secular high
school education, but also established schools for girls taught by women. The
course of study at one of the modern *madrasas* in Qom included jurisprudence,
law, religion, the study of the Qur'an, logic, philosophy, and ethics as well as
Persian and Arabic literature, foreign language (English), mathematics, sciences,
and humanities (including psychology, sociology, geography, history, and Islamic economics) (Fischer, 1980:249). Although modern *madrasas* were not
established to prepare students for entrance to the formal schooling system, the
very attention to the realities of modern times and the opportunity provided by
these schools for students from rural and religious backgrounds to continue their
education is important to note. Both married and unmarried students received a
stipend throughout their studies, the length of which depended on the progress
and effort of the individual.

A parallel system of higher education in religious studies was created during
the Pahlavi rule through the faculties of theology in the state-sponsored universities—a tradition that continues today. Twenty-seven faculty members, twenty-
one of whom held Ph.D. degrees, taught at the faculty of theology and Islamic
studies, Tehran University, in 1975. A general B.A. along with M.A. and Ph.D.
degrees in religion and speculative mysticism, Islamic law, Islamic philosophy,
and Arabic culture were granted at the time. English and French were also
offered as foreign languages. Observers have pointed to the absence of early
Islamic and European philosophy as well as non-Shi'i dialectical theology in
the university course of study (Fischer, 1980:249).

In 1991–92, a total of 10,669 or 3 percent of all university students were
studying religion and speculative mysticism, theology and Islamic studies, history and civilization of Muslim nations, Islamic education, Arabic language and
literature, Qur'anic studies, principles of Islamic law and jurisprudence, Islamic
philosophy, Islamic theology, Islamic economics, Islam and propagation, Islamic
political science, and Islam and management at the undergraduate and graduate
levels. Included among them were 3,399 undergraduate students trained at the

universities to teach theology and Islamic studies, and Arabic language and literature, and 147 graduate students being prepared to teach Islamic studies at the universities (*Amar-e Amuzesh-e 'Ali Iran 1370–71* [*Higher Education Statistics*], 1992).

Since the establishment of the Islamic Republic in 1979, the traditional *madrasas* have also added social sciences and humanities (political science, history, and education), mathematics, foreign language (English), and computer science to their curriculum (*Keyhan* [daily newspaper], May 30, 1990). Enrollment has also increased from 10,350 in 1975 to a total of 75,238 in 1990, among whom 90 percent are male and 10 percent female (*Salnameh-ye Amarí Keshvar* [*Statistical Yearbook*], 1990). Although the religious atmosphere of present-day Iran and the absence of restriction on traditional education are important factors in attracting students to the *madrasa*, one cannot but wonder whether the chance to obtain power through Islamic education and membership in the religious elite group is the real incentive.

A unique feature of *madrasa* education is its teaching method, a tradition worth exploring and adopting in other institutions. Historical accounts of the teaching method in the *madrasa* reminds one of the more innovative, participatory, learner-centered methods propagated today in the advanced countries of the West, in which debate, critical thinking, and questioning are encouraged.

According to Nakosteen, the teacher, the book, the lecture, and the debate were the "nerve centers" of early Muslim education, encouraging individualism, questioning, dispute, and experimentation as part of the learning process. Students were free to question the teacher, disagree with him, and even challenge and correct his statements (Nakosteen, 1964:46). The fact that students chose their teacher and traveled long distances to join a learning circle meant that the learner had the freedom to stay with a good teacher or leave him if his teachings were no longer useful or challenging.

Although memorization and recitation gradually replaced free and spontaneous discussion, students continue to be "partners in learning" as opposed to the "captive audiences" of the universities. The pedagogical style at the *madrasas* in Qom is still based on a "dialectic principle of argument and counter argument in which students are encouraged to participate" (Fischer, 1980:63). Students study with teachers of their own choice and are encouraged to ask questions and discuss/dispute the answers. The fact that there are no grades, and that each student can join classes according to his or her own ability and choice is yet another indicator of the openness of the *madrasa*, also called a "free university."

Modern/Secular Education

The duality between traditional and modern education reached its climax during the rule of the Pahlavi Dynasty (1925–79). Although modern schooling had its beginnings in the nineteenth century, it was not until the early 1930s that the monopoly of the religious establishment in educating the young at the higher levels was truly challenged. The establishment of Tehran University in 1935 by Reza Shah opened a new chapter in the history of schism between secular and religious education.

The challenge of Tehran University was in both its content and its product. Not only did the new institution offer modern sciences in a coeducational set-ting—unprecedented in Iranian history—but it was also set up to train a new elite to gradually replace the traditional one. The graduate of Tehran University was to be a skilled technocrat, whose expertise would serve a "new" Iran, a modern, industrial one. Tehran University was also a reflection of the changes in the broader sociopolitical context. Reza Shah had a plan to transform Iran from a traditional, religious, and feudal society to a modern, secular, Western-ized, and industrialized one, and education was to play a key role in this en-deavor. This was the real challenge to the traditional centers of power and elite formation, and thus led to an uneasy, long coexistence.

The establishment of modern universities based on the Western model con-tinued during the reign of Mohammad Reza Pahlavi (1941–79). The Universities of Isfahan, Mashhad, Shiraz, and Tabriz were established in 1949, followed by Ahwaz (1955), Jundishapur (1956), National University (1960)—the only pri-vate university at the time—and Aryamehr University (1966). The establishment of modern universities was accompanied by a transition from the French model, practiced by faculty members trained in Europe, to the gradual dominance of the American model through American-educated Iranian professors and U.S.-Iranian cooperation in higher education. The years prior to the 1979 revolution also witnessed the highest number of Iranian students abroad, many studying in the United States. In 1975, 14,000 Iranian students were enrolled at U.S. uni-versities, 80 percent of whom were undergraduates. Iranian-American liaison in higher education was not limited to Iranians studying in the United States. Fac-ulty exchange, transfer of educational technology, curriculum development, text-book preparation and translation, teacher education, collaborative research, and educational aid are further instances of the close link between the two countries before the 1979 revolution (American Council on Education, 1976:1–2, 160–71).

The adoption of the Western, particularly American, model in higher educa-tion marked the beginning of a new period of elite formation in Iran that began in the mid-1960s. A historical look at the education of the elite in Iran points to three distinct periods in Iranian history and reflects social transformation from a traditional/religious society to a modern/secular one. Accordingly, the training of traditional elite in the *madrasa* was replaced by elite formation in highly prestigious centers of education in the country, such as Dar al-Fjonun and Teh-ran University. The elite of the 1970s, however, were mostly educated in the West, representing Western culture and mannerism deemed as high culture at the time.

Another major difference between the traditional and the modern higher education system was the nearly total dependence of the latter on the state. Institutions of higher learning were no longer administratively independent and financially self-reliant as was the case with the *madrasa* system. The autonomous nature of higher education came to an end with the establishment of the centrally administered Ministry of Science and Higher Education in 1968, following major student protests that led to the closure of universities, calling in of security forces, and extensive arrests—a story that was to continue for a long time.

Further reliance on the state was brought about by the announcement of free, nationalized higher education in 1975. University students in Iran and abroad would receive free tuition, free board, and monthly cash subsidies in exchange for two years of "national service" for each year of support. The latter policy had two aims. First, the shah wanted to build a technocratic society, and the institutions of higher education were to educate the skilled manpower needed to serve this purpose. Technocrats—scientists, engineers, and technicians—were needed to bring about a "skills revolution." There was a dire need for expertise and specialization and universities were assigned this task. The second aim was to pacify the students. Iranian universities had long been centers of political activism and revolutionary fervor. Political dissidence was rampant among students, and making them dependent on state aid was a way to quiet them. The faculty members were not immune from state control either. Security forces had to "clear" professors before they were allowed to teach at universities.

It is true that the "externalist" view of higher education in Iran sheds light on the interaction between educational factors and societal forces. Yet it is only through an "internalist" view that one can gain insight into the internal dynamics of universities and problems faced by higher education.

The development of higher education during the Pahlavi period was marked by quantitative growth and expansion in the number of students and institutions. Tehran University enrolled 1,550 students in 1935. Forty years later, 135,354 students, 28 percent of whom were female, were studying in 10 universities and 133 institutions of higher education. Of the total number, 27 percent were enrolled in two-year programs, 62 percent in the undergraduate level, and 11 percent in graduate programs. In 1975, the highest rate of student enrollment was in the social sciences (23 percent), followed by engineering (19 percent), humanities (18 percent), mathematics and sciences (16 percent), medicine (11 percent), agriculture (5 percent), fine arts (3 percent), education (3 percent), and law (2 percent). Ironically, student preference for social sciences and humanities was contrary to the shah's plea for training skilled experts in the technical and scientific fields. In 1975, 12,310 faculty members taught at institutes of higher learning, 13 percent of whom were female and 2 percent non-Iranian (American Council on Education, 1976:28, 39, 48).

Higher education in prerevolutionary Iran faced major problems, some of which continue to plague the system today. Higher education has been characterized by immense pressure for admissions since the mid-1960s. A hierarchical system in which all education is supposed to lead to the university has created a mismatch between secondary school graduates seeking admissions and the limited number of seats available in institutes of higher learning. As a result, each year less than 10 percent of those taking the national university entrance examination are able to attend university.

The inability to gain admissions to universities and the "diploma disease" existing in Iranian society has led to the exodus of those who sought university degrees beyond the border, resulting in brain drain. Although emigration also occurred among Iranians who had studied in Iran yet chose to live and work abroad, brain drain during the shah's rule was mostly the result of overseas education and the choice of life in the host country upon graduation. Had higher education facilities been available in the country, there might have been less "outflow" of skilled personnel and much-needed specialists especially in the fields of medicine and engineering. Brain drain has mainly been a political issue since the 1979 revolution, yet one cannot but wonder whether the existence of a large number of universities and fully equipped research centers would have partly prevented the emigration of skilled Iranians.

Another long-term problem plaguing higher education in Iran is reflected in its priorities: the choice of quantity over quality; memorization and book learning over critical analysis and problem solving; theory over practice; and teaching over research. The prestige of obtaining a university degree has long overshadowed the importance of intellectual development and creativity in the teaching-learning process. Thus the eve of the revolution witnessed the university as mainly a teaching and degree-conferring institute, marked by limited intellectual discourse, research, and innovation and extensive political activism among the students. The situation was to change after the 1979 revolution.

POSTREVOLUTIONARY HIGHER EDUCATION

Iranian leaders often refer to the 1979 revolution as first and foremost a cultural revolution that was aimed at bringing about radical transformation in social and cultural values. Its mission was to change secular, Westernized Iran into an Islamic society ruled by *vali-ye faqih* (religious jurisprudence) and governed by Islamic law. Its elite would, therefore, no longer be "Westoxicated" intellectuals but rather devout Muslims loyal to the government. Obviously prerevolutionary universities could neither contribute to the cause of the revolution nor train ideal citizens of the Islamic Republic. This was deemed enough reason to dramatically alter the content and product of postrevolutionary higher education. The above was not to be achieved through gradual reform but rather by radical, often violent, measures to bring about an ideal Islamic university. The importance of the postrevolutionary university is such that Iranian authorities state "it is through the university that a nation may be reformed or destroyed" (Pazargadi, 1986:63).

Cultural Revolution

The 1979 revolution fundamentally changed the goals and functions of higher education in Iran. Whereas "skills revolution," formation of modern, secular elite, and training of experts and technocrats were the major aims of universities in the pre-1979 period, postrevolutionary higher education was assigned the task of bringing about a "cultural revolution" and educating pious, committed individuals. The choice of commitment (*ta'ahod*)—defined as piety and loyalty to the Islamic government—over expertise (*takhassos*) and specialization reflects the priorities of higher education in the Islamic Republic. Similar to the Chinese Cultural Revolution that favored "redness" over expertise, postrevolutionary Iranian leaders preferred devotion to Islam and support of the revolution to skill and specialization among university students (Mehran, 1990).

To achieve this end, the universities were closed in 1980 for three years; during this time fundamental transformation occurred in the selection of students, hiring of faculty members, and the curricular content. Through what is known as *enqelab-e farhangi*, or cultural revolution, the Iranian government launched a campaign to "purify" and Islamize the content of higher education and train committed students as opposed to "mere" experts.

Ayatollah Khomeini, founder of the Islamic Republic, criticized universities during the Pahlavi rule for being "imperialist," lacking Islamic morality, educating intellectuals "infatuated with the West," and serving the foreigners. He even declared Westernized faculty members as enemies of Islam, working for colonialists and imperialists, and named universities as "machines into which Muslims were thrown to come out as Communists" (Pazargadi, 1986:31). To change the above situation, Ayatollah Khomeini called for an educational revolution of an Islamic character, beginning with the establishment of an "ideal" university unattached to the East or the West—the socialist and capitalist camp, respectively—the product of which is "human, Islamic, and of service to the country."

Criticizing the Pahlavi regime for creating disunion and hostility between the university and the clergy, Ayatollah Khomeini stated that "at the university, the name of clergy was received as an opiate, and the mention of academicians among the theological students meant infidels" (Pazargadi, 1986:62). To reverse the situation, he asked for cooperation between universities and theological centers and assigned this task to the very same people who had received both traditional *madrasa* schooling and modern university education. The latter, along with other committed individuals, were to render universities independent and destroy the influence of the superpowers among students. The postrevolutionary Islamic universities were to be fundamentally transformed to provide Islamic education and spiritual/moral training as well as teach sciences to bring about self-reliance for the nation.

It is important to note that Islamized universities have never been opposed to science and technology. The search for an Islamic university based on Muslim culture and morality does not mean that "only Islamic learning should be taught in them or that each science comes in two varieties, one Islamic and the other non-Islamic" (Algar, 1981:296). Postrevolutionary higher education never rejected modern sciences; what was shunned was not industrialization and modernization, but Westernization, dependence on foreigners, and blind imitation of Western ways. Yet once faced with a choice between Islamization and specialization in the universities, the Iranian authorities chose the former. The early years of the revolution was a period during which the criteria for studying and teaching at the university were not knowledge and expertise, but moral refinement and political loyalty to the government.

To achieve this end, the universities were closed, the Headquarters of Cultural Revolution was established, and a seven-member team was assigned the task of determining the educational content and policy of universities on the basis of Islamic culture and the political exigencies of the government. Emphasizing Islamic ideology and deemphasizing Western norms and values were guidelines for changing the content of instruction, especially in the humanities and social sciences (Sobhe, 1982).

The Iranian cultural revolution was not limited to transforming the academic curricula and rewriting the textbooks. It also aimed at purging dissident students and expelling faculty members labeled as anti-Islamic and counterrevolutionary. Once known as a "battlefield" and a "military fortress," the Iranian university was transformed from a bastion of political activism to a center of quietism and conservation due to extensive purging of students and faculty and the introduction of a highly ideological university entrance system based on loyalty to the Islamic government.

At present, student selection in the Islamic Republic is based on passing written examinations that assess the knowledge and aptitude of those aspiring to enter the university as well as meeting certain religious and political requirements. Belief in Islam or membership in any of the recognized religious minorities in Iran (i.e., Christians, Jews, and Zoroastrians); practice of religious rites; absence of enmity and opposition to the Islamic government; and lack of moral corruption are the major criteria for entrance to the university (*Rahnema-ye Azmun Vorudi* [Guidelines for the Entrance Examination], 1992:1). Likewise, faculty members are selected on the basis of their academic/scientific ability as well as their political beliefs before and after the revolution and their moral conduct in the university setting.

It is ironic that institutions that were once centers of revolutionary fervor and important sources of support for the 1979 revolution were to become elements of stability and consolidators of the ruling power. In fact, universities reflected the existing sociopolitical realities of the time. The early years of the revolution were marked by tumult, parallel and competing sources of authority, and heated struggle for power. This was reflected at the university level, where many students were active members of various dissident political organizations. Along with the consolidation of the ruling power and the return to stability, universities began acting as stabilizers and became yet another tool in the hand of authorities to train Muslim elites imbued with the desirable religio-political ideology.

Two organizations were established to maintain quiet and ensure student activity along Islamic lines: the University Crusade (*Jihad-e Daneshgahi*) and Islamic Students Association (*Anjoman Islami*). Both were charged with Islamizing universities and administering extracurricular activities including political meetings and speeches, conferences, lectures, and book exhibitions while supervising the conduct of faculty members and students inside and outside the classroom.

Structure, Administration, and Planning of Higher Education

Despite efforts to Islamize higher education, Iranian universities have retained many of the structural and administrative features of the prerevolutionary period. Higher education remains a state function, marked by highly centralized planning and policy making. Two Ministries and three councils are in charge of planning, administration, and policy making.

The three councils are responsible for general educational strategies and policies. The Supreme Council for Cultural Revolution, established at the onset of the 1980 cultural revolution, is the highest policy-making body on cultural and educational matters. The Supreme Council for Higher Education Planning is in charge of the design and planning of higher education, the development of universities and other institutions of higher learning, the approval of new educational programs, curricula, and courses, and the drawing up of rules and regulations. The council is composed of eight specialized planning groups in agriculture, art, basic sciences, engineering, humanities, medicine, teacher training, and technology, each of which is responsible for curriculum development in the relevant field of study. The Council for the Development of Higher Education is responsible for the establishment, development, and dissolution of higher education institutes, educational programs, and courses of study.

The two Ministries—the Ministry of Culture and Higher Education and the Ministry of Health and Medical Education—act as executive and supervisory bodies in charge of the administration and implementation of all programs of study. The Ministry of Culture and Higher Education is responsible for holding the university entrance examination and governing and supervising all the public universities and institutions of higher education with the exception of medical education, which is directed by the Ministry of Health and Medical Education. Both Ministries are the only accredited bodies awarding higher education qualifications in the country (Beheshti, n.d.).

Higher education in Iran is composed of the following degree programs: associate degree (2 years), bachelor's degree (4 to 6 years), master's degree (2 years), professional doctorate degree in medicine, veterinary medicine, laboratory science, dentistry, and pharmacy (total of 6 years), academic doctorate degree (Ph.D.) (3 years), postgraduate medical diploma (2–5 years), and advanced postgraduate medical diploma (2 years).

The ranking of faculty members resembles that of the Western countries with assistant, associate, and full professor status. Although holding a Ph.D. degree is the prerequisite for becoming a full-time faculty member, due to the shortage of instructors in the postrevolutionary period, holders of a master's degree can also teach at the university. Professors are obliged to teach, conduct research, and perform administrative tasks. Given the heavy teaching load of faculty members, however, research has become a luxury for most. University teaching remains a low-paying yet prestigious profession.

All institutions of higher education follow an identical curriculum. The exact content of each course along with the textbooks are centrally determined. Faculty members, however, constantly change and revise the content and assign new textbooks. The academic year is comprised of two semesters of seventeen weeks' duration with the option of enrolling in the summer session. Higher education is based on a unit system and the grading is from 0 to 20. The language of instruction has always been and continues to be Persian, with the exception of the use of English at the American-modeled Shiraz University during the Pahlavi period.

The system of public education at all levels is financed from the stage budget. At present, 4.1 percent of the GNP and 22.4 percent of the total government budget are allocated to education. The budget is distributed among general education (primary and secondary levels), higher education, and technical-vocational education. In 1993, the expenditure on higher education was 1.08 percent of the GNP, while the percentage of higher education expenditure as that of the total national expenditure was 3.55 percent (*Education in the Islamic Republic of Iran*, 1993).

Problems

Despite major differences compared to the prerevolutionary institutes of higher learning in terms of content, ideology, and criteria for student and faculty selection, Iranian universities are still afflicted with some of the very problems that plagued them before the revolution. These include a highly competitive university entrance examination creating a backlog of rejected secondary school graduates; mismatch between higher education and national needs, especially in the technical and industrial fields; the dominance of book learning and theoretical studies leading to few practical training experiences; prevalence of the diploma disease such that receiving a university degree is deemed more important than benefiting from a rich learning experience; and, finally, the choice of quantity over quality, resulting in low intellectual standards among both students and faculty members.

The emphasis on obtaining a degree and the social as well as family pressure on the youth to attend universities has resulted in an ever-increasing number of high school graduates who attempt to enter institutes of higher learning. Yet the limited number of spaces and facilities at the universities has led to low admission rates such that only 7 percent of those who take the university entrance examination are accepted. The usual competition for limited space is further exacerbated by the political loyalty-morality checks and the postrevolutionary quota system that ensures the entrance of those who fought in the 1980–88 Iran–Iraq war, those who were maimed or crippled in the war, family members of the martyrs, and students from impoverished regions of the country.

The postrevolutionary years have witnessed unprecedented quantitative expansion in higher education, with numbers almost doubling during the past seven years. During the 1991–92 academic year, 138 universities and 69 higher education institutes existed, attended by 344,045 students specializing in 416 fields of study, taught by 25,208 faculty members. Compared to the 1990–91 academic year, the above figures show a 10.2 percent and 7.9 percent increase in the number of students and faculty, respectively (*Higher Education Statistics*, 1992). There has also been a 7.6 percent increase in the number of students admitted to the universities and a 11.9 percent increase in the number of graduates.

In 1991–92 the highest concentration of students was at the bachelor's level (70.58 percent), followed by 15.58 percent enrollment at the master's level, 12.54 percent at the two-year colleges, and 1.3 percent at the doctoral level. The unequal distribution of students at different levels and the shortage of skilled specialists led to the decision to increase master's and doctoral level enrollment throughout the country. Student selection of specialization has led to 34 percent enrollment in the humanities, 22.57 percent in medical sciences, 20.88 percent in engineering and technical fields, 15.54 percent in natural sciences, 4.81 percent in agriculture and veterinary sciences, and 2.2 percent in art and architecture (*Higher Education Statistics*, 1992). Increasing enrollment in the medical and technical specializations will rectify the shortage of manpower in the two key fields that can bring about self-reliance for the nation. The problem that remains, however, is the shortage of middle-level technicians that should be trained in technical-vocational centers. Yet the traditional disdain for manual labor continues to be a major obstacle to achieving this goal.

Response to Challenges

The annual increase in the number of students and the limited space at public universities led to three major changes at the higher education level: the establishment of private and distance universities and evening classes at public institutions. Whereas the Iranian Constitution states the provision of free education for everyone at all levels as one of the obligations of the Islamic Republic (Algar, 1980:28), private universities charging fees have been established since 1984. Free Islamic University (*Daneshgah-e Azad Islami*) was first established in the capital of Tehran and has rapidly expanded throughout the country ever since. It offers programs at all levels in fifty-two fields of study. Although its entrance examination is different from that of the public universities, the curricular contest is the same. The number of students enrolled at the Free University increased from 5,249 during the 1984–85 academic year to 60,397 in 1992 (*Statistical Yearbook*, 1992).

Another fee-for-service higher education facility is the opening of evening classes at public universities. The latter have always been free for students, some of whom even received further stipends. Yet the same universities today charge students who can attend classes in the evening. The establishment of institutes of higher learning that charge students reflects the nation's economic and educational shortcomings that have led to the reversal or revolutionary measures according to postrevolutionary realities. Privatization of universities in 1984 and schools in 1988 has been criticized by those who believe that the gap between rich and poor will be consolidated and even justified by private schooling that provides quality education at a high cost.

Another measure to meet the rising demand for higher education has been the establishment of the Distance Education University (*Daneshgah-e Payam-e Nur*) in 1987. With its headquarters in Tehran and 60 centers across the country, this university offers bachelor's degrees in several subjects through audiovisual instructional materials, correspondence, and meetings with instructors. Special textbooks that facilitate independent study have been prepared for Distance Education University courses by university professors. During the 1991–92 academic year, 47,063 students were studying through Distance University centers supervised by 1,691 faculty members (*Higher Education Statistics*, 1992).

It is also interesting to note that 317 foreign students are presently studying in Iran, the majority of whom are from Muslim countries such as Iraq, Sudan, Afghanistan, and Lebanon. In fact, Imam Khomeini International University has been established to attract foreign students by using English as the language of instruction.

The quantitative expansion of institutes of higher education has been accompanied by unprecedented brain drain immediately after the 1979 revolution, leading to shortage of faculty members at all levels. The purging of many faculty members during the cultural revolution period and the migration of many to the West left the universities with a shortage of 9,000 instructors (Jihad-e Daneshgahi, 1990). The result has been overloaded faculty members who teach at various universities. Teaching and administrative affairs have replaced research, leading to low-quality teaching and out-of-date instructional materials. To upgrade their knowledge, faculty members have been provided funds to travel to regional and international conferences and take leaves of absence to conduct research in Iran or abroad. To overcome the shortage of university professors in deprived provinces, a phenomenon called "flying professor" (*ostad-e parvazi*) has appeared: Faculty members are flown weekly or monthly from their place of work and residence to universities in other provinces to teach courses. In addition, male professors are not granted tenure unless they have first taught at universities in deprived provinces.

The response to shortage of instructors has been twofold. On the one hand, students at master's and doctoral levels are sent abroad to study and return to teach at universities. Although sending students abroad, particularly to Western countries, was severely condemned in the early years of the revolution, the lack of specialists especially in technical and professional fields has led to yet another reversal of policy such that at present many Iranian students are provided scholarships to study in foreign countries, except in the United States. Western Europe, India, Canada, and Australia are the countries with the highest concentration of Iranian university students.

On the other hand, an attempt has been made to strengthen the domestic capacity to train university-level instructors. Not only has education at the master's and doctoral levels been expanded, but the Faculty Training University (*Daneshgah-e Tarbiyat-e Modarres*) has been established with the sole purpose of training "committed" faculty members. During the 1991–92 academic year, 1,815 students were studying at the master's and doctoral levels at the Faculty Training University, taught by 776 professors in seven departments (*Higher Education Statistics*, 1992). Students are provided with the best educational facilities and ensured teaching and high-ranking administrative positions upon graduation. They are trained not only to overcome the shortage of professors, but also to gradually replace Western-educated, less doctrinaire faculty members, especially in the social sciences and humanities.

Educational Disparities

In addition to the problems of educational quality and shortage of faculty members, the Iranian system of higher education is characterized by gender as well as geographic inequality. The postrevolutionary period has witnessed active participation of female students and instructors at the higher level of education. Islamization and de-Westernization of the university setting have been important sources of encouragement for traditional, religious families who are now more willing to send their daughters to universities. Once a hotbed of political activism and the center of modern thinking and Western mannerism, the universities are today a continuation of the traditional lifestyle in a closely supervised and controlled Islamic atmosphere. Yet gender inequality still exists, leading to significant differences between male and female enrollment. In 1991–92, 28 percent of the students were female while women comprised only 17 percent of the faculty members, mostly at the assistant professor rank. Also fewer women than men continue their education at the higher levels—only 25 percent of master's level students are female and women comprise 30 percent of doctoral candidates (*Statistical Yearbook*, 1992).

Immediately after the 1979 revolution, Islamic authorities aimed at redirecting the education and professional choices of female students toward specializations deemed more appropriate for women. For instance, studies in heavy industry demanding fieldwork were closed to women, while they were encouraged to study what was considered "feminine" subjects such as teaching, nursing, and obstetrics-gynecology (Mehran, 1991). The above policy has been altered to a certain extent in recent years. Yet limitations still exist so that women cannot aspire to become judges—a highly rational profession that women are considered unable to perform given their "emotional character." Furthermore, women are barred from receiving scholarships to study abroad unless they are married and accompanied by their husbands. It should be noted that there is a heated discussion about this issue by women in Parliament who oppose such discriminatory policy.

Yet another difference between male and female academic and vocational choice is the difference between their choice of specialization at the university level. In 1991–92 women comprised 43 percent of students in medical sciences while only 4.8 percent of the total enrollment in engineering and technical fields were female.

The first three choices of women are humanities, medicine, and natural sciences (in the above order). It is interesting to watch the socioeconomic consequences of increasing female enrollment in medicine, a field that has traditionally been dominated by men and is accompanied by high income and social prestige.

Another source of inequality in Iranian higher education is geographical disparity. Large metropolitan centers of affluent provinces continue to have monopoly over educational resources. In 1991–92 one-fourth of the total student population were enrolled in universities located in Tehran, followed by Isfahan, Khorasan, Fars, and East Azerbaijan. In fact, 72 percent of all university students are located in five provinces, with the remaining 28 percent distributed in the other nineteen provinces. The heavy concentration of students in the key provinces has led to better educational facilities and a higher number of faculty members.

As mentioned before, to address the needs of university students in deprived regions, "flying" professors are sent to teach at regular intervals and newly appointed faculty members are encouraged to teach in less affluent provinces by providing them with low-cost housing and other facilities. Given the low salary of faculty members and the high cost of living in large urban centers, the provision of affordable housing and the reduced living expenses in smaller cities could be an effective incentive in attracting university instructors to other provinces.

In sum, one can state that higher education in Iran has been characterized by the choice of quantitative expansion over qualitative development; placing a priority on teaching over research; emphasizing rote memorization and book learning as opposed to analytical-critical thinking and problem solving; and the choice of repetition over innovation. This has not brought about an empowered higher education system that can solve domestic problems and challenge the established Western models, a task accomplished by some Asian countries.

FUTURE DEVELOPMENTS

A critique of the present situation in Iranian universities has led to an attempt to revise past policies. Yet future higher education trends need to be considered within a broader context. The Second Economic-Social-Cultural Development Plan of the Islamic Republic of Iran (hereafter referred to as the second plan) points to a shift from the expansion of the public sector to more emphasis on "popular activity and creativity," leading to reduced government activity and an increased role for the private sector. Higher education policies are to be changed accordingly. The following are the basic aims of higher education in the next five years:

1. Strengthening and consolidating the administrative, financial, and scientific independence of universities and other institutes of higher education and research.
2. Increasing the internal and external efficiency of higher education.
3. Increasing the role of the private sector and bringing about popular participation in the development of research and higher education.
4. Strengthening the scientific base of the institutes of higher learning.
5. Developing scientific cooperation at the national and international levels.
6. Bringing about geographic equilibrium with the purpose of creating social justice at the higher education level (*Second Plan*, 1992).

The above points indicate a serious rethinking of higher education policies in the Islamic Republic. The emphasis on quality, increased privatization of higher education, and granting independence to universities are signs of the response to internal demands on higher education. The expansion at regional and international linkages is also important not only because Iran should no longer remain scientifically isolated, but also because it will provide students and faculty much needed opportunities for exchange of information and updating of knowledge. Last but not least, bringing about social justice by reducing geographic disparity is reminiscent of the early revolutionary slogans that called for an end to deprivation and inequality. Coupled with the decision to charge fees for affluent university students, this is a clear sign of the transition to a phase in which the people, as opposed to the government, will be held responsible for the provision of educational opportunities. As such, this is a radical departure from the policy of free education for all at all levels as stated in the Constitution.

CONCLUSION

A historical review of higher education in Iran in its social, political, economic, and cultural context leads to two concluding remarks. First, higher education has developed mostly in response to internal demands rather than external changes. The relative isolation of Iran from the academic/scientific circles of the world in the postrevolutionary period has led to weak international links and less accountability to international standards. Moreover, internal demands have mostly been political in nature, resulting in weak links between higher education and economic development and an even weaker relationship between education and scientific-technological advancement. Therefore, although Iranian higher education has questioned Western supremacy, it has not been able to challenge Western science and technology. As a result, higher education in Iran has not been able to present an alternative model at the international scene.

Second, higher education in Iran has at all times reflected the status quo, aimed at training the elite that would serve the political ideology of the ruling power. Thus higher education has been used both as an element of Westernization, modernization, and secularization and as a tool for Islamization and politicization, depending on who was in power at the time. The exceptions have been the traditional *madrasa* system that long remained independent from the government and the dissident students who have continuously revolted against the establishment.

The link between higher education and the ruling ideology has never been as close as during the postrevolutionary period, when Iranian universities changed from centers of political activism to institutes of stability. After the 1980 cultural revolution Iranian universities have been assigned the triple tasks of education, political socialization, and Islamization. At times politics and ideology replaced skill and expertise, and morality and loyalty became more important than teaching and research.

At present, social realities and economic exigencies, the dire need for specialists and technocrats, and the consolidation of the ruling power have led to moderation in the radical policies of the early revolutionary years. Although commitment, piety, and loyalty to the government as well as Islamization and "purification" of universities are still important factors in determining higher education policy and practice, the realities of the Thermidorean period have led planners and policy makers to reverse some of the decisions that led to unprecedented brain drain and the lowering of educational quality among both faculty members and students.

Iranian universities have a long way to go until scientific self-reliance and total cultural and educational independence are achieved. Yet the groundwork is laid for the young generation to accomplish what has been left incomplete. In this endeavor, one should link modern science and knowledge with a view of one's cultural identity and historical roots so that the best of the past and present are combined to create a better future.

REFERENCES

Algar, Hamid, trans. 1980. *Constitution of the Islamic Republic of Iran.* Berkeley: Mizan.
———. 1981. *Islam and Revolution: Writings and Declarations of Imam Khomeini.* Berkeley: Mizan.

Amar-e Amuzesh-e 'Ali Iran 1370–71 [Higher Education Statistics of Iran 1991–92].
    1992. Tehran: Ministry of Culture and Higher Education.
American Council on Education. 1976. An Analysis of U.S.-Iranian Cooperation in
    Higher Education. Washington, D.C.: Overseas Liaison Committee.
Arasteh, Reza. 1962. Education and Social Awakening in Iran. Leiden: E. J. Brill.
———. 1963. "The Growth of Higher Institutions in Iran." International Review of
    Education, 7, 327–34.
Ayman, Iraj. 1974. Educational Innovation in Iran. Paris: UNESCO.
Barani, Amin. 1961. The Modernization of Iran, 1921–41. Palo Alto, Calif.: Stanford
    University Press.
Barnameh-ye Dovvom Tose'eh Eqtesadi, Ejtema'i va Farhangi Jomhuri-ye Islami Iran.
    [The Second Economic, Social, and Cultural Development Plan of the Islamic
    Republic of Iran]. 1992. Tehran: Planning and Budget Organization.
Beheshti, H. S. N.d. System of Education in the Islamic Republic of Iran. Tehran: Min-
    istry of Culture and Higher Education.
Clark, Burton R. 1992. "Comparative Higher Education." In Marvin C. Alkin, ed.,
    Encyclopedia of Educational Research. New York: Macmillan.
Education in the Islamic Republic of Iran. 1993. Tehran: Ministry of Education.
Farmarfarmayan, Hafez. 1968. "The Forces of Modernization in Nineteenth Century Iran:
    A Historical Survey." In W. R. Polk and R. L. Chambers, eds., Beginnings of
    Modernization in the Middle East. Chicago: Chicago University Press.
Fischer, Michael M. J. 1980. Iran: From Religious Dispute to Revolution. Cambridge,
    Mass.: Harvard University Press.
Jikhad-e Daneshgahi [University Crusade] 1990. Daneshgah-e Enquelab [The University
    of Revolution]. Tehran: Ettela'at Foundation.
Mehran, Golnar. 1990. "Ideology and Education in the Islamic Republic of Iran." Com-
    pare, 20, 53–65.
———. 1991. "The Creation of the New Muslim Women: Female Education in the
    Islamic Republic of Iran." Convergence, 24, 42–52.
———. 1992. "Iran." In Peter W. Cookson, Alan R. Sadovnik, and Susan F. Semel,
    eds., International Handbook of Education Reform. Westport, Conn.: Greenwood.
Nakosteen, Mehdi. 1964. History of Islamic Origins of Western Education, A.D. 800–
    1350. Boulder, Colo.: University of Colorado Press.
Nasr, Seyyed Hossein. 1987. Traditional Islam in the Modern World. London: KPI.
Pazargadi, Alaedin, trans. 1986. Educational Revolution as Regarded by Imam Khomeini.
    Tehran: Bonyad-e Be'that.
Rahnema-ye Azmun Vorudi [Guideline for the (University) Entrance Examination]. 1992.
    Tehran: Ministry of Culture and Higher Education.
Saliq, 'Isa. 1975. Tarikh-e Farhang-e Iran [History of Iranian Culture]. Tehran: Tehran
    University Press.
Salnameh-ye Amari Keshvar [Statistical Yearbook]. 1990, 1992. Tehran: Statistical Cen-
    ter of Iran.
Sobhe, Khosrow. 1982. "Education in Revolution: Is Iran Duplicating the Chinese Cul-
    tural Revolution?" Comparative Education, 18, 271–80.
Soltanzadeh, Hossein. 1985. Tarikh-e Madares-e Iran [History of Iranian Schools]. Teh-
    ran: Agah.
Szyliowicz, Joseph S. 1973. Education and Modernization in the Middle East. London:
    Cornell University Press.

8

JAPAN

Kumiko Fujimura-Fanselow

In the hundred years or so since the establishment of the first modern university in Japan, both the number and variety of institutions of higher education as well as the number of students have increased manyfold. Higher education in Japan has shifted from an elite to a mass system, with about 40 percent of all high school graduates pursuing higher education; the figure is 60 percent if we include all institutions offering some form of postsecondary education.

Today, however, Japanese higher education faces a number of serious challenges that have, over the course of the past ten years, led to a major effort emanating from the top level of government to bring about reforms. Many of the challenges are similar to those that face higher education in other highly industrialized societies. Others are unique to the Japanese case, and the pressures stem from internal changes and developments as well as from changes taking place in the larger international context.

The most serious challenge is posed by demographic changes, which, in the remainder of this decade, are expected to lead to a sharp decline in the population of eighteen- to twenty-two-year-olds, who make up 90 percent of college enrollment in Japan. Since more than 70 percent of the institutions are private and enroll about the same proportion of students, the very survival of many institutions is threatened by these changes. These changes, moreover, are taking place precisely at a time when, as in many other advanced industrialized countries, higher institutions are facing a reduction in financial resources and public funding. The competition for scarce resources in a tight economy has led to a growing demand for accountability and quality. Widespread concern and criticism have been expressed by political and economic leaders that while the educational system has been quite successful thus far in providing a relatively high level of basic education for the population and thereby helping bring about economic development and maintain social stability, it may not be up to meeting the challenges facing Japan in the next century. The rigidity and uniformity that mark the structure, curricula, and teaching methods within the educational system are viewed as hindering the cultivation of young people with the kind of creativity, diversity of talent, and broad, international outlook necessary for Japan to compete successfully in an increasingly complex and competitive world. Universities, in particular, which have hitherto functioned primarily as a mechanism for occupational selection, are being pressured to upgrade their educational function and to provide stronger, more useful training to students. Finally, various groups that have until now had limited access to higher education in Japan—women, older and returning students, and foreign students—are seeking their place.

In the face of these challenges, public policy makers as well as individual institutions have undertaken a very serious reexamination of current policies and practices. Recommendations proposed by the University Council and embodied in directives from the Ministry of Education have been aimed at improving the quality of higher education and promoting greater diversity and flexibility in order to better respond to existing students' needs and to attract a wider number of nontraditional students. The very survival of higher institutions will hinge on their ability to understand the nature and implications of the changes under way and to adopt innovative approaches both in administration and management and in teaching and curriculum in response.

PROFILE OF THE SYSTEM OF HIGHER EDUCATION

Historical Development

From the Meiji Period up to World War II. Challenges arising from rapid social and political changes within Japanese society as well as from external forces and factors shaped policies and initiatives in education from the very inception of Japan's modern system of education in the latter half of the nineteenth century. For the Meiji leaders who assumed power in 1868, the establishment of a comprehensive modern educational system was a key element in transforming Japan from a feudal to a modern, unified nation-state composed of a citizenry obedient and loyal to the new nation, as well as to building Japan's economic and military power so that it could ward off the challenge posed by the more powerful Western nations. Thus, a system of compulsory elementary education was established with an emphasis on indoctrinating the masses with a spirit of morality and nationalism. Simultaneously, a high priority was placed on the development of higher education in order to train an elite, who, equipped with the latest Western knowledge and techniques, would develop the science and technology necessary for Japan to catch up with the West.

The Fundamental Code of Education promulgated in 1872 called for the establishment of 8 universities, in addition to 256 middle schools and 53,760 elementary schools, with compulsory education set at 4 years. Despite a shortage of resources, the greatest part of the national education budget was given over to support for higher education and for sending students overseas. One-eighth of the first education budget was earmarked for overseas study, and support for Tokyo University, which was established in 1877, was the major item in the budget. Initially, the higher realms of education were dominated by foreigners, but they were increasingly replaced by Japanese trained either abroad or in the university itself.

The Imperial University Decree, promulgated by the first minister of education, Mori Arinori, in 1886, laid the official foundation of the national universities. It redesignated Tokyo University as "Imperial" and clearly stipulated that the ultimate purpose of research and education at the Imperial university was to engage in research and education that would serve the needs of the state. Tokyo Imperial University included schools of law, medicine, literature, and science, as well as a graduate school and a school of engineering. Four more Imperial universities, including Kyoto Imperial University, were established over the following thirty years.

While several private institutions of higher education, such as Keio and Waseda, were also established, several factors inhibited the growth of private schools. For one thing, they lacked full legal status; only the Imperial universities were given formal recognition as universities. Keio, in 1890, and Waseda, in 1905, became in substance multifaculty universities, but together with all other private schools, they remained *senmongakko* ("special schools") until the promulgation of the University Ordinance of 1918. Private institutions were also hampered by pressures, and at times interference, by the state and the steady growth of government universities, and they suffered from marked financial difficulties (Nagai, 1971).

The promulgation of the University Ordinance in 1918 marked an important period in the development of Japanese higher education by elevating a number of national, public, and private institutions to university status and giving legal recognition to the formation of single-faculty universities. The period between 1918 and the eve of World War II was one of marked expansion in higher education. At the same time, in the rapidly developing industrial society, higher education began to take on the new function of training of white-collar workers. Increased emphasis was placed on professional education and practical, occupation-related learning. One point of difference between the private and government universities was that the former placed major emphasis on the expansion of their humanities divisions, primarily because the establishment and maintenance of science and engineering courses would have required large sums of money. This tendency has persisted to this day.

In all, forty-five universities existed prior to World War II. A marked characteristic of these institutions was their hierarchical ranking. At the apex were the seven Imperial universities, which produced the nation's elite bureaucrats; among them Tokyo Imperial University ranked first. Next in the hierarchy were the remaining government universities plus a small number of private universities, such as Waseda and Keio. Well below these came the twenty-three remaining private universities. In order to enter a university it was necessary to complete five years of middle school following six years of elementary school; the next step was to pass a highly competitive examination for entry into the three-year university-preparatory school, or "higher school," from which entrance into university was virtually automatic. But in order to enter a high-ranking university, it was necessary to come through a high-ranking higher school. The state and public higher schools ranked above the private, and graduates of a government higher school were assured of getting into a leading national university. Once admitted, graduation was virtually guaranteed, and graduates, particularly those from the Imperial universities, could look forward to obtaining top positions in government and industry. The path leading to the university was extremely narrow. According to Passin, about one out of ten boys completing elementary school entered the five-year middle schools; only one out of thirteen middle school graduates could expect to enter higher school; and only one out of twenty-five was admitted to the prestigious higher schools that provided access to the Imperial universities (Passin, 1965:103–4). Other channels of postsecondary education for those who did not gain admission to higher school included normal schools or military schools, *senmongakko*, and *koto-senmongakko* (higher technical school). Graduate schools were not well developed in the prewar period. Though they did nominally exist, there was no fixed program or period of residence for candidates. Only after years of demonstrated scholarship were doctorates awarded.

It is important to note that universities, as well as the secondary school track that led to universities, were closed to women. A leading role in promoting female education beyond the elementary level was played by Christian missionaries from the United States, Canada, and Great Britain, who established secondary schools for girls in various parts of the country, including Ferris Seminary (1870) and Kobe Jogakuin (1875). Not until the 1880s did the government take steps to set up secondary schools for girls, and as late as 1894, only eight public girls' high schools existed throughout Japan. The Higher Girls' School Law of 1899 called on local governments to establish at least one girls' high school in each prefecture.

Institutions of higher education for women were again started by the private sector, the first of which was what is now called Tsuda College in 1900. By 1937, there were forty-two private women's colleges offering three-year courses of study. Two national women's higher normal schools were established to train teachers for girls' high schools and women's normal schools, and six public or prefectural colleges were established prior to World War II. Following the promulgation of the University Ordinance of 1918, some women's colleges applied for university accreditation, but their applications were rejected. Therefore women's colleges remained in the status of *senmongakko* (although many of them were called *daigaku* [university]), and as such could not award a recognized degree, merely a "certificate of achievement." Some of the men's universities opened their campuses to women; Tohoku Imperial University's Faculty of Science was the first of the Imperial universities to do so, in 1913. However, admission to the most prestigious Imperial universities, Tokyo and Kyoto Imperial Universities, was denied to women. On the eve of World War II, about 10 percent of girls graduating from elementary school went on to girls' high schools, and of those graduating from high school, fewer than one out of ten went on to some type of postsecondary institution.

Post–World War II Reforms in Education. Following the end of World War II, under the influence of the American Occupation, the entire educational system of Japan was reorganized, in both structure and curriculum. Compulsory education was increased from six to nine years, and a 6-3-3-4 structure was adopted (six years of elementary school, three years of lower secondary school, three years of upper secondary school, and four years of university). Coeducation was extended to all levels, including university, and a common curriculum was instituted for all schools. The system was shifted from a multitrack to a single-track structure, each level qualifying students for the next higher level. The separate tracks were consolidated at each level, and university status was granted to various existing institutions, including prewar higher schools, *senmongakko*, technical schools, and normal schools. By 1950, there were 201 universities, or four times the number recognized prior to the war. Whereas the universities of the prewar period provided three years of professional education to students who had finished three years of general or liberal education in the higher schools, the new universities provided two years of general education followed by two years of professional education.

Those institutions that did not meet the necessary standards for being elevated to the status of university were designated for the time being as *tanki daigaku*, or "short-term universities" (the equivalent of junior colleges), with courses of study lasting two or three years. Following years of negotiations between the Ministry of Education and the *tanki daigaku*, during which time numerous new *tanki daigaku* had been established, it was decided in 1964 that these institutions would be perpetuated within the framework of the university system.

Types of Institutions of Higher Education

Universities, numbering 523 in 1992, 591 junior colleges, and 62 technical colleges (*koto-senmongakko* or *kosen* for short) comprise the traditional higher education sector in Japan. In addition, there is a wide variety of technical and vocational schools, including the "miscellaneous schools" (*kakushugakko*), numbering over 3,200, and more than 3,400 "special training schools" (*senshugakko*), many of which provide postsecondary-level training.

Universities offer an undergraduate degree program consisting for the most part of four years of study, as well as six-year programs in medicine, dentistry, and veterinary science. Ninety-one of the universities are single-sex, women's universities, and they enroll about 25 percent of all female university students. Junior colleges tend to be small and to offer limited programs of study for a predominantly female clientele. The technical colleges, established in 1962 in response to demand by business and industry for technological manpower, combine the last three years of high school with two years of college and provide students with intensive vocational and technical training. The "miscellaneous schools" and "special training schools" generally provide specialized vocational and technical training varying in length from one to three years. The "special training schools" in particular have grown rapidly in popularity since their inception in 1976. Their professional program, which comprises the largest of their three programs, is geared to students who have graduated from upper secondary school.

A defining characteristic of Japanese higher education is the dominance of private as opposed to national public (established, funded, and operated by the national government) and local public (prefectural or municipal) institutions. As of 1992, 73 percent of all universities, 84 percent of junior colleges, 90 percent of "special training schools," and 97 percent of the "miscellaneous schools" are private, enrolling, respectively, 73, 92, 94, and 98 percent of all students in those institutions. The technical colleges are an exception: 95 percent of them are public and enroll 94 percent of all students (Mombusho, 1993:74, 77–79, 108, 110).

An alternative form of higher education is available through the University of the Air, founded in 1983, which, via television and radio programs, enables people of different ages and backgrounds to pursue a university education and also serves as a vehicle for recurrent education. Students can take a full load of courses leading to a bachelor of arts degree program or simply take selected courses for a semester or a full academic year. In 1988, to take an example, two-thirds of the students enrolled in the university were in the over-thirty age group, and 70 percent were enrolled in a degree program; in addition, about 75 percent were working (Ministry of Education, 1989:113, chart LIII-A).

Graduate education has thus far remained underdeveloped in Japan. Fewer than 8 percent of students graduating from university in 1992 entered graduate school (Mombusho, 1993:94–95). A new system of graduate education was established by the government in 1953, and since 1961, a number of the newer universities began to offer an American-style master's degree and the new doctorate degree. However, even today, over 60 percent of all graduate degrees are conferred by national universities. The master's degree is granted after two years of full-time study beyond the bachelor's degree, including thirty credit hours and a thesis. The doctorate requires completion of three or more years of study beyond the master's and a total of fifty credit hours in graduate work. Each student must also complete a major research project, submit a dissertation, and pass a final examination. Customarily, though, young scholars must also prove themselves in research and publication before actually receiving the degree.

Table 8.1
Enrollment in Postsecondary Education by Type of Institution, 1992

Type of institution	All Students		Female Students	
	Enrollment	percent of total	Enrollment	percent of all students
University*	2,293,269	62.6	672,337	29.3
Junior College	524,538	14.3	481,044	91.7
Technical College**	20,713	0.6	2,014	9.7
Special Training Schools***	691,343	18.9	354,091	51.2
Miscellaneous*** Schools	132,387	3.6	36,646	27.7
Total	3,662,250	100.0	1,546,132	42.2

*Figures include students enrolled in master's and doctoral degree programs.
**Figures refer to students enrolled in the fourth and fifth years of the five-year courses in technical college.
***Figures refer to those enrolled in programs that require graduation from upper secondary school for admission.
Source: Mombusho (1993:74, 78, 79, 108, 110).

Enrollment Rates

As table 8.1 shows, 2.8 million Japanese are enrolled in universities and junior colleges today. If we include all of the various types of postsecondary institutions, the figure comes to over 3.6 million.

Behind the general expansion in postsecondary school enrollment has been the achievement of 100 percent attendance through nine years of compulsory schooling, and a steady rise in the proportion entering and graduating from upper secondary school, to the point where today that figure is over 90 for both sexes. Looking more closely at changes in college enrollment figures over the postwar years (table 8.2), there was a steady increase culminating in a peak in the late 1960s and early 1970s as the first baby boomers reached college age. A number of factors were behind this rapid expansion. One was the growing prosperity of the Japanese people made possible by the unprecedented economic growth experienced in the 1960s; between 1950 and 1968, the average annual growth rate of national income attained a level of nearly 10 percent. General improvement in living standards, coupled with reduction in the number of children per family (from 5.14 in 1940 to 2.30 in 1960, to 1.81 in 1975) that accompanied the

Table 8.2
Enrollment Ratios of Females and Males of the Corresponding Age Group by Level of Education, 1955–91

Year	Upper Secondary School*		University**		Junior College**	
	Females	Males	Females	Males	Females	Males
1955	47.4	55.5	2.4	13.1	2.6	1.9
1960	55.9	59.6	2.5	13.7	3.0	1.2
1965	69.6	71.7	4.6	20.7	6.7	1.7
1970	82.7	81.6	6.5	27.3	11.2	2.0
1975	93.0	91.0	12.5	40.4	19.9	2.6
1980	95.4	93.1	12.3	39.3	21.0	2.0
1985	94.9	92.8	13.7	38.6	20.8	2.0
1990	95.6	93.2	15.2	33.4	22.2	1.7
1991	95.8	93.5	16.1	34.5	23.1	1.8
1992	96.2	93.9	17.3	35.2	23.5	1.8

*These figures represent the number of students going on to upper secondary school or technical college, including those combining school attendance with employment, divided by the total number of students who graduated from lower secondary school in a given year, multiplied by 100.

**These figures represent the number of students going on to either junior college or four-year university divided by the total number of students who graduated from lower secondary school three years prior to each year (which represents basically the total of all those in the 18-year-old age group), multiplied by 100.

Source: Mombusho (1993:36–37, 38–39).

appearance of the urban nuclear family as the predominant family model, meant that more resources were available to educate sons and daughters. Meanwhile, there was a growing demand within the industrial economy for those with university training, especially scientific and technical training.

While higher education has subsequently continued to expand, enrollment has not shown a steady rise, as was anticipated by many. In the mid-1970s higher education entered a phase of nonexpansion, due in part to a decline in the college-age population but also to a reduction in resources brought on by the decline in economic growth in the wake of the 1973 oil crisis and the ensuing cutback in government support for higher education. In 1976, the government issued a policy restricting further growth of higher institutions, maintaining that their number had reached a sufficient level, and called instead for improvement in the quality of existing institutions. The following years saw a decline in admission rates to colleges and universities. Enrollment increased once again in the latter part of the 1980s as those born during the second baby boom (from 1971 to 1974) reached college age. To forestall the prospect of ending up with a large number of young people unable to find a place in any university or junior college, the Ministry requested private universities to increase their admission quotas temporarily, starting in 1991, in order to accommodate this increased demand. At the same time, there was a rush to establish new higher institutions: Forty-one new universities and forty-three new junior colleges were established within the five-year period between 1985 and 1990. The number of eighteen-year-olds is expected to drop sharply, from over 2 million in 1992 to 1.5 million in the year 2000.

Apart from these demographic changes that will affect college enrollment, there is also some indication of changes in social attitudes regarding college attendance. A growing, though still relatively small, number of young people appear to be rejecting what in the past amounted almost to a faith in the value of formal education and the university diploma. This is evidenced, for example, by a rise in the number of high school dropouts. Public perception of universities, in particular, has become increasingly negative—universities are viewed as expensive "leisure lands" where students merely enjoy four years of doing everything but studying, while the professors in turn demand little work from the students. Also significant is that while the cost of financing a college education has become increasingly higher, the market value of college education appears to have diminished.

Competition for admission into the elite universities continues to be very keen. At the same time, however, we are seeing the growing popularity of alternative, newer institutions of postsecondary education, notably the "special training schools." The popularity of these institutions is attributable to the fact that they provide training of a more practical and specialized nature than that generally provided in colleges and universities. Students can obtain licenses or certifications in various fields during the course of their study or upon graduation. Quite a few students enter these schools after they have graduated from a junior college or university while still others attend both types of institutions simultaneously. It is likely that these schools will assume a growing role in providing postsecondary education.

Graduate students represent only 3 percent of total enrollment in universities; moreover, more than 50 percent of these students are concentrated in a few dozen universities. In 1992, 63 percent of master's level and 66 percent of doctoral level students were enrolled in national universities (Mombusho, 1993:

82–83). Those who do go on for graduate study generally plan either to pursue an academic career or to go into research work in the scientific, technological, or engineering field. Thus in 1992, 56 percent of all master's level students were in engineering and science, while 66 percent of the doctoral students were studying either medicine, dentistry, engineering, or science (ibid.). The tendency thus far in Japan has been for society at large not to reward those who elect to go on for advanced degrees; industry tends to hire graduates immediately after they receive their bachelor's degrees, preferring to provide further training on the job.

THE CHANGING FUNCTION AND PATTERNS OF HIGHER EDUCATION

Policy, Planning, Finance, and Organization of Higher Education

From the very inception of the university system in the Meiji period, educational policy has been based on, and shaped by, political and economic policy needs. More specifically, the government has pursued a policy of concentrating resources in a highly limited and elite public sector and supporting research in areas seen as vital to national interests, while leaving quantitative expansion to private institutions. Between 1960 and 1970, when expansion in enrollment was most dramatic, the number of national and public universities and junior colleges remained almost unchanged, whereas the number of private ones nearly doubled. Today, privately run institutions make up three-fourths of all universities and junior colleges.

The government has nevertheless exercised major influence and control over the establishment and administration of higher institutions, both private and public, through the Ministry of Education. Standards for the establishment of a university, junior college, or technical college are prescribed by ministerial regulations, and applications must be approved on the basis of those standards set by the Council for University Chartering and School Juridical Person, which is appointed by the Ministry of Education. The Ministry prescribes standards for universities with respect to curricula, number and qualifications of teachers, student:faculty ratios, size of buildings and grounds, the number of library books, and the like.

The Ministry of Education also controls the budgets of all national higher institutions and associated research institutes. Public universities, junior colleges, and colleges of technology are financed for the most part by funds from respective establishing local public bodies and partly by subsidies from the national treasury. Private institutions are in principle self-supporting. Until 1970, when the national government started a subsidy system to help with current expenses, they were obliged to depend on tuition fees paid by students as virtually their sole source of income. Rising tuition charges were, in fact, one cause of the student protests during the late 1960s. Subsidies, which are granted through the Private School Promotion Foundation, developed rapidly from 1970 to 1981, at one point covering nearly 30 percent of annual expenditures. Since 1981, however, the total amount of subsidies has increased only slightly, and their share of current expenditures has declined to below 20 percent. Today, private institutions are dependent on tuition and fees paid by students for more than half of their budgets.

Tuition and fees at the private universities is close to three times that charged at national universities—830,000 yen compared to 290,000 yen on the average in 1990 (Mombusho, 1993:162–63); yet in terms of teacher:student ratios, current expenditures per student, floor space per student, and number of library books per student, they fall far behind public institutions.

Traditionally, university faculties were organized along the European chair system, and this practice has been maintained at many of the national universities. There is a fixed number of faculty members of each rank for each chair, and this is the basis for determining budget allocations, including annual research budgets, and student quotas. The majority of universities, however, follow a newer model whereby teaching staff needs and budget allocations are determined on the basis of the number of students in different fields and the number of instructors of different ranks required in order to teach the various courses offered in each subject field.

Stratification within Higher Education

Stratification among different universities is a marked feature of higher education in Japan. As Amano has pointed out, because so many new universities were launched following World War II without adequate preparation, they varied greatly in quality. Moreover, "the new universities inherited not only the campuses and staff but also the traditions, social functions, and social prestige of the former institutions that they succeeded and were integrated into. Thus the new university was designed to have an extremely hierarchical structure from its beginning" (Amano, 1986:32). The government's policy with respect to the establishment and financing of higher education has served to maintain this hierarchy and to exacerbate competition for those institutions at the top of the pyramid, namely, the national (particularly the former Imperial) universities and the more prestigious private ones.

Also significant in terms of maintaining this stratification is the personnel policy of businesses, the most important employers of university graduates. A degree from a first-class university has been viewed as the most important criterion in securing a stable career with top-ranking corporations. A hierarchy exists not only among universities but also among faculties; the faculties of medicine and law at national universities tend to be the most selective.

This competition for admission to prestigious universities, epitomized by the term "examination hell," has been brought to bear on students at progressively lower grades as increasing numbers of youngsters attempt to gain entry into the—often private—secondary schools that in turn have high success rates in preparing students for these highly competitive universities. Recognizing this trend, the Central Council for Education, in a report dealing with reforms pertaining to the high school level, advocated a drastic view of university entrance examination methods as well as business recruitment policies. One proposal for reducing competition for entry into certain high schools known for producing a large number of successful applicants to the top universities was that universities limit the number of students admitted from any one high school—a proposal that was met with considerable skepticism.

As indicated earlier, junior colleges have become in effect the "women's track" in higher education, and although they enjoy the title of "university," they are seen as forming the bottom layer of the university pyramid. Although it is theoretically possible for graduates from junior colleges to transfer to four-year universities, few in fact are able to do so.

Curriculum

The curriculum at colleges and universities and requirements for graduation are prescribed by the Ministry of Education. Curricular offerings vary considerably, however, at the different types of universities and junior colleges. A notable difference between private and national universities is that science, engineering, and medical faculties are much more predominant at the national universities. Private universities have, in general, placed major emphasis on developing their humanities and social science programs because they are much less costly. Thus, in 1992, engineering students made up 30 percent of all students enrolled in national universities, compared to 17 percent at private universities; the corresponding figures for students in medicine and dentistry were 7 percent and 2 percent. On the other hand, 64 percent of all students at private universities were enrolled in the literature and social science faculties, in contrast to just 23 percent at national universities (Mombusho, 1993:80–81).

The majority of women's universities are comprised exclusively of the faculties of literature and home economics—fields traditionally considered appropriately "feminine"—while professional subjects such as engineering, accounting, economics, and law are almost totally absent. The bias in curriculum has been even more pronounced at private junior colleges, which have been commonly viewed as "bride-training schools." Professional education has been limited to preschool teacher training. The national junior colleges (which numbered 39 out of a total of 591 junior colleges in 1992) offer courses predominantly in the technical and vocational fields, but they enroll primarily male students. More recently, however, in response to demand for more specialized and job-related training, junior colleges and women's universities have begun to offer programs in such fields as information processing, international relations, and health care services. (Recent reforms pertaining to college and university curricula are discussed in the "Current Reforms" section.)

Brief mention should be made of the introduction of women's studies into the curriculum at many colleges and universities within the past fifteen years. Women's studies-related courses first made their appearance in the mid-1970s. In 1990, about 23 percent of all junior colleges and four-year universities offered courses in women's studies (Kokuritsu Fujin, 1991), although none had a department devoted to women's studies or awarded a degree in women's studies.

Pressures toward Internationalization

One of the major challenges facing Japanese higher education is how to respond to the many pressures posed by the "internationalization" of Japanese society. Although this term, so frequently heard in Japan today, can be (and is) interpreted in different ways even among the Japanese people, we can identify a number of dimensions. One is a recognition of the need to make higher institutions more open and accessible to students from other countries, an issue discussed later in the chapter. Another issue centers around the concern that Japanese universities are not effective in producing students with the kind of creativity and breadth of understanding required for working and competing on an international level in business and politics. In this regard, one specific shortcoming is in the area of foreign language education (particularly English), and strong emphasis has been placed recently on teaching "oral communication"— another popular catchword these days. Related to this is a somewhat belated recognition of the growing demand throughout the world for Japanese language study and the need to train more teachers and develop instructional materials, methods, and facilities. Providing Japanese language instruction to foreign students, as well as to foreign workers and their children living in Japan, refugees from Indo-China, and returnees from China, is another aspect of this issue demanding urgent attention.

Still another dimension of internationalization is that Japanese colleges and universities are encountering competition for a declining student population not only among themselves but also from the increasing numbers of foreign (especially American) universities that have begun to recruit Japanese students for their home campuses or for branch campuses in Japan. In addition, more and more students who can afford to do so are opting to attend college (and in some cases even high school) abroad. For example, the number of Japanese students enrolled in American institutions (as undergraduates and graduate students and in practical training, nondegree, or intensive English programs) doubled between 1987–88 and 1990–91, from 18,000 to 36,000; the figure for undergraduates alone jumped from about 9,700 to more than 25,000 (The Japan-U.S. Educational Commission, 1992:2). This phenomenon reflects in part a dissatisfaction with various aspects of the educational system in Japan as well as an attraction to the wide variety of programs offered at American colleges. Another factor that has promoted this trend is the change in employment practices among Japanese companies. Whereas traditionally, they preferred graduates from Japanese universities and viewed those educated abroad as not fitting in, within the past ten years or so, with rising pressures toward internationalization, more companies have begun to recognize the value of such individuals for both their knowledge of other cultures and their language abilities.

Degree of Emphasis on Research

Research is carried out in university faculties and graduate schools, as well as in interuniversity research institutes, research institutes attached to universities and university faculties, research institutes under the direct supervision of the Ministry of Education, and private research institutes. As noted earlier, graduate education in Japan has been much less developed than in the United States and most European countries, largely because of the limited prospects for suitable employment upon completion of graduate work. Resources available for advanced research have been extremely limited. Recently, however, the realization that fundamental research must be promoted in order for Japan to compete in fields in which the state of the art is evolving rapidly has spurred growing concern. The Ministry has called for the implementation of several policies to promote scientific research, among them the establishment of more structure in graduate education and significant expansion of graduate education, expansion of grants-in-aid for scientific research and for postdoctoral fellowships, and improvement of interuniversity research institutes; expansion of cooperative research involving industry, government, and the universities; and the promotion of international exchange and cooperation, including international joint research.

Current Reforms

Many of the recent changes and developments in higher education that have been referred to in the above discussions reflect efforts currently under way to bring about reform at all levels of Japanese education. This reform movement can be traced back to the early 1980s, when Prime Minister Yasuhiro Nakasone, responding to widespread public concern and dissatisfaction with the educational system, took up educational reform as a major policy issue. Citing the need for a solid commitment from the executive branch, he called for the establishment of an ad hoc Council on Educational Reform that would have a three-year term and report directly to him. The council was charged with making a comprehensive study of various government policies and practices in education and related areas and presenting recommendations for reforming the education system. The council (whose name was changed in April 1986 to the National Council on Educational Reform) presented its recommendations in a series of four reports submitted between 1985 and 1987; after the final report was presented, the government announced a cabinet resolution to accept the recommendations and to move immediately to implement them.

The council's proposals for reform dealt with three main points: (1) replacing the uniformity, rigidity, and narrowness that characterize education at all levels with an emphasis on promoting individuality and creativity; (2) restructuring the education system to provide for lifelong learning; and (3) making education more responsive to changes and new challenges, particularly those posed by internationalization and the information age. With regard to higher education specifically, the council made several recommendations: further diversification, with each institution having greater freedom to develop its own programs; changes in eligibility requirements and entrance examinations so as to make admission to postsecondary institutions more flexible; revision of regulations so that students can switch from one institution or department to another more easily; expansion and improvement of graduate education and research and promotion of joint research by industry, government, and higher education; greater effort toward internationalizing education, such as facilitating enrollment of foreign students and improvement of foreign language instruction; and improvement of the university entrance examination system through the establishment of a new uniform examination that would replace the current Joint First-Stage Achievement Test.

In October 1987, the Ministry appointed a University Council composed of representatives of the universities and the business community to begin concrete planning for the reform of higher education. In February 1991, the University Council issued a report that set forth the themes "liberalization," "diversification," and "quality improvement." The report called for a relaxation of requirements currently regulating colleges and universities, and at the same time urged institutions to establish a system of self-evaluation and make public their evaluations. It further called on higher institutions to open their doors to the public, by, for example, allowing those outside the traditional college population to study on a part-time basis and establishing quotas to allow for admission of more transfer students (Mombusho Kotokyoiku kyoku, 1991). The council's May report warned of the anticipated crisis facing Japanese universities in the wake of declining enrollments and urged institutions to prepare for the upcoming struggle for survival by upgrading their quality—reducing class sizes, developing new and distinctive curricula, improving teaching methods, and employing specialists from outside academe as instructors. The report also called for restrictions on the establishment of any new colleges or universities. Many of these proposals were reflected in the revisions in ministerial regulations pertaining to standards for the establishment of higher institutions announced in June 1991.

At least some of the proposed reforms have begun to be put into practice. Many institutions have begun to initiate some form of self-evaluation of their organizational structures, admission procedures, curricula, teaching methods, and the like, although there is considerable resistance, especially among faculty members, to the idea of having students evaluate classes and professors.

Most significant have been the curricular changes undertaken at several institutions within the past few years in response to revisions in ministerial regulations referred to above. The most far-reaching revision was the elimination of the existing distinctions in college and university curricula between courses in general education, foreign languages, health and physical education, and specialized education and the requirement that all students take a prescribed number of credits in each category. Henceforth, while students would be required to take a certain number of credits in order to graduate, it would be up to each institution to determine which courses would be required. One byproduct of these changes is that faculties and departments of general education have either been eliminated at several universities and their professors reintegrated into other faculties and departments or else made into a separate faculty or department.

Moreover, institutions were granted greater freedom to set up faculties, departments, and programs of study based on their particular goals and needs. As a result, several new faculties and departments, including many offering interdisciplinary and multidisciplinary programs, have sprung up, such as the faculties of "environment and information" and "comprehensive policy" (at Keio University's Fujisawa campus), and the "comprehensive human studies faculty" at Kyoto University made up of the departments of "international culture," "basic sciences," "natural environment," and "human studies."

RESPONDING TO INTERNAL DEMANDS

Students

Nearly four out of ten young people in the relevant age group enter university or junior college (see table 8.2). If we include those who go into technical and vocational types of postsecondary institutions, the total figure is almost 60 percent. A closer examination of these figures reveals that despite the dramatic expansion in enrollment, opportunities for higher education have not been made equally available to all segments of the population. Recent recommendations for reform have addressed some, though not all, of the issues concerning the need to respond to the demands of different social groups in Japanese society.

Opening Higher Education to Nontraditional Students. The tendency thus far in Japan has been to conceive of formal education as something one undertakes during a limited period in one's life—in youth—and on a full-time basis. Universities, therefore, are extremely youth-centered and closed to adult learners. Unlike the United States, Canada, Australia, and many European countries, where people aged twenty-five and older comprise a substantial proportion of enrollment in higher education, in Japan 90 percent of enrollment is drawn from the eighteen- to twenty-two-year-old population. As a rule, students enter university immediately upon high school graduation, or a year or two later in the case of those who have failed earlier entrance exams. It is almost impossible to gain admission to a university after more than that length of time. In addition, programs of study at both the undergraduate and graduate levels are offered only on a full-time basis.

It was not until 1978 that older or returning students were first admitted to universities, and then, only in the evening division and on the basis of special recommendations. In the following year the law faculty of Rikkyo University in Tokyo became the first university to admit nontraditional students to its regular program through a special system of entrance examinations. Since then the number of such institutions has increased to the point where in 1989, nineteen national universities, eight local public universities, and over sixty private universities were admitting such students. So far, however, the number of students admitted has been quite limited; in the case of Rikkyo, the number of admitted to its law faculty is restricted to roughly 5 percent of the total.

Given the anticipated decline in the traditional college population, colleges will increasingly be forced to make efforts to attract nontraditional, part-time students in order to survive. A substantial proportion of this clientele is likely to be women—housewives in their thirties and forties who want to return to school now that their children are older, as well as employed women who wish to acquire or upgrade knowledge and skills required for their current jobs or to make a career change. One way for women's colleges and universities to survive in the coming years is to emphasize and strengthen their functions as institutions for women's lifelong or recurrent education. Similarly, junior colleges might attempt to become more like American community colleges. As Kitamura (1991: 318) emphasizes, the influx of large numbers of nontraditional students into Japanese colleges and universities will inevitably pose a serious challenge to traditional Japanese higher education and demand that they reexamine many of their existing assumptions and practices, including curricula and teaching methods.

Issue of Gender Inequality in Higher Education. Another marked feature of Japanese higher education, and one that has persisted since the inception of higher education, is gender differentiation. Today, more than 96 percent of girls finish high school; the proportion of females in the relevant age group entering colleges and universities has risen from just 5.5 percent in 1960 to more than 40 percent in 1992, overtaking males since 1989 (see table 8.2). Nevertheless, as Fujimura-Fanselow (1989, 1985) has emphasized elsewhere, significant gender differences persist.

A majority of females pursue higher education in junior colleges rather than four-year universities. In 1992, for example, six out of ten females entering college went into junior colleges, whereas among males, 94 percent went on to four-year universities. The rate of female entry into four-year universities today is about what it was for males twenty-five years ago.

Females accounted for 92 percent of the junior college student population, but only 29 percent of university undergraduates (see table 8.1). Women who enter four-year universities tend to be a much more select group than their male counterparts both in terms of social class and academic ability.

The comparatively low rate of female enrollment at four-year universities means that women continue to comprise a small minority in graduate schools. Only 4.2 percent of all women graduating from university in 1992 went on to graduate school, compared to 9.1 percent of males (Mombusho, 1993:94–95); women comprised just 18.5 percent of students enrolled in master's degree programs and 16.6 percent of those in doctoral degree programs in 1992 (Mombusho, 1993:82–83).

Women continue to cluster in traditionally female fields of study, namely, the humanities in four-year universities and the humanities and home economics in junior colleges, although since the mid-1980s the proportion of women going into the social sciences, especially university departments of law, economics, and commerce, has shown a pronounced increase.

Social Class Differences in Educational Opportunities. There is also considerable inequality in terms of educational opportunity among different social strata. Fujita (1989), for example, cites several surveys that suggest that the pattern of differences in academic achievement (including attainment of higher education) according to father's education and occupation has remained unchanged during the period in which secondary and higher education underwent major expansion. Universities, particularly those that enjoy the highest prestige and therefore provide access to desirable employment, have become increasingly dominated by those from the upper strata. At Tokyo University, for example, the majority of students originate from the upper strata, and this has become more pronounced in recent years (Amano, 1986). One factor is that an increasingly large proportion of entrants into the top universities are coming out of the top private high schools. The many years of study and parental support in terms of psychological support and tuition for private tutors or *juku* (cram schools) necessary in order to prepare for the competitive entrance examinations required for admission to these high schools function to limit opportunities for many within Japanese society.

The cost of higher education, particularly at the private institutions, is also a significant factor. Public provision for student financial aid is not as extensive as in some countries, and most of it takes the form of loans rather than grants. Additional expenses are entailed in preparing for the entrance exams.

Urban–Rural Differences in Access to Higher Education. As is common in many societies, opportunities for young people to pursue higher education vary by region or place of residence. Thus, the percentage of graduating high school seniors in 1993 going on to universities and junior colleges ranged from a high of between 40 percent and 44 percent in 11 of the 47 prefectures and other administrative divisions in Japan, to less than 30 percent in 12, with Okinawa showing the lowest figure, 20.1 percent ("Kanri juken ni," 1993). One important factor is the greater availability in the larger cities of private preparatory schools (*juku* and *yobiko*) that many aspiring students attend after school, on weekends, and during vacations in order to get special training in preparation for university entrance examinations. In recent years several of the prefectures that have lagged behind in rates of college entry have sought to improve their standing by allocating resources for the establishment of special classes within public high schools designed to produce higher rates of successful entry into universities ("Tokushu kurasu," 1993).

Another factor underlying regional differences in college attendance is the imbalance in the distribution of higher institutions throughout the country, with a heavy concentration, particularly of universities, in the large cities. This again is the result in large part of the government's policy of relying on the private sector to expand facilities in response to growing demand. There is at least one national university in each administrative division, but less than half have local public universities. Private universities vary in number, from just one in Tottori prefecture to 106 in Tokyo. More than half of all universities are located in Tokyo, Osaka, Kyoto, Yokohama, and a handful of other large cities. Junior colleges are distributed somewhat more evenly, but they, too, show strong concentration in the heavily populated urban centers. The financial burden on the families of students who are forced to live away from home in order to attend college or university presents a significant obstacle. The unavailability of colleges within commuting distance is a more serious impediment for young women, since many parents are reluctant to allow their daughters to attend school away from home and parental supervision, especially if they are not able to reside in a college dormitory or the home of close relatives.

Opening up Higher Education to Students from Abroad. Students and faculty from foreign countries have constituted a very small presence in Japanese higher institutions. In 1983, the Ministry of Education announced a plan to institute comprehensive measures to increase the number of foreign students studying in Japan from the then current figure of 10,428 to 100,000 by the beginning of the twenty-first century. In 1992, there were 46,000 foreign students in Japan, of which about 41 percent were enrolled in undergraduate programs in junior colleges and universities, 31 percent in graduate programs, and the rest in postsecondary technical and vocational schools (Nishizawa, 1992:55). The figure of 46,000 is low compared to that in the United States (366,000 in 1988), France (126,000 in 1988), West Germany (92,000 in 1988), and Great Britain (59,000 in 1987). Over 90 percent of the foreign students in Japan are from other Asian countries, just 3 percent from North America, and 2 percent from Europe. The number of Asian students who come to study in Japan is still small, however, compared to those going to Europe and North America. For example, while students from China constitute the largest group of foreign students in Japan (18,000) and those from Korea the second largest group (6,500), their numbers are small in comparison to those going abroad to study in the United States (50,000 and 18,000, respectively) (Takei, 1992:32).

Since the launching of the previously cited plan to increase the number of foreign students in Japan to one hundred thousand, the Ministry of Education has sought to reach this goal through various measures, such as creating a system through which foreigners can receive preparation, including Japanese language study, in their own countries prior to coming to study in Japan, increasing the number of government scholarship students and providing assistance to privately funded students through scholarships, tuition waivers, and assistance for medical expenses, and constructing foreign student dormitories at national universities. In addition, since 1989, the Ministry of Education has held Japan Education Fairs in China, Malaysia, Thailand, and Indonesia to provide information on various aspects of study in Japan.

Several factors limit foreign study in Japan, including the high cost of living, but language is the dominant impediment. Instruction in nearly all universities is in Japanese, with the exception of a few such as the International Christian University, the international divisions of Sophia University and Waseda University, and the International University located in Niigata Prefecture (a graduate university). Although the number of people studying Japanese as a foreign language has been rapidly increasing in many countries, the opportunity to achieve mastery in the language continues to be very limited, so that foreign students coming to Japan face a major language problem. Much needs to be done, obviously, in the way of providing Japanese instruction to foreign students prior to beginning a program of undergraduate or graduate study as well as after they have entered a Japanese university.

Overseas Education and Education for Returnee Students. In recent years, as the number of Japanese going abroad to live and work as academics, businesspersons, and government officials for a number of years has grown rapidly, the number of accompanying children has also grown. The number of children of compulsory school age residing abroad reached 50,000 in 1992, and the number of elementary, lower secondary, and upper secondary school age children who returned to Japan during the fiscal year 1991 exceeded 13,000 (Mombusho, 1993:112–13). The education of children living abroad and returnee children (*kikokushijo*) has, therefore, become an important educational policy issue.

Returnee children have faced various difficulties in terms of adjusting to schooling back in Japan and having to take the examinations required for admission to upper secondary schools and universities. Since these issues came to public attention in the mid-1970s, the Ministry of Education has established special classes for returnee children in schools attached to national universities and set up a system of special "reception schools" (*ukeireko*). In addition, it has designated pilot schools for the study of the education of returnees. At the university level, since the mid-1980s, a number of universities have set up special quotas for returnee students. Those who meet the necessary criteria gain entrance either through a special entrance examination, evaluation of their overseas qualifications and reports, or an interview. The number of universities offering such a special quota has increased considerably, from forty-three in 1984 to one hundred in 1986. While Goodman (1993), for one, has argued that, far from being disadvantaged as they once were, returnee students today are enjoying preferential treatment in terms of admission to universities and employment, the education of both Japanese residing overseas and those returning to Japan remains an issue fraught with dilemmas and conflicts for young people and their parents.

Occupational Prospects of Graduates. Occupational selection has been one of the most important functions of higher education in Japan. Occupational prospects for university graduates differ considerably by gender, faculty, and institutional ranking. In the case of males, graduates from the most prestigious national and private universities are most likely to be recruited by the major companies, which offer better salaries, bonuses, and fringe benefits, as well as stability, while those from less prestigious universities find jobs in smaller companies. Moreover, graduates from the top-ranked national universities such as Tokyo, Kyoto, and Hitotsubashi and private ones such as Keio and Waseda are also more likely to rise to elite positions in business and the national bureaucracies (see, e.g., Ishida, 1993; Ushiogi, 1986). Employment opportunities differ also by faculty, with graduates from the faculties of law, economics, business management, commerce, and engineering getting preferential treatment over those from the humanities and social science faculties. Many major companies have permitted only certain departments or faculties of particular universities to take their entrance examinations, although recently many of them have adopted more open policies. The way in which graduates are hired also varies by faculty; companies hiring graduates from a faculty of technology tend to rely heavily on the faculty recommendations, while social science graduates normally take a company-administered entrance examination.

Looking more closely at patterns of employment among graduates, in 1992, about 80 percent of both male and female university graduates took up employment; among junior college graduates a higher percentage of women than men took up employment (87 percent versus 71 percent), while more males went on for more advanced education. In the case of male university graduates, of the 247,000 who took up employment, 38 percent went into office/clerical work and 37 percent into professional-technical occupations (of which over 80 percent went into technical occupations) and about 21 percent went into sales work (10 percent among females). In the case of junior college graduates, about 42 percent of the 11,000 male graduates went into technical occupations, while among the 183,000 female graduates, more than 60 percent went into clerical work, with the rest going into teaching (mostly at the preschool level), health-related occupations, and sales. As a general trend, the number of those going into the teaching profession has declined in recent years with the fall in birthrates. Employment patterns by industry show that among university graduates, over the past twenty to twenty-five years, the relative proportion going into the service industry has increased while that going into production and manufacturing has fallen. In the case of junior college graduates, the service industry is the largest employer, followed by manufacturing and production.

The employment situation among women graduates, particularly those from universities, merits some explanation. While companies hire high school or junior college graduates as "office ladies" (OLs) to perform routine clerical work, graduates from four-year universities have been excluded from such positions because they are more expensive and presumably will have fewer years before they leave their jobs to get married or start a family. At the same time, most employers have been reluctant to hire female graduates to perform tasks comparable to those assigned to male university graduates. A major legal step in promoting employment opportunities for women was the passage of the Equal Employment Opportunity Act (EEOA) in 1986, which coincided with a period of labor shortage in a flourishing economy. More companies began to hire female four-year university graduates, in some cases for management-track positions, prompting in turn a trend away from junior colleges toward four-year universities, and from women's universities toward coed universities, which offer a greater variety of study options in more directly job-related fields. However, the recent downturn in the economy has virtually wiped out the gains made by female university graduates: The employment rate among these women, which had reached 86 percent in 1991, fell to 80 percent in 1992. These women have clearly borne the brunt of cutbacks in new worker hiring. This is a clear reflection of the shortcomings of the EEOA, which "forbids" only certain discriminatory practices (e.g., with respect to retirement, benefits, and certain types of on-the-job training), while with respect to recruitment, hiring, job placement, and promotion, it demands only that employers "make an effort" to end discrimination.

Some recent developments with respect to employment among Japanese college graduates should be noted. One is that, with so many young people now going on to college, "prestige and privilege is no longer at the disposal of every university graduate" (Amano, 1989:120), and differential in lifetime earned income between high school and college graduates overall has become smaller (see, e.g., Kamishiro, 1993). Another is that hiring and employment based on the concepts of lifetime employment, seniority, and educational credentialism have gradually begun to break down in the face of declining economic growth and growing domestic and international competition. As more companies find themselves forced to cut back on hiring, they are showing more interest in potential employees' personal qualifications rather than which school they attended. Simultaneously, graduates' criteria and considerations for choosing employment are also undergoing changes. For example, the tendency to seek positions within large corporations located in Tokyo is giving way. Within the past few years, the percentage of male university graduates from the humanities and social science faculties taking up employment with companies with less than one thousand employees has shown an increase, from 34 percent among 1991 graduates to 40 percent among 1993 graduates, as has the percentage who have returned to their home prefectures to take up employment—up from 30 percent in 1991 to over 34 percent in 1993 (Kobayashi, 1993:54, figure 5 and 55, figure 6). In addition, today's young people seem to be more concerned about choosing a job or position that appeals to them, is interesting, and provides an opportunity for personal growth, and they show much less hesitance about changing jobs should they find themselves dissatisfied. According to figures released by the Ministry of Labor in 1991, 28.4 percent of those who had graduated from college in 1989 had left their jobs within three years (among women alone the figure was almost 46 percent), and one in three had changed jobs within that time (Kosugi, 1993:58, figure 1). One factor promoting this new trend is that differentials in salary and other benefits and in opportunities for advancement have become much less significant than in the past.

Faculty

Ranks and Ratio, Salaries, and Social Status. Teachers, particularly university professors, have tended to enjoy high prestige in Japanese society. When university attendance was limited to a small elite, university professors tended to come from well-to-do-families that could afford to have a son in a profession that, though highly respected, was by no means high paying. Competition for full-time university teaching positions is very high today, but the social status enjoyed by professors appears to have declined considerably. Full-time faculty numbered 129,000 at universities. Notable is the fact that even though private universities enroll 73 percent of all students, only 52 percent of the 129,000 teach at private universities (Mombusho, 1993:86). This underscores the point made earlier that amenities at private universities are on the whole inferior to those at national and local public universities. Of the 129,000, 36 percent were full professors, 22 percent professors, 13 percent lecturers, and 26 percent assistants (ibid.). Junior colleges employ about 21,000 teachers full-time (ibid.: 87). Both universities and junior colleges have a large part-time teaching staff (99,000 and 36,000, respectively, in 1992) that consists of many who have a full-time teaching position elsewhere.

Personnel practices in universities, particularly those where the chair system prevails, tend to be characterized by the principle of inbreeding, lifetime employment, and seniority. It is common for an aspiring scholar to become an assistant at his or her alma mater, then gradually move up to assistant professor and professor with the passage of years. Many, therefore, spend their entire professional career with the institution from which they graduated. There is much less mobility than in the United States, for example. Teaching positions at many of the top universities are almost completely monopolized by their own graduates. The result is that many university teachers lack a variety of work experiences. While many universities do advertise publicly for faculty openings, a system of patronage and the "old boys network" function to restrict open competition.

The salaries of faculty at national universities are based on a scale used for national civil servants, and this same scale is generally used as a model by the private universities. Actually, salaries tend to be higher at the private universities, but as national civil servants, faculty members at national universities receive considerably better benefits, including inexpensive housing and a larger retirement pension. Salaries do not vary a great deal across institutions and is determined primarily on the basis of years of experience and age; academic qualifications and individual performance or merit are given much less weight. There is basically no such thing as tenure, except in the case of foreign faculty. Generally one is hired with the understanding that the position is permanent. In the case of national universities, an assistant becomes eligible for promotion to assistant professor after about three years; he or she must teach for seven more years before becoming eligible for promotion to full professorship. Actual promotion depends on whether there is a position available at a particular rank, evaluation of one's research, and so on. At many private universities even when there is an institutionalized system of review for promotion, promotion generally takes place automatically on the basis of age and years of service. These practices are viewed as contributing to the stagnation and low quality of teaching and research in many higher institutions and have come under severe criticism in recent years not only from without but also from within (see, e.g., Shadan Hojin Nihon Shiritsu Daigaku Renmei, 1991).

Gender Inequalities in Faculty Representation. Sex differences in university enrollment described earlier are manifested in women's lack of representation on college and university faculties. More women teach in junior colleges than in universities: in 1992, women made up roughly 40 percent of all faculty members in junior colleges, under 10 percent of four-year university faculty, and less than 5 percent of graduate-level faculty. The higher the professional rank, the smaller is the representation of females: Women comprise just 5 percent of full professors at universities and 26 percent of those at junior colleges, and 4 percent of university and 12 percent of junior college presidents (Mombusho, 1993:86–87). Moreover, within universities, women's representation on faculties is higher at the private than at the national universities, at women's universities than at coeducational universities, and at the more recently established ones than at the older, more prestigious institutions.

Women's underrepresentation in college and university faculties is a manifestation of the closed nature of Japanese universities and the custom of inbreeding. Women have tended to be excluded from the networks through which faculty and research staff are often recruited, while at the same time they have not been able to build their own women's networks. There are, moreover, no affirmative action programs designed to promote the hiring of women and to redress gender imbalances. As a consequence, fewer women are able to obtain employment following completion of master's and doctoral degree programs. Many women continue teaching for years as adjuncts at two or three institutions without ever obtaining a full-time position. The various forms of discrimination that exist in academia are likely to prove much more difficult to attack than those found in business and industry. It is significant to note that none of the various recommendations and proposals for educational reform set forth by the

National Council on Educational Reform or by the University Council has addressed these and other gender issues.

Foreign Faculty. The number of non-Japanese on the academic staff of all the four-year universities in 1992 was 2,685 out of a total of 130,000. At the national universities, the figure was 819, or 1.5 percent of the total (Mombusho, 1993:86–87), and of these the majority were employed on a contractual basis as assistants, in many cases as foreign language teachers. Tokyo University had only 7 foreign professors on its regular faculty, while Osaka University, also a national university, had just 4 in 1991 (Ozaki, 1992:22). Foreign nationals have been allowed to hold regular positions at national or public universities only since 1982, when a special law was enacted making this possible. As the figures show, however, their number has shown a very modest increase, a reflection again of the restrictive personnel practices common to many Japanese universities. Recent reform proposals have advocated doing away with the closed personnel system and broadening recruitment by adopting flexible qualifications and hiring more nonacademics as well as foreign nationals.

Teaching versus Research. Japanese universities have traditionally tended to emphasize their research function over their educational function. Kitamura (1986) has offered some important historical explanations for this. One is that from the very inception of Japan's modern system of education in the Meiji period, compulsory education has been heavily directed and controlled, whereas the university has been viewed as an institution catering to an elite group of students who presumably come with definite goals for pursuing study and the capacity to learn independently in an atmosphere of relative freedom. Another factor Kitamura notes is the predominance of the idea that "the function of research and teaching are in harmony, cannot be separated, and are not in a conflicting relationship with each other," and the assumption that "the professors' research activities automatically contribute to their students' educational progress." It is up to the students to learn from what the professors "profess" and to integrate what they learn from the various courses they study into their total university experience (Kitamura, 1986:165).

These traditional notions regarding the function of university education and teaching, which were maintained at the mere handful of elitist universities before World War II, have continued to mold the consciousness of a great number of the professors who teach in today's greatly more expanded system of higher education. The problem is, of course, that universities no longer cater exclusively to students who are more or less homogeneous in terms of social background, motivation, and ability levels; they now encompass a diversity of students.

Universities and professors have come increasingly under criticism in recent years for neglecting their teaching function, as is evidenced by the predominance of large lecture classes, especially at the mammoth private colleges, a high incidence of class cancellations by professors, and the generally inferior quality of teaching. The low rate of class attendance and lack of academic motivation exhibited so frequently by students are seen as at least in part attributable to the uniform and uninspiring teaching methods characteristically employed by professors (see, e.g., Kitamura, 1992; Hara, 1992). While teacher training at the elementary and secondary school levels is well developed, there is no systematic training for those entering teaching in higher education.

Until recently, universities and faculty have for the most part overlooked these issues, in large part because of the absence of any pressures to do so, given that universities have been in the position of being able to pick and choose students in a sellers' market and because the faculty at Japanese universities has considerable power and autonomy in matters pertaining to teaching and research as well as in governance and administration. As discussed in the section on current reforms, the anticipated competition for an increasingly diminishing student market, plus growing pressures from the Ministry of Education to improve the quality of university teaching, have impelled institutions to begin reexamining their curricula and teaching practices. Institutional and faculty self-evaluation, staff development, and research on teaching and learning, which have for too long been neglected, are essential tasks facing Japanese higher education.

FUTURE DEVELOPMENTS

The challenges confronting Japanese higher education today emanate from many sources: an anticipated sharp decline in the traditional college-going population, leading to growing competition among and within different types of higher institutions for students; the rising influx of students varying in age, needs, and interests; and growing dissatisfaction over the level and quality of higher education provided and demand on the part of business and political leaders and society as a whole for more accountability. Higher institutions face the task of redefining, diversifying, and expanding their functions to meet the needs of new clientele while at the same upgrading the quality of both research and teaching. Adding to the pressures is the fact that these challenges are being posed precisely at a point when funding for higher education is becoming increasingly tight in a shrinking economy facing growing international competition.

The survival of higher institutions will depend on the ability of administrators and faculty to fully grasp the nature and scope of the changes and to respond to the new challenges in a visionary way. Not all institutions will be up to the task. Kitamura, citing common strategies pursued by some university administrators to counter declining enrollments such as establishing new departments and programs thought to be popular among prospective students, cautions, "These approaches are, most often, based on the same assumption as the traditional expansion model and have merely been 'added on' to the existing structure of higher education. What is really needed is a basic structural change which will include significant innovations for strengthening the functions of education" (Kitamura, 1991:315). Finally, it is worth noting that while the Ministry of Education has liberalized many of the regulations governing the structure and organization of higher education in an effort to encourage institutions to adapt to new challenges, at the same time, it is not entirely clear how much initiative and autonomy the Ministry is willing to grant them and how much control it intends to maintain over the actual direction and content of change.

REFERENCES

Amano, Ikuo. 1986. "Educational Crisis in Japan." In William K. Cummings et al., eds., *Educational Policies in Crisis*. New York: Praeger.

———. 1989. "The Dilemma of Japanese Education Today." In James J. Shields Jr., ed., *Japanese Schooling—Patterns of Socialization, Equality, and Political Control*. University Park: Pennsylvania State University Press.

Fujimura-Fanselow, Kumiko. 1985. "Women's Participation in Japanese Higher Education." *Comparative Education Review*, 29 (4), 471–89.

———. 1989. "Japan." In Gail P. Kelly, ed., *International Handbook of Women's Education*. New York: Greenwood.

Fujita, Hidenori. 1989. "A Crisis of Legitimacy in Japanese Education—Meritocracy and Cohesiveness." In James J. Shields Jr., ed., *Japanese Schooling—Patterns of Socialization, Equality, and Political Control*. University Park: Pennsylvania State University Press.

Goodman, Roger. 1993. *Japan's 'International Youth.'* Oxford: Clarendon.

Hara, Kazuo. 1992. "Jugyo keikaku to jugyo hyoka" (Class Planning and Evaluation). *IDE, 332*, 5–13.

Ishida, Hiroshi. 1993. *Social Mobility in Contemporary Japan*. Stanford: Stanford University Press.

The Japan–United States Educational Commission, Educational Information Service. 1992. *EIS Annual Report*.

Kamishiro, Kazuyoshi. 1993. "Daigakusotsu no rodoichiba—genjo to tembo" (The Labor Market for University Graduates—Present Situation and Future Outlook). *IDE, 345*, 5–11.

" 'Kanri juken' ni hashirigachi." 1993. *Asahi Shimbun*.

Kitamura, Kazuyuki. 1986. "The Decline and Reform of Education in Japan: A Comparative Perspective." In William K. Cummings et al., eds., *Educational Policies in Crisis*. New York: Praeger.

———. 1991. "The Future of Japanese Higher Education." In Edward R. Beauchamp, ed., *Windows on Japanese Education*. New York: Greenwood.

———. 1992. "Gakusei ni yoru jugyo hyoka" (Class Evaluation by Students). *IDE, 332*, 18–26.

Kobayashi, Shinichi. 1993. "Maker banare wa tomattaka" (Has the Trend Away from Manufacturing and Production Ceased?). *IDE, 345*, 46–51.

Kokuritsu Fujin Kyoiku Kaikan. March 1991. *Heisei ninendo koto kyoiku kikan ni okeru joseigaku kanrenkoza kaisetsu jokyo chosa kekka hokoku* (Survey of Courses on Women's Studies and Related Subjects in Institutions of Higher Education in Japan [fiscal 1990]). Saitama-ken: Kokuritsu Fujin Kyoiku Kaikan (National Women's Education Centre).

Kosugi, Reiko. 1993. "Daisotsusha no ritenshoku" (Job-Changing among University Graduates). *IDE, 345*, 58–62.

Ministry of Education, Science and Culture. 1989. *Education in Japan—A Graphic Presentation*. Tokyo: Gyosei.

Mombusho (Ministry of Education). 1993. *Mombu Tokei Yoran* (Digest of Educational Statistics). Tokyo: Okurasho Insatsukyoku.

Mombusho Kotokyoiku kyoku kikakuka Daigaku Shingikai shitsu. 1991. *Daigaku Shingikai News, 8.*

Nagai, Michio. 1971. *Higher Education in Japan: Its Take-off and Crash*. Tokyo: University of Tokyo Press.

Nishizawa, Yoshiyuki. 1992. "Ryugakusei gyosei no gendankai" (The Current Stage in Foreign Student Administration). *IDE, 335*, 54–60.

Ozaki, Hitoshi. 1992. "Gakujutsu kokusai koryu no hoko" (The Direction of International Exchange in Arts and Sciences). *IDE, 335*, 19–26.

Passin, Herbert. 1965. *Society and Education in Japan*. New York: Teachers College Press.

Shadan Hojin Nihon Shiritsu Daigaku Renmei. 1991. *Daigaku Kasseika e no Teigen* (Proposal for Activating Universities). Tokyo.

Shiritsu Daigaku Renmei. 1991. *Daigaku kasseika e no teigen—kyoin jinji seido no kaizen ni mukete* (Proposals for Activating Universities—Toward an Improvement of the Faculty Personnel System). Tokyo: Shadan Hojin Shiritsu Daigaku Renmei.

Takei, Kazuyoshi. 1992. "Nihon ryugaku fair" (Japan's Study Abroad Fair). *IDE, 335*, 31–36.

"Tokushu kurasu settchi de daigaku shingakusha ga kyuzo." 1993. *Asahi Shimbun*.

Ushiogi, Morikazu. 1986. "Transition from School to Work: The Japanese Case." In William K. Cummings et al., eds., *Educational Policies in Crisis*. New York: Praeger.

9

LAOS

John C. Weidman

With a 1992 per capita GNP of U.S.$250, the Lao PDR is among the group of countries designated by the World Bank as "low-income economies." It has a population of 4.4 million with an average life expectancy of fifty-one years (World Bank, 1994b:162, table 1). The adult illiteracy rate of 36 percent is much lower than the rates in two other low-income Asian countries, Bhutan (62 percent) and Nepal (74 percent), but considerably higher than the 12 percent illiteracy rate in Sri Lanka (ibid.:54, table 2.5).

Despite its low per capita GNP, the economy of the Lao PDR has shown healthy growth over the past several years that was stimulated by a program of economic reform initiated by the government in 1986 called the New Economic Mechanism (NEM). The NEM emphasized "reorienting the economy away from central planning and its emphasis on public ownership towards a market-oriented economy led by a vigorous private sector" (ibid.:1). While the shift to a more market-driven economy has not been without its problems, especially in financial institutions where the shift away from total government control has been difficult, considerable progress has been made.

Between 1988 and 1993, the real annual growth rate averaged 7.5 percent. With a population growth rate of 2.9 percent, real per capita income growth has been near 5 percent. Nearly 90 percent of the workforce is employed in agriculture, which includes livestock and fisheries (ibid.:5), but the share of agriculture in the total GDP has declined from 63 percent to 56 percent since 1987 while the industrial share has grown from 11 percent to 17 percent. Even though the share of GDP attributable to the service sector has remained around a quarter over this period, "the composition of services has shifted away from public services towards commercial services, largely privately provided" (ibid.:3). In 1992, 25 percent of the workforce was employed in urban areas and the average monthly salary of urban workers was 30,000 kip or approximately U.S.$43 (ibid.:61–62).

The educational system in the Lao PDR that prepares students for postsecondary education includes a preschool sector (creche and kindergarten), a 5-year primary school sector, a 3-year lower secondary sector, and a 3-year upper secondary sector. In 1991–92, there were 121 creches with 1,725 students; 922 kindergartens with 22,372 students; 7,101 primary schools (of which only 1,927 had all 5 primary grades) with 574,038 students; 707 lower secondary schools with 87,167 students; and 118 upper secondary schools with 30,172 students (Murugasu, 1993:11).

Net enrollment ratios (percent of age cohort enrolled) for each level were 61.6 percent for primary (ages 6–10), 7.4 percent for lower secondary (ages 11–13), and 3.6 percent for upper secondary (ages 14–16) (ibid.:14, table 6). Currently, only 40 percent of an age cohort complete primary education, 30 percent of them move on to lower secondary school, and 12 percent move from lower to upper secondary school (ibid.:10). Less than 2 percent go on to postsecondary education. While females outnumber males at the preschool level, all succeeding levels are predominantly male: 56.4 percent in primary, 60.2 percent in lower secondary, and 63.8 percent in upper secondary (ibid.:12, table 2). Enrollment ratios are highest in the urban areas (4 of the country's 17 provinces), but they were below the national average in all of the remaining 13 provinces (ibid.:18).

PROFILE OF THE HIGHER EDUCATION SYSTEM

Teacher Education

Teachers for primary and secondary education are trained in specialized pedagogical institutions, only a small number of which provide instruction that would be considered to be at the postsecondary level. Most teachers have completed only the level of education immediately above the one at which they are teaching. It is common to find many of the teacher training institutions sharing facilities under a single management structure. There are 50 institutions enrolling 4,820 students preparing teachers for the preschools and primary schools. They tend to provide a 3-year program for students who have completed lower secondary school.

For the preparation of secondary school teachers, there are 18 institutions enrolling 4,610 students preparing to teach in lower secondary schools. They tend to be either 3-year programs for lower secondary school graduates or one-year programs for upper secondary school graduates. There are 3 postsecondary institutions enrolling 3,100 students preparing to teach in upper secondary schools. Most of these are 3-year training programs open to upper secondary school graduates (Murugasu, 1993:28–29).

Postsecondary Technical Education

This sector includes two types of institutions, technical colleges and higher technical colleges, which are open to students who have completed upper secondary education. The 35 institutions included in this group prepare middle- and higher-level technicians. Located strategically around the country, 7 are under the supervision of the Ministry of Education and the rest fall under other Ministries. In 1988, enrollment was 5,265 in the 28 technical colleges and 1,136 in the 7 higher technical colleges. About 80 programs ranging from 1.3 to 3 years in length are offered in the technical colleges and 14 programs ranging from 1.5 to 5 years in length are offered in the higher technical colleges (Murugasu, 1993:21–22).

The Ministry of Health operated 4 technical colleges with 3-year, health-related programs that enrolled 1,071 students in 1988. The Ministry of Agriculture and Forestry operated 7 technical colleges that enrolled 928 students. The Ministry of Communication, Transport, Post, and Construction had 7 institutions that enrolled 382 students. The Ministry of Economy, Planning, and Finance ran 2 institutions that enrolled 535 in programs in planning, banking, finance, and accounting. The Ministry of Culture operated 3 institutions that enrolled 135 students in courses in Lao arts and music, sculpture, metal and ceramic arts, dancing, and voice. A total of 1,136 students were enrolled in 1988 in the 7 higher technical colleges. The Ministry of Communication, Transport, Post, and Construction accounted for about 63 percent of this total (ibid.:22).

University-Level Postsecondary Education

There are three institutions that are considered to provide university-level programs: the University Pedagogical Institute, the National Polytechnic Institute, and the University of Health Sciences. Each of these institutions provides specialized professional training of at least four years' duration that is open to graduates of upper secondary schools. There is no national university providing programs in the arts and sciences. Admission to these institutions is based on a provincial quota system determined by the Ministry of Education (Asian Development Bank, 1989b:66; Spaulding, 1990:117).

University Pedagogical Institute (UPI). The University Pedagogical Institute (UPI) was founded in 1964 as the National Institute of Pedagogy of Vientiane for the training of primary and lower secondary school teachers. In 1975, it was merged with the Normal School of Viengsay to become a higher education institution providing 4-year programs for the training of upper secondary school teachers and was renamed the UPI in 1988. The UPI has a teaching staff of 260 and enrolls 2,500 students in 6 faculties: mathematics and physics, biology and chemistry, geography and history, psychology and educational sciences, Lao languages, and foreign languages. In addition to the main campus on the outskirts of the capital city of Vientiane (Dong Dok), there are campuses in the cities of Luang Prabang (the traditional royal capital) and Savannakhet, each enrolling 400 students (Can, 1991:173). About 80 percent of the students complete their programs (Spaulding, 1990:117).

National Polytechnic Institute (NPI). The National Polytechnic Institute (NPI) was founded in Vientiane in 1984 to train engineers. NPI has a teaching staff of 100 in 4 faculties: fundamental sciences, civil engineering, mechanical engineering, and electrical engineering. Programs take 5 years to complete (Can, 1991:174). All quota students must take a qualifying examination prior to enrollment and approximately 25 percent of the students are required to take a year of preparatory work prior to attending higher education courses (Asian Development Bank, 1989b:27, table 5.14; 32). Enrollment in 1991–92 was 590 students (Murugasu, 1993:27). The program completion rate for the NPI is only 52 percent (Asian Development Bank, 1989b:29).

University of Health Sciences (UHS). The University of Health Sciences (UHS) was founded in 1969 (Asian Development Bank, 1989b:66) as the Royal School of Medicine in Vientiane and renamed in 1975 (Can, 1991:173). There are about 1,000 students (ibid.:191) enrolled in 3 programs staffed with about 50 full-time and 50 part-time teachers. General medicine is the largest, with about 700 students enrolled in a 6-year course. Pharmacy has about 200 students enrolled in a 5-year course, and dentistry has about 100 students enrolled in a 4-year course. Program completion rates are 85 percent for general medicine, 79 percent for pharmacy, and 92 percent for dentistry (Asian Development Bank, 1989b:68–69).

Changing Function and Pattern of Higher Education

The fundamental reform of postsecondary education in the Lao PDR that is currently being implemented with funding from the Asian Development Bank is the consolidation and rationalization of the system (Lamoureux, 1994). As originally proposed, the reform was to focus on expanding the scope of the programs and academic staff in the University Pedagogical Institute, Dong Dok. The aims of this university were:

1. to offer programs of studies leading to degrees in arts and sciences for meeting the manpower demands of such graduates

2. to offer limited programs of postgraduate studies in arts and sciences, as well as carry out applied research in these areas

3. to develop curriculum, textbooks, and other instructional materials for the courses offered

4. to organize and/or conduct in-service training programs for its own faculty as well as the teachers of upper secondary schools and teacher trainers of the lower secondary teacher training schools

5. to collaborate with other institutes of higher learning inside and outside the country to develop new knowledge and innovations in different related fields/subjects (Asian Development Bank, 1989b:75).

The first aim also implies the need to provide instruction in all programs that is not too highly specialized in order to prepare students more adequately for a changing world in which market forces will be increasingly important in shaping opportunities, both individually and collectively. It also suggests that the curriculum should be expanded to cover the needs of the emerging market economy, an example of which would be the development of a degree program to train managers (ibid.:76). The second aim speaks to the need to provide advanced training for academic staff in university-level institutions within the country as costs of sending students to foreign universities become prohibitive.

The third aim reflects problems with outdated curriculum and materials, again due to extremely high costs in the international marketplace. It is reflected in poor libraries and laboratory facilities as well as in the limited access by students even to basic textbooks (Asian Development Bank, 1992:67–68). As a consequence, most instruction is little more than transmission of content in lectures during which students are expected to take copious notes that will be their primary source material for subsequent examinations. It also implies the importance of expanding the use of technology, including computers (Spaulding, 1990). The fourth aim emphasizes the need to provide in-service as well as continuing education for maintaining the knowledge and skills of the professionals being trained. Finally, the fifth aim reflects the need for building linkages with sister institutions in other countries.

Subsequent deliberations supported by another Asian Development Bank technical assistance project resulted in the formulation of a much more ambitious plan that seeks to phase in, over a period of several years, the consolidation of several existing postsecondary education institutions into a multicampus national university under a single administrative structure (Lamoureux, 1994). This new institution would include as organizational units, rather than independent institutions, faculties of education, engineering, and medicine. Additional faculties, in part from existing institutions, anticipated include economics and management, agriculture, and law. Also anticipated is a change in the structure of degree programs, with all sharing a common two-year general education component, followed by a specialization of three to four years' duration.

All of this will require careful deliberation and planning within the particular cultural traditions of the Lao people in order for implementation to be effective. Additional funds will also have to be obtained, which will prove very difficult in the face of increasing demands on governments to pay for goods and services at unsubsidized prices.

Two of the ways in which funding for higher education has been expanded and diversified is through charging fees to students and allowing the establishment of private sector higher institutions. Both of these methods are being used in Mongolia, another Asian country in which higher education was highly subsidized by the Soviet Union (Weidman, 1995). The establishment of student fees has usually been accompanied by government loan schemes so that poor students are not prevented from going on to higher education. The Asian Development Bank is funding a project in the Lao PDR to expand education through the private sector. While this project will initially focus on primary and secondary education, it may be extended to higher education at some future time. The Asian Development Bank is also committed to funding improvement of the higher education system.

RESPONSES TO INTERNATIONAL DEMANDS

Following the devastation of the Vietnam War, the part of the former French colony of Indochina in Southeast Asia known as Laos emerged from a civil war in which the victorious Pathet Lao established a communist government and renamed it the Lao People's Democratic Republic (PDR) in 1975. Because of the continuing animosity of the United States and former French colonials as well as the Lao fear of Chinese intervention, the Lao PDR aligned itself with the Soviet Union. Consequently, the newly emerging country received a substantial amount of aid from the Soviet Union and other Eastern European countries during the first decade and a half of its existence as a republic under communist rule.

With the fall of the Soviet Union in 1991, not only were its constituent republics forced to fend for themselves at the mercy of an uncontrolled world economy but also many of the countries that had been under its sphere of influence (among them, the Lao PDR) were forced to do the same. For higher education institutions, this included having to pay world market prices for books and equipment that had been provided either free or at very low cost as part of Soviet aid packages. It also meant severely reduced opportunities to send academic staff to universities in the Soviet Union or other Eastern European countries for advanced degrees, also at very minimal cost to the sending university.

While the government has been making good progress in the transition to a socialist market economy, there is a serious shortage of professional and technical personnel (e.g., administrators, accountants, lawyers, engineers). The exodus of many professionals after the 1975 revolution and the very limited capacity for education and training have led to serious skill shortage, currently estimated at twenty thousand graduates from higher education. The total supply of graduates at relevant levels was less than 850 in 1993, with none in economics and management (Asian Development Bank, 1995:3).

The system has suffered from a proliferation of institutions of questionable quality. As is the pattern in many current and former socialist countries, ministries tended to establish their own highly specialized training institutions. While providing personnel for the respective ministries, these institutions have not been responsive to the manpower demands of the rapidly changing economy in which the government is slowly ceasing to be the employer of last resort (ibid.:4).

Quality of institutions is poor because of inadequate secondary school preparation of students as well as dilapidated facilities, outdated equipment, and underqualified teaching staffs. At the country's flagship higher education institution, the University Pedagogical Institute, less than 15 percent of the staff have postgraduate qualifications, with an additional 5 percent currently in training. The remaining 80 percent have either bachelor's degrees or diplomas. Because of the absence of appropriately trained technical support staff (e.g., librarians, lab technicians), inadequate facilities, and severely limited book and periodical collections, libraries and laboratories are barely functional (ibid.: 4).

FUTURE DEVELOPMENTS

The rationalization of the higher education system was enabled by a prime minister's decree establishing the National University of Laos (NUOL). Implementation will entail: (1) amalgamation of four postsecondary institutions (University Pedagogical Institute in Dong Dok, National Polytechnic Institute in Vientiane, University of Health Sciences in Vientiane, and the Agricultural College in Nabong); (2) consolidation by gradual integration of six partner campuses; and (3) development of regional colleges through which NUOL relates to the provinces. Programs will be strengthened (including developing a foundation program for the first two years of undergraduate study and improving science laboratories and equipment) and a new Faculty of Economics and Management will be developed (Asian Development Bank, 1995:6, 14).

The prospects for consolidation and rationalization of higher education in the Lao PDR seem reasonably good because this reform is being supported financially by the Asian Development Bank as is expansion of education through the private sector. What remains to be seen is how long reform might take and whether there will be sufficient financial resources, both internal (via diversification of funding) and external (donor agencies), to accomplish the level of quality improvement that is necessary for graduates to be competitive in a world economy.

REFERENCES

Asian Development Bank. 1989a. *Lao People's Democratic Republic Education Sector Study*. Vol. 4: *Teachers and Their Training*. Manila, Philippines: Author.

———. 1989b. *Lao People's Democratic Republic Education Sector Study*. Vol. 5: *Technical, Vocational, and Higher Education*. Manila, Philippines: Author.

———. 1992. *Lao People's Democratic Republic*. Education and Development in Asia and the Pacific Series. Vol. 1. Manila, Philippines: Author.

———. 1995. *Report and Recommendation of the President to the Board of Directors on a Proposed Loan to the Lao People's Democratic Republic for the Post-secondary Rationalization Project*. Manila, Philippines.

Can, Le Thac. 1991. "Higher Education Reform in Vietnam, Laos, and Cambodia." *Comparative Education Review, 35* (1), 170–76.

Lamoureux, Marvin E. 1994. *Post-Secondary Education Rationalization Project—Lao PDR (Asian Development Bank T.A. No. 1957–Lao)*. Vol. 1, "Design Report." Prepared for Asian Development Bank, Manila, and Ministry of Education, Lao PDR. Middlesex, England: Serco Education Limited.

Murugasu, V. 1993. *Encouraging Private Sector Education Study (TA No. 1776–LAO)*. Manila, Philippines: Asian Development Bank.

Spaulding, Seth. 1990. "Educational Development and Reform on the Soviet Periphery: Mongolian People's Republic and Lao People's Democratic Republic." *Journal of Asian and African Affairs, 2* (1), 109–24.

Weidman, John C. 1995. "Diversifying Finance of Higher Education Systems in the Third World: The Cases of Kenya and Mongolia." *Education Policy Analysis Archives, 3* (5).

World Bank. 1994a. *Lao People's Democratic Republic Country Economic Memorandum*. Report No. 12554–LA. Washington, D.C.: World Bank, Country Operations Division, Country Department I, East Asia and Pacific Region.

———. 1994b. *World Development Report 1994: Infrastructure for Development*. New York: Oxford University Press.

10

MALAYSIA

Molly N. N. Lee

Malaysia is an ex-British colony that did not obtain its political independence until 1957.[1] It is a multicultural society with an estimated population of 16 million in 1990. The racial composition is 55 percent Malays and other indigenous people,[2] 34 percent Chinese, 10 percent Indians, and one percent "others" (Sri Lankans, Eurasians, and other communities) (Malaysia, 1986). Malaysia has a democratic government, dominated by the Malay elites. At the time of independence, "the Malays had the numbers, the Chinese the wealth and the English-educated the control of the government" (Wang, 1970:245). These three groups of contending elites formed the first coalition government under the banner of the Alliance Party, which later became the National Front (Barisan National) and is currently ruling the country. The Malay language is the national language; since 1970 the sole official language and the main medium of instruction in the education system has been Bahasa Malaysia.[3]

Malaysia is a society divided by race, language, religion, culture, and, to some extent, occupational and regional differences. During the first ten years of independence, there was a great disparity in income distribution between the Malays and non-Malays, which led to the outbreak of racial riots on May 13, 1969. Since then, the Malaysian government has implemented the New Economic Policy to restructure the occupational composition of the economy and to redress the economic imbalances among the races (Malaysia, 1971a). Education, especially higher education, is expected to help achieve these aims by being an agent of social mobility. The Malay ruling elites undertook a policy of sponsored mobility, whereby greater access to higher education is made available to the Bumiputras[4] through the "racial quota system." The objective of this policy is to increase the educational opportunities of the Bumiputras so that they can increase their representation in industry and commerce.

Malaysia is rapidly developing an industrialized economy. While in the past it has depended on its natural resources like tin, oil, and timber, and agricultural products like rubber, palm oil, and cocoa, Malaysia has now joined the other newly industrializing countries in Asia by expanding its industrial sector. Malaysia is aggressively pursuing an export-oriented growth strategy by encouraging foreign investments in its manufacturing sector. Today, besides raw materials, Malaysia also exports manufactured products like electronic chips, air-conditioners, televisions, and cars. As the Malaysian economy becomes industrialized, the need for high-level human resources is a definite impetus for the expansion of the higher education system. This has been reflected in the increase in the number of universities and private colleges in the past two decades. However, Malaysia's human resource development strategies have focused largely on achieving a genuine expansion of ethnically balanced manpower at all levels and in all areas of specialization, a policy that has often resulted in shortages of quality high-level manpower in key areas (Jasbir, 1989).

The rapid expansion of higher education is not only a response to internal factors like rising social demand and manpower needs, nor is it unique to the Malaysian context. Many Asian countries are also witnessing this trend and there are exogenous contributing factors like the interrelationship of national economies to a global economy and attempts by individual nation-states to modernize and transform their societies (Selvaratnam and Gopinathan, 1984). According to the human capital theory, there is a close relationship between economic growth and human capital, and higher education is seen as playing a role in training the human resources. Every nation-state is organized around economic growth objectives; therefore, it is not surprising to witness each government mobilizing its financial and material resources toward the expansion of higher education. But, on the other hand, the institutional perspective places great emphasis on the cultural and ideological dimension of the world system. According to Meyer (1980), the world system is not simply a collection of nation-states engaged in economic exchange; it is also an overarching social system of institutional rules and structural properties. These rules define the parameters within which nations operate and strongly influence the behavior of other nations. The worldwide belief in the importance of science and technology in fostering national development has resulted in many governments committing their resources to the expansion of tertiary education, especially in the production of scientifically and technically skilled personnel. In other words, as part of the world culture, university education becomes institutionalized in nearly every country throughout the world. Some would even go further and say that the university in many Third World countries is a symbolic asset in the process of nation building, like a national flag or a national airline (Van Den Bor and Shute, 1991).

University education may have its roots in the West, but as it becomes institutionalized in developing countries, it tends to become "indigenized" in one way or another. This chapter is a critical overview of the development of higher education in Malaysia, analyzing the extent to which this development is shaped by internal social demands as well as external forces in the international arena.

PROFILE OF THE HIGHER EDUCATION SYSTEM

Historical Development

As an ex-colony, Malaysia has inherited many British legacies, including the political, legal, administrative, and education systems. The university system took root during the colonial period when the King Edward VII College of Medicine was first established in 1905. In 1929, the second tertiary institution was established under the name of the Raffles College. Both these colleges were amalgamated in 1949 to form the University of Malaya in Singapore with degree-granting status. In 1959, the university started an autonomous division in Kuala Lumpur that became a separate entity in 1962.[5]

In the same year, a Higher Education Planning Committee was formed to study the development of higher education based on foreseeable needs and financial resources of the country. The recommendations of this committee gave the initial impetus for a sudden expansion of higher education in Malaysia. Between 1969 and 1972, four new universities were founded. Two of them were converted from existing colleges and two were brand-new. The University of Agriculture (Universiti Pertanian Malaysia) was converted from the College of Agriculture in 1971; similarly, the Technical College was given university status in 1972 and became the University of Technology (Universiti Teknologi Malaysia). In 1969 the Science University of Malaysia (Universiti Sains Malaysia) was established in Penang, and in the following year the National University of Malaysia (Universiti Kebangsaan Malaysia) was established in Kuala Lumpur. Two additional universities, the International Islamic University (Universiti Islam Antarabangsa) and the University of North Malaysia (Universiti Utara Malaysia), came into being in 1983 and 1984, respectively. The latest additions are two new universities in Sarawak and Sabah—University of Malaysia Sarawak (Universiti Malaysia Sarawak) was started in 1993 while University of Malaysia Sabah (Universiti Malaysia Sabah) was founded in 1995.

All in all, there are eight local universities, one international university, two colleges, and six polytechnics in Malaysia. The two colleges are the MARA[6] Institute of Technology, which was established in 1967 to train Bumiputras in middle-level management and technical positions, and the Tunku Abdul Rahman College, which was established in 1969 to meet the higher education demands of predominantly Chinese students who had no access to the limited number of university places. These are only the public institutions of higher learning. However, in the 1980s, there was a rapid expansion of private colleges that offer a whole host of postsecondary education, ranging from certificate to diploma and degree levels. To date, there are about two hundred postsecondary private institutions registered with the Ministry of Education (Tan, 1994) and over 175 types of programs or courses offered by these institutions, many of which are affiliated with foreign universities. This indicates that Malaysia has joined other Asian countries in expanding its higher education system to include both the public and private sectors as well as a binary system of tertiary education.

Higher Education

The term "higher education" means the various types of formal postsecondary education institutions that train middle- and high-level professional personnel in degree-, diploma-, and certificate-granting programs. Although traditionally higher education may have meant only university education, today one of the main concerns in many Asian countries is how to adapt an elitist university system to meet the increasing social demand on higher education. There are increasing pressures from rural areas, minority groups, and women for higher education to fulfill more adequately the claims of equity and social justice (Selvaratnam and Gopinathan, 1984). Most countries have responded by expanding a lower tier of higher education, which involves the establishment of polytechnics, colleges, technical institutes, and other new institutions of higher learning. Unlike the traditional universities, these new institutions are more likely to offer new curricula that include more professional programs and more technologically based learning systems. Although the main functions of higher education have remained unchanged (to train and develop human resources and to produce and disseminate knowledge), these functions are now being carried out by various types of institutions of higher learning. The diversification of higher education is not only reflected in the emergence of many private institutions but is also accompanied by various kinds of educational innovations like the open university model, distance learning, study-service schemes, twinning programs, and many others.

The higher education system in Malaysia may have originated from a few elitist public institutions that led to credentials that enable employment in the upper echelons of the occupational structure. Today higher education has diversified through the creation of the first- and second-tier institutions as well as the privatization of education. According to Altbach and Gopinathan (1982), governments find it easier to build up educational institutions to meet some of the needs of newly articulate segments of the population than to rapidly develop the economy. The expansion of higher education in Malaysia has been fueled partly by social demand and a belief in the intrinsic values of higher education. The enrollment rate at the university level remains low, around 3.0 percent, but is about 16.5 percent if other types of postsecondary education are taken into account (see table 10.1). In 1990, the total enrollments in public higher education institutions at the certificate, diploma, and degree levels were 9,180, 28,000, and 60,010, respectively (see table 10.2). The rate of increase in higher education is about 33 percent at the certificate level, 12 percent at the diploma level, and 59 percent at the degree level. These figures did not take into account the number

Table 10.1
Enrollment Rate in Government-Assisted Educational Institutions by Level of
Education, 1989

Level of Education and Age Groups		
Primary 6+ - 11+	Enrollment	2 390 920
	Population*	2 415 400
	Enrollment Rate	98.99%
Lower Secondary 12+ - 14+	Enrollment	938 518
	Population*	1 132 600
	Enrollment Rate	82.86%
Upper Secondary 15+ - 16+	Enrollment	358 608
	Population*	730 500
	Enrollment Rate	49.09%
Post Secondary & College 17+ - 18+	Enrollment	121 042
	Population*	736 800
	Enrollment Rate	16.43%
University 19+ - 24+	Enrollment	53 476
	Population*	2 007 800
	Enrollment Rate	2.66%

*Estimated.
Source: Ministry of Education (1991:table 1.2).

of students studying overseas, which is about 52,000, and the enrollment in private education, which totals about 35,600. However, it is interesting to note that Malaysia produces more degree-holders than certificate- and diploma-holders put together. This is probably due to the fact that there are great discrepancies in the wage schemes between the first- and second-tier qualifications,

Table 10.2
Enrollment in Public Higher Educational Institutions, 1985–95

	1985	1990	1995*
Certificate	6,880	9,180	18, 290
Diploma	25,050	28,000	44,230
Degree	37,840	60,010	89,680
Total	69,770	97,190	152,200

*Projected figures.
Source: Malaysia (1991:table 5.1).

thus leading to more demand for degree than for diploma or certificate qualifications.

CHANGING FUNCTIONS AND PATTERNS OF HIGHER EDUCATION

Knowledge is at the heart of higher education. Universities, polytechnics, and colleges are organized to produce and disseminate knowledge. These institutions of higher learning are charged with the responsibilities of enhancing knowledge continuously through research and teaching in various disciplines. According to Husen (1991), the primary role of higher education should be to emphasize underlying intellectual, scientific, and technological principles rather than provide narrow specialist knowledge because specific knowledge can quickly become outdated. Like in other Asian countries, the functions and patterns of higher education in Malaysia have changed in response to both global influences and internal demands. This section discusses changes that have occurred in the following aspects of higher education: stratification, governance and finance, curriculum, research, and training.

Diversification of Higher Education

The rapid expansion of higher education in Malaysia has been fueled by a strong social demand, for higher education is seen as the main avenue for social mobility and social justice. As the system of higher education expands it has also typically added new kinds of institutions, resulting in stratification within the system. At the apex are the universities, whose functions are to promote national integration and unity; to provide trained and skilled manpower; to rectify existing imbalances in educational opportunities among racial and income groups; and, through research, to study and find solutions to serious national problems (Sharom, 1985). Next come the colleges, polytechnics, and other academic institutions designed to meet specialized needs and to meet the ever increasing demand for postsecondary education.

In the past, the Malaysian government had very strict control over the establishment of new institutions of higher learning, but in recent years, it has been more liberal in allowing the "privatization" of the education sector. In the 1980s, there was phenomenal growth in private education, especially at the postsecondary level. Today, private education covers a whole range of professional, technical, and managerial courses available at various educational levels. This has come about for various reasons, which include the growing demand for higher education, the limited number of places in public institutions of higher learning, and the greatly increased cost of overseas education. Over the years, the development of private education in Malaysia has grown into an industry with huge investment from large corporations.

In 1990, there were 35,600 students enrolled in the private institutions of higher learning, out of which 14 percent were studying for a degree, 46 percent for a diploma, and 40 percent for a certificate (Malaysia, 1991). Besides, the number of students studying abroad nearly doubles this number. These figures reflect a great shortage of places in the public institutions of higher learning. Only about 4.6 percent of the college age cohort is enrolled in a public institution of higher learning (Young and Ng, 1992). This enrollment rate is relatively low when compared to other Asian countries like Singapore (12 percent), Thailand (16 percent), Japan (31 percent), and South Korea (38 percent) (World Bank, 1991).

Governance and Finance

With the expansion of higher education, public policy is expected to move toward differentiation of functions, financial support formulas, and governance mechanisms (Selvaratnam and Gopinathan, 1984). An emerging feature in the higher education system will be its diversity in terms of institutional arrangements, sources of financing, administrative structures, and student clienteles. In many countries, public institutions of higher learning find it more and more difficult to maintain complete autonomy. Instead, they are becoming more and more financially dependent and are subject to the laws of the land.

The governance of all Malaysian universities and colleges comes under a common legislative framework known as the Universities and University Colleges Act of 1971. No university is to be established except in accordance with the provision of this act. Under this act, the government has full authority over student enrollments, staff appointment, curricula, and financing. For example, no faculty or course may be introduced in any of the universities without prior consultation with the minister of education. Furthermore, the minister of education is responsible for the general policy direction of higher education in the country. The political and administrative control of the universities in Malaysia by the state is legally enshrined.

In general, the administration and academic structure of the Malaysian universities are based on the British system, with some American influences among the newer ones. The academic activities are organized and revolve among core disciplines that form the body of knowledge used in teaching and research (Selvaratnam, 1989). The authorities of the university include the court, the council, the senate, the faculties, the institutions, the boards of studies, the boards of selection, the board of student welfare, the guild of graduates, and other such bodies (Malaysia, 1971b). The vice chancellor is appointed by the university council as the principal of academics and executive officer of the university. The council is the governing body of the university and is the principal authority in that it determines broad policies of the whole university. The senate is in charge of academic matters and is made up solely of academics. The registrar takes care of academic and administrative affairs and the bursar deals with financial matters. In sum, the administration takes care of the technical aspects of the functioning of the university whereas the governance concerns itself with the policies and procedures of decision making in the academic context (Altbach, 1982). Usually, basic academic decision making is in the hands of the governance structure while the implementation of policy is the responsibility of the administration. As pointed out by Altbach (1982), the universities have emerged as major national institutions and have been given large amounts of money; governments have increasingly tried to assert their authority, not only over broad policy but often in detailed operations of the universities.

All the public institutions of higher learning are financed by the government whereas the private institutions are self-sustaining. Malaysia has always placed a high premium on education, devoting an average of 6 percent of its GNP to education compared with 3.6 percent for developed nations (Dean, 1992). The total educational expenditure came to 5,262 million ringgits under the fifth Malaysia plan (1985–90); a total sum of 7,724 million ringgits was allocated to education under the sixth Malaysia plan (1991–95). However, the total expenditure assigned to higher education remains the same, that is, a sum of 2,591 million ringgits under both these plans. This implies that there is a relative decline in the financial resources for higher education from 49 percent of the education budget to 33 percent. While the cost of higher education continues to increase, there has been a budget cut for higher education due to keen intersectoral competition for public funds. Therefore, each public institution of higher learning needs to move away from its present heavy dependence on public funds and seek alternative sources of funding.

Curricula

Universities throughout the world look to the major metropolitan institutions for leadership, and often follow the curricular and other practices of these universities (Altbach, 1982). Asian universities are no exception because academics from these countries are often trained in the metropolitan centers and bring back with them the ethos, orientations, and practices of the universities in which they have been trained. Likewise, the Western model of higher education, particularly the British model, permeated and dominated the higher education system in Malaysia especially in terms of its knowledge structure and organization, its curricula and standards, and its social functions (Selvaratnam, 1989). However, efforts have also been made to link the development of higher education to the local social, political, and economic context.

One such effort is to change the medium of instruction from English to Bahasa Malaysia throughout the whole education system. As noted by Altbach and Gopinathan (1982:33), "the university is inevitably involved in broader issues of politics, public policy and cultural contestation. The choice of the language of instruction is then a matter of great sensitivity and also of immense consequence to the university." Today, all public institutions of higher learning use the Malay language as the medium of instruction. Much effort has been made to adapt the Malay language for scientific purposes and to ensure that vocabularies are appropriate for academic and scientific instruction. Many resources have been channeled to the translation of foreign textbooks into Bahasa Malaysia, and the writing and publication of Malay textbooks at all levels of education, under the auspices of Dewan Bahasa dan Pustaka (Language and Literature Agency). Although progress has been slow and despite the high cost and problems encountered, Malaysia has committed to the use of an indigenous language for undergraduate instruction. However, for advanced studies and research, English remains a necessity and there has been great concern that the standard of English has deteriorated over the years.

Another feature of the Malaysian university system is that the development of courses is well coordinated so that there is no duplication of courses of study in the different universities unless there are convincing reasons that this is necessary. The Ministry of Education, through the Committee of Vice Chancellors, which is chaired by the minister of education, tries to ensure that this principle is adhered to by requiring that any new courses of study are to receive its authorization (Sharom, 1980). For example, programs like agriculture, architecture, law, dentistry, pharmacy, housing, building, and planning are offered in only one of the universities. Furthermore, efforts have been made to offer indigenous curricula like Malay literature and Islamic studies. A certain amount of internationalization has also occurred with the establishment of the International Islamic University, which uses Arabic and English as the mediums of instruction. The purpose of this university is to strengthen cooperation and friendship among Islamic countries by providing facilities for Islamic studies

Table 10.3
Comparison between Off-Campus and On-Campus Programs in Universiti Sains Malaysia, Penang

Programme	Average cost per student	Number of students (1990)
Off-campus	RM 1,404*	2,847
On-campus	RM 12,087	8,303

*This figure is computed from the annual recurrent expenditure for the Centre of Off-Campus Studies, which is about 3.14 percent of the university budget. This does *not* include the cost of many human resources and physical facilities that are shared by both on-campus and off-campus students.

and training skilled manpower on the basis of Islamic principles. In line with the worldwide Islamic movement, the stress is on the philosophical assumptions and beliefs of Islam concerning knowledge, which is basically an attempt to break away from the dominance of Western knowledge (Selvaratnam, 1989). This university opens its door to many foreign students and academic staff from other Islamic countries.

Although in the past the university curricula may have followed the British model, the trend now is toward adopting many aspects of American higher education. The academic year in each Malaysian university is divided into two semesters instead of three terms. Both the "unit/credit" system and continual assessment throughout the course have been implemented in most of the universities. Some of the universities have schools instead of faculties, and many of the programs are multidisciplinary in approach. The minimum number of years for a first degree is four years, not three years. At the postgraduate level, various master's programs like master's of business administration (MBA) are taught by coursework. It can be said the university education in Malaysia is a hybrid British and American model.

There are also some innovative programs in the Malaysian higher education system. One is the off-campus program in the Universiti Sains Malaysia, Penang, which was first established in 1971 with the aim of providing an opportunity for working adults to have a university education through distance learning (Wong and Lee, 1992). Here distance education is used to expand opportunity to receive higher education because it is cost-effective. A comparison of the annual recurrent expenditure of the off-campus program with that of the on-campus program shows that for a small extra cost of RM 1,404 per student, the university was able to expand its academic education to an additional 3,000 students approximately (see table 10.3). Another innovation is the twinning programs that are found in many private colleges. In Malaysia, the Higher Edu-

Table 10.4
Enrollment at Degree Level in Local Universities, 1985–95

	1985	1990	1995
Arts	20,350 (54%)	34,660 (58%)	51,410* (57%)
Science	12,330 (33%)	16,450 (27%)	24,210* (27%)
Technical	5,160 (14%)	8,920 (15%)	14,050* (16%)
Total	37,840	60,030	89,670*

*Projected figures.
Source: Malaysia (1991).

cation Act does not allow private institutions to confer degrees, restricting them to diploma courses and degrees conferred by foreign universities through the twinning program (Kamal, 1992). As such, there is no choice but for many private colleges to twin with overseas institutions in the United States, the United Kingdom, Australia, Canada, New Zealand, and other countries to offer various types of degree courses and professional qualifications.[7]

Research and Training

The traditional roles of the university are training and research. However, these two academic functions are often in conflict in the Third World context (Altbach, 1982). Most universities expect their academic staff to be involved in research, but in the Third World there is often a lack of time, facilities, or infrastructure. The emphasis on teaching tends to be greater in developing countries because of expanding enrollment and shortage of academic staff, and these heavy teaching loads sometimes interfere with the commitment to research. In this section, we examine how the Malaysian universities attempt to fulfill these two functions.

In terms of training, the dual aim of the university is to produce liberally educated ''all-rounders'' who could serve the growing public sector, private sector, and teaching profession, and to produce a core of professionals with a rigorous and specialized training in medicine, dentistry, engineering, accountancy, and so forth to meet the growing needs of the country (Selvaratnam, 1989). The enrollment at degree level in the Malaysian universities according to their fields of study is shown in table 10.4. Like in many other Asian countries, the proportion of students enrolled in the arts are higher than in the sciences. The

Table 10.5
Female Graduates in Local Universities, 1991

Level of Studies	F	T	%
Non-degree program	15	30	50.0
Certificate	29	101	28.7
Diploma & Integrated	558	2,161	27.2
First Degree	4,845	10,188	47.5
Post-Graduate Diploma	1,016	1,667	60.9
Masters	130	375	34.6
Doctor of Philosophy (Ph.D.)	18	48	37.6
Total	6,611	14 570	45.0

Source: Adapted from Malaysia (1993:table 11).

move now is to produce more scientific and technologically skilled manpower to meet the needs of a rapidly industrializing economy. However, this is not going to be an easy task because a recent study shows that there has been a decline of the ratio of science to nonscience students at the secondary level (Sharifah and Lewin, 1993). Part of the reason may be due to the pull of the labor market, where accountants and business administrators get higher pay than scientists and engineers.

Overall participation in higher education according to gender is quite even. The number of female graduates in Malaysian universities is slightly less than male graduates (about 45 percent; see table 10.5). Among the level of studies, it is interesting to note that the percentage of females at the postgraduate diploma level (60.9 percent) exceeds that of male graduates. This is not surprising because the majority of the students at this level are being trained to be graduate teachers by the diploma of education programs, and most of them are women. If we look at the breakdown according to field of study, the number of female students with technology majors is still comparatively low (see table 10.6).

The Malaysian universities have a relatively low rate of research productivity (Jasbir, 1989; Cheong, 1989; Haris, 1985). This is a common problem among Third World universities, which simply do not have the resources for advanced scientific research in most fields. According to Altbach (1982:52), "the development of research capacity is a manifold problem related to indigenous Third World personnel and financial resources, the rapid growth and increased cost of research in the industrialized countries, and the difficulty of developing indigenous models in a world dominated by Western thought and orientation." The subculture of research and scholarship has been slow to develop in the Third World, for academic traditions are not only foreign but are fairly new too.

In the Malaysian case, the universities have been faced with considerable

Table 10.6
Undergraduate Female Students with Science and Technology Majors in Local
Universities, 1992

University	Science			Technology		
	F	T	%	F	T	%
Universiti Malaya	1597	3203	49.9	96	804	11.9
Universiti Pertanian Malaysia	1406	3071	45.8	57	528	10.8
Universiti Kebangsaan Malaysia	1164	2490	46.7	45	380	11.8
Universiti Sains Malaysia	1571	3602[1]	43.6	152	340[3]	44.7
Universiti Teknologi Malaysia	380	1829	20.8	1570	7882	20.0
Universiti Utara Malaysia	-	-	-	-	510	0.0
Institute Teknologi MARA[2]	1837	3740	49.1	1117	4038	27.7

Source: Universiti Sains Malaysia (1994).

challenges regarding rapidly increasing enrollments, rapid expansion in the number of institutions, and the change in the medium of instruction from English to Bahasa Malaysia. These pressures have placed great strains on the universities and have probably been responsible for the relatively low rate of research productivity (Altbach, 1989). The inability of Malaysian universities to produce research has led to the proliferation of scientific research institutes set up by the government to study specific problems relating to national development. In Malaysia, the key to its economic success has been its efforts to diversify and upgrade the quality of its agricultural products like rubber, palm oil, cocoa, pineapples, coconuts, and forest products. Thus, the earlier research institutes were established to support the growth and development of the primary commodities and natural resources (see table 10.7). Later, other institutes that deal with nuclear energy, industrial research, and microelectronics were added to the list together with think-tanks like the Institute of Strategic and International Studies and Malaysia Institute of Economic Research. These research institutes are well funded by taxpayers' money, and they are expected to do the bulk of research and development work since they are allocated about 50 percent of the government research fund while the universities are allocated a mere 22 percent (Jasbir, 1989). Through default, the Malaysian universities have to compete with other public research institutes for funding and personnel if they are to maintain their role as "knowledge production" centers instead of being relegated to the status of mere teaching and training institutions.

The seeming reluctance of local academics to get involved in research is basically due to the weak research environment that prevails in Malaysia. A study on the research productivity among the Universiti Pertanian Malaysia academic staff shows that they spent about 30 percent of their time on research and, among the active researchers, they produced on average only one article per annum (Haris, 1985). Most of the staff ranked research as second priority

Table 10.7
Major R&D Institutes

Institution	Year of Establishment	Ministry	Status
Institute of Medical Research (IMR)	1901	Health	Statutory
Rubber Research Institute (RRI)	1925	Primary Industry	Statutory
Forest Research Institute	1929	Primary Industry	Statutory
Veterinary Research Institute (VRI)	1948	Agriculture	Departmental
Mines Research Institute	1951	Primary Industries	Departmental
Malaysian Agriculture Research and Development Institute (MARDI)	1969	Agriculture	Statutory
Fisheries Research Institute	1972	Agriculture	Departmental
Nuclear Energy Unit	1972	Prime Minister's Department	Departmental
Standards and Industrial Research Institute of Malaysia (SIRIM)	1975	Science and Technology and Environment	Statutory
Palm Oil Research Institute of Malaysia (PORIM)	1979	Primary Industry	Statutory
Malaysian Institute of Microelectronic System (MIMOS)	1984	Prime Minister's Department	Departmental
Institute of Strategic and International Studies (ISIS)	1983		
Malaysian Institute of Economic Research (MIER)	1986		

Source: Adapted from Jasbir (1989:table 3.1).

behind teaching. Many reasons were given for this poor performance, including lack of time, finances, training, equipment, research assistants, motive, and leadership from senior academics. As observed by Cheong (1989), there appears to be much research capability among the academic staff, but due to a lack of leadership in research and a lack of effort to organize and mobilize people, the Botany Department in Universiti Malaya has yet to utilize the expertise of its academic staff. The lack of academic leadership in many departments and faculties is partly due to the government policy of greater Bumiputra's representation, especially in key administrative positions in the universities (Jasbir, 1989). Such a practice has not always resulted in the appointment of senior scholars and experienced scientists to these key posts. For those who have moved early in their careers into administrative positions, research activity often receives low priority. Therefore, they are not able to provide strong research direction for their departments or schools because they do not have much time to consolidate their own research capabilities. Furthermore, those who have the expertise but are outside the power structure were reluctant to provide this kind of leadership.

The lack of motivation to do research can be contributed to several factors. First, there are no formal regulations in the university system to specify that research, unlike teaching, is compulsory for all and that appointments of tenured staff can be terminated if found inactive in research (Cheong, 1989). The majority of the academicians believe that research and publications make little difference to their promotion. Second, because of the small scientific community, very often researchers work individually in a lonely enterprise lacking stimuli from and interactions with colleagues who are studying the same problems. Linkages with industry are weak. Research funding is scarce and difficult to obtain, especially from outside funding agencies. In brief, the academic staff's commitment to research is at best weak and the research environment is far from satisfactory.

Another feature of Malaysian research is that most is commissioned by various government agencies, statutory bodies, and private companies (Haris, 1985). This kind of research does have its advantages and disadvantages. On the positive side, the research may be relevant to the client's social or national needs. It also brings in financial rewards to both the researchers and universities concerned. In some cases, it involves access to information that would otherwise be unavailable to academics. However, there are many negative effects too. This kind of research tends to act as a strong disincentive for universities to act as independent critics and commentators in society. Academics may be tempted to do little or no independent research, which means many other important issues will be unresearched. Moreover, research quality is likely to fall because most commissioned research remains unpublished and thus cannot be reviewed and evaluated by peers. Therefore, not only the research environment in Malaysia is weak, but the kinds of research that are being carried out need to be diversified.

RESPONSES TO INTERNAL DEMANDS

Equity Issues

Access to higher education is a very salient equity issue as higher education is often perceived as an avenue for social mobility. The Malaysian government views access to higher education as a means of restructuring the society to eliminate the identification of ethnic community with economic functions. This has been one of the primary objectives of the New Economic Policy implemented in 1970, which involves providing more educational opportunities to the Bumiputras so that there will be greater Bumiputra representation in the various professions and occupations in the modern sector. To achieve this objective, the government implemented the racial quota system whereby the ethnic composition of the student population in the universities as a whole and in each of its faculties should reflect the ethnic composition of the country. Under the amendment of the Universities and University College Act of 1971 in 1975, the universities and other public tertiary institutions were required to admit more Bumiputra students so as to redress the economic imbalances between the Bumiputras and non-Bumiputras. To administer this policy effectively, the government established the Central University Admission Unit (Unit Pusat Universiti) whereby the selection and admission into the country's universities were tightly controlled and based on racial quota. The implementation of this policy has eroded one of the deeply entrenched university traditions, that is, the admission of students based on merit (Selvaratnam, 1989).

To ensure that poor Bumiputras, especially those in the rural areas, can gain access to higher education, they were given special assistance in terms of secondary and preuniversity education and financial aid. There are 16 residential science schools, with a total enrollment of 17,000 Malay students in 1987, and 11 MARA (Majlis Amanah Rakyat Asli) junior science colleges that provide special secondary science education to Bumiputra students. In addition, each of the universities runs preuniversity, matriculation, premedical, prescience, and preengineering programs for rural Bumiputra students (Selvaratnam, 1988). These moves were aimed at improving the supply of suitable Bumiputra candidates to be admitted to science-based courses at the tertiary level. Furthermore, more than 80 percent of all the government scholarships and bursaries were given to Bumiputras. In 1982–83, a total of 20,526 students or 66.7 percent of the aggregrate enrollment of 30,844 students in five selected universities were on government scholarships. In addition, there were 12,800 Malaysian students overseas, sponsored by the government, pursuing higher education (Mehmet and Yip, 1985). These government scholarships are aimed at creating and nurturing a class of Bumiputra professionals, commercial entrepreneurs, and industrial entrepreneurs so that they can participate actively in the rapidly industrializing economy.

This policy has been extremely successful in increasing the Bumiputras' participation in tertiary education. Table 10.8 shows that the proportion of Bumiputra students enrolled in the universities increased from 28.8 percent in 1966–67 to 63.0 percent in 1985. It is interesting to note that over 90 percent of the students studying at the diploma level are Bumiputra students (see table 10.9). This has come about because the MARA Institute of Technology, which has an enrollment of 23,165, consists of mainly Bumiputra students. The quota system

Table 10.8
Ethnic Enrollment Figures At Universities, 1966–67 and 1985

	Bumiputras	Chinese	Indian & Others	Total
Universiti Malaya* (1966/67)	1,038	2,034	531	3,603
	(28.8%)	(56.5%)	(14.7%)	(100%)
All universities (1985)	23,841	11,241	2,756	37,838
	(63.0%)	(29.7%)	(7.2%)	(100%)

*The only university then.
Source: Karthigesu (1986:table 1).

may have succeeded in aligning the overall enrollment at the tertiary level with the racial composition of the country, but this policy has also had many other unforeseen consequences.

This preferential treatment policy in favor of the Bumiputras has led to the emergence of an even more polarized society instead of promoting national harmony. Because of the quota system and the limited number of places in public institutions of higher learning, many non-Bumiputra students who are just as qualified are denied places locally and are forced to go overseas at their own expense or to seek further education in the private colleges. The 1985 figures showed that out of a total of 22,684 students studying overseas, 73.4 percent of them were non-Bumiputras (Malaysia, 1989). Locally, most of the students in the private colleges are non-Bumiputra students who have failed to gain admission in the public institutions of higher learning or who were offered places but not in courses of their choice (Young and Ng, 1992). The Tunku Abdul Rahman (TAR) College has about 5,000 students, mainly non-Bumiputras. Racial polarization is bound to rear its ugly head when different ethnic groups seek their higher education at different institutions. Thus, this politically motivated policy has resulted in a polarization of races.

Apparently, the admission of large numbers of Bumiputras into the institutions of higher learning implies that many of them gain entry not entirely on merit but on socioeconomic grounds (Karthigesu, 1986). Currently, students are admitted to the universities based on two kinds of selective examinations. One is the higher school certificate examination (Sijil Tinggi Pelajaran Menengah, STPM), which is set by the Malaysian Examination Syndicate and taken by all the students in the national school system; the other is sometimes known as the matriculation examination, set by each of the universities for their own pre-university classes. Most of the students registered in these matriculation classes are Bumiputra students. Unfortunately, there is great discrepancy in the quality of students that are admitted to the universities based on these two kinds of

Table 10.9
Participation by Ethnic Group in Local Tertiary Public Institutions, 1988

Level of Education	Enrollment	Bumiputra %	Chinese %	Indian %	Others %
Post-secondary	53,578	54.3	39.5	5.4	0.8
Certificate	7,043	70.2	25.3	3.7	0.8
Diploma	26,225	92.8	6.4	0.5	0.3
Degree*	48,539	61.8	31.1	6.6	0.5

*Includes enrollment in postgraduate courses.
Source: Adapted from Malaysia (1989:table 13.2).

examinations. This discrepancy is further reflected in the results at the end of their degree programs in the universities. A study by Karthigesu (1986) shows that the percentage of Bumiputra students obtaining the higher classes of degrees is comparatively less than non-Bumiputra students no matter if it is an arts degree, science degree, or professional degree. This goes to show that in giving greater attention to equity issues in educational and occupational opportunities, the quality of skilled manpower produced at the local universities has been neglected (Jasbir, 1989).

This positive discrimination policy not only generates interethnic conflict and tension, but also results in greater intraethnic inequalities. An empirical study by Mehmet and Yip (1985) shows that the Malaysian scholarship policy fails badly because it discriminates in favor of the richer and more powerful households, which is contrary to the original objectives of the New Economic Policy. Their findings show that the intra-Malay inequality of opportunity in higher education is significant. For every one chance that the poor Malay household has for being awarded a scholarship, the rich Bumiputra household has twenty-one chances. They concluded that scholarships are regressively distributed, favoring the richer households, and this is true for all ethnic groups. This has come about because the criteria used for awarding these scholarships are based on race and merits, and usually children from well-to-do families perform better academically than those from poor families. Consequently, the scholarship policy has contributed to reproducing and maintaining the socioeconomic status of the upper strata of the Malay community rather than helping the social mobility of the poor Malays (Selvaratnam, 1988). Another disturbing trend is that Bumiputras with good academic results are invariably sent overseas, leaving those with lesser qualifications to enter local universities. Furthermore, the more affluent non-Bumiputras who can afford the high fees charged by foreign universities prefer to study overseas. This, in turn, creates two groups of Malaysian graduates: one group from local universities who are more rural and comfortable with Malay and one group of overseas graduates who are more urban and comfortable with English (Dean, 1993). This "dualism" can be threatening to the government's effort to build a united Malaysian society.

External Efficiency

The external efficiency of the higher education system is determined by the labor market outlook. It is important that the training and research programs in these institutions of higher learning match the evolving demands of the economy. Both structural adjustment and technical changes have an impact on the level, type, and spatial location of occupations available to higher education graduates (Salmi, 1991). A good indicator of external efficiency of the higher education system is to examine the match between graduates and occupations. Many developing countries have used manpower planning techniques to estimate future occupations and training needs and to plan their higher education outputs accordingly. Unfortunately, these techniques are usually flawed from both methodological and theoretical standpoints. The failure of manpower planning often results in massive graduate unemployment or underemployment.

The external efficiency of the Malaysian higher education system is problematic as reflected by a certain amount of mismatch between graduates and jobs. A study on higher education and employment recorded a fair degree of mismatch between high-level scientific manpower and the needs of the labor market (Fatimah et al., 1985). In the case of science graduates, only 28.9 percent worked in science-related jobs while the rest worked in administrative and managerial jobs as well as in banking, business, or commercial enterprise. A smaller study by Cheong (1989) also shows that 23 percent of the botany graduates were involved in work that did not fully utilize their knowledge and competence in botany. These findings lend support to the "credentialing" function of universities whereby graduates are ensured entry into high-paying jobs by virtue of their qualifications.

The scholarship policy also generated a mismatch in the high-level manpower market (Mehmet and Yip, 1985). The government scholarships are not geared to the development of the professional, but rather to the production of the generalist. Graduates in the professional fields represented only 23.3 percent of the total. There is a serious lack of coordination between manpower planning and economic planning. As a result, there is a surplus of generalist graduates and an acute shortage of scientific and professional graduates. This problem is further exacerbated by an imbalance in the higher education system where graduates at the diploma level, who are greatly needed for subprofessional employment, are *fewer* than graduates with degrees (see table 10.2).

Brain Drain

Academicians enjoy a relatively high social status in the Malaysian society but this is not reflected in the salaries they earn. Faculty members are paid and treated like any other civil servants. The recently implemented New Remuneration Scheme may have offered a better deal to senior faculty members but it is not attractive to junior members. Thus, the public institutions of higher learning are encountering the problem of recruiting new lecturers despite the fact that nearly all the universities have their own academic training schemes for Bumiputras that provide special opportunities to selected Bumiputra graduates to undertake overseas postgraduate studies leading to higher degrees so that they can return to serve the universities.

Not only do the institutions of higher learning have to compete with the private sector for new graduates; they are also losing many of their experienced academic staff to private firms who can offer much higher salaries. In trying to explain why academicians left the universities, Khairuddin (1993) remarks: "universities—the bastion of the abstract and the pragmatic, was just not nimble enough to keep up with competition. Short of being sanctified with saintly virtues, who indeed could compete with conspicuous consumption, ostentatious display of wealth and with social values for instant gratification?" It has been reported that since 1985, a total of six hundred lecturers have left to join the private sector (*New Straits Times*, September 22, 1993). The problem of brain drain is so acute that Universiti Utara Malaysia (UUM) has cited the shortage of academic staff as the reason for decreasing its intake of new students. This exodus of academic staff into the commercial and industrial sectors and the inability of the universities to attract new graduates into academic positions will be a major constraint on the expansion of higher education in Malaysia.

This problem is further compounded by the shortfall of female participation in academia. The 1994 figures show that the percentage of female lecturers in the local universities ranges from 20.8 percent (International Islamic University) to 38.8 percent (University of Malaya). The percentage of women academicians obtaining promotion from lecturer to associate professor also decreases significantly from their overall representation in the academic staff (Universiti Sains Malaysia, 1994).

Student Activism

Student activism can be said to be nonexistent in Malaysia. Five years ago when tuition fees more than doubled, there was no protest from the students. This definitely was not the case during the heyday of student activism during the late 1960s and early 1970s. In those years, students took to the streets to protest against government economic and educational policies. The Malaysian government has resorted to legislation to curb the power of student unions from involving themselves in what the government terms political activities. Under the Universities and University Colleges Act of 1971, no student or faculty can be involved in any political activities or affiliated with any political party or trade union. Under this law, every student organization has to inform the university authorities of their activities. The tight control of student activities in the universities has reduced the campus to a high school, where activities like scouting, Red Crescent, St. John's Ambulance, and other such mild activities are encouraged, and where even the students' dress is governed by the "dress code" of the university. The government's attempt to gag both the dons and students from being key participants in shaping public discourse has resulted in a very passive and subdued campus population. If one of the functions of higher education is to produce future leaders for the country, then students should be allowed to organize and participate in social and political activities that would enhance their personal development.

FUTURE DEVELOPMENTS

Malaysia will continue to develop its higher education system by improving its quality, increasing its efficiency, and achieving greater equality. Currently, there is a public discourse on how to review the Universities and University Colleges Act of 1971 so that a more independent governance structure can be established. Academicians have been calling for the adoption of a university charter whereby universities would be run by a council of higher education instead of by the Ministry of Education. The shift will be from a "state control" model to a "state supervisory" model (World Bank, 1993). It is hoped that the state will change its dominant role in the provision and financing of institutions to a less interventionist role whereby it supervises and monitors the development of higher education. Its main responsibilities would be to provide a conducive environment establishing the broad parameters to guide public and private higher education institutions and to offer incentives to meet national training and research needs.

The share of education in public spending has already become very large and it is increasingly difficult to compete for additional resources. Malaysia devotes as much as one-fifth of its national budget to education, and much of this goes to higher education. However, with the continual expansion and increasing costs of higher education, Malaysia will have to formulate policies geared toward greater cost recovery. The latest move in this direction is the idea of "corporatization" of the local universities. Each local university has been directed by the Ministry of Education to conduct its own feasibility study on how it can be "corporatized" (*The Star*, 1995). The objectives of corporatization are to increase the efficiency of management and reduce the government's financial burden in funding the universities. Policy alternatives like increased university fees, graduate tax, selective pricing, and setting up endowment and salary structures for each university may be introduced in due course. Student loans may replace scholarships.

Furthermore, the government may stop sponsoring students to study overseas at the undergraduate level so as to reduce the outflow of foreign exchange. The private sector is to play a more active part in the provision of higher education so that there will be increased access to higher education within the country. Currently, the government is amending the Universities and University Colleges Act of 1971 so that foreign universities can set up branch campuses in Malaysia. The government's move to liberalize its tight control over the provision of education is aimed at making Malaysia the regional center of higher education. In line with this move, the Immigration Department has come up with new rulings to make it easier for foreign students to come to study in Malaysia. There are about 3,600 foreign students studying in Malaysia now, and this figure is expected to increase when foreign universities begin to set up branch campuses in various parts of the country (*The Star*, 1995).

The 1961 Education Act will also have to be reviewed so that English can be used as the medium of instruction in these private institutions of higher learning. With increased globalization of the economy, the Malaysian government realizes the importance of English as an international language for trade and the transfer of knowledge. Lately, there has been a move to arrest the decline of English in the education system. At the tertiary level, local universities are encouraged to adopt a bilingual policy. For example, every undergraduate in the University of Science Malaysia has to take a certain number of English courses, and faculty members are encouraged to use both Bahasa Malaysia and English in their instruction.

Tertiary education in Malaysia will be rapidly expanded in the coming years. The government is taking steps to make tertiary education available to three out of every ten students by the year 2000 (*The Star*, 1995). The current undergraduate ratio of one out of every ten (for 19–24-year-old age cohort) is very low when compared to other Asian countries. To meet this target, every existing local university will increase its student population to twenty thousand by the year 2000. At the undergraduate level, there will be a move to increase the number of certificate- and diploma-holders so that there are enough blue-collar workers to support the rapidly industrializing economy. Another five new polytechnics are going to be built under the current development plan. Furthermore, another two new universities are going to be built under the seventh Malaysia plan (1995–2000). One of the two proposed universities would be an open university, and existing universities would also expand their distance learning programs so that more students can have access to higher education at a lower cost.

To improve the research productivity of the country, there is an urgent need to expand the postgraduate programs. In 1990, the number of postgraduate students was 3,500, and this number is expected to increase by 70 percent to about 6,000 by 1995 (Malaysia, 1991). Under the sixth Malaysia plan (1990–95), a sum of 6 million ringgits has been allocated to research and development. A strong commitment to graduate training and research will help build up an academic system that will serve both national needs and the international scientific community. In short, Malaysia will continue to expand its higher education system, widen its access, and improve its quality and efficiency in accordance with the changing needs of the Malaysian society and the global environment.

NOTES

1. The Federation of Malaya gained its independence in 1957 and formed Malaysia with Sabah, Sarawak, and Singapore in 1963. But Singapore seceded in 1965 to become an independent republic.

2. Other indigenous people include the Orang Asli in Peninsular Malaysia; the Kadazans, Muruts, Bajaus, and other tribes in Sabah; and the Dayaks, Ibans, Penans, and others in Sarawak.

3. Bahasa Malaysia is the official name for the Malay language.

4. Bumiputra means "native of the soil." This term is used to mean the Malays and other indigenous tribes such as the Kadazans and Dayaks. The Bumiputras enjoy the "special privileges" as enshrined in the Malaysian Constitution (see Article 152 of the 1957 Malaysian Constitution).

5. See Ahmad (1972) and Selvaratnam (1986) for a more detailed description of the historical development of the University of Malaya in Kuala Lumpur.

6. MARA stands for Majlis Amanah Rakyat Asli, which means the Council of Trust for Indigenous People.

7. See Lee (1994) for more detailed descriptions of these twinning programs.

REFERENCES

Ahmad Ibrahim. 1972. "Higher Education in Malaysia." *Bulletin of the UNESCO Regional Office for Education in Asia*. Bangkok: UNESCO.

Altbach, Philip G. 1982. *Higher Education in the Third World: Themes and Variations.* Singapore: Maruzen Asia.

———. 1989. "Higher Education and Scientific Development: The Promise of Newly Industrialized Countries." In Philip G. Altbach et al., eds., *Scientific Development and Higher Education: The Case of Newly Industrializing Nations.* New York: Praeger.

Altbach, Philip G., and S. Gopinathan. 1982. "The Dilemma of Success: Higher Education in Advanced Developing Countries." In Philip G. Altbach, ed., *Higher Education in the Third World: Themes and Variations.* Singapore: Maruzen Asia.

Cheong Siew Yoong. 1989. "Research and Productivity in the Malaysian University: A Case Study of the Department of Botany, University of Malaya." In Philip G. Altbach et al., eds., *Scientific Development and Higher Education: The Case of Newly Industrializing Nations.* New York: Praeger.

Dean, A. R. 1992. "A High Premium on Education." *New Straits Times*, August 31.

———. 1993. "The Challenges Facing Malaysian Universities." *New Straits Times*, August 31.

Fatimah Hamid Don, Jasbir Sarjit Singh, Mogana Dhamotharan, and Moses Samuel. 1985. *Higher Education and Employment in Malaysia: The Experiences of Graduates.* Kuala Lumpur: Institute of Advanced Studies, University of Malaya.

Federation of Malaya. 1957. *Federal Constitution.* Kuala Lumpur: Government Printer.

Haris, G. T. 1985. "Constraints on Research in Malaysian Universities." *Southeast Asian Journal of Social Science, 13* (2), 80–92.

Husen, Torsten. 1991. "The Idea of the University: Changing Roles, Current Crisis, and Future Challenges." *Prospects, 21* (2), 171–88.

Jasbir Sarjit Singh. 1989. "Scientific Personnel, Research Environment, and Higher Education in Malaysia." In Philip G. Altbach et al., eds., *Scientific Development and Higher Education: The Case of Newly Industrializing Nations*. New York: Praeger.

Kamal Salih. 1992. "Economic Growth and Education Reform: Some Fundamental Issues of Education Policy." Paper presented at the seminar on "Educational Restructuring and Economic Growth: Role of the Private Sector," organized by Malaysian Institute of Economic Research, November 3–4, Kuala Lumpur, Malaysia.

Karthigesu, R. 1986. "Distribution of Opportunities in Tertiary Education in Malaysia: A Review of the Fifth Malaysia Plan." *Pendidik dan Pendidikan, 8*, 34–47.

Khairuddin Yusof. 1993. "Rise and Fall of the Academician." *New Straits Times*, July 16.

Lee, Molly N. N. 1994. "Private Education in Malaysia: Social Implications." *Education Journal, 21* (2), 22 (1), 157–67.

Malaysia. 1971a. *Second Malaysia Plan: 1971–1975*. Kuala Lumpur: Government Printer.

———. 1971b. *Universities and University Colleges Act, 1971*. Kuala Lumpur: Government Printer.

———. 1989. *Mid-Term Review of the Fifth Malaysia Plan, 1986–1990*. Kuala Lumpur: Government Printer.

———. 1991. *Rancangan Malaysia Ke-enam: 1991–1995*. Kuala Lumpur: Government Printer.

Malaysia, Ministry of Education. 1991. *Education Statistics of Malaysia, 1989*. Kuala Lumpur: Dewan Bahasa dan Pustaka.

———. 1993. *Education Statistics of Malaysia, 1991*. Kuala Lumpur: Dewan Bahasa dan Pustaka.

Malaysia, Ministry of Finance. 1986. *Economic Report, 1986/87*. Kuala Lumpur: National Printing Department.

Mehmet, Ozay, and Yip Yat Hoong. 1985. "An Empirical Evaluation of Government Scholarship Policy in Malaysia." *Higher Education, 14*, 197–210.

Meyer, John W. 1980. "The World Polity and the Authority of the Nation-State." In A. Bergesen, ed., *Studies of the Modern World-System*. New York: Academic.

Salmi, Jamil. 1991. "The Higher Education Crisis in Developing Countries." Background Series. No. PHREE/91/37. Washington, D.C.: World Bank.

Selvaratnam, V. 1986. "Dependency, Change and Continuity in a Western University Model: The Malaysian Case." *Southeast Asian Journal of Social Science, 14* (2), 29–51.

———. 1988. "Ethnicity, Inequality, and Higher Education in Malaysia." *Comparative Education Review, 32* (2), 173–96.

———. 1989. "Change Amidst Continuity: University Development in Malaysia." In Philip G. Altbach and V. Selvaratnam, eds., *From Dependence to Autonomy: The Development of Asian Universities*. Dordrecht: Kluwer Academic.

Selvaratnam, V., and S. Gopinathan. 1984. "Higher Education in ASEAN Towards the Year 2000." *Higher Education, 13*, 67–83.

Sharifah Maimunah bt Syed Zin, and Keith M. Lewin, eds. 1993. *Insights into Science Education: Planning and Policy Priorities in Malaysia*. Paris: IIEP (International Institute for Educational Planning).

Sharom Ahmat. 1980. "Nation Building and the Universities in Developing Countries: The Case of Malaysia." *Higher Education, 9*, 721–41.

———. 1985. "The Relevance of the American Higher Education Model for Malaysia." In Philip G. Altbach, ed., *An Asean-American Dialogue: The Relevance of American Higher Education to Southeast Asia*. Singapore: RIHED (Regional Institute of Higher Education Development).

Tan Mui Hong. 1994. *Education Guide Malaysia*. Kuala Lumpur: Challenger Concept.

The Star. 1995. February 9, March 1.

Universiti Sains Malaysia. 1994. *Malaysia: Fact Sheets*. Penang: Woman and Human Resources Studies Unit, School of Social Sciences.

Van Den Bor, Wout, and James C. M. Shute. 1991. "Higher Education in the Third World: Status Symbol or Instrument for Development?" *Higher Education, 22*, 1–15.

Wang, Gungwu. 1970. "Malaysia: Contending Elites." In Wang Gungwu, ed., *Community and Nation: Essays on Southeast Asia and The Chinese*. Kuala Lumpur: Heinemann Educational Books (Asia).

Wong, Suk-Ying, and Molly N. N. Lee. 1992. "Bridging the Formal and Non-Formal Mode: A Comparative Study of Distance Higher Education in Asia." Paper presented at the VIIIth World Congress of Comparative Education, July 8–14, Prague, Czechoslovakia.

World Bank. 1991. *World Development Report*. New York: Oxford University Press.

———. 1993. *Policy Options for Higher Education Reform*. Washington, D.C.: Author.

Young, Mei Ling, and Ng Siew Kiat. 1992. "Balancing the Roles of Public and Private Sectors in Education and Training." Paper presented at the seminar on "Educational Restructuring and Economic Growth: Role of the Private Sector," organized by the Malaysian Institute of Economic Research, November 3–4, Kuala Lumpur, Malaysia.

11

MONGOLIA

John C. Weidman,
Regesuriin Bat-Erdene,
Ochir Gerel, and D. Badarch

Mongolia is a landlocked country of 2.4 million inhabitants living in an area of
1.6 million square kilometers. The country is sandwiched between Russia and
China, each of which also has a Mongolian population (0.5 million and 3.5
million, respectively). Among the 20 different ethnic groups living in Mongolia,
the largest is the Halh (more than 75 percent), followed by the Kazakh (5.3
percent), the Dorvod (2.8 percent), and the Bayad (1.9 percent). In 1989, more
than 40 percent of the population was under the age of 14 (*Mongolia Human
Resource Development and Education Reform Project: Sector Review*, 1993: 1–
12 and table 1–4). About 25 percent of the population resides in the capital city
of Ulaanbaatar, 25 percent resides in other urban areas, and a large segment of
the remainder is nomadic.

Its estimated 1992 per capita GNP of U.S.$299 places Mongolia among the
poorest countries in the world. GDP in 1992 was distributed as follows: 34.5
percent agriculture, 41.7 percent industry, and 23.8 percent services (ibid.: table
1–5). Real GDP growth was about 2 percent in 1994, the first year since 1989
that there had been positive economic growth. In 1994, over 20 percent of the
population was living below the official poverty level (Asian Development
Bank, 1995:87).

The People's Government of Mongolia was declared in 1921 under a single-
party government that held power until 1990. The Mongolian People's Republic
was established in 1924 as the world's second communist country. Mongolia
maintained close political and economic ties with the Soviet Union, but was
never one of its constituent republics. At the peak of this relationship, almost a
third of Mongolia's GDP was provided by the Soviet Union. This included
significant support (e.g., books, equipment, training of academics and researchers) for Mongolian higher education. Following the fall of the Soviet Union in

1991, the external financial support evaporated and a new, democratic political structure was established to guide the country's transition to a democratic government and a market economy.

The period since 1990 has been one of rapid political, economic, and social change. Bat-Erdene, Costa, and Yeager (1996) summarize the changes in each of these areas as follows:

Political Transitions

From:

- strong ideological monitoring
- single-party rule
- ultimate authority held by party
- symbolic Parliament
- isolation
- centralization
- limitation of human rights

To:

- tolerance of pluralism
- multiparty democracy
- Constitution-based authority
- working Parliament
- open-door policy
- decentralization
- freedom of human rights

Economic Transitions

From:

- centrally planned (command) economy
- government controls on prices of goods and services
- turnover taxes and profit taxes on state enterprises and cooperatives
- state ownership of all property

To:

- market-oriented economy
- liberalization of pricing
- taxation reform (personal income and private enterprises)
- private ownership of property

Social Transitions

From:

- "classless" society, social equity, collective well-being
- socialist/communist ideal
- communist model of collective responsibility
- government-provided health care and social "safety net"

To:

- class based on personal achievement, capitalism, individual well-being
- personal value system/worldview
- personal responsibility
- individually paid health insurance program, limited government involvement

Mongolia has had a very high literacy rate, largely because the communist government provided all schooling free of charge, including boarding schools for children of nomadic parents. The educational system includes ten years of basic education (currently four years primary, four years intermediate, and two years secondary or vocational). Until recently, higher education was also entirely free, but with student selection based on entrance examinations administered by the higher education institutions. Enrollment quotas for the various specializations were set by the government and allocated to the various provinces (*aimags*) on the basis of projected manpower needs. The language of instruction throughout the entire educational system is Mongolian.

PROFILE OF THE HIGHER EDUCATION SYSTEM

Historical Development

The first nationally funded institution for formal higher learning, the Mongolian State University, was established in 1942 in the capital city of Ulaanbaatar. Modeled after universities in Russia, it had three departments: pedagogy (for preparation of secondary school teachers), medicine, and veterinary medicine. The primary emphasis of this new institution was teaching in the departments represented. Most of the limited advanced research was done under the auspices of the National Committee of Science, which was not directly affiliated with the university. Over the years, the Mongolian State University developed several faculties: physics and mathematics (including meteorology); natural science (chemistry, biology, and geology); social science (philosophy, history, and sociology); economics; law; and languages and literature (Mongolian, Russian, and English). In order to meet the country's increasing needs for secondary school teaching personnel, the State Pedagogical Institute was founded in 1951.

By the mid-1950s, there was a joint recognition by the government-supported agency for overseeing scientific research, the National Committee of Science, and researchers in the university of the need to establish research programs in several of the academic areas represented among the faculty teaching at the Mongolian State University. Thus, the first major reform of Mongolian higher education involved moving faculty at the Mongolian State University into partially autonomous research institutes where both teaching and research would take place but which would emphasize research. In 1958, the zoological-veterinary medicine faculty at the Mongolian State University was the first unit to be so transformed and renamed the Agricultural Institute.

Even though the National Committee of Science was amalgamated into the Mongolian State University in 1959, this structure lasted only until 1961, when the Mongolian Academy of Sciences was founded, thereby perpetuating the pattern of concentrating advanced research in the Institutes of the Academy of Sciences rather than in the university. The Academy of Sciences, in conjunction with the Supreme Council for Academic Degrees and Titles, also controlled awarding of the highest scientific research titles—the candidate of science (roughly equivalent to a Ph.D. degree) and the doctor of science (roughly equivalent to a postdoctoral degree). Until 1992, the Supreme Council for Academic Degrees and Titles was under the Council of Ministers (the main government policy body) and controlled by the Ideological Secretary of the Central Committee of the Mongolian People's Revolutionary Party. Since 1992, the chairperson of the Supreme Council has been the minister of science and education. Because scientific degrees are awarded by a nonuniversity body and are not necessarily tied to a university-based program of study and research, it is also still possible for individuals to earn advanced degrees by presenting a completed research project/research report for consideration.

Continuing this trend toward unit autonomy, the Medical Institute was formed from the medical faculty of the State University in 1961. The polytechnic faculty was established as part of the State University in 1969 and became the Polytechnical Institute in 1982. The Russian Language Teachers' College, established as part of the State University in 1979, became the independent Russian Language Institute in 1982. There was also some effort to establish higher education institutions in provinces (aimags) with sizable populations located far from Ulaanbaatar. One example of this is the training institution for secondary school teachers, the Pedagogical Institute at Khovd, located near the western border of Mongolia. In other cases, institutions were founded as specialized secondary schools (grades 9 and 10) to serve regional needs, such as the Teachers Colleges in Dornod and Arkhangai for the preparation of primary school teachers, the Economics College in Zavkhan, and the Agricultural Colleges in Khovd, Darkhan, and Bayanchandman. Such institutions were initially authorized to offer specialized secondary education, and postsecondary programs were added as required for national development. A few were ultimately authorized to award certificates considered the equivalent of academic degrees. Under this system of higher education, all costs were fully subsidized by the Mongolian government which, in turn, received subsidies from the Russian government in the form of instructional materials and scientific equipment.

The strong Russian influence on Mongolian higher education continued until the breakup of the Soviet Union. Legislation for the second major reform of higher education, passed in late 1990, mandated major restructuring. The three institutes that had been founded as parts of the Mongolian State University became independent universities in 1991: the Mongolian Agricultural University, the Mongolian Medical University, and the Mongolian Technical University. The State Pedagogical Institute became the Mongolian Pedagogical University. The Russian Language Institute was renamed the Foreign Language Institute and became part of the Pedagogical University. The creative and performing arts faculty at the Pedagogical University became the Institute of Art.

At this time, the Mongolian State University was renamed the National University of Mongolia, and the Pedagogical Institute at Khovd became a branch of it in 1993. The National University has had a faculty for the preparation of secondary school teachers since its founding; thus, bringing the Khovd Pedagogical Institute, which has similar programs, under its umbrella rather than that of the Pedagogical University was not unreasonable. A new public higher education institution was created in 1991 by combining sixteen institutes from the Academy of Sciences in Ulaanbaatar into the Mongolian Institute of Technology. In addition to the National University, which had been the only university authorized to award advanced scientific degrees, all of the newly designated universities and the Institute of Technology were authorized to begin developing postgraduate degree programs.

Two degree-granting colleges designed to prepare students for various business, commerce, and finance positions in the developing market economy of Mongolia were also established in Ulaanbaatar in 1991: the College of Commerce and Business and the Economic College. These two colleges were originally established as *technikums* (specialized secondary schools) by the Ministry of Trade and the Ministry of Finance, respectively. These two colleges were initially run jointly by the responsible Ministries and the Ministry of Education. Two special purpose higher education institutions also received a "university" designation in the 1990 higher education law: the Military Institute became the Military University, and the Art Institute became the University of Art.

In addition to the administrative shifts already mentioned, several regional specialized secondary schools were incorporated into the higher education sector and received the designation of "college" in the 1990 legislation. In the interim, most of these institutions have been brought under the administrative umbrella of a Mongolian university. The Transportation Institute, formerly a school run by the Mongolian Ministry of Roads, Transportation, and Communication, became part of the Technical University. A branch of the Technical University was also established in Darkhan. A specialized secondary school in Zavkhan called the Economic College became a branch of the National University. Medical Colleges in Central Gobi and Gobi Altai *aimags* were brought under the Medical University.

Several institutes and colleges for the preparation of teachers that were located in Ulaanbaatar were brought under the umbrella of the Pedagogical University, including Teachers College, Kindergarten Teachers College, Music Teachers College, and the Institute of Physical Education. The Institute of Foreign Languages in Erdenet and two regional teachers colleges (at Arkhangai and Dornod) also became branches of the Pedagogical University. The Music College, Culture College, and Arts College were brought under the Art University. Finally, the Agricultural Colleges at Darkhan, Bayanchandman, and Khovd were designated branches of the Agricultural University.

Yet another important result of the 1990 education reform was legislation enabling the establishment of private higher education institutions. The first of these, all of which must receive operating approval from the Ministry of Science and Education, were founded in 1991. There are currently more than thirty authorized private higher education institutions.

Institutional and System Structure

Each public institution of higher education in Mongolia is relatively autonomous, with its own administration and budget. The chief administrative officer is the rector, appointed by the minister of science and education, usually from recommendations made by duly constituted search committees. While institutions differ in some ways, the general pattern in the national universities is for the rector to appoint up to three deputy rectors, most commonly one for academic affairs, one for financial affairs, and one for research.

Faculties are organized into departments with chairs and a dean. There are also directors of the various research institutes. This group of deans and institute directors, along with the vice rectors, tends to comprise the Rectors' Council and meets two or three times per month to advise on various procedural issues. A second group, the Learned Council, is larger and represents the senior scientific people in the institution. This council meets only two or three times per year and advises primarily on academic policy issues. Finally, there is a University Council, which is representative of all major constituencies—faculty, students, staff, and administrators. This body tends to meet twice a year and provides advice to the rector on institutional quality of life. Members of all councils are appointed by the rector, who is the primary decision maker in all aspects of institutional management.

Most major decisions are, however, subject to approval by the Ministry of Science and Education, often in consultation with other responsible Ministries. For instance, budget requests submitted by the university rectors to the Ministry of Science and Education must also receive subsequent approval by the Ministry of Finance; requests for student spaces in the various fields of study must receive subsequent approval by both the Ministry of Finance and the National Development Board. While there is no "system-level" administrative structure, the Ministry of Science and Education is responsible for oversight and regulation of both the public and private sectors of higher education.

Two other bodies that play advisory roles in Mongolian higher education are the Higher Education Reform Commission and the Council of Rectors. The Higher Education Reform Commission (HERC) was established by the Great Khural in 1990 to provide advice on facilitating the reform of higher education, with a special emphasis on making it more responsive to the demands of a market economy. The chairman of this commission is a member of the Great Khural and reports to the chairman of the Standing Committee on Education, Science, and Culture Policy. Members include representatives from the Ministry of Science and Education and the Academy of Sciences, as well as several university rectors.

The Rectors' Council was established by the Ministry of Science and Education and includes all of the rectors of the public universities, the rector of the College of Commerce and Business, the chairman of the Association of Private Higher Education Institutions, and the general director of the Postsecondary Education Department in the Ministry of Science and Education. The rector of the National University is chairman of the Rectors' Council. It advises the Ministry primarily on regulations and operational procedures related to public and private higher education.

There is also the Foundation for the Improvement of Higher Education, established primarily to support the Higher Education Reform Commission through fund raising, liaison with the developing private enterprises, and working on international cooperation. Members include representatives from the Great Khural, the Ministry of Science and Education, and the Academy of Sciences, as well as several university rectors.

The impact of these bodies is very hard to judge. Each is perceived to be a "nongovernment" agency because each has no direct decision-making authority even though members of decision-making bodies are represented. There seem to be no effective mechanisms for structuring the work of such advisory bodies. Hence, each has difficulty in determining the extent to which its work is being taken into consideration by either the Ministry of Science and Education or the Great Khural. There is also considerable overlap of membership among the three entities, with several people serving on all three groups.

Student Enrollment

Student enrollments for 1993–94 in each type of higher education institution are shown in tables 11.1 and 11.2. Trends in enrollments at the public universities and two leading colleges preparing students for positions in the evolving market economy are shown in table 11.3. All of the universities have had stable enrollments during the transition from dependence on Soviet resources, except for the Agricultural University, which has lost half its students. Presumably, the privatization of agriculture has reduced the need to obtain advanced academic credentials since workers can receive the direct financial benefits of their labor rather than simply being employed as government workers on collective farms.

Table 11.4 shows the 1992–93 enrollment for first academic and graduate degrees by field (UNESCO classifications) and gender. Not surprisingly, education and teacher training had the largest number of students, followed by engineering; commerce and business; and humanities, religion, and theology. What is very unusual for a developing country is the very large proportion of female students (almost 64 percent overall, and 40 percent to 50 percent in science and engineering). Men seem to be much more likely than women to forego advanced education in favor of moving into the labor market. It remains to be seen if parents will continue to be as willing to have their daughters pursue higher education when it is no longer free.

Following the withdrawal of Soviet support and the economic shock of the transition to a market economy in Mongolia, especially coping with the relatively high costs of goods on the world market, the government was no longer able to subsidize the full costs of higher education. Consequently, a tuition structure has been implemented. Beginning with the fall semester of 1993, all students in Mongolian institutions of higher education were required to pay tuition. Those students who are studying in specializations that have been identified as manpower needs by the National Planning Board are eligible for loans from the government to pay their tuition fees. Institutions are now permitted to

Table 11.1

Full-Time Enrollment in University-Level Institutions, 1993–94

	Graduate Students %		Undergraduate Students %		Specialized Secondary-Voc. %	
	Total	Female	Total	Female	Total	Female
National Universities						
National University of Mongolia	116	16.4	3,158	58.5		
Pedagogical Institute-Khovd			446	78.9		
Economics College-Zavkhan			213	77.9	142	76.1
Agricultural National University	89	9.0	1,157	46.4		
Agricultural College-Bayanchandman					183	43.7
Agricultural College-Darkhan			143	77.6	82	84.1
Total	**205**	**13.2**	**5,117**	**58.9**	**407**	**63.1**
Other Public Universities						
Technical University	66	16.7	3,055	44.0	374	9.9
Technical University-Darkhan			221	48.0	41	65.9
Pedagogical University	37	27.0	1,805	65.5		
Foreign Language Institute			742	80.3		
Kindergarten Teachers' College			456	98.7		
Pedagogical College			639	92.6	72	79.2
Music Teachers' College			169	71.6	25	56.0
Foreign Language Institute-Erdenet			110	84.5		
Joint Mongolian-Russian College			71	59.2	28	7.1
Medical University	75	0.0	2,416	78.1		
University of Art			342	76.7		
Total	**178**	**11.8**	**10,026**	**65.9**	**540**	**25.4**
Other Public Higher Education Institutions						
Institute of Technology			100	35.0		
University of Eastern Literature			51	76.5		
Khar Khorum University			106	33.0		
Total			**257**	**42.4**		

Source: Ministry of Science and Education, Ulaanbaatar, Mongolia.

Table 11.2
Full-Time Enrollment in College-Level Institutions, 1993–94

	Undergraduate Students		Specialized Secondary-Voc.	
	Total	% Female	Total	% Female
Public Colleges				
Economics College	648	55.7		
College of Commerce & Business	392	72.4	201	79.6
Railway College	14	21.4	427	52.5
Fine Art College	39	25.6	245	21.6
College of Culture	33	84.8	223	81.6
Pedagogical College-Arkhangai	407	90.9	52	82.7
Pedagogical College-Dornod	248	95.2	37	94.6
Medical College-Dornogobi	136	88.2	263	94.3
Technical College-Darkhan	34	35.3	267	40.8
Agricultural College-Khovd			143	61.5
Music College	184	69.6	35	45.7
Total	**2,135**	**72.7**	**1,893**	**61.2**
Private Higher Education Institutions				
Mongol Business School	80	51.2		
University of Mongolian Knowledge	193	73.6		
Institute of National Sport	249	19.3		
Otgontenger Foreign Language College	384	83.6		
Mamba Datsun Medical College	10	60.0		
Shikhikhutag College of Law	65	53.8		
Orkhon Foreign Language College	347	80.1		
Onol Foreign Language School	127	82.7		
College of Eastern Philosophy	91	74.7		
Tsog Foreign Language College	512	82.9		
Mandakh Accountancy Institute	145	75.2		
Tsagan Lavai Pedagogical Institute	165	93.3		
College of Natural Science	15	80.0		
College of European Languages	193	80.3		
College of Mongolian Script	226	94.2		
Gurvan Erdene Pedagogical College	130	91.5		
College of Tsagaan Shuvuut Co. Ltd	396	72.0		
Gobi College	99	84.8		
Ireedui College	54	79.6		
Khan Khukhyi College of Interpreters	153	82.4		
Bers College	66	51.5		
College of Social Science & Economics	75	72.0		
Institute of Mongolian Civilization	100	64.0		
Total	**3,875**	**76.0**		

Source: Ministry of Science and Education, Ulaanbaatar, Mongolia.

Table 11.3
Higher Education Student Enrollment and Graduation Data, 1990–93

	1991 1990 Total	1992 1991 Total	1992 Total % Fem	Grads Total	Grads % Fem	1992 Total	Total % Fem	Grads Total	Grads % Fem
National Univ	1896	2126	60.4	393	59.5	2430	60.1	363	63.6
Ped Inst-Khovd	443	470	58.9	84	63.1	413	67.8	88	51.1
Technical Univ	3089	3053	39.3	551	39.7	3083	41.8	607	47.9
Pedagogical Univ *	2654	2650	81.1	584	71.2	2722	68.0	529	72.8
Medical Univ	3037	3075	73.3	432	81.9	2666	79.1	443	82.6
Agricult Univ	1910	1515	40.9	399	47.4	976	49.9	345	40.6
Inst of Technol						41	19.5		
Art Univ 255	321	48.9	44	31.8	358	51.7	58	58.6	
Economic Coll		304				476	50.8		
Coll Comm & Bus		188				299	68.5		

*Data for students at the Pedagogical University include those enrolled in the Institute for Foreign Languages.
Source: Ministry of Science and Education, Ulaanbaatar, Mongolia.

admit additional students on a demand basis who must pay tuition fees from their own (or parents') resources or obtain commitments from potential employers to cover costs (with or without obligation for repayment, depending on the company). Tuition fees are based on the total estimated costs incurred by each institution (e.g., salaries, maintenance, materials and equipment, etc.; see Bray et al. [1994] and Weidman [1995] for more detailed discussions of financial issues).

Initially, higher education institutions were restricted by the Ministry of Science and Education to admitting only a small percentage of additional students over and above the established quotas, usually 10 percent to 15 percent. However, as pressures increased to raise more of their budgets from nongovernment sources, institutions admitted increasingly larger numbers of self-paying students. Using the data in table 11.4 as a base, the total number of students enrolled in undergraduate-level programs in public higher education institutions rose by 41.1 percent (from 16,917 to 23,869) between 1992–93 and 1995–96. During this period, the proportion of females continued to increase (from 63.8 percent to 67.7 percent). In private higher education institutions, enrollment more than doubled (from 3,875 shown in table 11.2 to 8,104) between 1993–94 and 1995–96. The proportion of females enrolled in private higher education decreased about 5 percent (from 76.0 percent to 70.8 percent). These data suggest that both public and private institutions of higher education are responding to a very strong student demand for higher education.

Academic Staff

The gender, experience, and age composition of teachers at the public universities and two of the leading public, business-oriented colleges is shown in

Table 11.4
Enrollment Rates in Field of Study by Level and Gender, 1992–93

Field of Study[1]	ISCED[2] Level 6		ISCED Level 7	
	Total	%Female	Total	%Female
1. Education and Teacher Training	4775	73.8	2	
2. Humanities, Religion, Theology	1679	73.6	29	6.9
3. Fine and Applied Arts	412	49.0		
4. Law	282	46.5	4	25.0
5. Social and Behavioral Science	255	65.9	10	20.0
6. Commercial and Business Admin.	1705	59.2	1	
7. Mass Communication, Documentation	86	69.8	1	
9. Service Trades	116	75.9	3	66.7
10. Natural Science	727	54.3	49	12.2
11. Mathematics and Computer Science	455	41.1	11	
12. Medical Science, Health-related	2748	79.3	4	50.0
13. Engineering	1973	40.3	33	12.1
14. Architecture	38	26.3		
15. Trade, Craft, and Industrial	241	49.0	15	40.0
16. Transport and Communications	469	35.8		
17. Agriculture, Forestry, Fishery	956	54.1	28	28.6
18. Other and Not Specified			2	
Total	16,917	63.8	192	17.2

[1]UNESCO categories.
[2]ISCED = International Standard Classification of Education; Level 6 = program leading "to the awarding of a first university degree or equivalent qualification"; Level 7 = program leading to a "higher postgraduate degree or equivalent qualification."
Source: Ministry of Science and Education, Ulaanbaatar, Mongolia.

table 11.5. Rank and degree distribution of teachers in the public universities are shown in table 11.6. Even though women predominate among the undergraduates, teachers in higher education are predominantly men, except for pedagogy and business. This mirrors the low enrollment of women in postgraduate degree programs (table 11.4). The average age of professors and those with doctoral degrees is fifty-seven; associate professors and those with master's degrees average forty-seven. Successors for these teachers are not being prepared in sufficient numbers to take their places. Professors and teachers spend most of their time in classroom instruction and have little time for or inclination toward research. About 10 percent of all students do, however, take part in research work and creative project development. Only 4.2 percent of the higher education institutions use computers.

Student:full-time faculty ratios for public higher education in 1995–96 averaged 12:1; for private higher education, 22:1. Private institutions of higher education make much more extensive use of part-time instructors (60 percent of all teachers as opposed to 18 percent in public institutions).

Table 11.5

Higher Education Teachers by Gender, Years of Experience, and Age

	1990 Tchrs	1991 Tchrs	1991 % Fem	1992 Tchrs	% 21+ Yr Ex	%Age 50+
National Univ.	271	279	33.3	289	42.2	28.7
Ped. Inst-Khovd	50	49	18.4	38	26.3	7.9
Technical Univ.	354	304	23.4	398	32.4	14.5
Pedagogical Univ.	164	165	27.9	153	32.7	17.0
Inst Frgn Lang.	94	74	82.4	72	23.6	19.4
Medical Univ.	266	272	45.6	275	24.7	12.0
Agricult. Univ.	177	138	20.3	95	32.6	25.3
Inst. of Technol.				9	44.4	22.2
Art University	51	60	51.7	93	29.0	20.4
Economic College		34	50.0	37	8.1	5.4
Coll Commerce&Bus		51	76.5	40	20.0	12.5

Source: Ministry of Science and Education, Ulaanbaatar, Mongolia.

Changing Functions and Patterns of Higher Education

The entire educational system has been shifting from a government-driven, highly centralized policy and administrative structure that was fully government-funded to one that is much more decentralized with increasing responsibility shifting to the provincial (*aimag*) level. While the number of places in each field of study for students in higher education who are supported by government loans is still being determined by the National Planning Board, institutions are now able to admit large numbers of other students who are able to pay their own way. Graduates will now be able to seek jobs in the emerging market-driven economy rather than being assigned to jobs by the government. Curriculum reforms are also now under discussion to move from a lock-step pattern to one in which there is much more flexibility for both students and teachers.

More attention will now be paid to providing a combination of both public and private education institutions, with special encouragement to the development of private institutions of higher education. There will be a more open and flexible structure for management, with higher education institutions expected to generate their own revenue sources through enterprises, training, research, and consulting services.

Plans and programs for training of students will be determined on the basis of diversified demand considerations of individuals (according to ability and interests), the government, private enterprises, and co-operatives. Conditions are being created to enable more individualized programs in which students are expected to read and study independently rather than relying solely on didactic instruction and copious note taking. Finally, there will be more comprehensive preparation of teachers with greater emphasis on subject area competence as

Table 11.6
Rank and Academic Degree Distribution of Teachers in Universities, 1991–92

	Total Tchrs 1991	Rank		Academic Degree	
		% Prof.	% Assoc. Prof.	%D.Sci.	%Ph.D.
National Univ.	279	4.3	13.6	3.6	31.9
Ped. Inst-Khovd	49	2.0	2.0		10.2
Technical Univ.	304		9.5	1.0	21.4
Pedagogical Univ.	165	1.2	7.9	1.2	17.6
Inst Frgn Lang.	74		2.7		10.8
Medical Univ.	272	.7	4.4	.7	23.9
Agricult. Univ.	138	2.9	7.2	2.2	29.7
Art University	60	5.0	1.7		6.7

Source: Ministry of Science and Education, Ulaanbaatar, Mongolia.

opposed to ideological commitment to the Communist Party. These transitions can be summarized as follows:

Educational Transitions

From:

- rigid, standardized curriculum determined by government
- strong ideological influence

- fully funded by the state

- centralized administration

- based on societal and manpower needs

- compulsory involvement in education

- teacher-centered instruction

To:

- diversified curriculum determined by local community needs
- oriented toward common values of humanity and science

- participatory financing, with cost recovery from students/parents

- decentralization

- based on personal demand

- right to choose, voluntary involvement

- student-centered instruction

Another reform has been an effort to change the academic degree structure to resemble an American-style pattern (e.g., bachelor's, master's, and Ph.D.). The bachelor's degree requires four to five years of postsecondary education (depending on the specialization and the institution); the master's degree requires another two years. Because secondary school in Mongolia ends with grade 10, there is concern that the bachelor's degree may represent a level of attainment lower than that of bachelor's degrees earned in more advanced Asian countries such as Korea and Japan.

A graduate student who continues with doctoral study after completing the master's degree will be required to study at least three more years and write a dissertation in order to earn a Ph.D. Several more years of study, research, and a major piece of research will be required to earn the doctor of science (D.Sci.) degree. For students who completed degrees under the old system, the following equivalencies are being used to classify different levels of study: bachelor's degree = four years of full-time study and a diploma; master's degree = five years of full-time study; Ph.D. degree = two to three years beyond the master's; and doctor of science (D.Sci.) = two to three years beyond the Ph.D. All post-graduate students except for those in medicine and law must earn the Ph.D. prior to beginning study for a D.Sci. degree.

A law passed in 1992 sought to incorporate a research mission into Mongolian higher education institutions by bringing the Academy of Sciences Institutes into a much closer relationship with the universities. The Ministry of Education was renamed the Ministry of Science and Education and a new Department of Science and Technology was established. The pattern of financing the Academy of Sciences was also changed, with the newly created Department of Science and Technology responsible for approving funding requests. This law also provided the impetus for developing closer relationships among the universities, the research institutes, and private enterprises.

RESPONSES TO INTERNATIONAL DEMANDS

The serious economic crisis due to the country's shift from a command economy closely aligned with the Soviet Union to a market economy oriented toward the larger international community has had serious consequences for higher education in Mongolia. All indications are that facilities and equipment present major problems across all levels of education in Mongolia. Buildings and other facilities are in increasingly poor repair due to lack of funds for maintenance. Heating costs have increased so rapidly that many educational institutions are forced to spend half or more of their budgets simply to keep buildings warm in winter. In higher education, scientific equipment tends to be outdated (much of it received from Russia a decade or more ago) and computers are in short supply. It is not unusual to have computer labs in which three or four students share a single computer. Maintenance problems are common.

Another significant effect is the drastic decrease in the number of books and periodicals that can be imported from abroad, including textbooks. The allocation for the National Library in Ulaanbaatar was reduced by 50 percent between 1989 and 1993. After adjusting for inflation and devaluation of the local currency based on international markets, the net library allocation in 1993 was less than 25 percent of what it had been in 1989. In the universities, most textbooks are in Russian and are not the most recent editions. A majority of the volumes in university libraries are textbooks (30 percent of the 240,000 library books at the National University; over 66 percent of the 150,000 books in the Technical University library; and 60 percent of the 54,000 books in the library of the

Foreign Language Institute of the Pedagogical University). There are virtually no resources to translate books into the Mongolian language, let alone to print them.

Students in higher education must rely heavily on rote learning and careful note taking as opposed to studying material in current textbooks or using library resources for independent study and research. There is an expectation that students will be supplied with all needed information and learning materials by the higher education institutions rather than having to purchase any textual materials themselves. Hence, virtually all student learning appears to take place in the classroom, where material is delivered by teachers. There appears to be only very limited supplementary work expected in the library. Even so, access to books is strictly controlled, so there is little opportunity for students to explore materials in their fields of study. This means that students in higher education are almost entirely dependent on their teachers for the content of their academic programs. Further, higher education in Mongolia is becoming increasingly self-contained. Neither students nor faculty can afford the costs of travel outside the country for advanced training.

Current scientific publications are very scarce, except in some of the institutes of the Academy of Sciences which, until the early 1990s, had its own special budget for such materials. Academy of Sciences research institutes also tended to have better laboratory facilities than the universities. There are also virtually no funds to support the acquisition of materials on electronic databases. In short, access to current research findings through periodicals or electronic databases is severely limited.

In spite of the limitations of facilities and equipment, the higher education system manages to be remarkably effective. Instruction is delivered, students seem to be reasonably successful at finding employment after graduation, and some faculty even manage to undertake programs of research. There does, of course, appear to be considerable variation in quality across programs within institutions as well as across institutions. In the absence of any real evidence on quality of the curriculum, it is very difficult to judge the level of preparation in Mongolia in comparison with bachelor's degree study, either in other Asian countries or in Europe and the United States.

With respect to gender equity, there is a fascinating anomaly in Mongolian higher education. Women constitute two-thirds of the undergraduates, but the proportion of women teachers does not reach the proportion of women studying for bachelor's degrees in any of the universities except at the Institute of Foreign Languages, which is now part of the Pedagogical University. This stands in sharp contrast to the newly developing Economic College and College of Commerce and Business, where women are well represented on the faculty. However, the distribution of students at the post-bachelor's level from which higher education faculty are primarily drawn provides a very different picture. In 1992–93, only 16 percent of those studying for an advanced degree beyond the bachelor's were women, and fewer than 10 percent of the advanced degree recipients in 1993 were women. This suggests that concerted efforts will have to be made to increase the number of women enrolled in advanced degree programs if their representation on the higher education faculties is to begin moving toward the proportion of female graduates at the bachelor's degree level.

Women are also not well represented in university administration; only one woman—a vice rector at the University of Art—holds a senior administrative position in any of the public higher education institutions. Things are quite different, however, in the private higher education sector. The founders (all also the current rectors) of four private institutions (Otgon Tenger, Orkhon, Onol, and Gurvan Erdene) are women, as is the rector of a fifth (Mongolian Script Institute). With respect to other types of jobs, there is no difference in the employment rates of men and women with higher education, largely because, until the past two years, student spaces have been allocated solely on the basis of manpower needs determined by the National Planning Board.

FUTURE DEVELOPMENTS

Higher education is the most rapidly changing segment of the education sector in Mongolia. In less than three years, the higher education sector changed from an essentially single, multipurpose university into a decentralized set of very specialized universities, each with its own mission and resources. At the same time, a number of steps were taken to bring the research enterprise, formerly housed primarily in independent institutes of the Mongolian Academy of Sciences, directly under the umbrella of the universities, thereby attempting to integrate the teaching and research functions within universities.

There is an ongoing attempt to "consolidate" and "rationalize" the system by bringing several regional specialized secondary and postsecondary "colleges" under the administrative oversight of the university-level institutions. This has also included discussion of bringing all of the specialized, university-level institutions located in the capital city (Ulaanbaatar) under a single administrative structure. All of this has been accomplished primarily by government law and regulation rather than through a systematic planning and design process. Consequently, there are serious questions about the extent to which this rapid change has actually resulted in desired system simplification and improvement as opposed to making it more complex and fragmented.

It is no longer possible for the government to assume responsibility for fully funding all costs of higher education. Consequently, beginning with the 1993–94 academic year, all students in higher education had to pay tuition fees for the first time. Further, the high costs of scientific equipment and instructional materials along with withdrawal of resources formerly available from the Soviet Union have caused serious problems for the delivery of high-quality instruction as well as for conducting research.

Despite all of the problems, the higher education sector in Mongolia has been functioning reasonably well, considering the serious shortages of instructional materials, the deterioration of the physical plant, and the need for retraining of academic staff. It is, however, rapidly losing its capacity to prepare students whose training is competitive with world standards. The scientific research establishment in Mongolia is also suffering because it, too, is increasingly not competitive with world standards. Hence, if graduates of Mongolian higher education institutions are to be prepared adequately for the demands of a world economy and for the future development needs of the country, these issues will need to be addressed. Efforts will have to be made to improve scientific communication through the use of computer networking and machine-readable databases, and to develop more effective coordinating mechanisms (including institutional consolidation) to improve efficiency and reduce duplication of programs among institutions. This will also entail developing the capacity for quality assessment and periodic accreditation of institutions, and integration of the research and teaching functions in higher education. Funding to support reform and development of the Mongolian higher education system has been committed in the form of a loan from the Asian Development Bank.

NOTE

Much of the information for this chapter was collected during the summer of 1993 as part of an education and human resources sector review in which Weidman and Bat-Erdene participated. The sector review was funded by the Asian Development Bank with financial assistance from the Japan Special Fund that was conducted under contract with the Academy for Educational Development, the University of Pittsburgh School of Education, and DanEduc Consulting. The opinions presented in this chapter are those of the authors and do not represent official policy of the Asian Development Bank, the contractors, or the government of Mongolia.

REFERENCES

Asian Development Bank. 1995. *Asian Development Outlook: 1995 and 1996*. New York: Oxford University Press.

Bat-Erdene, R., Vincent Costa, and John Yeager. 1996. "The Impact on Structural Adjustment in the Ministry of Science and Education, Mongolia." Paper presented at the annual conference of the Comparative and International Education Society, March 8, Williamsburg, Va.

Bray, Mark, Surengiin Davaa, Seth Spaulding, and John C. Weidman. 1994. "Transition from Socialism and the Financing of Higher Education: The Case of Mongolia." *Higher Education Policy, 7*, 36–42.

Mongolia Human Resource Development and Education Reform Project: Sector Review. 1993. Prepared for the government of Mongolia by the Ministry of Science and Education, the Academy for Educational Development, the University of Pittsburgh School of Education, and DanEduc Consulting. Support for this activity was provided by the Asian Development Bank with financial assistance from the Japan Special Fund.

Weidman, John C. 1995. "Diversifying Finance of Higher Education Systems in the Third World: The Cases of Kenya and Mongolia." *Education Policy Analysis Archives, 3* (5).

12

NEPAL

Murari Prasad Regmi

Nepal, the Everestland and birthplace of the Buddha, has always been an independent kingdom. Situated on the central southern slopes of the mid-Himalayas, it covers 147,000 square kilometers and has some 19 million inhabitants. Nepal's geopolitical importance lies in its strategic location between two giant nations, China and India. Rich in cultural heritage, it is a land of diverse ethnic groups. Tibeto-Burman people like the Kirat, Gurung, Magar, Limbu, and Tamang live in the northern parts of the country; Hindus and other minor tribes like the Sunwar, Dhimal, Danuwar, Satar, Tharu, and Santhal live in the southern part. Historically there were three types of religious systems of education: the Hindu/Vedic tradition of Sanskrit education, the Buddhist tradition of education, and the Islamic Urdu-Persian-Arabic religious tradition. The Vedic tradition was handed down by Brahmans in the southern *tarai*; northern *gompas* Buddhist lama monks and priests taught Buddhist philosophy, logic, and Tantra; and Muslim *maulavis* taught in the *madarsa*.

From ancient times to A.D. 1768, from the Kirata Dynasty to the Malla Dynasty, there was religious education. Nepal was divided into many feudal states before its unification by King Prithvi Narayan Shah, forefather of the present king, in 1769. He emphasized military education. There was a four-tier system consisting of tillers (peasants), petty landlords, higher landlords, and the king. The king under feudalism had nothing to do with the people at the grassroots level (Thapa, 1992). There was a large gap between the ruled and the ruler. Nepalese peasants became poorer because of the land system and the gap between common farmers and the rulers. This feudalism was at its zenith during Rana rule (A.D. 1846–1950), characterized by opposition to the expansion of education. Education was available to the ruling class only, achieving the hegemony of the ruling class while exploiting the peasants. The specific landowning systems also oppressed peasants, as well as fostered and strengthened feudalism. Peasants secured their right of ownership certificate after the implementation of the Land Reform Act (1964).

Nepal had no formal school system before the Anglo-Nepal War (1814–16). Prime Minister Jung Bahadur Rana's visit to Great Britain in 1850 gave rise to his dream of Western-type English schooling for Rana children. Jung Bahadur's dream was realized when in 1854 Durbar School came into existence. Gradually this school was opened to the common people's children too, and brought with it a system of education that demanded new needs and values like political awareness, democratic ideals, international understanding, and knowledge and skills relevant to science and technology (Joshi, 1990). The Rana society decided very late to transform its elitist educational system into one that might serve the masses. At first, Rana decided to use that system as an instrument for their own development, not for national development.

A Sanskrit school was set up in 1877 and popularized in Kathmandu by Ranodeep Singh. This school helped in the preservation of traditional values. Dev Shamsher in 1901 pioneered vernacular liberal education for all, which promoted literacy and arithmetic skills among children. Dev Shamsher was exiled to India by his successor, Chandra Shamsher, because liberal education was perceived as a threat to the Rana regime in Nepal. Padma Shamsher in 1947 started Basic Gandhian Education in the villages. He emphasized craft education—spinning, weaving, woodcraft, and agriculture. Padma Shamsher was also opposed by his successors; ultimately he left Nepal and found asylum in India.

Education in Nepal gathered momentum after India's independence in 1947. Many Nepali students found admission to Indian schools, colleges, and universities. People also demanded human rights and freedom. The Rana autocracy came to an end after a century. This long period is one of the darkest periods in Nepali history. Democracy was followed by the rapid growth of education (1951–70); a reconstruction of education was introduced after 1971.

The Nepali economy is predominantly rural, based on agriculture and related activities with close interdependency within the "man-land-forest-livestock" continuum for meeting the requirements of food, fuel, and fodder (Bajracharya, 1992). As shown in the World Development Report of 1989, Nepal's estimated population, with U.S.$160 per capita income, was 17.6 million in mid-1987. It increased at the rate of 2.7 percent a year. From 1982 to 1992, GNP per capita virtually remained stagnant, barely exceeding the population growth rate (Dahal, 1992). Sixty percent of the total population falls below the absolute poverty line. So the first and foremost challenge in Nepal is to reduce the level of poverty. The second is to increase the literacy rate, which was 54.5 percent for males and 25 percent for females in 1991–92. In 1951, Nepal had a literacy rate of only one percent. The challenges posed by the goal of universal literacy by the year 2000 are many and formidable. Nepal faces four problems: lack of a strong political will, financial inadequacy, lack of manpower resources, and low motivation among students and teachers (G. S. Pradhan, 1992).

Hayes (1993) states that Nepal has become increasingly open to the outside world and interlocked with extranational social and cultural systems; "modern" ideas about how to live have been introduced through trade, tourism, foreign assistance, and technology. Nepal's economy is increasingly monetarist, and the signs of increasing "commodification" and "consumerism" are apparent in the urban areas. The "democracy movement" in Nepal can be viewed as both an expression and a reinforcement of these rising aspirations. Nepal may be a long way from becoming one of the newly industrializing countries in the region, but it can claim a place in the vanguard among what we might call newly democratizing countries (NDCs).

Nepali people have faith in the power of education to engineer social change. However, how much to press for change and how much to keep in the way of traditional educational practices remains a constant challenge for educators. Their interests lie typically in using education as a means of producing a fairer, more equitable society.

PROFILE OF THE HIGHER EDUCATION SYSTEM

The defining functions of the system of higher education in Nepali society are to produce and train manpower at different levels, to raise the living standards of the people, and to preserve the traditional knowledge, values, and norms of Nepal. The National Education Committee (NEC, 1988) has proposed separate centers of learning for the study of Ayurvedic and Buddhist philosophy. The Nepali education system aims to preserve democracy, peace, and culture and to create the infrastructures for building up the skills, attitudes, personalities, and understandings necessary for various occupations, professions, jobs, and services. The specific goals of technical education are to enable the trainee to grasp the impact of scientific and technological innovations and transformations of human civilization, society, policy, and environment, as well as to develop in the individual the capacity to assume leadership in any community or group activities. Higher education encourages and promotes research in the fields of arts and sciences, management, and vocational education. It aims at counteracting the elitist bias of the inherited system of education by linking it more effectively to productive enterprises, egalitarian principles, and plans to unify education into one entity that serves the country's needs and aspirations.

Education in Nepal was influenced by the second world wave of democratization. Tribhuvan University remains the premier institution of higher education. It symbolizes the deepest aspirations of the nation for a life of quality and culture. The traditional sectors of the economy have not created jobs and opportunities significant enough to attract or absorb men and women who have come out of educational institutions. Disparity between the growth in education and that in the rest of the economy has heightened concern about the state and nature of education itself. A state of virtual anarchy reigns in the educational world. Competence in teaching and administration has declined. Politicization is unchecked. Political ideologies are instruments of partisan political actions rather than matters of free, legitimate, and dispassionate discussions.

Ramsey (1991) states that education is also a tool of social justice and quality of life. It can contribute to a lessening of the national debt, and it faces substantial economic challenges. Education is viewed as an "industry" that cannot be separated from the economy in general. It is a major employer.

HISTORICAL DEVELOPMENT

Very few colleges were founded before the first democratic revolution in 1951 gave new impetus to accelerate the pace of educational development in the country. Tribhuvan-Chandra College, now Trichandra Campus, was founded in 1918. It was the first college of higher English-style education. In 1929, formal training in medicine began with Ayurvedic School at Naradevi, Kathmandu, by the Department of Education. In 1947, training in forestry started under the Department of Forestry. Nepal Law College was started in 1954. In 1956, Nurses Training School at Mahaboudha began, and a College of Education was founded under His Majesty's Government. Nepal National College was also established in the same year.

Tribhuvan University was established on July 14, 1959, at Tripureswor. The university was formally declared open on the fifty-third birthday of His Late Majesty King Tribhuvan Bir Bikram Shah Dev. Before that, all the colleges were affiliated with Patna University in India. Tribhuvan University was shifted to Kirtipur in November 1966. The university premises cover an area of about four hundred acres. The university buildings were erected in cooperation with friendly countries like India and the United States (Regmi, 1987). The Tribhuvan University Act of 1971, which made the university the sole controller, stands as a landmark in higher education.

The main aims of university higher education are to preserve the historical and cultural heritage of the nation; to accumulate, advance, and disseminate knowledge; to encourage and promote research in various areas; and to help students build character. There are four levels of higher education: (1) proficiency certificate (2 years minimum); (2) bachelor's degree (2 years minimum); (3) master's degree (2 years minimum); (4) doctor of philosophy (3 years minimum). The university runs its academic programs through its five institutes (medicine, forestry, engineering, agriculture and animal sciences, and science and technology) and four faculties (management, education, law, and humanities and social sciences).

The academic session normally starts in mid-July. At the end of each academic year the students take the annual examination conducted by the office of the Controller of Examinations. Seventy percent class attendance is a requirement for taking the annual examination. The students must pass all subjects offered to obtain diplomas and degrees.

TYPES OF HIGHER EDUCATION:

The types of higher education in Nepal are as follows.

1. Higher Secondary Education (classes 11–12 or 10 + 2) began in 1992. In the first phase thirty-six schools were provided for students who had passed tenth grade or earned a school leaving certificate (high school). Higher Secondary Education will balance the expansion of enrollment in the university. All proficiency certificate level courses under the university should be brought under the wing of higher secondary education by the year 2000 (NEC, 1992).

2. The Cambridge 'O' level (10 + 1) and 'A' level (11 + 2) curricula in the Budha Nilkantha School have achieved international recognition, and the high achievements of the students reflect the excellent academic standards that have been maintained over the years. Many of the Cambridge course graduates are presently studying in reputable colleges and universities, mainly in the United States and the United Kingdom (Kansakar, 1993). Budha Nilkantha School is an institution supported jointly by Her Majesty's Government/British Government. It is not only a national school but also a model school at the national level.

3. Higher Education (University) is imparted by the three universities in Nepal: Tribhuvan University, Mahendra Sanskrit University, and the newly started Kathmandu University. The latter was established in 1992 and some four hundred students were enrolled in the undergraduate science, bachelor's of management, and pharmacy programs. At present its focus is to run science classes. The medium of instruction is English. Teaching is supported by computer training courses.

4. Mahendra Sanskrit University was established in January 1987. This university is expected to play a unique role in the preservation and promotion of the rich treasures of knowledge and of the quintessential cultural heritage of Nepal through advanced study and research in Sanskrit learning. It has eight campuses. Higher Sanskrit education confronts some special problems like a low percentage of student enrollment, lack of teacher training programs, and lack of dormitory facilities for students. In Sanskrit education the medium of instruction is Sanskrit from higher secondary education (post-Madhyama to Acharya) degrees. But in general education, Sanskrit is taught through the national language, Nepali.

5. Nepal's technical school education dates back to the late 1920s. In 1929, Ayurvedic School was established, and in 1934, Civil Medical School was opened. In 1942, a technical training school for producing suboverseers and forest training centers for rangers were set up. The major trades offered by technical schools include general mechanics, electricity fitters, sanitary fitters, cabinet makers, automechanics, and office workers. There are three levels in the technical school scheme: higher secondary technical school, secondary technical school, and lower secondary technical school. In 1992, the National Education Committee planned to develop technical and vocational training so as to double its present annual capacity to train 9,342 persons within the next five years and triple it within ten years. The Technical Education and Vocational Training Council is expected to fulfill its institutionalized responsibilities concerning the development of curricula, training, standardization, certification, consultancy, quality control, and coordination.

The technical institutes of Tribhuvan University offer bachelor of engineering (B.E.) and bachelor of medicine and bachelor of surgery (M.B.B.S.) courses. The other agencies are the training centers of the cottage and rural industry development, training institutes under the Ministries and Departments of Tourism, Communication, Land Reform and Management, Forest, Local Development, and Health.

The history of curriculum development starts from 1877, when the position of director of education was first created to oversee the management of Durbar school. The Board of School Leaving Certificate Examination, established in 1934, publishes results for grades 9 and 10. The Department of Education determined the syllabus for lower grades. A minimum curriculum for all levels of schools was prescribed for the first time in 1948 under the recommendations of the National Educational Planning Commission. In 1960, under the Ministry of Education and Culture (MOEC), the section for curriculum and textbooks was established. The Department of Education formed committees of subject specialists, educators, and teachers to discuss and draft the curriculum in detail. The curricular aspects of an educational system deserve a closer chronological scrutiny in order to provide a clear image of the trends, potential, and future prospects of a sound educational program in keeping with the needs and demands of the changing Nepali society.

Every university has a curriculum development center (CDC). The rector of the university looks after its functions and programs. There are subject committees to take care of curriculum development and changes in each faculty/ institute. The task of designing and renewing university curricula is a continuous one that requires creative and innovative intervention on appropriate occasions. Thus the efforts at curriculum renewal will continue to focus on sensitivity and responsiveness of the academic programs. In recent years Nepali has been used as a medium of instruction for undergraduate classes. Parity or equivalence in degrees is maintained with specific reference to Indian and foreign universities. The system of external examiners also helps maintain general links, parity, or equivalence with Indian universities (Regmi, 1987).

ENROLLMENT IN HIGHER EDUCATION

In 1994–95 there were 102,018 students attending Tribhuvan University (table 12.1), excluding students from 131 private campuses. The current data for private campuses are not available. However, total number of students enrolled on the private campuses was 43,621 in 1992–93.

In 1951, there were only two colleges and 250 students. In 1971, there were 49 colleges and the recorded student enrollment was 17,200. The enrollment figure for undergraduate level was 20,658 in 1974–75. This figure rose to 47,882 in 1981–82. Similarly, enrollment at the graduate level was 3,474 in 1981–82 as compared to only 801 in 1974–75.

Table 12.1
Higher Education Enrollment, 1994–95

Faculty/Institute	Students	Percent
Tribhuvan University		
Engineering	2,029	1.98
Agriculture	675	0.66
Medicine	1,098	1.07
Forestry	541	0.53
Science & Technology	14,109	13.82
Law	6,117	5.99
Management	27,054	26.51
Humanities	38,243	37.48
Education	12,152	11.91
Total	**102,018**	**100(Approx)**

HIGHER EDUCATION: CHANGING PATTERNS

Tribhuvan University is the first university in the country to offer and conduct academic and training courses and programs in various disciplines. The other two universities are Mahendra Sanskrit University (1987) and Kathmandu University (1992). These universities receive major financial assistance from His Majesty's Government of Nepal and operate in conjunction with the Ministry of Education, the National Planning Commission, and related Ministries.

The highest government body of Tribhuvan University is the Tribhuvan University Council. The council is represented by constituencies such as teachers, businesspeople, students, the press, and other sectors of the intelligentsia. The rector serves as member-secretary of the council. The council facilitates critical examination of academic policies and programs. The major responsibilities of the academic council include determining admission criteria, establishing standards of instruction and research, and setting examination standards. It is also interested in the task of monitoring and evaluating academic programs of the university.

In recent years the Nepali people have begun to rely on higher education to help sustain the nation's economy and quality of life. In a global society this role clearly requires higher education to prepare the next generation for the challenges of working and competing with people from other nations and cultures. On an average five students get selected for Fulbright scholarships to the United States each year. The educational problems of suburban towns and villages are increasing largely due to population growth. To venture a solution in this area, some schools are well equipped to develop new approaches to educational delivery. Tribhuvan University has to some extent become an organization that provides education of equal quality to all the regions. Another major educational experiment is under way at Kathmandu University. This experiment also hopes to maintain the standard and quality of higher education.

The first democratic Nepalese government was formed in 1950. Since then the government has taken a number of measures to expand and consolidate the educational system in order to fulfill the rising social demand for education. Thus on the basis of enrollment projections of the Education and Human Resources Sector Assessment, it can be estimated that by the year 2000, a 2.8 percent and 3 percent growth rate per annum is needed to accommodate the specific age cohort for primary and secondary schools, respectively. The teacher requirements by the year 2000 are 2.8 percent and 4.3 percent per year to employ teachers for primary and secondary schools, respectively (R. M. Pradhan, 1992).

Analysis of the present high school curriculum shows certain elements irrelevant to the student's life and society. Students should study six subjects instead of seven. The introduction of vocational subjects like the seventh is irrelevant. This extra load on students hinders their growth. The curriculum is a mixture of many odd combinations lacking specialization in science, arts, and commerce courses. The school curriculum has no provision for "sports" education, except a rudimentary course on health and hygiene. This shows that there is no clearcut, long-term educational policy in Nepal. Also, examiners follow no objective and scientific evaluation rules. The controller's role is unproductive and nonconstructive.

Democracy is one of the most powerful bases of legitimacy for government. It is "government of, by, and for the people." However simple this definition may sound, it sets forth two conceptual elements fundamental to democratic theory: first, the system should be as participatory as possible; second, it should facilitate the general well-being of people (Dahl, 1956; Schattschneider, 1960).

Education in Nepal is planned and organized within the framework of the government. The national assembly as the highest legislative body in the country is responsible for policy deliberations and legal provisions in the education sector. Major administrative units and agencies related to the various aspects of education in Nepal are as follows: National Education Committee, Ministry of Education and Culture, education directorates and district education offices, Curriculum Textbook Supervision, development center, and universities and research centers. The National Education Committee is independent and the highest body set up by the government to formulate plans and policies on education. At present, the committee is organized under the chairmanship of the minister of education, culture, and social welfare. This committee formulates policies and issues directives in all aspects of the education sector, presents reports to His Majesty the King on matters of educational development from time to time, evaluates the progress of education in Nepal, and coordinates the activities of Tribhuvan University, the Ministry of Education and Culture, and other Ministries in the formulation and implementation of educational policies and programs.

RESPONSES TO INTERNAL DEMANDS

In 1994–95, the enrollment of students in five technical institutes was 18,452 and the enrollment in the four general education faculties was 83,569. Thus total enrollment is 102,018 students. This excludes enrollment on private campuses. The representation of various caste/ethnic groups according to the 1991 census is as follows:

Caste/Ethnic Group	% of Total Population
Brahmans	13
Chhetris	16
Thakuris	2
Newars	6
Thakalis	*
Moslems	3
Marbadis	*
Tarai Communities	27
Low castes (Hill)	8
Other Hill castes/ethnic groups	25
Total	**100**

* Less than one percent.

Brahmans are the dominant caste group in the population, and they had the largest legislative representation in the national assembly of 1991. The Indo-Aryan Brahmans (39.7 percent) were first in representation to Parliament, followed by Indo-Aryan Chhetri (17.7 percent) and the Tibeto-Burman tribal group (23.3 percent) (table 12.2). In 1991–92 Nepal's GNP per capita was U.S.$180. One of the objectives envisioned in the eighth plan (1992–97) is poverty alleviation. A large proportion of people (50 percent to 70 percent) live in abject poverty (Dahal, 1992).

The population distribution of Tribhuvan University teachers in 1992 is shown in table 12.3. There are 5,400 teaching staff in the university, with 154 professors, 853 readers, and 1,849 lecturers. There are 65 constituent campuses in 5

Table 12.2
Ethnic/Caste Representation in the Legislation, 1991

	Ethnic/caste	Percent
1.	Brahman	39.7
2.	Chhetri	17.7
3.	Newar	8.3
4.	Tribal	23.3
5.	Trader	3.4
6.	Landed	5.3
7.	Muslim	2.3
	Total	**100**

Development Regions in Nepal. The Central Development Region (CDR) has the highest (30) number of campuses; there are only 2 campuses in the Far Western Development Region (FWDR). Regional distribution of campuses is not uniform. Because of paucity of information, data on race/ethnicity and social class are not available. Graduate students take up school teaching because it is an easily available profession. Job opportunity is high in the urban areas, while farming is the chief profession in the rural areas. Private educational institutions pay more salaries than the government. In Nepal, students from Japan, China, Germany, the United States, and Norway come to study the language, culture, and anthropology of Nepal.

Inequality is observed in the education of minority groups (Tibeto-Burman groups and Tharu groups). However, overt discrimination is not found among education institutions. The system of higher education is dominated by Brahmans, Chhetris, and Newars; higher education is stratified among these three caste groups. These people play the leading role in administrative, legislative, and other services. Conflicts among student groups have been reported in the engineering, law, and management campuses of Kathmandu. "Protest-proneness" among urban students is rising but rural students are calm and quiet. Many students believe that racial discrimination is no longer a problem in Nepal society. Hurtado (1992) states that across all groups, perceptions of student-centered priorities were important predictors of perceptions of low racial tension. Campuses should seek opportunities to reconfigure resources and rewards to

Table 12.3
University Teachers' Status, 1992

Position	Total	Percent
Professor	154	2.85
Reader	853	15.79
Lecturer	1,849	34.24
Assistant Lecturer	1,939	35.90
Senior Instructor	47	0.87
Instructor	118	2.18
Deputy Instructor	201	3.72
Assistant Instructor	181	3.35
Others	58	1.07
Total	**5,400**	**100 (Approx)**

create student-centered properties that will benefit all students. University teachers are politically liberal and are indifferent regarding their welfare and promotion. They are incapable of showing their merit and worth in research and excellence in teaching. Teachers express mistrust and lack of commitment. There are 2,276 administrative staff, 3,129 utility staff, and 1,528 technical staff; thus, the total number of nonteaching staff comes to 6,933. The teaching versus nonteaching staff ratio is 1:1.28 for Tribhuvan University. The nonteaching staff, therefore, contributes to the hegemony of administration over teaching.

Teaching versus Research

In Nepal, little investment has gone into educational projects and educational research. Challenges facing the university are connected with objective evaluation in matters concerning teachers' rewards/punishments and a lack of adequate opportunities to increase teachers' academic qualifications and professional competence. Improvement is needed in the quality, effectiveness, and efficiency of the university organization and administration.

Salaries are too low to meet minimum requirements. A professor in Tribhuvan University receives U.S.$118 per month. Sometimes in Nepal, university teachers are honored by being appointed as ambassadors. A professor retires at the age of sixty-three with a meager pension.

At present Tribhuvan University has close affiliations with many institutions and universities in different countries including Shimase University, University of Bergen, Boston University, Cornell University, Indian Institute of Technology, and the Free University of Brussels. These universities are helping with the training of faculty teachers and collaborative research.

FUTURE DEVELOPMENTS

The tradition of appointing scholars to head university systems has increased since the mid-1980s. Legislators and party leaders play their roles in the replacement of department heads throughout the nation. Nepal has recently embarked on the path of progress and development. It requires competent manpower in various walks of life. To a large extent, universities have been fulfilling this responsibility by producing skilled professionals and technicians in agriculture, forestry, medicine, engineering, administration, and business.

Tribhuvan University and Kathmandu University have been initiating and encouraging dialogue on pressing contemporary issues such as ecological degradation, population growth, and poverty. This interactive process helps create public awareness through dialogue and consultations. Universities in Nepal are strengthening a corporate identity by loosening caste, linguistic, and regional barriers. The promotion of national integration remains a major commitment of the universities.

Multicultural education is the first step toward empowering all students in a Nepalese global society. For the achievement of multicultural goals, reeducation of teachers can and should be shared by the college or university. The educational messages are disseminated through various media, including newspapers, magazines, television, and radio. Effort is being made to break the stereotypes in the curricula of schools and universities.

The application of digital technology has revolutionized the classroom, fundamentally altering patterns and types of interactions among students, faculty, researchers, community problem solvers, and other campuses and universities. Interactive multimedia, including video discs, compact disc-read only memory (CD-ROM), high-definition televisions, and advanced computers, have made their way into academic instruction. Equally important, advanced technology will allow students, faculty, and researchers in colleges and universities to interact in collaborative learning and problem solving with colleagues at other institutions and in other organizations.

Minority students' language policy is hailed as an enhancement of the status of the indigenous language communities (Sherpa, Tamang, Magar, Rai, Tharu, and Dhimal) as a significant part of national development. Empowerment comes when pedagogy encourages critical, independent thinking, and when the aim is to build on a child's strengths rather than identify weaknesses (Cummins, 1986).

Nepali educators are conscious of the acute crisis caused by scarcity of resources and the inertia of an educational system that lacks practical utility to life. Access to education in remote hill areas is hindered because societies are facing extreme poverty. Success in these areas will be a hard task to achieve.

Nepal needs efficiency, which is a concomitant of rapid industrialization, economic rationalism, and the goal of meritocracy. Nepal conveys the importance of human values like well-being, peace, friendship, and coexistence to other people of the world. This is only possible through education.

REFERENCES

Bajracharya, K. M. 1992. "Forest Resources and Environment in Nepal." Paper presented at the National Seminar on "Environment and Sustainable Development Issues in Nepalese Perspective," February 10–11, Kathmandu.

CERID (Center for Educational Research and Development). 1993. *Newsletter*, Tribhuvan University. Kathmandu: Research Centre for Educational Innovation and Development.

Cummins, J. 1986. "Empowering Minority Students: A Framework for Intervention." *Harvard Educational Review, 56*, 18–36.

Dahal, M. K. 1992. "Population and Development: Issues in Nepalese Perspectives." In B. K. Karki Chhetri, ed., *Population and Development in Nepal*. Central Department of Population Studies.

Dahl, R. A. 1956. *A Preface to Democratic Theory*. Chicago: University of Chicago Press.

Gilley, J. W. 1991. *Thinking about American Higher Education*. New York: Macmillan.

Hayes, A. C. 1993. "The Changing Demand for Children and Socioeconomic Development in Nepal." Paper presented at the National Seminar on Population and Sustainable Development in Nepal, March 22–26, Tribhuvan University.

Hurtado, S. 1992. "Tribhuvan University: Challenges and Remedies." *Education and Development 1991–92*. Kathmandu: Centre for Educational Research Innovation and Development.

Joshi, R. K. 1990. "Education and Polity: A Historical Perspective." *Education and Development 1989–90*. Kathmandu: Centre for Educational Research Innovation and Development.

Kansakar, T. R. 1993. "Setting Priorities for Budha Nilkantha School." *Rising Nepal*, September 26.

National Education Committee (NEC). 1988. *A Glimpse of Education in Nepal*.

———. 1992. Report of The National Education Commission. Keshar Mahal, Kathmandu, Nepal.

Pradhan, G. S. 1992. "University Literacy—Challenges for the 1990s." *Education and Development 1991–92*. Kathmandu: CERID.

Pradhan, R. M. 1992. "Population and Education in Nepal." In Bal Kumar, Karki Chhetri, ed., *Population and Development in Nepal*. CDPS, Tribhuvan University.

Ramsey, G. 1991. "The Need for National Policies in Education." *Unicorn, 17* (1), 34–41.

Regmi, M. P. 1987. "Historical Development of Psychology in Nepal." In G. H. Blowers and A. M. Turtle, eds, *Psychology Moving East*. A Westview Special Study. Boulder, Colo.: Westview Press.

Schattschneider, E. E. 1960. *The Semisovereign People: A Realist's View of Democracy in America*. New York: Holt, Rinehart, and Winston.

Thapa, K. B. 1992. "Feudalism in Nepal: A Perspective of Socioeconomic History." *Tribhuvan University Journal*, 67–73.

13

NORTH KOREA

Gay Garland Reed
and Bong Gun Chung

Producing an overview of higher education in the Democratic People's Republic of Korea (DPRK) presents some methodological problems. This is due to several factors: (1) Data are not collected and reported in North Korea in a form consistent with Western scholarship and most of the statistical data are over a decade old. (2) Primary sources like the works of Kim Il Sung and books by North Korean scholars are highly politicized, obscuring the line between reliable data and ideology. (3) Our research dilemma is similar to that of China watchers two decades ago. Since we have not traveled to North Korea ourselves, we are relegated to relying on the eyes, ears, and writings of those who have.

The DPRK is a highly literate country. U.S. government analysts estimated in 1979 that North Korea had achieved a literacy rate of over 90 percent. A more recent source estimates the figure at 95 percent (Thomas, 1983:236). Bordered by the People's Republic of China and The Republic of Korea, the DPRK has an ethnically, linguistically, and ostensibly ideologically homogeneous population of approximately 22 million. It is noted for its rigid communist stance, its insularity, and its promotion of the cult of Kim Il Sung and, more recently, of his son and successor Kim Jong Il.

All aspects of the revolution, ideological, technical, and cultural, are dependent on the North Korean "cradle to grave" education system. While most authors who write about North Korean education agree that the system is quite developed in terms of allocation of resources and universal access to free education, it must be stressed that the officially stated purpose of education is to produce a socialist mind and body; academic freedom is nonexistent.[1]

The present school system consists of general schools, special schools, and adult schools. In 1972 universal eleven-year compulsory education was instituted. Aside from the formal education system, there are very potent and per-

Figure 13.1
History of North Korean Education

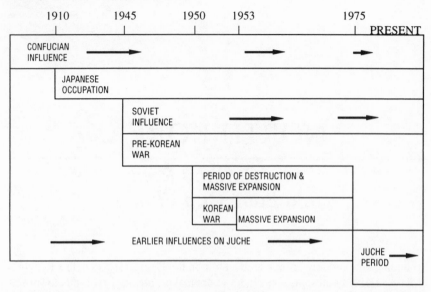

vasive nonformal and informal systems that promote the *Juche* principle, which
has become the defining factor of North Korean communism. *Juche*, which we
define in detail below, is a Korean word that broadly means ''self'' or ''subject.'' It denotes a modified practice of Marxism and Leninism in the unique
context of North Korean culture and politics, strongly emphasizing self-reliance
and independence. The *Juche* principle is central to a study of higher education
because it is simultaneously the philosophy that guides North Korean education
and the object of intense scholarly research at institutions of higher learning in
the DPRK.

Since all education in North Korea is designed to serve the socialist cause, it
is important to examine the principles that undergird North Korean education
and guide educational policy. We propose to do this by examining relevant
materials in *The Works of Kim Il Sung*, including the *Theses on Socialist Education*, as well as other publications about North Korean education from both
North and South Korea as well as the United States.

PROFILE OF THE HIGHER EDUCATION SYSTEM

As a prelude to the discussion of higher education, it is useful to take a look
at the historical, social, and ideological context of education in the DPRK. For
the purpose of this study we have divided the history of North Korean education
into five periods: the Confucian period, the Japanese Occupation period, the Pre-
Korean War period, the Destruction and Massive Expansion period (Kim, Tong-
gyu, 1990a:99–114), and the *Juche* period. (See figure 13.1.)

Confucian Period (Ancient Korea to 1910)

Like other countries in Northeast Asia, Korea has Confucian roots. Chinese thought and culture had an enormous impact on Korea, especially among the *yangban* (aristocratic) class. Although the Korean alphabet (*hangul*) was developed by a group of scholars during the reign of King Sejong in 1446, Chinese characters were imported into the Korean language and used in official documents, scholarly texts, and poetry. To be educated was to know the Chinese classics. In South Korea even today, in order to lead an "intellectual life" one is expected to know between 1,500 and 2,000 Chinese characters. This is not the case in North Korea, which instituted the exclusive use of *hangul* immediately following the Japanese occupation as a means of ridding the country of the legacies of past feudalism.[2]

Although Chinese characters are no longer used in the North, the DPRK maintains close ties with China and certain aspects of Confucianism are still apparent. Paternalism, authoritarianism, and respect for learning are aspects of Confucianism that continue to influence educational thought and pedagogy in North Korea. Figure 13.1 suggests that this influence has continued despite the communist repudiation of Confucianism as a feudalistic belief system that denigrates manual labor and maintains class stratification.

Japanese Occupation Period (1910–45)

Although Korea maintained a system of very sophisticated Confucian schools for many centuries, higher education in the modern sense did not exist until the establishment in 1925 of Kyoungsung Imperial University, the predecessor of Seoul National University. Although this institution for higher learning was built on Korean soil, the majority of the students who attended were Japanese. Since most higher-order jobs were taken by Japanese, there was little need to provide the local Koreans with tertiary education. It is important to remember that during the Japanese occupation, Koreans were forbidden from speaking their native language in schools and endured a period of systematic deculturalization that has left deep psychological scars. This experience of cultural imperialism was relived for decades in the speeches of Kim Il Sung and contributed to the formation of the *Juche* principle, the belief in self-reliance, which became a central feature of Korean communism.

During the Japanese occupation of Korea there were strong anticolonial forces at work. Two important centers of resistance were Korea University, which was founded with local capital, and Yonsei University, which was founded by American missionaries. Both of these universities are located in the South.

Pre-Korean War Period (1945–50)

In the period after liberation from the Japanese, enormous advancements were made in the DPRK in eradicating illiteracy. Adult schools, evening schools, workshop schools, and Korean alphabet schools were set up all over the country for this purpose (President, 1992:54). North Koreans designate this period as the "peaceful building up period and democratization of schools and education" (Kim Tong-gyu, 1990a:101–4).

This was also the period when Soviet influence began to be felt in schools.[3] Pictures of Russian heroes appeared in Korean schools and students were exhorted to "learn from the Soviet Union" (Yang and Chee, 1963:126). Famous Soviet pedagogues such as N. K. Krupskaya, who was the wife of Lenin, and A. S. Makarenko were noted and quoted in North Korean educational materials used in teachers' colleges. The combination of theory and practice and collectivism in education, which are major themes in North Korean education, originate from these sources (Kim, Tong-gyu, 1990a:102; 1990b:76–77).

All schools, including those that had been used by the Japanese living in Korea, those that had religious affiliations, and those that were privately owned, were consolidated into a single government-controlled system. Educational advisors, some of whom were Soviet Koreans, went to North Korea to revolutionize the system (Scalapino and Lee, 1972:900). These Soviet educational advisors trained teaching cadres in teachers' colleges. At the same time, college students from DPRK went to the Soviet Union for higher education (Yang and Chee, 1963:127).

Destruction and Massive Expansion Period (1950–75)

This broad designation spans the period from the beginning of the Korean War in 1950 to 1975, when the eleven-year compulsory education policy was fully implemented.

The Korean peninsula was devastated by the war, which lasted from 1950 to 1953. Ninety percent of all cultural and educational facilities were destroyed and 850,000 students from the north, about half the total number, were mobilized for the war effort (Yang and Chee, 1963:127).

The period following the Korean War was marked by successive reforms in the field of education. Universal primary education was established in 1956 (Scalapino and Lee, 1972:1105). This was gradually increased over the next two decades until 1972, when the eleven-year system was introduced. The period between 1972 and 1975 was marked by massive expansion in the educational sector. State investment increased 1.7 times, 60,000 teachers were trained, and 30,000 more classrooms were built. By 1975 there were 60,000 kindergartens and nurseries, 4,700 primary schools, and 4,100 senior middle schools in the DPRK (Universal, 1981:12). The year 1975 marked the end of this period of massive educational expansion and the full implementation of the eleven-year compulsory education system.

Juche Period (1975–Present)

We have chosen to designate 1975 as the beginning of the Juche period even though the seeds were sown much earlier. North Korea traces the origin of Juche to the Manchu armed resistance period; the desire for self-determination was a natural response to Japanese colonialism. Kim Il Sung, who became the North Korean premier and chairman of the Korean Workers' Party in 1948 and ruled until his death in 1994, made national dignity and identity objectives of his political movement from its start (Yang and Chee, 1963:127).

For several decades the *Juche* principle was defined and discussed in the copious *Works of Kim Il Sung*. The official adoption of *Juche* as a statement of principle was made in 1970 in a Korean Workers' Party resolution and again in 1972 in the North Korean Constitution (Chung Young Soo, 1990:29). On the occasion of the First Youth Day on August 26, 1991, Kim Jong Il, son of Kim Il Sung, made the following statement to the League of Socialist Working Youth: "The *Juche* idea is the sole guiding ideology of our revolution and the lifeblood of our nation. All the revolutionary struggle of our party and our people is to implement the *Juche* idea" (*North Korea Quarterly*, 1991:257).

Since the objective of North Korean education is the creation of "*Juche* type revolutionaries" and *Juche* is the principle that undergirds the political and economic systems, it is useful to understand what this term means and to discuss its implications for the education system.

Juche is most often translated as "self-reliance" or "self-identity," but the meaning is imprecise. It can also refer to national pride, national assertiveness, or national identity, depending on the context (Bunge, 1981:176). Kim Il Sung's often-reiterated position on *Juche* was that it represented an independent stance that rejected dependence on others and required self-reliance and acknowledgment of one's own strength.

The principle is further illuminated in Kim Il Sung's *Theses on Socialist Education*, which was released at the 14th Plenary Meeting of the Fifth Central Committee of the Workers' Party of Korea on September 5, 1977. This document is perhaps the most quoted of all documents in North Korean writings dealing with the educational system. In the theses, Kim Il Sung reiterates themes from his collected works and encapsulates his views on the principles, pedagogy, content, and policies of North Korean socialist education. The document also stresses that the *Juche* principle is a "scientific and revolutionary world outlook indispensable for men of a communist type" (Kim J.S., 1977:17).[4]

In the *Theses on Socialist Education, Juche* appears to be synonymous with communism although at a later time Kim Il Sung suggests that it actually supersedes communism:

The guiding idea of our socialist education is communism, the *Juche* idea. Communism, the Juche idea, is the ideological, theoretical and methodological basis of socialist education. Communism, the *Juche* idea, gives correct answers to all theoretical and practical problems arising in educational work and shows the direction in which socialist education should develop. (ibid.:8)

Later in the same document, Kim Il Sung explains that the unique environmental, social, and cultural characteristics of a nation demand that it train its people to conform to that reality and thus, education must focus on the history, culture, nature, and geography of one's own country. Even subjects like science and technology, which are imported from other countries, should be studied from the standpoint of the Korean situation (ibid.:10ff.). "The purpose of learning and introducing foreign things should always be to get better acquainted with our own things and to carry out our revolution and construction more efficiently" (ibid.:12).

The emphasis on *Juche*, or the nationalist orientation, as the central principle of North Korean communism represented a shift in emphasis from the North Korean Marxist-Leninism of the post-liberation days, which took a more internationalist stance (Scalapino and Lee, 1972:847–48). This narrow focus on self-interest and self-study has also been relatively successful in sustaining the personality cult of Kim Il Sung.

TYPES OF INSTITUTIONS OF HIGHER EDUCATION

There are multiple models of tertiary education in the DPRK. Some courses of study are completed in as little as two years; others might take as long as twelve years if the student moves through all of the levels to take the terminal doctoral degree. The options include: factory colleges (5 to 6 years), factory vocational junior colleges (4 years), vocational colleges (3 years), university and college (2 to 6 years), research institutes (equivalent to master's degree—3 to 4 years), and doctoral institutes (2 years) (Kim and Ahn, 1993:32; Kim Tong-gyu, 1990b:126–27). Of course this list also includes teachers colleges (3 to 4 years) and medical schools. Political elites of the Workers' Party of Korea are retrained at special schools that include the Socialist Working Youth University (3 years), the Politics University of the North Korean CIA (3 years), and the Kim Il Sung High Level Elite School (Lee Chung-gak, 1990:292).

Most colleges and universities have daytime, evening, and correspondence classes. Higher education expanded significantly in the 1980s. The number of colleges and universities including teachers colleges and factory colleges was 170 in 1980, but in 1989 the number reached 270. Two- and three-year junior colleges increased from 516 to over 600 during the same period (Kim Sun-ho, 1990:279–96; Lee Chong-gak in Hwang et al. 1990:292–94). These numbers are consistent with statistics found in Kim and Ahn (1993) (see table 13.1).

Expansion of the tertiary education system has continued into the 1990s. In April 1994 the minister of finance of the DPRK, Yun Ki Chong, delivered a report on the 1993 budget in which he indicated that more than twenty universities and colleges made their appearance in 1993, including universities of technology, agriculture, and physical education (*SWB*, 1994).

Table 13.1 also provides data regarding student enrollment. Although Kim and Ahn did not provide statistics for student enrollment in 1987, the UNESCO statistical yearbook of 1992 indicates that in 1987 there were 390,000 students enrolled in higher education institutions. UNESCO also notes that 2,468,000

Table 13.1
Expansion of Higher Education in North Korea

Year	Number of Institutions	Number of Students	Number of Professors	Students per Professor
1945	4	3,130	140	22.4
1950	15	10,240	980	18.6
1955	17	12,860	1,180	10.9
1960	76	97,000	3,900	24.9
1965	98	156,000	7,810	20.5
1970	129	71,000	3,450	20.5
1972	140	77,000	3,760	20.5
1975	150	92,000	4,490	20.5
1980	170	258,000	7,100	36.1
1982	186	256,000	7,100	36.1
1988	235	n.a.	n.a.	n.a.

Source: Adapted from Kim and Ahn (1993).

students were enrolled in secondary education in the same year. Given the large number of institutions of higher education and the national emphasis on tertiary education for all, the enrollment is surprisingly low and the percentage of students who go on for higher education is also low. This might be partly explained by the fact that 70 percent[5] of the freshman class is comprised of those who were recently discharged from compulsory military service, a commitment that may last from five to ten years (Kim Tong-gyu, 1990b:429).

UNIVERSITY AND COLLEGE ADMITTANCE

Admission to institutions of higher education is based on political considerations and scholastic achievement, in that order (Kwon, 1993:5). In this respect the DPRK resembles the People's Republic of China in the late 1960s and early 1970s, a period characterized by Susan Shirk (1982) as a "virtuocracy." She used this term to describe the system in China in which access to education and jobs in the society was dependent on demonstrated political purity as shown by adherence to state orthodoxy. China has departed from this approach of rewarding people within the system, but North Korea is still very much a "virtuocratic" system.

In the past, applicants to college sent their documents, including a list of five preferred colleges or schools, to the education department of the local administrative committee in the city or county of their residence. The applications included recommendations by an employer or school, a performance record, an evaluation of political attitude written by the chairman of the local youth league, a statement of social origin (peasant, worker, or intellectual), family situation, "trend of thought," and general calibre. Screening of the applications was done by a selection committee composed of Party cadres and staff members of the administrative, social, and educational organizations of that district. This committee then assigned the applicants to colleges based on the quota set by the provincial organizations. Once assigned to a college, the student took the entrance examination. The results of this examination, along with the student's social status and political activities, determined whether or not the student would be accepted (Vreeland, 1976:118).

STRATIFICATION WITHIN THE SYSTEM

North Korea's most prestigious institution of higher learning is Kim Il Sung University (KISU), which was founded in 1946, two years before the official establishment of the North Korean government. As of 1980, KISU had 50 departments in 13 schools and 10 research institutes with 1,200 faculty members. The 13 schools are: history, philosophy, politics and economy, law, foreign languages and literature, Korean language and literature, mathematics, energy and dynamics, physics, chemistry, biology, geography and geology, and automation science (Kim and Ahn, 1993:33).[6]

The continued emphasis on communist ideology is evident in the curriculum. For example, all one thousand students in the school of history of Kim Il Sung University study the history of the people's revolution for four and one half years according to Choe Yong-sik, the dean of that department, who was interviewed in Paris at a Korean Studies meeting in 1991.

Far less prestigious than Kim Il Sung University or any of the other established provincial universities and colleges throughout the country are the study-while-working colleges, whose numbers have grown exponentially over the past several decades. Theoretically, 100 percent of factory workers attend school part-time while they are working (Scalapino and Lee, 1972:1289). This study-while-working model was the result of an on-the-spot inspection by Kim Il Sung at Kim Chaek Engineering College in 1960. At the time he noted that study was detached from practical production and proposed the union of education and productive work with an emphasis on technical training (Scalapino and Lee, 1972:1288). Besides promoting technical expertise, these schools also served the ideological purpose of "critiquing exploitive capitalism."

In the *Theses on Socialist Education*, Kim Il Sung suggested that tertiary institutions that promote "ideological, technical and cultural revolutions" should be distributed in rural as well as urban areas and in industrial and agricultural zones so as to maintain a developmental balance throughout the country and address unique regional characteristics (Kim Il S. 1977:45). He was clear that the intellectualization of the society would only be complete when higher education became compulsory. In 1992 the process of "assimilating the whole society to intelligentsia" was reiterated at the Sixth Congress of the Workers' Party of Korea. At that time it was noted that over one hundred higher education institutions had been expanded or set up in cities, industrial zones, rural areas, and fishing villages within a period of ten years (*FBIS*—EAS, 1992:22). Most of these institutions were factory or farm-attached colleges.

The curriculum of factory colleges is divided into two broad categories: theoretical training, which includes political training, and technical training. In the early 1970s, political training consisted of five hours a week studying Kim Il Sung's *History of Struggle* and the history of the Korean Workers' Party, four hours a week for foundations of Marxism-Leninism, and five hours a week of Russian language training. This accounted for 60 percent of the time. The rest of the time was spent in specialized technical training (Scalapino and Lee, 1972: 1289–90).

EDUCATIONAL FUNDING

The free compulsory eleven-year education system is a source of great pride to North Korean leaders, who regularly compare themselves with other countries of the world and in particular with the Republic of Korea to the south. Kim Il Sung has described the system in the DPRK as the "most advanced system of free compulsory education" (*FBIS*—EAS, 1993:19). According to a statement released in 1993, each student is granted a benefit of 16,000 won from the state for the entire period from kindergarten to university. This figure is equivalent to the wages of an average worker who is paid 130 won per month for ten years and three months.

Students in the study-while-working system at the tertiary level are paid full wages and pay no tuition for their studies. Stipends are paid to students at colleges and universities who are not part of the study-while-working program. The DPRK government notes that these stipends grew 33 percent on average between February 1992 and February 1993. Given the impact of the collapse of the Soviet Union on the North Korean economy, this percentage seems a bit inflated.

Another institution of higher education is the Academy of Social Sciences, which was established in December 1963. Its forerunner, the Academy of Sciences, was established during the Korean War in 1952. The purpose of this institute according to Kwak Son-up, the director of external affairs, is "to study the line and policy of the Korean Workers' Party and to systematize the *Juche* idea." Studies at the Academy of Social Sciences include: *Juche* idea, history, linguistics, archaeology, literature, philosophy, law, and world economy. Within the academy there is also a Folklore Institute (*FBIS*—EAS, 1991:23).

It must be emphasized that an important characteristic of the education system of the DPRK for the past several decades has been the close, sustained interrelationship between educational policy and the personality cult of Kim Il Sung and later, though to a lesser degree, his son, Kim Jong Il.

RESPONSE TO INTERNAL DEMANDS

Intelli (intellectuals), as they are known in North Korea, is a category that includes not only those who are engaged in the humanities, sciences, and social sciences but also managers, technicians, engineers, and numerous professionals that require some higher education. The dearth of competent manpower in industry as well as in political revolution has led North Korea to emphasize the fostering of *intelli* as an elite group involved in the process of nation building (Chong Sung Jin, 1984:6–11).

Historically, the role and status of intellectuals in North Korea are somewhat different from the Chinese case. Unlike Mao Zedong, who harbored a continuing mistrust of intellectuals and targeted them for persecution, Kim Il Sung nurtured intellectuals. Since many of the most capable had relocated in Japan during the Japanese occupation or fled to the south during the Korean War, Kim Il Sung realized that the success of his regime was contingent upon maintaining the loyalty of those intellectuals who remained. The importance of the historic contributions of North Korea's intellectuals is recognized in the symbol of the Korean Workers' Party, which is a hammer and sickle with a writing brush superimposed over it signifying the "three-class alliance" of workers, peasants, and intellectuals (Cumings, 1990:55). Despite this recognition, however, South Korean scholar Kim Tong-gyu points out that until 1969 teachers received lower wages than coal miners (Kim Tong-gyu, 1990b:359).

The central role of North Korean intellectuals in the process of socialist construction was reiterated in 1992 when Pyongyang released a statement that "One million, six hundred thousand intellectuals in Korea are now living a worthy life as eternal companions, faithful helpers and good advisers in the building and activities of the Workers Party of Korea" (*FBIS—EAS*, 1992:30). The tone of this passage is characteristic of North Korean ideological management. The larger statement from which this passage is drawn uses the historical perspective to remind readers of the contributions made by intellectuals from the period following liberation in 1945 to the present. These contributions include fighting alongside the People's Army in the "Fatherland Liberation War" (Korean War), the rebuilding of the country during the postwar period, contributions made during the period of socialist industrialization (1957–70), and their contributions to successfully solving scientific and technological problems concerned with modernization and the "scientification of the national economy" (ibid.).

INTERNATIONAL STUDENT EXCHANGES

The ideological rigidity of the DPRK has made international student exchanges difficult. Nevertheless there have been, and continue to be, educational exchanges, primarily between North Korea and other communist countries. Both North Korean student returnees who were often ''corrupted'' by their overseas associations and introductions to less rigid forms of communism, and international students in the DPRK who interacted with and ''corrupted'' students at home, have been a source of problems for the DPRK government.

In particular, students who traveled outside North Korea posed problems. Scalapino and Lee report that as early as 1961, all but a few students were recalled from Eastern Europe and the Soviet Union for fear that they would give in to the power of revisionism (1972:899). Later, when students were once again allowed to study in Eastern Europe, they were again recalled after the fall of the Berlin Wall. It became clear that there were no ''safe'' countries. Albania, China, and Mongolia, which were once only tainted by ''revisionism,'' have increasingly fallen into ''capitalistic tendencies.'' According to reports, some of the students who studied in other countries ''began suffering the doubts of an apostate when they saw the world beyond the world that Kim Il Sung had built'' and even ''lost their faith'' (Shapiro, 1994:40). An American acquaintance who taught in China from 1987 to 1992 reports that on two separate occasions North Korean students studying at leading universities in China approached him requesting his help in gaining political asylum in the United States. Since only the most politically trustworthy students are sent abroad to study, this anecdotal information suggests that there are ideological struggles within the DPRK that are not publicly acknowledged.

Similar concerns of ideological corruption are raised when students from other countries go to North Korea to study. It was reported, for example, that a Chinese student was involved in some of the student unrest at Kim Il Sung University in 1993. Considering the fact that it has traditionally been the students who were the vanguard of dissent and political change in Korea, these signs must be disquieting for the DPRK government.

FUTURE DEVELOPMENTS

The collapse of the Soviet Union, which precipitated severe economic hardship in the DPRK, the succession of Kim Jong Il to the position of leadership after his father's death in 1994, the complex international negotiations related to the nuclear issue, and the continuing discussions regarding reunification of the Korean peninsula will all have inevitable repercussions for the higher education system.

We suggest three possible scenarios for the future of higher education in North Korea. The first is ideological retrenchment and continued isolationism punctuated by infrequent student exchanges with communist, former communist, and nonaligned nations. In this case the DPRK would maintain its higher education system as is, while continuing to promote study-while-working programs and to emphasize ideological training. The second scenario would come about as a result of the reunification of the Korean peninsula. In this case, we would expect to see rather dramatic structural and ideological changes in the tertiary education system and a general democratization of the system at all levels. The third scenario that we posit is more gradualist in nature. It would begin with an increase in the number of cultural and scholarly exchanges between North Korea and countries throughout the world. The emphasis would be on fostering understanding and developing ties that would promote economic well-being while maintaining the educational sovereignty of the North Korean nation.

Among these three scenarios, the latter seems most probable. A gradualist approach would strive to balance ideology and technology. The fear of Western contamination of the *Juche* ideology will inevitably accompany an open-door policy, but the need for technological and economic infusion from outside makes taking such a risk necessary.

NOTES

1. For example, Rhee Yong Bok's (1984) *Education in the Democratic People's Republic of Korea*, published in Pyongyang, quotes heavily from the works of Kim Il Sung and is highly propagandistic in nature.

2. Disconnection from the feudal past is also disconnection from thousands of years of cultural and intellectual achievements. Abolishing the use of Chinese characters has created a discontinuity of culture.

3. At the end of World War II, Korea, which was regarded as Japanese territory, was divided into two military occupation zones. The Soviet Union controlled the North and the United States controlled the South. Military governments were temporarily set up on either side of the 38th Parallel and this division of Korea was the foundation of two politically, economically, and educationally estranged societies.

4. The timing of this document is significant because it comes just after the death of Mao Zedong, the fall of the Gang of Four, and the period of ideological retrenchment in China when Hua Guofeng was establishing his right to succeed Mao Zedong.

5. Lee Chong-gak (1990) uses a figure of 30 percent to 40 percent based on testimony of North Korean defectors.

6. In *North Korea: A Country Study* (1981:88), the list for the same year is somewhat different. That list includes: automation sciences, biology, geography, geology, history, law, literature, mathematics, philosophy, physics, and political economics. The same article indicates that there are 3,500 faculty, of which 1,200 are teaching faculty (p. 88).

REFERENCES

Bunge, Frederica M. 1981. *North Korea: A Country Study.* U.S. Secretary of the Army.
Cumings, Bruce. 1990. *The Two Koreas: On the Road to Unification?* Headline Series. New York: The Foreign Policy Association.
Developments in North Korea. 1993. Seoul: Naewon.
Federal Broadcast Information Service (FBIS)—EAS. 1991. March 27, p. 23.
———. 1992. October 19, p. 22.
———. 1993. February 16, p. 19.
Kim, Il Sung. 1977. *Theses on Socialist Education.* Pyongyang, Korea: Foreign Languages Press.

Kim, Ransoo, and Yong Sop Ahn. 1993. "Higher Education in South and North Korea." *Higher Education Policy, 6* (2), 29–36.

Kwon, Hyuk Kie. 1993. "University Education in North Korea." *Vantage Point.*

———. 1991, Summer–Fall. *North Korean Quarterly* (61–62). Hamburg, Germany: Institute for Asian Affairs.

———. 1992. *President Kim Il Sung and Development of Education in Korea.* Pyongyang: Kyowon Sinmun.

North Korean Quarterly. 1991. Nos. 61&62, Summer/Fall. Hamburg, Germany: Institute for Asian Affairs.

President. 1992. *President Kim Il Sung and the Development of Education in Korea.* Pyongyang, Korea: Kyowon Sinmun.

Scalapino, Robert, ed. 1963. *North Korea Today.* New York: Praeger.

Scalapino, Robert, and Lee Chong-sik. 1972. *Communism in Korea:* Part II, *The Society.* Berkeley: University of California Press.

Shapiro, Michael. 1994. "Annals of Authoritarianism: Kim's Ransom." *The New Yorker,* January 30, pp. 32–41.

Shirk, Susan. 1982. *Competitive Comrades: Career Incentives and Student Strategies in China.* Berkeley: University of California Press.

Summary of World Broadcasts (SWB). BBC. 1994. April 9, D/5.

Thomas, R. Murray. 1983. "The Democratic People's Republic of Korea (North Korea)." In R. Murray Thomas and T. Neville Postlethwaite, eds., *Schooling in East Asia: Forces of Change.* New York: Pergamon.

———. 1981. "Universal Eleven-Year Compulsory Education." *Indo-Korean Friendship.* New Delhi: Om Prakos Mantri.

Universal. 1981. "Universal Eleven-year Compulsory Education." *Indo-Korean Friendship, 12* (8–9). New Delhi: Om Prakos Mantri.

Vreeland, Nena. 1976. *Area Handbook for North Korea.* 2d ed., Washington, D.C.: Foreign Area Studies of American University.

Yang, Key P., and Chang-boh Chee. 1963. "The North Korean Educational System: 1945 to Present." In Robert Scalapino, ed., *North Korea Today.* New York: Praeger.

KOREAN LANGUAGE REFERENCES

Chung, Sung Jin. 1984. *Fostering the Huge Corps of Intellectuals in the Democratic People's Republic of Korea.* Pyongyang: Social Science Publishing.

Chung, Young-soo. 1990. "Pukhan ui kyoyuk yinyum" (Educational Ideology of North Korea). In Chung Kyu Hwang, Huh Suk, Chung Young-soo, Lee Sung-ho, and Lee Chung-gak, eds. *Pukhan kyoyuk ui chomyong (Spotlight on North Korean Education).* Seoul: Pommunsa.

Hwang, Chung Kyu, et al. 1990. *Spotlight on North Korean Education.* Seoul: Bobmunsa.

Kim, Chang Ho. 1990. *History of North Korean Education.* Pyongyang: Social Science Publishing.

Kim, Dong Kyu. 1990. *Pedagogy of North Korea.* Seoul: Mun Maek Sa.

Kim, Hyong Chan. 1990. *North Korean Education.* Seoul: Ulyoumunhwasa.

Kim, Sun-ho. 1990. "Kodung Kyoyuk" (Higher Education). In Kim Hyong Chan, ed., *Pukhan ui kyoyuk (North Korean Education).* Seoul: Uryumunhwasa.

Kim, Tong-gyu. 1990a. "Kyoyuksa" (Educational History). In Kim Hyong-chan, ed., *Pukhan ui kyoyuk (North Korean Education)*. Seoul: Ulyoumunhwasa.

———. 1990b. *Pukhan kyoyukhak (Pedagogy of North Korea)*. Seoul: Munmaeksa.

Lee, Chung-gak. 1990. "Pukhan ui kyoyuk chungchaek gwa hengchung mit kodung kyoyuk" (Educational Policy, Administration, and Higher Education of North Korea). In Chung Kyu Hwang, Huh Suk, Chung Young-soo, Lee Sung-ho, and Lee Chung-gak, eds., *Pukhan kyoyuk ui chomyong (Spotlight on North Korean Education)*. Seoul: Pommunsa.

Rhee, Dong Gun, and Su Il Choi. 1979. *Juche Ideology in the Ideological and Methodological Foundation of Socialist Education*. Pyongyang: Science Encyclopedia Publishing.

Rhee, Yong Bok. 1984. *Education in the Democratic People's Republic of Korea*. Pyongyang: Social Science Publishing.

14

PAPUA NEW GUINEA AND THE PACIFIC ISLANDS

Mark Bray

The Pacific Ocean and the countries that lie within it comprise 35 percent of the earth's surface. However, the total population of these countries is just 13 million, which is only 0.03 percent of the world's total. The higher education systems that serve these countries are diverse and multifaceted, and face major challenges of size, resourcing, and orientation.

The various countries of the Pacific are formed from thousands of islands. The largest island is New Guinea, of which the western half is part of Indonesia and the eastern half is part of Papua New Guinea. Other islands are very small; some are separated from each other by huge expanses of sea.

As might be expected in so vast an area, the Pacific contains peoples of diverse cultures. It also contains nations with varied colonial histories, economic circumstances, and political inclinations. For present purposes, the region is taken to include the twenty-one countries listed in table 14.1. Of these, nine are full sovereign states, five are sovereign states in free association with other states, and seven are dependencies. The chapter will exclude discussion of Hawaii and Rapanui (Easter Island) since although these are certainly Pacific Islands, they are parts of larger states. The chapter also excludes discussion of New Zealand and Australia, which are on the Pacific Rim but really form a category by themselves.

Table 14.1 also provides figures on population, land area, and both total and per capita GNP. The populations and areas vary widely, from Tokelau with just 2,000 people and 12 square kilometers to Papua New Guinea with 3.8 million people and 461,690 square kilometers. The figures on total GNP also show wide variation, though some of the small territories have fairly high levels of per capita GNP. The statistics on land area disguise the fact that some states are compact while others are composed of very scattered islands. Niue and Nauru,

Table 14.1
Pacific Island Countries: Population, Land Area, Total GNP and Per Capita GNP

	Population (Thousands)	Land Area (Sq. Kms.)	Total GNP (US$ Million)	Per Capita GNP (US$)
America Samoa	38	197	190	5,000
Cook Islands	18	234	25	1,400
Federated States of Micronesia	91	702	128	1,400
Fiji	717	18,274	1,130	1,600
French Polynesia	189	4,000	1,370	7,250
Guam	126	549	670	5,320
Kiribati	68	861	40	670
Marshall Islands	45	181	n.a.	n.a.
Nauru	7	21	70	10,000
New Caledonia	154	19,058	860	5,580
Niue	2	259	4	2,000
Northern Mariana Islands	20	475	n.a.	n.a.
Palau	12	460	n.a.	n.a.
Papua New Guinea	3,800	461,690	3,444	900
Solomon Islands	319	29,785	130	410
Tokelau	2	12	n.a.	n.a.
Tonga	99	697	80	800
Tuvalu	8	26	5	630
Vanuatu	162	12,129	120	740
Wallis & Futuna	12	124	12	1,000
Westerm Samoa	159	2,934	100	630

Notes: N.a. = not available. Most figures refer to the late 1980s.
Sources: The Europa World Yearbook (London: Europa Publications, 1990); *The Statesman's Year-book* (London: Macmillan, 1989).

for example, are single islands, whereas the Federated States of Micronesia consist of several hundred islands. The north–south dimensions of Kiribati, which has 33 islands, stretch 2,000 kilometers and the east–west dimensions stretch 3,900 kilometers. Since the country crosses the international dateline, when it is Tuesday in the west it is only Monday in the east.

The implications of population, area, and both total and per capita GNP for higher education will become clear in subsequent sections of this chapter. A major question for the countries of the Pacific is how to operate higher education institutions that are large enough to secure economies of scale. One way, which will be given some prominence, is regional cooperation. However, regional cooperation faces many obstacles and is not an easy solution. The countries composed of scattered islands also face challenges concerning physical access to education. These are especially problematic in countries with low total and per capita GNP.

In addition to the diversity in population, area, and economic features is great diversity in cultures and histories. The major cultural groupings are Melanesian, Polynesian, and Micronesian (Crocombe, 1987:17–21). Melanesia includes Papua New Guinea, Solomon Islands, Vanuatu, New Caledonia, and parts of Fiji. Its peoples are generally dark-skinned and have curly hair. The points of the Polynesian triangle are New Zealand at the bottom, Hawaii at the top, and

Rapanui in the far east. Polynesians generally have lighter skin and straight hair. Micronesia embraces Kiribati, Nauru, Marshall Islands, Palau, Guam, and the northern Mariana Islands. Micronesians also generally have light skin and straight hair, though differ in facial features from Polynesians.

Further diversity exists within each group, especially within Melanesia. Papua New Guinea alone has over seven hundred distinct languages, and its peoples differ widely in their physical features and customs (Dorney, 1991). Solomon Islands has nearly eighty languages and corresponding cultural diversity (Laracy, 1989). Because none of the indigenous languages has sufficient dominance, in both of these countries almost all education is conducted in English. Some other countries have greater linguistic homogeneity, of which Tonga and Western Samoa are prominent examples. However, because of the need to access international literatures, even in these countries English is the dominant language at the postsecondary level.

Mention of the English language requires reference to the colonial history of the region. Here again, as indicated in table 14.2, diversity is the keynote. Within the Pacific are countries that at various points in history have been colonized by the United States, the United Kingdom, France, Japan, Spain, Germany, New Zealand, and Australia. The period of German colonialism was terminated by the First World War, and the period of Japanese colonialism was terminated by the Second World War. Although legacies from these periods do remain, they are not prominent in the education systems. However, the legacies of American, British, and French colonialism are very clear, both in the structures of education systems and in the languages of instruction.

PROFILE OF THE HIGHER EDUCATION SYSTEMS

While much of this chapter focuses on universities, the region also has many other institutions of higher education. Papua New Guinea, for example, has over sixty such institutions, including teachers' colleges, nursing colleges, seminaries, and agricultural colleges. Most of these institutions are government-funded (under the umbrellas of as many as fifteen different Ministries), though ten are private. Fiji has a school of medicine, an institute of technology, two schools of agriculture, a nursing school, and two teachers' colleges. Even Tonga has six postsecondary institutions; Vanuatu has five.

The seven universities in the region are:

• the University of Papua New Guinea, founded in 1966

• the Papua New Guinea University of Technology, which evolved from an institute of technology in 1969

• the University of the South Pacific, founded in 1968

• the *Universite Francaise du Pacifique*, founded in 1988

• the University of Guam, which evolved from a teachers' college in 1968

• the National University of Samoa, founded in 1984

• 'Atenisi University, in Tonga, which evolved from a lower-level institute in the 1980s

All but the last of these institutions are government-funded. The two Papua New Guinean universities are national institutions, as is the National University of Samoa. However, the University of the South Pacific (USP) was established to serve eleven countries, and since 1991 has served twelve. The eleven countries forming the original membership are Cook Islands, Fiji, Kiribati, Nauru, Niue, Solomon Islands, Tokelau, Tonga, Tuvalu, Vanuatu, and Western Samoa. The twelfth country is Marshall Islands. The *Universite Francaise du Pacifique* is also a regional institution, serving both New Caledonia and French Polynesia. About half the student body of the University of Guam comes either from other parts of Micronesia or from outside the region altogether.

It will be observed from the foundation dates of the universities that tertiary education in the Pacific is a relatively recent phenomenon. This reflects the fact that economic and social development in the region as a whole has occurred later than in most other parts of the world. The region was the last to commence the process of decolonization, which has still not been completed (Crocombe, 1987; Robie, 1989). This fact continues to have implications for the scale and nature of educational provision (Bray, 1993).

However, in all territories the creation of universities was preceded by other forms of postsecondary education. The earliest institutions were theological colleges established in the nineteenth century by the London Missionary Society. As the Society's influence moved east across the Pacific, colleges were established first in the Society Islands (now part of French Polynesia), then in the Cook Islands, Western Samoa, and the Loyalty Islands (now part of New Caledonia), and finally in Papua New Guinea. Other churches set up theological colleges in Tonga, Fiji, Vanuatu, Solomon Islands, and Pohnpei. Since the churches also ran schools, the colleges were concerned with teacher training as well as theology (Crocombe, Baba, and Meleisea, 1988:20–21).

For the historical record, it is also important to mention the Suva Medical School, established in Fiji in 1885. This institution began admitting regional students in 1914, and was given a formal regional mandate in 1928. At that time it became known as the Central Medical School, though it is today called the Fiji School of Medicine. The institution was supplemented by a special medical program at the University of Sydney for Papua New Guineans, but for several decades it remained the only medical school actually located in the Pacific Islands.

The postwar period brought the establishment of a number of secular teachers' colleges. One such college, founded in 1952, was the basis of what is now the University of Guam. Others were set up in Solomon Islands, Vanuatu, and elsewhere. The Micronesian Teacher Education Center was established in 1963, and in 1970 evolved into the Community College of Micronesia serving the

Table 14.2
Present Statuses and Colonial Histories of Pacific Island Countries

Country	Present Constitutional Status	Principal Colonial Rulers*
American Samoa	Unincorporated US Territory	USA (since 1899)
Cook Islands	Self-governing in free association with New Zealand	UK (1888-1901); New Zealand (since 1901); self-government since 1965
Federated States of Micronesia	State in free association with USA	Spain (1885-99); Germany (1899-14); Japan (1914-45); 1947-86 part of the US Trust Territory of the Pacific Islands
Fiji	Independent sovereign state	UK (1874-1970)
French Polynesia	Overseas Territory of France	France (since 1847)
Guam	Unincorporated US Territory	Spain (1565-1898); USA since 1898
Kiribati	Independent sovereign state	UK (1892-1979)
Marshall Islands	State in free association with USA	Germany (1878-1914); Japan (1914-45); 1947-86 part of the USA Trust Territory of the Pacific Islands
Nauru	Independent sovereign state	Germany (1888-1914); Australia (1914-68)
New Caledonia	Overseas Territory of France	France (since 1853)
Niue	Self-governing in free association with New Zealand	New Zealand (since 1901); self-government since 1974
Northern Mariana Islands	Commonwealth of the USA	Spain (1565-1899); Germany (1899-1914); Japan(1914-45); 1947-76 part of the US Trust Territory of the Pacific Islands
Palau	State in free association with USA	Spain (1885-99); Germany (1899-14); Japan (1914-45); since 1947 USA
Papua New Guinea	Independent sovereign state	UK (British New Guinea [later called Papua] 1884-1906); Germany (New Guinea 1884-1914); thereafter Australia till 1975.
Solomon Islands	Independent sovereign state	UK (1893-1978)
Tokelau	Dependency of New Zealand	UK (1889-25); New Zealand (since 1925)
Tonga	Independent sovereign state	Treaty gave UK control over foreign affairs (1901-70)
Tuvalu	Independent sovereign state	UK (1892-1978)
Vanuatu	Independent sovereign state	Anglo-French Condominium (1906-80)
Wallis & Futuna	Overseas Territory of France	France (since 1887)
Western Samoa	Independent sovereign state	Germany (1899-1914); New Zealand (1914-62)

*This summary excludes many details. For example, between 1947 and 1968 Nauru was formally a UN Trust Territory of Australia, the United Kingdom, and New Zealand, though Australia provided the administration. The summary also omits mention of Japanese occupation, e.g., of Nauru (1942–45), and of the Solomon Islands, Papua, and New Guinea (1942–44). Further, during the nineteenth and early twentieth centuries many islands were affected by lesser treaties that cannot be mentioned here.

Source: Douglas and Douglas (1989).

Federated States of Micronesia, Palau, and Marshall Islands. The year 1970 also saw foundation of a comparable college in American Samoa.

Despite the large number of institutions in Papua New Guinea, postsecondary enrollment rates are low. This is partly a function of low enrollment rates at primary and secondary levels. Only two-thirds of children aged seven to twelve attend primary school, and enrollment rates for lower and upper secondary education drop still further to 16 percent and one percent, respectively (Papua New Guinea, 1990:15). The majority of those who complete upper secondary education (grade 12) do continue to higher education, but it will be evident from the above figures that the enrollment rate is below one percent. Enrollment rates are also low in the other Melanesian countries, particularly Solomon Islands and Vanuatu. However, they are higher in the Polynesian and Micronesian countries.

One challenge facing almost all the higher education institutions in the region, especially those conceived as national institutions serving countries with small populations, has been their small size. For example, in 1991 the Tungaru Nurse Training School in Kiribati had just 29 students, while the Tarawa Teachers' College had only 58 and the Tarawa Technical Institute had 103. Some governments have sought to reduce this type of fragmentation by amalgamating institutions. One example is the Solomon Islands College of Higher Education (SICHE), which was formed in 1984 by combining the Solomon Islands Teachers' College, the Honiara Technical College, the Marine Training School, the School of Nursing, and the Public Service Training Centre. In 1992 the college had 3,000 students. Many of them studied on a short-term or part-time basis, however, and the college had only 1,200 full-time equivalents (FTEs).

Papua New Guinea also has many small institutions. A major watershed in that country was the creation in 1983 of a Commission for Higher Education (CHE). At that time the total student load of the 65 institutions was equivalent to only 10,500 FTEs, and 46 institutions had fewer than 200 FTEs (Murphy, 1989:175). Rationalization has been a major task for Papua New Guinea's CHE, but still faces many obstacles.

Like the Solomon Islands College of Higher Education, some universities have many part-time students. USP, for example, had 13,000 students in 1991 but only 3,350 FTEs. Many of the part-time students took extension courses. One way through which USP serves its member states is through distance education, and almost every country has either a campus or an extension studies center. Some classes are held via satellite. In 1971 the U.S. National Aeronautics and Space Administration (NASA) offered its Applications Technology Satellite for free use to the peoples of the Pacific Basin, and USP was among the first institutions to take up the offer. The satellite ceased to be operational in the mid-1980s, but was then replaced by another operated by the International Telecommunications Satellite Organisation (INTELSAT). The use of such technology to reduce the problems caused by distance is of considerable significance. The organization of classes is not easy, for they must cope not only with different time zones but also with the fact that member states of USP are on both sides of the international dateline. Despite such difficulties, however, USP's extension services network has become an operation of considerable effectiveness (Kacimaiwai, 1988; Monsell-Davis and Naidu, 1989).

The University of Papua New Guinea (UPNG) also has a network of extension centers. The first three were created in the early and mid-1980s, and by 1990 had been joined by another seven (Van Trease, 1990–91:113–14). These centers rely on funding from their provincial governments, and have not always operated smoothly. However, in 1990 they had over 4,500 students and were an important form of outreach. Many of the extension students were taking adult matriculation courses, which helped expand the pool of applicants for full-time on-campus study. Other students studied for diplomas of various kinds, and for the first year of the two-year in-service bachelor of education degree. The pass rate of those who actually took the examinations (excluding those who withdrew during the programs) was approximately 33 percent. This was much lower than that of students in full-time institutional study, but extension courses were still seen by the government as highly cost-effective (Papua New Guinea, 1990:48).

Finally, it is desirable to say a few words about 'Atenisi University, which was mentioned above, chiefly because it is different from all the other institutions and thus represents a form of counterpoint. The institution is the brainchild of its director, Futa Helu. Its origins lie in a small night school started in 1963 for staff of the Tonga civil service who wished to improve their English, algebra, geometry, bookkeeping, and mathematics skills. 'Atenisi is Tongan for Athens. Helu (1988:204) explains that he chose this name "as a symbolic recognition by the people of Tonga and the South Pacific of the great contribution made to universal culture by the ancient Greeks when they evolved philosophy and science." The institution is small, having in 1989 just sixteen staff and one hundred students, of whom twenty were part-time. The institution is also highly idiosyncratic. Nevertheless, it is worth mentioning not just for the sake of completeness but also because its existence as the South Pacific's only private university highlights the fact that all others are public institutions. 'Atenisi also presents a model for higher education that is just as viable in small states as in large ones (Bray and Packer 1993:68–70).

THE CHANGING FUNCTIONS AND PATTERNS OF HIGHER EDUCATION

Manpower and Political Development

Higher education in the Pacific plays an obvious role in production of qualified manpower. Indeed Papua New Guinea's Commission for Higher Education has described manpower development as the chief objective of higher education (CHE, 1986, quoted in Papua New Guinea, 1990:17). Qualified manpower continues to be needed not only for economic growth but also for localization. The latter has remained an important goal even in the 1990s, for the speed at which national governments have been able to replace expatriate workers by locals has been much slower than predicted in the 1970s and early 1980s (Curtin, 1989; Gannicott 1990; World Bank, 1992).

However, leaders in the Pacific countries resist the notion that higher education should be driven solely by manpower demands. For example, the 1990 plan for higher education in Papua New Guinea recognizes (p. 22) that "We must [also] produce more well-educated people with a sense of social responsibility; more historians, artists, authors, environmentalists, social scientists, youth and community workers, industrial relations practitioners, journalists, philosophers, theologians—people able to understand and contribute to Papua New Guinea other than through its economic development." Such a view would be echoed in other parts of the region (Throsby, 1987; Jones, Meek, and Weeks, 1991).

Allied to this perspective, albeit receiving less emphasis in the 1990s, is the perceived function of national integration. The early development plans of both UPNG and USP noted the great cultural diversity of the peoples that the institutions served. UPNG was established following the 1964 report of a team led by Sir George Currie, former vice chancellor of the University of Western Australia. That report (quoted by Murphy 1989:176) noted that the institution could easily become a victim of partisan politics, but added: "conversely, such an institution, given time to build up a tradition of autonomy, academic freedom, and useful service to the community at large, could be one of the most powerful factors of unity imaginable."

A similar goal was held by the architects of USP, though they aspired to regional as well as national unity. Both purposes were achieved to at least some extent. Writing as a Solomon Islander, for example, Maenu'u (1988:314) reported that "The growing up together, sharing, giving and taking at USP brought a new outlook to Solomon Islanders who have been there. And this encouraged more national awareness which creates a strong and real concern for one another, and which continues beyond the time spent together at the University." He added: "Not only did USP foster the cementing together of Solomon Islands students there, but being a regional institution they meet students from other countries of the South Pacific. Apart from the formal programmes, they also learn a lot from each other, and about their cultural backgrounds. Such interaction and understanding is very healthy for the South Pacific as a whole."

Some writers warn against overestimation of the nation-building factor (e.g., Crocombe and Meleisea, 1988:375; Murphy, 1989:181). Nevertheless, the political function has certainly been of importance, and is likely to remain so.

Stratification within the System

One result of the priorities for higher education during the 1960s and 1970s has been a structure that contains inherent inequalities. In the early years, the demands for manpower and political development were preeminent. Urgent needs remained in the 1990s, but attention had begun to turn to aspects of social stratification that were exacerbated by the higher education system. This included rural-urban, class, and gender stratification.

Papua New Guinea's 1990 higher education plan (p. 13) noted that unemployment already afflicted at least 25 percent of the urban population of working age. It stressed that "education—including higher education—must avoid reinforcing the viewpoint that national development and individual fulfilment are inevitably linked with urban residence." Yet while this is a noble goal, it is difficult to implement. The plan did emphasize extension services, which are able to reach people in smaller centers in addition to the main towns. However, extension centers cannot resolve the basic problem. The fact remains that not only in Papua New Guinea but also in the other Pacific countries, education *is* oriented to urban life. This is a function not only of curriculum but also, for the bulk of higher education, in the location of provision.

A similar point has been made by Crocombe and Crocombe (1994:126) with reference to Solomon Islands. Although only 10 percent of people live within thirty minutes' drive of the USP Center in the capital town, 76 percent of extension students were in the capital. Rural people lacked access to the center; the few who did enroll in USP extension courses suffered high dropout rates because of the lack of support services. Crocombe and Crocombe comment (1994:127) that "this concentration of educational privileges in the capital is noticeable in almost all [Pacific] island nations."

A second aspect of social stratification concerns the income groups that mainly benefit. Because the government of Papua New Guinea was anxious to expand access to higher education during the 1960s and 1970s, it introduced a system of fee-free education accompanied by generous scholarships. By the 1980s, the authorities had become more critical of this system, viewing it as costly and of questionable benefit even in promoting equity (Murphy, 1989:181; Papua New Guinea, 1990:34–35). As in other countries, change to a fee-charging system with more selective support to students has been a slow and controversial process. However, it seems inevitable that in the long run such change will occur; and it will be justified on the grounds of *greater* social equity in so far as resources will be channeled to students who are in most need rather than to all students, including those with little need. Similar developments are likely to occur in the USP region. For example, one recommendation of a 1992 World Bank study (p. 36) was that "governments should abolish general allowances for post secondary students and institute mechanisms which ensure that post secondary students and their families with the capacity to make a significant contribution to the costs of post secondary education pay for such education."

A third aspect of stratification concerns gender. Murphy (1985) presented a detailed analysis of output by sex from UPNG. During the 1970s and the first half of the 1980s, she pointed out (p. 147) that the overall output of female graduates was approximately 12 percent of the total. The annual percentage peaked in 1978 at 17 percent and again in 1981 at 16 percent, but fell again in

1982 to 12 percent. In 1974, she noted, female output formed just 3 percent of the total. Within degree studies, female output was relatively high in social work, education, and the arts, but was extremely low in agriculture, economics, law, and medicine. Murphy pointed out (pp. 151–52) that these patterns not only implied that national resources were going to men rather than women, but also that the situation was being perpetuated: "Through UPNG awards, localization of the upper echelons of the public bureaucracy including the key decision-making positions has taken place. Undoubtedly females form only a small percentage of these incumbents. It is self-evident that unless females participate in the decision-making process the interests of females in general tend to be overlooked."

Concentrating on UPNG, Murphy's paper did not in fact expose the worst-case scenario. At the University of Technology, proportional output of females was only a third of that at UPNG. The situation did improve so that by 1993 female enrollments at UPNG formed 23 percent of the total, and at the University of Technology 16.3 percent of the total (Commission for Higher Education, 1993). However, it was clear that enrollments remained very unbalanced.

A comparable pattern existed in the other Melanesian countries, particularly Solomon Islands and Vanuatu. However, as noted by Crocombe and Crocombe (1994:130), in Micronesia and Polynesia patterns were very different—to the extent that at the University of Guam and the Tahiti campus of the *Universite Francaise du Pacifique*, females were in the majority. To some extent this reflects a correlation between female enrollment rates and high per capita income.

TENSIONS AND RESPONSES: NATIONAL, REGIONAL, AND INTERNATIONAL

National Tensions

All societies in the Pacific face considerable tension between the traditional and the newly imported Western ways of life. Universities are part of the latter. They are linked to the wage economy and to what is called the modern sector; they transmit values that often conflict with those held in indigenous cultures (Colletta, 1980; Falgout and Levin, 1992). Extension of the wage economy, and the education system that accompanies it, also brings dependence on a larger world order. This has been vividly expressed by Habu (1985:10–11) with reference to Solomon Islands:

In our College we have a School called the School of Industrial Development. One of its important duties is to train mechanics to maintain all the imported machinery we bring in from other countries. Outboard motors and fibre-glass canoes are all over the place. . . . In exchange for these things we send timber to some people who depend on us for timber, and fish to those who like our fish.

Isolation gave Pacific societies the advantage of wanting only the things that could be procured from the immediate environment. Today, the economy has enabled them to have foods that can only be produced by people in other countries. This has led those who did not have these things to request these things, and become dependent on manufactured goods. Much of education is devoted to trying to learn about these new things—why they are made, how they are made, how they should be looked after. Instead of planting yams for dinner, many people now buy and sell imported goods in order to buy yams, or sell yams to buy rice.

Wasuka (1989:99) is similarly ambivalent:

Schooling is often talked about as being the key to well being and prosperity. It is an irony of modern Solomon Islands that it has instead become for many people an occasion of failure and disappointment, a sign of their exclusion from the development to which they aspire. Increasingly since the 1960s the obtaining of material rewards, higher social status and power has come to be dependent on educational achievement. But access to the education system is not available to everyone. As a result schooling, whatever benefits it confers, and they are innumerable, also works to increase social divisions.

Although comparable tensions may be found in all countries that are the focus of this book, in the Pacific region they are more acute because of the recent development of the cash economy and its accompaniments (Amarshi, Good, and Mortimer, 1979; Crocombe, 1987).

Some of the early architects of the university systems in the Pacific perceived this problem and sought to build on indigenous cultures rather than undermining them. Albert Wendt, from Western Samoa, was among these people. He joined the staff of USP in 1974, aspiring, he says (1989:92), "to help create and develop a university that was based on our visions and aspirations, to cater to our needs; a catalyst which would help develop the arts of our region." Sadly, by the time the university was twenty years old, Wendt could only report disillusion (p. 92):

Universities are about universities. . . . I should have remembered that. But in my youthful enthusiasm and belief that new things can be created I forgot. I also forgot that colonialism leaves its cultural baggage and imagery in our lives, thinking and visions of our power-makers and leaders who then recreate that imagery or support its recreation in our countries. I did not know then that USP had been conceived out of that imagery, planned and established by expatriates, modelled on the universities they knew and considered suitable for us.

Wendt and others who are concerned about such issues are not optimistic about the extent to which the universities of the Pacific region can resolve this tension. Thus, although the *Universite Francaise du Pacifique* endeavors to reflect and develop the cultures of the region through courses in Polynesian languages and the civilizations and cultures of Oceania, the architects of the university have carefully imitated the structures and retained links with universities elsewhere in the world, particularly in France (Borzeix, 1991). Similar tensions are evident in the University of Guam, which nurtures close links with the United States. Even the National University of Samoa, which had conservation of Samoan culture and language very high on the list of reasons for its establishment (Uili, 1988:210), is substantially developed in the Western mold. Wendt refers to the fact that the USP was conceived by expatriates. However, the tensions also exist in institutions conceived by Pacific Islanders.

Regional Tensions

At the regional level, particularly within the USP region, major tensions exist between the demands of nationalism and the basis of regional institutions. These have been especially evident in the University of the South Pacific itself. Although Western Samoa remains a member of USP, as already mentioned it has set up its own national university to provide local leadership in a way that USP is felt unable to do. The government of Solomon Islands aspires to follow suit by upgrading its College of Higher Education into a university; similar goals have been expressed in Tonga. Even Fiji has at times felt frustrated by the regional structure of USP, and has considered establishing a separate, national university (McCall, 1984:60).

These tensions are perhaps inevitable in regional institutions, and are also felt in the University of the West Indies (Sherlock and Nettleford, 1990). However, USP is more centralized than its West Indian counterpart.

For some, centralization has an inescapable logic:

Fiji is by far the largest country in terms of population, it is the most economically diverse and stable, and geographically it lies at the approximate centre of the region. Furthermore, the USP structure maps precisely onto the basic patterns of trade, transport, communications and regional politics in the South Pacific. . . . One of the strengths of the hub campus has been the capacity of the USP to build up a strong teaching and resource base so essential to the provision of effective academic programmes. A more decentralised model could have created particular difficulties for extension teaching, probably resulting in diffusion of effort. (Teasdale, 1993:146)

Others are less complimentary and confident. It is again worth quoting Wendt's perspective (1989:92–93): "I landed in a supposedly regional institution which, even though it was only a seven year old infant, was already centralized in Suva and would continue to become more centralized there, to be caught in the issue which plagues the USP to this day: centralization versus decentralization (and the pace of decentralization)."

Crocombe and Crocombe (1994) are among authors who have highlighted the ways in which Fiji has benefited from being the chief host to USP. Although Fiji has only 44 percent of people in the USP region, it has over 70 percent of students and regional staff posts, and over 90 percent of postgraduate students. Foreign donors have provided almost all the USP's capital funds and staff training, a high proportion of its scholarships, many of its staff salaries, and substantial contributions to the recurrent budget. Ostensibly these donations have been for the benefit of all USP member countries, but Crocombe and Crocombe argue that they have exacerbated regional inequalities. Had resources been allocated directly to USP member countries, they suggest, those countries could have insisted on a more equitable spread of both physical plant and benefits, as a condition of contributing to the regional network. Crocombe & Crocombe (1994:126) conclude that

Most island countries will be marginalised if they become pressured into a single Pacific islands regional system, and can only approach the world beyond through that system. Their leverage is their sovereignty, their ability to negotiate freely. And in a complex situation, flexibility, multiplicity, and freedom of choice are essential ingredients if the islands are to avoid being locked into the kind of bureaucratic straitjacket from which Eastern Europe is trying to escape.

The challenge for the institutions, and for the governments, therefore, is to find the best balance between competing forces. As might be expected, Geoffrey Caston, former vice chancellor of USP, takes a rather different view from Crocombe and Crocombe. He has attempted to respond positively to the tensions, and has been quoted as saying (Caston, 1989:52) that the university

was set up to do for its member countries those of their educational tasks which cannot effectively or economically be done nationally, or on a small scale. I hope national institutions like the Solomon Islands College of Higher Education, the National University of Samoa and the Fiji Institute of Technology, will continue to develop and free the resources of USP to do the work, at degree, and increasingly, at post-graduate level which only we can do. At present our development is hampered by the very pressing need for us to continue to fill gaps at sub-degree level in national educational provisions, with the result that much of the more advanced work continues to be done at overseas universities, often less appropriately. But this cannot be achieved unless more resources can be invested by national governments in national institutions without, of course, reducing their investment in their own regional institution. That is the way we should be going, but it will be hard.

It will indeed be hard; and the extent to which the optimum balance can be found will be a major determinant of the future at both regional and national levels.

International Tensions

Mention has already been made of the tension between aspiration on the one hand to serve and develop local cultures and on the other hand to retain international links. In their early years, all the universities of the Pacific region were conscious of international scrutiny and whether they would be considered "real" universities. One way to withstand this scrutiny was to build links with institutions in Australia, North America, and Europe through recruitment of expatriate lecturers and appointment of external examiners. These strategies have paid dividends, but have also created tensions.

Further tensions have arisen from the activities of external donors. For Papua New Guinea and the USP region this particularly means Australia and New Zealand. For American Samoa, Guam, Palau, the Northern Mariana Islands, the Marshall Islands, and the Federated States of Micronesia it means the United States; and for French Polynesia, New Caledonia, Wallis & Futuna, and to some extent Vanuatu, it means France. Each of these donors has perceived strategic reasons for assisting higher education, both directly in the recipient countries and through scholarships tenable in the donor countries (Hindson, 1987; Luteru, 1993). Many governments in the region have also taken loans from the World Bank and the Asian Development Bank.

For the recipients, such aid provides welcome budgetary support and linkages to the economies of more developed countries. However, not only may the assistance undermine efforts to link education more closely to national cultures and priorities; it may also undermine the ability of regional and national institutions to recruit good students.

Perhaps the strongest example of the latter is the Equity and Merit Award Scheme launched by the Australian government in 1990. Ostensibly this is a form of aid, but it also gives guaranteed revenue to Australian universities, which have been encouraged to become more market-oriented. The scheme allows students to apply directly to Australian universities, who make offers to students according to academic criteria. Unlike most other aid schemes, the final decision on offers is made by the Australian Universities International Development Program rather than the governments of the countries from which the students are recruited. Of the awards given in 1990 and 1991, 46 percent were for courses that were already available in the region (World Bank, 1992:58). In these cases, the scheme substantially had the effect of taking the best students out of the region and leaving only the lower-quality ones for USP and the other institutions.

More positively, it should also be mentioned that some regional training is provided for the smaller states by the higher education institutions in Papua New Guinea. Solomon Islands has sent significant numbers of students to UI'NG, and most other countries have sent smaller numbers. However, Papua New Guinea's external image has been negatively affected by its domestic security problems, and these enrollments fell markedly in the late 1980s and early 1990s.

FUTURE DEVELOPMENTS

Higher education in the Pacific region is set for considerable quantitative expansion. This is partly a function of population growth, but also reflects shortages of skilled manpower. Papua New Guinea's 1990 plan for higher education reports (p. 21) that many employers responding to a survey indicated a great need for "keen, well-educated and flexible young people, qualified in just about anything." The plan envisaged (p. 77) that the number of graduates would expand by 47 percent in ten years. At the same time, the number of academic staff would increase by only 22 percent, implying a higher education sector that operated more efficiently and had lower unit costs.

Comparable developments are envisaged elsewhere in the region. The 1992 World Bank study of Fiji, Kiribati, Solomon Islands, Tonga, Vanuatu, and Western Samoa noted (p. 13) that despite the slow economic growth over the 1980s, skill constraints were a major issue in all six countries. The study highlighted persistent vacancies in the public services, the slow pace of localization of senior positions, and the fact that many employees were inadequately trained for their current positions. There were of course variations among the countries, but the nature of the problem may be illustrated by the situation in Fiji. According to that country's Civil Service Management Information System, in 1991 there were 1,895 vacant posts (10.2 percent of the establishment) with most at middle and senior levels. The infrastructure sections of the Ministry of Works had a vacancy rate of 32 percent (267 posts) in an establishment of 839; and there was a 21 percent vacancy rate (209 positions) in the Ministry of Primary Industries. The World Bank envisaged that, as in Papua New Guinea, much of the increased higher education output could be achieved through increased efficiency in the existing institutions, including through filling of places currently lying vacant.

One mechanism through which governments plan to increase enrollments is through distance education. All countries of the region already have some distance education programs, which are an important mechanism for combatting the vast distances of the Pacific region. The government of Papua New Guinea (1990:48), for example, considers distance education a highly cost-effective way to reach large numbers of people. However, the 1992 World Bank study (p. 47) stressed the need within the USP region to strengthen existing extension services, select more carefully the range of courses offered, ensure provision of tutorial staff for all students, and hold regular academic reviews. The report also emphasized the need to assess the full cost implications of proposals to upgrade telecommunications/video capability, observing that in at least three countries the present radio/satellite service at the USP centers was not working because the countries could not finance the small recurrent costs of existing communication capabilities. The same sort of caution is needed in other parts of the Pacific. Distance education has much potential, but is not the answer to all problems.

Returning to the full-time face-to-face studies, all governments are actively concerned about quality as well as expansion. The government of Papua New Guinea (1990:55), worried about the number and quality of entrants to higher education, stresses the need to expand enrollments in the national high schools. The government is also concerned about the quality of processes of higher education, and in 1993 embarked on a U.S.$28 million project with assistance from the Asian Development Bank partly aimed at qualitative upgrading.

Shortcomings in both student intakes and training processes have also been identified in smaller countries in the region. For example, the teacher training course in Kiribati requires only completion of Secondary Form 3 for entry, and in addition to the limited output of secondary education, quality is often especially poor in science and mathematics (World Bank, 1992:23). Trainers in the higher education institutions are also commonly underqualified, with 60 percent holding qualifications at the same level that they teach.

Finally, the pace of localization of staff has been much slower than anticipated in the 1970s and early 1980s. In 1993, 23.9 percent of staff in Papua New Guinea's universities were noncitizens (Commission for Higher Education, 1993); respective figures were 29.0 percent in the community (primary) school teachers' colleges, and 25.3 percent in the nursing schools. Comparable figures were found in many of the smaller countries of the region, which in many cases lose many qualified people through emigration. At least until the early 1990s, Papua New Guinea had not suffered seriously from brain drain, but there was some danger that loss of talented personnel could reach much higher proportions. Thus although the future is likely to bring much greater localization, that too should not be overestimated.

Finally, higher education in the Pacific region will continue to experience tensions in the search for its own identity. The institutions on the one hand endeavor to meet national and regional needs and to be relevant to the cultures of the societies in which they operate, but on the other hand are linked to an international, Western-dominated network that both confers benefits and imposes constraints. The legacies of colonialism are still very apparent in the Pacific region, and are likely to remain so for many decades.

NOTE

The author acknowledges receipt of financial support from the Centre of Asian Studies of the University of Hong Kong for preparation of parts of this chapter.

REFERENCES

Amarshi, Azeem, Kenneth Good, and Rex Mortimer. 1979. *Development and Dependency: The Political Economy of Papua New Guinea*. Melbourne: Oxford University Press.

Borzeix, Jacques. 1991. "A French University in the South Pacific." In David R. Jones,

V. Lynn Meek, and John Weeks, eds., *Explorations in Higher Education: A South Pacific Critique*. Melbourne: Centre for the Study of Higher Education, University of Melbourne.

Bray, Mark. 1993. "Education and the Vestiges of Colonialism: Self-determination, Neo-colonialism and Dependency in the South Pacific." *Comparative Education, 29* (3), 333–48.

Bray, Mark, and Steve Packer. 1993. *Education in Small States: Concepts, Challenges and Strategies*. Oxford: Pergamon.

Caston, Geoffrey. 1989. Quoted in "Educating the Pacific." *Pacific Islands Monthly*, July.

Colletta, Nat J. 1980. *American Schools for the Natives of Ponape: A Study of Education and Cultural Change in Micronesia*. Hawaii: University Press of Hawaii.

Commission for Higher Education. 1993. Unpublished data on enrollments in institutions of higher education. Waigani: Commission for Higher Education.

Crocombe, Ron. 1987. *The South Pacific: An Introduction*. 4th ed. Auckland: Longman Paul.

Crocombe, Ron, and Marjorie Tuainekore Crocombe. 1994. *Post-Secondary Education in the South Pacific: Present Patterns and Future Options*. London: The Commonwealth Secretariat.

Crocombe, Ron, Tupeni Baba, and Malama Meleisea. 1988. "The Development of Higher Education in the Pacific Islands." In Ron Crocombe and Malama Meleisea, eds., *Pacific Universities: Achievements, Problems and Prospects*. Suva: Institute of Pacific Studies, University of the South Pacific.

Crocombe, Ron, and Malama Meleisea. 1988. "Achievements, Problems and Prospects: The Future of University Education in the South Pacific." In Ron Crocombe and Malama Meleisea, eds., *Pacific Universities: Achievements, Problems and Prospects*. Suva: Institute of Pacific Studies, University of the South Pacific.

Curtin, Timothy. 1989. "The Evaluation of Human Capital: A Comment on Recent Literature Relating to Papua New Guinea." *Papua New Guinea Journal of Education, 25* (2), 51–55.

Dorney, Sean. 1991. *Papua New Guinea*. Sydney: Random House.

Douglas, Norman, and Ngaire Douglas. 1989. *Pacific Islands Yearbook*. 16th ed. Sydney: Angus and Robertson.

Falgout, Suzanne, and Paula Levin, eds. 1992. *Socialization and Schooling Research in Pacific Societies*. Special issue of *Anthropology and Education Quarterly 23* (1).

Gannicott, K. G., ed. 1990. *Education for Economic Development in the South Pacific*. Pacific Policy Paper 6. Canberra: National Centre for Development Studies, The Australian National University.

Habu, Mostyn. 1985. "The Impact of Scale, Isolation and Dependence on Educational Development: Solomon Islands." Paper presented at the Pan-Commonwealth Experts' Meeting on Educational Development for the Small States of the Commonwealth, Mauritius.

Helu, Futa. 1988. "'Atenisi Institute and University." In Ron Crocombe and Malama Meleisea, eds., *Pacific Universities: Achievements, Problems and Prospects*. Suva: Institute of Pacific Studies, University of the South Pacific.

Hindson, Colin. 1987. "Educational Aid in the South Pacific: A Look at Priorities." *Directions, 9* (1), 26–41.

Jones, David R., V. Lynn Meek, and John Weeks, eds. 1991. *Explorations in Higher*

Education: A South Pacific Critique. Melbourne: Centre for the Study of Higher Education, University of Melbourne.

Kacimaiwai, Pamela. 1988. "Reaching the Off-Campus Majority." In Ron Crocombe and Malama Meleisea, eds., *Pacific Universities: Achievements, Problems and Prospects.* Suva: Institute of Pacific Studies, University of the South Pacific.

Laracy, Hugh, ed. 1989. *Ples Bilong Iumi: Solomon Islands, The Past Four Thousand Years.* Suva: Institute of Pacific Studies, University of the South Pacific.

Luteru, Pa'o H. 1993. "Aid and Education in Small Systems: A South Pacific Perspective." In Kevin Lillis, ed., *Policy, Planning and Management of Education in Small States.* Paris: International Institute for Educational Planning.

McCall, Grant. 1984. "The University of the South Pacific: Context, Purpose and Prospect." *Vestes* 27 (2), 55–64.

Maenu'u, Leonard. 1988. "Solomon Islands." In Ron Crocombe and Malama Meleisea, eds., *Pacific Universities: Achievements, Problems and Prospects.* Suva: Institute of Pacific Studies, University of the South Pacific.

Monsell-Davis, Michael, and Som Naidu. 1989. "Reaching Out: Distance Teaching and Higher Education in the South Pacific." *International Journal of Educational Development, 9* (3), 183–94.

Murphy, Penelope. 1985. "UPNG as an Agent of Social Stratification: An Analysis of Output by Sex." In Mark Bray and Peter Smith, eds., *Education and Social Stratification in Papua New Guinea.* Melbourne: Longman Cheshire.

———. 1989. "Universities, Government Intervention and the Commission for Higher Education in Papua New Guinea." *International Journal of Educational Development, 9* (3), 175–82.

Papua New Guinea, Government of. 1990. *National Higher Education Plan.* Boroko: Commission for Higher Education.

Robie, David. 1989. *Blood on Their Banner: Nationalist Struggles in the South Pacific.* London: Zed.

Sherlock, Philip, and Rex Nettleford. 1990. *The University of the West Indies: A Caribbean Response to the Challenge of Change.* London: Macmillan.

Teasdale, Robert. 1993. "Higher Education in Small Systems: A Pacific Island Perspective." In Kevin Lillis, ed., *Policy, Planning and Management of Education in Small States.* Paris: International Institute for Educational Planning.

Throsby, C. D., ed. 1987. *Human Resources Development in the Pacific.* Pacific Policy Paper 3. Canberra: National Centre for Development Studies, The Australian National University.

Uili, Tau'ili'ili. 1988. "Le Iunivesite Aoao O Samoa (Le IAOS)" (The National University of Samoa). In Ron Crocombe and Malama Meleisea, eds., *Pacific Universities: Achievements, Problems and Prospects.* Suva: Institute of Pacific Studies, University of the South Pacific.

Van Trease, Howard. 1990–91. "Distance Education at the University of Papua New Guinea: Issues and Developments." *Papua New Guinea Journal of Education, 26* (2) / 27 (1), 111–28.

Wasuka, Moffatt. 1989. "Education." In Hugh Laracy, ed., *Ples Bilong Iumi: Solomon Islands, The Past Four Thousand Years.* Suva: Institute of Pacific Studies, University of the South Pacific.

Wendt, Albert. 1989. "Personal Reflections on the University of the South Pacific." *Papua New Guinea Journal of Education*, 25 (2), 91–94.

World Bank. 1992. *Pacific Regional Post Secondary Education Study*. Washington, D.C.: Population and Human Resources Division, World Bank.

15

PHILIPPINES

Andrew Gonzalez

Before 1969, the policy governing the Philippines' system of higher education was one of laissez faire, to the point where almost 85 percent of students were attending private universities supported for the most part by student fees alone. After World War II, private higher education in the Philippines expanded by allowing the private sector to open new institutions without tuition regulations or even efforts to direct students toward specific fields. In 1969, however, the government decided to conduct a survey and evaluation of the system with the aim of avoiding a mismatch between graduates and available jobs. At the same time, students' complaints about high tuition fees culminated in a legislative act by which the Department of Education began regulating tuition and fees. For more than a decade after 1969, private higher education tuition and fees were regulated and an attempt was made to follow a central plan. However, it soon became evident that in regulating a service industry at its source of expansion, the department was in effect regulating the institutions to a point of nonviability. By the end of the Marcos administration (1965–86), the time was ripe for the gradual deregulation in fees and new programs. Also, new institutions opened to the point where at the beginning of the Ramos administration, the secretary of education in effect deregulated tuition fees, programs, and curricula, and encouraged the opening of new institutions, thus restoring the policy of laissez faire to the system. The beginnings were evident in the deregulation steps taken by Secretary Onofre D. Corpuz during the twilight of the Marcos years; the law providing for state aid to private higher education under Secretary Lourdes R. Quisumbing during the Aquino administration (1986–92); and full deregulation by Secretary Armand E. Fabella at the start of the Ramos administration (1992–). Laissez faire had come full circle.

THE PHILIPPINE HIGHER EDUCATION SYSTEM

Structure

Government institutions of higher education are separately chartered by an act of Congress and are governed by boards of trustees, with the secretary of education, culture, and sports as the ex officio chairman of the board. For these individually chartered state colleges and universities (de Guzman et al., 1987), the only linkage with the Department of Education, Culture, and Sports (DECS) is through the secretary, who is ex officio chairman of the board, including the board of regents of the University of the Philippines system. Obviously the secretary has no time to chair the quarterly meetings of all state colleges and universities, so only sits on the board of the principal ones and delegates the chairmanship for others to an undersecretary, an assistant secretary, or a regional director.

For private colleges and universities, in addition to internal control by their respective boards of trustees, external control is vested in the regional director, who usually designates someone on staff to be in charge of the private higher education institutions in the region or under his area of supervision.

Aiding the secretary of education, culture, and sports in this task of overseeing private higher education is the Bureau of Higher Education, which supervises the opening of new programs and quality control of existing programs through technical panels. These technical panels (from the government, private sector, business, and industry) prescribe minimum standards and oversee curricular change in professional fields. The Professional Regulation Commission licenses certain courses for which an examination is needed to practice in the following professional fields: engineering, architecture, medicine, dentistry, nursing, physical therapy, medical technology, and accountancy. DECS administers its own licensing examination for teachers but is scheduled to turn over this function in the near future to the Professional Regulation Commission. Private institutions are governed like corporations—stock or nonstock—by an annual meeting of the corporate membership and the election of members of the board of directors or board of trustees.

Since the end of 1994, the Bureau of Higher Education of the Department of Education, Culture, and Sports, by an act of Congress (R.A. 7722) signed on May 18 of the same year, was abolished. In its stead, a Commission on Higher Education (CHED), directly under the Office of the President, was established, in effect establishing Higher Education as a separate department under a chairman of CHED with cabinet rank.

Basic Statistics

As of the 1994–95 academic year, the total number of institutions of higher education was 1,090. Table 15.1 summarizes the numbers and the categories.

Table 15.1
Number of Higher Education Institutions, 1994–95

Type	Classification		Total
	Main	Branch Campus	
Public			
Chartered	87	83	170
DECS-Supervised	95	1	96
Community College	29	1	30
Private			
Sectarian	242	5	247
Non-Sectarian	527	20	547
TOTAL	**980**	**110**	**1,090**

Source: Bureau of Higher Education, Department of Education, Culture, and Sports.

The number of teachers in these institutions as calculated in the 1991–92 academic year was 36,877 (see table 15.2). The number of students in tertiary education is provided in table 15.3. The qualifications of faculty in these institutions is given in table 15.4 in terms of degrees completed.

Types of Institutions

There are both degree-granting institutions (bachelor's degree, master's degree, doctorate) and nondegree-granting institutions (two or three years in duration where one completes a two-year certificate or a three-year diploma).

Distance education programs are offered by the University of Mindanao (using mailed lessons and radio broadcasts), the Asian Institute of Distance Education (AIDE), and the College Assurance Plan College (CAP College). At AIDE, lessons are sent by mail; at CAP College, mailed lessons are supplemented by examinations on site at the college in Makati, Metro Manila. A special education program for the deaf at CAP College offers classes taught in sign language.

There is a Bureau of Nonformal Education in the general offices of DECS that administers nondegree programs. These programs usually teach livelihood skills, literacy, and other basic skills. The DECS network of schools located throughout the country are the usual sites of these nonformal programs.

In addition, the Department of Labor and Employment administers short-term (usually 6-month) programs at its National Manpower and Youth Council with special places all throughout the fifteen regions of the country where these oc-

Table 15.2
Teachers in Higher Education, 1991–92

REGION	TYPE OF SCHOOL					TOTAL
	PRIVATE		PUBLIC			
	Non-Sectarian	Sectarian	Chartered State Univ. & Colleges	DECS Supervised	Community College	
I	743	275	2247	35	126	3426
II	179	134	354	00	0	667
III	2241	604	1133	246	47	4271
IV	1305	615	827	198	30	2975
V	1183	758	1113	163	167	3384
VI	910	1455	1203	366	53	3987
VII	842	736	476	37	0	2091
VIII	319	515	708	252	53	1847
IX	376	247	611	233	0	1467
X	1698	879	540	29	63	3209
XI	732	1006	309	15	17	2079
XII	156	347	1046	0	0	1549
NCR	2278	1908	NDA	92	182	4460
CAR	306	570	525	64	0	1465
TOTAL	13268	10049	11092	1730	738	36877

Notes: NDA = no data available; NCR = national capital region; CAR = cordillera autonomous region.

cupation-oriented courses are offered; many of the students enrolled in these courses obtain employment in industrial concerns.

Moreover, both public and private individual institutions through their extension services not only organize short-term training courses for teachers (through workshops and seminars during the semester and long summer vacations) but likewise offer short-term nondegree courses of immediate relevance to livelihood generation through the extension services units of these institutions.

An Evaluation of the Present Situation

The current state of higher education in the Philippines has been characterized as a system where there is more quantity than quality. In other words, the output in March each year of degree-level graduates is about 250,000, with about 750,000 secondary school graduates. The Philippines ranks among the top ten countries of the world in terms of the percentage of the relevant age group in higher education. It has attained the level of a developed country in terms of the proportion of students enrolled in higher education institutions, along with the United States, Japan, and some Latin American countries. However, labels are deceiving. The number of years of preparation for a secondary school grad-

Table 15.3
Enrollment by Program, 1994–95

COURSES	TOTAL PHILIPPINES	DISTRIBUTION
Arts and Sciences	160,651	10.52%
Teacher Education	178,122	11.67%
Engineering and Technology	205,715	13.48%
Medicine and Health-Related	242,084	15.86%
Commerce/Business/ Management/Accountancy	392,959	25.74%
Agriculture/Fishery/Forestry/ Veterinary Medicine	46,439	3.04%
Law	15,882	1.04%
Religion/Theology	7,199	0.47%
Criminology	25,006	1.64%
Information Technology	83,572	5.47%
Maritime Education	145,655	9.54%
Graduate Level	23,352	1.53%
Total	**1,526,636**	**100.00%**

Source: Bureau of Higher Education, Department of Education, Culture, and Sports.

uate entering university is the shortest in the world: six years of elementary and four years of secondary schooling, or only ten years. Among more affluent students, there are as many as two years of preparatory studies before elementary school plus an extra year at the end of elementary school, thus making a total of thirteen years. The affluent who can afford to be in school longer are at a decided advantage in pursuing higher studies. Usually graduates of private secondary schools (except for excellent government high schools such as the Philippine Science High School, the Metro Manila Science High Schools, and some provincial schools) score much higher on the National College Entrance Examination (NCEE)—usually in the 90th percentile range.

The NCEE was established as a national secondary school leaving examination in 1973, with the cutoff score initially stipulated at the 45th percentile and moving up subsequently to the 55th percentile and even higher in some professions such as medicine and nursing. Under a policy set for 1993–94, with the NCEE examination taken in 1993, a 10th percentile cutoff has been prescribed by the DECS secretary to restore the spirit of free market competition. This move, though controversial, was expected to increase enrollment in 1994–95, the only constraint being the ability of the secondary school graduate to pay tuition and fees. Each university had the option of imposing its own cutoff percentile.

A substitute for the NCEE was administered at the end of 1994–95. Known

Table 15.4
Qualifications of Faculty

	TOTAL	PERCENTAGE
Bachelor's degree	7,905	63%
Master's degree	3,578	28%
Doctorate	1,142	9%
Total	12,625	100%

Source: National Inter-University Forum on Education (NIUFE) Newsletter, 1991–92 issues.

as the National Secondary Achievement Test, it is weighted according to the percentage of the general average score of a secondary school leaving student.

While the Philippines has been described as overproducing graduates who cannot be employed, graduates for the most part have had only fourteen or at most fifteen years of schooling by the time they graduate from a tertiary-level institution. The first two years of collegiate or university work in the Philippines consist of general education courses that are usually taken in other countries during the final two years of secondary school. Thus the period of specialization is only two to three years and given the relatively low qualifications of the faculty (63 percent of whom have no advanced degrees and have earned only the bachelor's degree), the level of competence of many graduates leaves much to be desired. It is really only upon passing the professional board examinations that one can feel assured of certain competencies. However, in specializations where no state examinations are prescribed, such as in the sciences (except for chemistry), humanities, and social sciences, one cannot be sure of the quality of the graduates in terms of their minimum competencies.

If one considers the ratio of students only among the third to fifth year of university, and allowing for wastage in certain difficult fields (such as engineering and physical therapy, where there is a mortality rate higher than 50 percent) usually after two years, then the ratio of university undergraduates to the relevant age group can be halved. This presents a more realistic picture and removes the Philippines from the dubious distinction of being among the top countries in terms of the proportion attending higher education. This in turn reduces the proportion of the educated unemployed found in international agency reports.

Given the relatively general level of education without desirable specialization (because of the shortness of formal schooling) among tertiary-level graduates in many fields, the problem of the educated unemployed proves to be less severe, since de facto most tertiary-level graduates have the equivalent training and qualification of a *Habitur* student in Germany, a baccalaureat in France, a *bachillerato* in Spain, or a matriculation student in former Commonwealth countries. These students, although finding it initially difficult to obtain a job, eventually do obtain one, though often one that has little to do with their qualifications. Moreover, usually there is a de facto downgrading of the graduate to the level of a clerk or a technician: engineers end up being technicians, unexamined accountancy majors become bookkeepers and clerks, humanities graduates work as front-desk people or even waitresses at five-star hotels and restaurants, teachers become floor managers in the household services of hotels, and medical technologists become orderlies in a foreign hospital. Fields for which there is demand abroad easily guarantee jobs: nursing, physical therapy, medical technology, and, until the market dropped in North America, medicine. While the criticism of having educated unemployed needs qualification in light of the above observations, it is nevertheless still true that Philippine higher education suffers from a problem of quality easily inferable from the lack of qualifications of faculty and from a mismatch between country needs and university output.

To begin with, there is a shortage of pure scientists in the Philippines. The country needs pure scientists for research and development departments in industries. It also needs to improve the teaching of science in elementary and secondary schools as well as tertiary-level institutions, and to train its corps of graduate faculty in the sciences and technology so as to be able to do local research for Philippine industry. Since the study of science and technology is difficult and since most available jobs in science are in teaching and simple industrial research, the enrollment in the pure sciences by the few institutions willing to subsidize such expensive teaching programs is quite small and often undersubscribed.

The same holds true for higher technology studies except that in technology there is no shortage of undergraduate first degree students. Yet there is little or no demand for graduate studies in engineering, which is needed for the adaptation and indigenization of technology.

On the other hand, while the country has enough engineers (though only a small percentage are trained to the level of international standards), there are not enough technicians and vocational graduates to staff Philippine manufacturing. Moreover, with the lure of work overseas, especially in the Middle East, many able technicians and trained vocational graduates are now working overseas. Though they send back precious foreign exchange that has kept the Philippine economy moving in spite of exports and a large international as well as domestic public debt, the absence of skilled manpower in the country has made quality control a problem for local industries.

Finally, while there are many undergraduate programs, graduate programs in the country are underdeveloped. Thus, university teaching positions are not staffed by adequately qualified faculty; research except for agriculture and the life sciences is inchoate precisely because of a neglected graduate component in the higher education system. Many of these deficits have resulted from a laissez-faire approach and the lack of adequate educational planning.

THE PAST REVISITED:
ETIOLOGY OF THE PRESENT SITUATION

The Philippine education system is the result of multiple influences, beginning with the period of Spanish colonization from 1521 to 1898.

The lasting legacy of Hispanic education is the University of Santo Tomas, dating back to 1611, which by the end of the Spanish period was empowered to grant degrees even up to the doctorate. The other legacy of Spain was parish schools teaching basic literacy and religion in over one thousand places (Bazaco, 1953), seminaries (which admitted nonclerical students), secondary-level convents for girls, and nationally known secondary schools such as the Ateneo Municipal and the Colegio de San Juan de Letran for boys. These institutions granted European secondary schooling degrees called the *bachillerato*.

The American period (1898–1946) brought in the system of public elementary schools (which have been responsible for the growth of literacy and the present level of education of Filipinos). This system has been maintained intact except for the reduction from seven to six years of elementary schooling (reduced for economic reasons but never restored since 1940), provincial high schools of good quality, and a series of tertiary-level institutions to meet immediate needs. Among them are the University of the Philippines (comprised of the agricultural college in Los Banos; the medical school in Manila; the program of arts and sciences transferred from the Philippine Normal School to the new university while the Philippine Normal School became the national institution for teacher training). For industrial education, the Philippine Colleges of Arts and Trade was founded; for the commercial skills or the "distributive sciences," the Philippine College of Commerce was established. In addition, arts and trades schools and agricultural schools were established throughout the country.

Thus, at the end of the American period before the outbreak of World War II and the Japanese period (1941–45), the system was complete in its basic structures and was adequate for the population at that time.

Private schools were permitted, but at the time private colleges and universities served only 11 percent of the college population while the government institution served 89 percent of the students; the proportion was 1 to 8 in favor of the public schools.

The postwar period saw a nation attempting to recoup its losses after a physically devastating period. During the census of 1939 (the last under the Americans), the total population of the country of 300,000 square miles was 16 million; in 1990, during the last census, the population had risen to 60 million and is expected to increase to 72 million by the year 2000. The strain on the system has been overwhelming; more than two-thirds of the population is twenty-five years and younger. There are 1.5 million students in the tertiary system and this number is expected to increase by at least 50 percent in the coming decade because of better retention rates as well as free secondary education offered under the 1987 Constitution. The value placed by the Filipino on formal schooling and the attainment of academic degrees is another contributing factor to the expected increase in tertiary-level enrollment.

Because of this continuing demand, the postwar independence governments took the line of least resistance through adopting a laissez-faire policy. This increased the establishment of private schools supported by tuition fees alone without state aid, but with state supervision for compliance to minimum standards. This has been responsible for the growth in numbers of colleges and universities, public and private, from 96 (Aldana, 1949:40–41) before the war to 1,090 in 1994–95.

While laissez-faire educational permissiveness has solved the social problem of providing facilities for the college age population desirous of schooling, there has not been a corresponding structure to monitor the market in such a way that it will produce the needed types of manpower for development. Thus, since 1969, survey after survey has shown that there is a deficit in the quality of secondary schools (especially in science and mathematics), an oversupply of graduates in business and the general bachelor of arts degree (in the humanities), a shortage of mathematics and natural sciences graduates, and a deficit in enrollment of suitable students for vocational-technical education which, because of its expense, has now been moved to the tertiary level. Moreover, graduate education (and therefore research) has been neglected. Where graduate programs exist, they are mostly in education and business. There are four universities in consortium offering a master's degree and eventually a doctorate in the basic engineering sciences. There is an ongoing Ph.D. program in environmental engineering at the University of the Philippines. Three universities in consortium offer a master's and a Ph.D. degree in computer science. There are also three universities in consortium that offer Ph.D. programs in mathematics, chemistry, and physics.

Attempts at Reform

There have been many efforts at reform of higher education during the past quarter century. A Presidential Commission to Survey Philippine Education was organized in 1969 and submitted a report (PCSPE, 1970). There were subsequent studies of the private (Private Higher Education [PHE] Study Group, 1975) and public (The Presidential Study Committee on State Higher Education, 1976) higher education systems, and an analytic study attempting to see how the two should complement each other (Dizon, 1976). The problems of Philippine higher education have been analyzed many times, but unfortunately there has been a lack of political will to make the needed changes. Thus, the attempts at reform have yielded little substantive improvement. Each new administration at the Department of Education, Culture, and Sports has prescribed another survey yielding basically the same findings and the same recommendations. In 1986, another study of the state colleges and universities was completed (de Guzman et al., 1987) and in 1991, a congressional commission came up with its own report (EDCOM, 1991) and recommendations.

Because the present senate president was head of the EDCOM, he has made a special effort to present legislation to implement some of the EDCOM recommendations. Some of these measures are now at the committee level of both Houses of Congress for study and several educational laws have been enacted as a result of the EDCOM report, including the establishment of a separate Commission on Higher Education (CHED).

Evaluation of the Past

The lessons of the postwar period indicate that a laissez-faire attitude toward higher education, with reliance on the private sector to meet the needs in a free market system, has temporary advantages at best. It ultimately results in a mismatch between the country's needs and the system's output. There is an overproduction of graduates in some fields and a shortage of graduates in others. Some of these latter fields (undergraduate sciences, graduate technology, graduate research, vocational-technical programs) are costly to run and call for expensive equipment. They are not easily offered because they require subsidies and are nonviable if one relies only on tuition income.

What is politically acceptable—satisfaction of the perceived educational demands of the masses—does not necessarily result in a better match between country needs and educational system output. There is thus a need for a central body to redirect enrollment and output along needed fields. It takes leadership, political will, and strong executives to implement reform to redirect the system toward heightened productivity.

FUTURE DEVELOPMENTS

A forward-looking view is necessary to deal effectively with the issues facing Philippine higher education. The system needs to be better rationalized to help the country move toward development with higher education as an ally rather than a dysfunctional partner in the process.

Quality and Quantity:
The Custodial Role of Higher Education

If the status quo is maintained, most of the 1,090 colleges and universities will continue to play a necessary custodial role for Philippine society at no government expense. Were the country to adopt a policy of restraining its secondary school graduates from attending courses of their choice at the tertiary level (at their own expense or at the expense of their parents), then political and social problems will most likely arise that would be counterproductive to development. In short, social unrest would be inimical to progress.

Tampering with access to higher education at the expense of parents will be politically hazardous and counterproductive. Moreover, it could be challenged on constitutional grounds.

If for the sake of quality there were a drastic reduction of university students, what would Philippine society do with its idle student-age youth (Philippine *ronin*, from the Japanese term, borrowed from the samurai term for unemployed soldiers and used to refer to university students waiting for admission, sometimes for long periods)? From idle youth will spring future leaders of anti-establishment forces that will be difficult to deal with, for they constitute a fertile seedbed for social revolution and new forms of terrorism and revolution as experience elsewhere has so vividly demonstrated. Therefore, the institutions of higher education should be encouraged and even assisted, since they now exercise this essential custodial social function with no expense to the government.

Dealing with the Educated Unemployed: The Remedies Taken

About 250,000 individuals receive college and university degrees each year. The nation must provide 800,000 new jobs each year for all those entering the workforce (Gonzalez, 1992). Presently it is difficult to absorb those without special skills. There is an unemployment rate of approximately 8.8 percent and an underemployment rate of almost 18.6 percent. In Philippine labor terms, the underemployed are those who already hold jobs but would like to work more since the income from their present jobs (which could be part-time) is insufficient for their needs.

Studies conducted by the Institute of Planning (a UNESCO affiliate) in Paris and the International Labor Organization, in cooperation with the Fund for Assistance to Private Education (FAPE), show that college graduates take from six months to twelve months to obtain a job (Sanyal, 1979, 1990; Arcelo and Sanyal, 1983). The better university graduates can obtain a job almost immediately, within three to six months at most. Some fields are so much in demand (computer science, physical therapy, manufacturing, engineering) that students begin on-the-job training during their final year in college.

The jobs obtained, however, are not always relevant to the fields studied. Accountants, especially if they have passed the certified public accountant's professional examination, easily obtain jobs in business offices; those unable to pass their licensure begin as bookkeepers. Commerce or business management graduates begin work as clerks and tellers in banks. Psychology and marketing majors begin jobs as salespeople either within the establishment or as field representatives. Humanities graduates begin as secretaries but when their management talents are recognized even as their language abilities blossom, they easily become executive secretaries and eventually part of management. Engineers either go into marketing (as sales representatives of technical products) or as practicing engineers in their fields in large companies, or if unable to pass the board examination are recruited as technicians on the manufacturing or production floor. Lawyers not practicing end up as freelancers, as assistants or staff, and if able, take on managerial roles as personnel or legal officers in companies. Nurses, physical therapists, and medical technologists mostly go abroad; fewer doctors leave the country because the North American market has become less open. However, dentists are beginning to go to the United States after sitting for a series of examinations that permits them to be able to practice in specific states.

Thus the term "educated unemployed" is a misnomer insofar as the Philippine situation is concerned. Truly educated students who finish with distinction or prove themselves innately competent either on the job or through public professional examinations have no trouble getting employment if they are genuinely interested in work. There are many underemployed in the Philippines but these are usually weaker students who finish up at the lower end of a rank-ordered list. Able students do get employed but sometimes with jobs at the lower end of the social scale and have to prove themselves so that better use of their training in more demanding jobs becomes possible. However, the Philippine experience is such that an able worker, even if not academically brilliant, if diligent and industrious and professional in fulfillment of duties, soon rises to the top either by promotion within the organization or transfers to another company for a better job.

Even college graduates who end up as clerks or waiters and waitresses in five-star hotels have opportunities and can easily obtain better jobs within the establishment, though the advantages are more available to those who have finished courses in the more affluent schools with a better reputation.

Perhaps the most unfortunate downgrading of university graduates that has occurred in the past ten years has been the hiring of teachers as domestics abroad in Asia, the Middle East, and Western Europe. Yet this is primarily due to the low salary scale of Philippine teachers and the low per capita income of the country. In fact, there is presently a shortage of teachers at the elementary and secondary levels. It is therefore not an educational unemployment issue but an economic issue that cannot be solved by the higher education system but by the Philippine economy.

Inertia of a System Where Political Intervention Is Endemic

The pressure placed on the educational system by politicians, especially in Congress, has a negative influence on educational development. This problem permeates all of Philippine society.

Specifically, what makes educational rationalization and planning very difficult for the Department of Education, Culture, and Sports is the desire of every representative in Congress to establish a state institution of higher learning, initially a college, subsequently a university, in his bailiwick, for obvious political reasons. The education secretary under the Aquino government made it a point to call for a moratorium on the establishment of new institutions. The Board of Higher Education was to be used as a screening body. But under the first secretary of the Ramos administration, a laissez-faire policy with market forces dictating the results has once more returned. The Commission on Higher Education's initial task is to discourage the upgrading of provincial secondary institutions to colleges and subsequently to universities, and to find incentives for existing universities, public and private, to upgrade their programs and faculty.

With a very limited budget allocated by Congress yearly as appropriation for higher education, more institutions means sharing the same pie among a greater number, in effect diluting the appropriation and largely reserving it for recurrent expenses (mostly salaries) with little or no funds for academic development and needed academic teaching materials such as books and scientific equipment.

In addition, influential individuals either politically well connected or legislators themselves and line officials such as provincial governors and mayors sometimes exert political pressure to have friends or relatives appointed to academic positions (teaching and administrative) even if undeserving or unqualified. This wreaks havoc on a rationalized ranking scale as well as on a system of promotions based on merit and achievement. Moreover, people appointed to academic ranks without aptitude or qualification and without real dedication often become agents of graft and corruption in state institutions, resulting in academic paralysis. The appointment of presidents in many state colleges and universities has become politicized, making a wise choice almost impossible and leading to divisive situations where factions attempt to dislodge an incumbent instead of taking care of their academic duties.

Again, while solutions to these problems are urgently needed, one must go beyond the university system for long-term remedies. A change of values and orientation as well as top-down and bottom-up ethical reform are needed.

Institutionalization of the Academic Lifestyle among the Faculty

The style of living that is ideal for faculty in higher education (what I have earlier referred to as the "academic lifestyle") is a cultural innovation in Asia and the Pacific (Gonzalez, 1993a). Other than in India and China, which have a long tradition of encouraging intellectuals and socially rewarding them to the point where the "profession" of intellectual has been institutionalized, other countries of Asia are without such a tradition (though the British tradition of university life has been adapted in Hong Kong, Singapore, and Malaysia). Similarly, borrowing from the German and later the American tradition, Japan has come to revere its intellectuals. The profession of *sen-sei* has a long tradition of reverence in Japan, which the Meiji Restoration transferred from the traditional monastery teacher to the European-trained university professor when Meiji Japan began opening its doors to Western knowledge.

The difficulty lies with countries such as the Philippines, Indonesia, and to some extent Thailand (though Buddhist monasteries have a long tradition, teaching and learning were not systematically organized along the Western model until King Mongkut's reign in the nineteenth century). In these countries there is no tradition of the institutionalized intellectual life to speak'of and therefore it has been difficult in spite of colonial influence to internalize the lifestyle that goes with academia. In the Philippines, for example, tertiary-level teachers are for the most part paid by the hour; the rates are quite low compared to other professions. Moreover, tertiary teachers have little time for research because of the heavy teaching load they have to accept to eke out an existence. The qualifications of the professoriate leave much to be desired since up to now only 37 percent (9 percent doctorates, 28 percent master's degrees) have advanced degrees. The situation with regard to qualifications is better in Thailand, but the rates in Thailand are not much better than those in Indonesia and the Philippines. In all places in ASEAN where the British tradition has not taken root, research is only at its beginning stages; certainly this is true in the Philippines.

Thus the most basic task confronting Philippine higher education in its quest for quality is faculty development. It must work to enable the majority of the faculty in tertiary education to obtain at least a postgraduate degree. It must also change the working conditions of teaching staff to permit more time for reading and research work. It goes without saying, of course, that salaries likewise have to be raised on a monthly basis for the entire calendar year, at a level in keeping with the dignity of the profession.

Extension Programs

While there must be teaching, research, and service, in developing countries the extension or service function takes on increased importance since often universities located in special regions must provide not only the manpower pool to carry on the task of development but must likewise provide the intellectual inputs into the process by supplying scientific expertise in planning, implementation, and evaluation as well as providing the technical manpower staff necessary for project implementation.

This task is relatively new to the university tradition and has been the main contribution of the American land-grant university, which was adopted in the Philippines by the College of Agriculture at Los Banos, which later became a constituent college of the University of the Philippines in 1908.

The extension function has now been incorporated into the mission of most tertiary-level institutions in the Philippines, which have taken on the special role of providing nonformal education through nondegree courses, social development projects, and social action projects by students under the supervision of their faculty. Where the university is especially equipped to handle extension programs, through its expertise among the faculty, such as in agricultural programs in rural universities and special conservation programs by the College of Forestry of the University of the Philippines and the Gregorio Araneta University Foundation, the extension function has taken on salience and prominence.

New Initiatives in Response to Contemporary Developments

Certainly one very positive reaction within the past ten years in Philippine higher education has been the relatively rapid response to new challenges through initiatives in the field of computer science, technical education, in-company schools, and academe-university research links.

In response to the need for manpower in the field of computer science, especially information technology, a large number of schools offer both degree and nondegree programs. They employ a free market mechanism to respond to the needs of rapidly growing industry especially in cooperation with Japan and the United States. These countries contract special software to be produced in the Philippines and then it is exported to international customers. The Philippines, because of its large number and trainability of graduates in software production skills, has been able to respond rapidly to this growing market and has seen these cooperative ventures multiply.

In addition, a breakthrough has been made in vocational-technical and technician education through dualtech schemes patterned after the German model and brought to the Philippines by the Hans Seidel Foundation in cooperation with MANTRADE, a car assembly and marketing corporation. Schools of this type, where student employees are sent by their companies to improve their skills according to predetermined specifications, have been found to be not only effective for skills transfer but also more stable for the maintenance and retention of newly trained staff. This is more preferable than the migration of skilled workers as overseas contract workers. The retention rate has been excellent; there is a move to enroll full-time students for the program under company sponsorship. It remains to be seen whether this scheme will succeed with the younger postsecondary group, since the experience with the students under the earlier scheme without the employment component has been their migration as overseas contract workers upon the completion of their government-sponsored or private industry-sponsored studies.

Even more interesting are the new schools organized by large companies to supply their own manpower skills needs: Toyota has opened a school for its car assembly and parts manufacturing industry; the Magsaysay Institute of Seamanship, in partnership with Mitsui Osaka, a large shipping company, has established a school of seamanship whereby students are recruited and then given full financial support, six months of formal training, and six months of apprenticeship on board ship with pay. Atlas Mining Company has a special postsecondary nondegree program for metal crafts, in line with its needs; similarly, a newsprint manufacturing company called PICOP has a program in a company-sponsored school that is geared to a nondegree sequence and gives preference for employment to graduates of its sponsored postsecondary school. Company-industry-sponsored schools will probably see continued expansion in the future.

There are also plans for implementation of joint research institutes between academic departments and leading companies for in-company research guided by academicians and including doctoral candidates as researchers. There are sixteen priority areas (Department of Science and Technology, 1992a, 1992b) that will provide relevant research projects for doctoral and postdoctoral students in suitably equipped laboratories. The doctoral and master's level candidates will be trained by the Department of Science and Technology in cooperation with a consortium of academic institutions. These include the University of the Philippines, Ateneo de Manila University, De La Salle University, and University of San Carlos. Cooperation will occur among these institutions and industries that will fund research institutes. These institutions include San Miguel Corporation, Engineering Equipment, Toyota, Mitsubishi, and Matsushita.

CONCLUSION

From the point of view of comparative education, the Philippines represents an interesting case. It is a system manifesting both strengths and weaknesses as it tries to cope with the reality of population growth and an economy painfully attempting to inch its way toward newly industrializing country (NIC) status, as well as economic tiger status within ASEAN. The present administration has announced its goal of reaching NIC status by the end of the century.

Relying heavily on the American tradition of higher education but at the same time aware that no tradition can be imported without adaptation to the social ecology of the recipient country, the Philippines is grappling with an educational structure to bring it in tune with its development targets (Gonzalez, 1989). Thus, since 1975 it has been moving from overcentralization toward localization and devolution of educational structures to the regions. Moreover, from an over-regulated system where so many permits and clearances had to be obtained in Manila, it is now turning toward deregulation even on the most sensitive issue, tuition fees, which were regulated beginning in 1969.

For a long time the state refused to accept the essential role of the private sector in higher education; recognition finally became official with the Education Act of 1982 and the 1987 Constitution. The full meaning of this recognition has yet to be spelled out in detail, although a law (R.A. 6728) has provided for some form of aid to private education through a service scheme whereby students who cannot be accommodated in public institutions may be sent to private institutions with state funds. Other provisions of the law have yet to be implemented, the most crucial being support for faculty development and special priority programs such as science.

The system has gone from a laissez-faire one that prevailed from independence in 1946 to regulation in 1969, which de facto stymied the system through overregulation. Strengths and weaknesses of a laissez-faire system in higher education readily come to mind when examining the Philippine experience: The permissiveness with regard to the private sector being allowed to open as many schools and programs as are financially viable resulted in imbalances in the system. It produced an overproduction of graduates in some fields and underproduction in others. Thus the Magic Hand of the free market is not present at all times; incentives are needed to make priority programs more attractive and to right the imbalance in needed graduates, particularly for certain nondemand fields such as pure science and higher-level technology. Thus, laissez faire must be accompanied by timely and limited interventions on behalf of certain deficit fields to keep adequate manpower available for the development of the economy.

While education is a public need and should be met by public resources, in developing economies that are unable to provide necessary academic services to all its citizens, the ability of the private sector in a free market economy to supply this need and to make a reasonable return on investment should be accepted, especially based on the experiences of the Philippines and other developing countries like Indonesia and Thailand. Contrary to the cliché and the charges leveled against the "commercialization of education," the citizenry should be grateful to the private sector because it has invested much resources due to the inability of the public sector to meet the demand. The free market philosophy is being adopted to reap more benefit from the law of supply and demand, with schools offering inferior programs dying a natural death and those offering superior programs able to charge higher tuition to maintain and enhance the quality of the programs they offer.

While there is a valid criticism about quality leveled against the products of Philippine higher education, the fact is that the country does produce adequately trained graduates to meet not only in-country needs but also out-of-country needs for certain fields; the skills of Philippine graduates in nursing, physical therapy, medical technology, medicine, accountancy, higher-level management, dentistry, pedagogy, vocational-technical fields, technology, engineering, and computer science are in much demand. The market for overseas contract workers remains large and is expanding; the sums earned by Filipino overseas workers have strengthened the economy and provided foreign currency to render a surplus in the balance of payments (though not in balance of trade). Hence, while quantity might be exaggerated, functional quality renders the graduates able to be of service globally as well as within the country. The level of certain professions such as accountancy and medicine, as well as computer science, management, and technologies for certain processes, is very high since the elites provide the leadership for these professions. This means that the majority of these functional graduates finish from purely teaching institutions with little or no research base. A case can be made for promoting teaching institutions at the tertiary level in developing countries. But empirical inquiry must show the proportion of higher education institutions that need to be research-oriented (such as the University of the Philippines at Los Banos). It seems that relatively few institutions are required to provide higher education needs (the training of staff for universities) and that the high-level scientific research needed to move from transfer of technology to adaptive technology to indigenous technology might best be served by a few high-quality research institutions. The American and Japanese systems of research in higher education are too expensive for a country like the Philippines. The suggestion has been made that even in a country of 63 million like the Philippines, one does not need more than one Ph.D. program of quality in every major field; these programs can be lodged in a few institutions (or in one institution), each specializing in one field. At these centers of excellence, in cooperation with industry, relevant research needed for development can be done and properly funded instead of spreading resources so thin that they end up without impact.

Thus though research is essential for eventually developing indigenous technology and being able to compete within the world market for specific products of export quality that meet international requirements, the structuring of research in a developing country, especially the research done through academic institutions or through academic-industry cooperative projects, has to be specific. It must avoid duplication and concentrate resources so that it can be effectively done in one institution or in a network of cooperating institutions rather than allowing the free market to operate, at least at the initial stages of research generation and activity. Alternatively, the model could be a research institute totally separate from academia; the problem here is that there are not enough research scientists outside academia to make this arrangement viable. If research institutes pirate academics, the supply of new manpower will be stopped. The formula calls for cooperation so that the scientists can continue their links with academia. The university could make provision for advanced research and at the same time attract the research funds for honoraria and equipment, while serving the needs of industry. This model for science and technology limits the versatility of the country's scientists and directs their efforts rather narrowly; nevertheless, it is the only way to start research activity in an area where it does not yet exist (Gonzalez, 1993b).

It is possible, based on the Philippine experience, to carry on education at a mass level, rather cheaply, with poorly paid and inadequately qualified faculty. The results of course will yield little in quality at least among the majority of the graduates. If reform is to start, it has to begin with the upgrading of faculty qualifications, a change of status for faculty, and improved working conditions to a point where teaching in higher education is sufficiently rewarded and esteemed. Hence, while the system after the postwar period was needed because of the exigencies of the postwar situation, one must now pay attention to radical reform in faculty maintenance (providing opportunities for improvement through study leaves and fellowships) and through restructuring of the profession to make it a vehicle for the nurturing of academic life in the Philippines.

For reforms in the curricula, there is a need to update and rewrite materials, and to retrain faculty to use these materials. While the Philippines will have a primarily teaching rather than research faculty for at least one more generation, a system of upgrading faculty by nonformal means is necessary. This must occur not only through access to current publications and subscriptions to journals but also through continuous in-service programs. Opportunities for younger faculty to work for advanced degrees will have to be integrated into the ongoing operations of the system. For the students, the instructional system has to move away from memorization and passive listening to an active and critical dialogue with teachers. Finally, provision of teaching materials must go beyond textbooks and classnotes.

Because extension programs have proven to be successful in building credibility for the social mission of the institution and providing a laboratory for learning among students and faculty, this positive feature of Philippine academia should not be neglected in favor of academic upgrading but made even more meaningful through systematic linkages with academic activities.

REFERENCES

Aldana, B. 1949. *The Educational System of the Philippines*. Manila: University Publishing.

Arcelo, A., and R. C. Sanyal. 1983. *Employment and Higher Education in the Philippines* (HELMS II Report). Manila: Ministry of Education, Culture and Sports; Fund for Assistance to Private Education; International Institute of Educational Planning.

Bazaco, Evergisto. 1953. *History of Education in the Philippines*. Manila: University of Santo Tomas.

de Guzman, Raul, et al. 1987. Report on state universities and colleges in the Philippines prepared by the task force to study state higher education. Manila: Ministry of Education, Culture and Sports (vols. 1, 2, 3).

Department of Science and Technology. 1992a. *Philippines Engineering and Science Education Project*. Manila (Manuscript).

———. 1992b. The DOST–World Bank Project on Engineering and Science Education. Bicutan (Manuscript).

Dizon, Amado C. 1976. "Facing the Dilemma in Higher Education." *FAPE Review, 6*, (3), 23–17.

EDCOM (Educational Commission). 1992. Report of the Commission of Education (EDCOM). Manila: Congress of the Republic of the Philippines.

Gonzalez, Andrew. 1989. "The Western Impact on Philippine Higher Education." In Philip G. Altbach and V. Selvaratnam, eds., *From Dependence to Autonomy: The Development of Asian Universities*. Dordrecht, The Netherlands: Kluwer Academic.

———. 1992. "Higher Education, Brain Drain and Overseas Employment in the Philippines: Towards a Differentiated Set of Solutions." *Higher Education, 23*, 21–31.

———. 1993a. "The Apostolate of the Mind in the Asian Setting: The Culture of Higher Education and Personnel." *Perspective 13* (3); *13* (4), 12–16.

———. 1993b. "Identifying Research Priorities in the Philippines." *Tanglaw, 2* (1), 7–9.

Presidential Commission to Survey Philippine Education (PCSPE). 1970. *Education for National Development: New Patterns, New Directions.* Report of the Presidential Commission to Survey Philippine Education. Manila: Department of Education and Culture.

Presidential Study Committee on State Higher Education (THE). 1976. "A Proposed Policy on Governance." *FAPE Review, 6* (4), 47–54.

Private Higher Education (PHE) Study Group. 1975. "The Strategic Role for Private Higher Education: An Educational Service Complementary to the Public." *FAPE Review, 6* (2), 12.

Sanyal, Bikas. 1990. *Changes in Higher Educational Management* (Notes). Paris: International Institute of Educational Planning, UNESCO.

Sanyal, Bikas, et al. 1979. *Higher Educational Labor Market in the Philippines.* Metro Manila: Ministry of Education, Culture and Sports.

16

SINGAPORE

Eng Thye Jason Tan

Singapore is an island state in Southeast Asia with a land area of 639 square kilometers. With 49 percent of the total land area built up, it is a highly urbanized society, with a population density of 4,397 persons per square kilometer. The population of just under 3 million consists of 78 percent Chinese, 14 percent Malays, 7 percent Indians, and one percent belonging to other ethnic groups. In addition to this ethnic mix, there is also diversity along the lines of language, religion, and culture.

After its founding as a British commercial and trading post in 1819, Singapore remained a colony until it attained full internal self-government in 1959. This was followed by a brief period as part of Malaysia from September 1963 until the establishment of an independent republic in August 1965. The People's Action Party, which captured power in the 1959 general elections, has been in power ever since.

Independence brought along with it the twin challenges of sustaining economic growth and nation building. The present government has made it clear that education has a key role to play in meeting both these challenges. Higher education institutions, as the pinnacle of the formal education system, are especially important in this regard.[1]

Two important features of Singapore higher education are the overriding importance of economic relevance and the dominant state presence in decision making and planning. By the early 1980s Singapore had entered the ranks of the newly industrialized countries, as well as "Asia's Four Little Dragons." The government launched its second industrial revolution in 1979, which involved restructuring the economy to focus on high-technology, skill-intensive manufacturing and service sector activities. Higher education enrollments were correspondingly increased to meet the anticipated manpower demands. Several government economic reports published since the mid-1980s have stressed the role of higher education institutions in maintaining Singapore's international competitiveness in the global economy alongside the developed nations and the other newly industrialized nations.

Sustained economic growth over the past three decades has also meant increasing social demand for access to higher education. The government has consistently adopted a cautious attitude toward expanding higher education enrollment, citing among other reasons the negative social consequences of graduate unemployment and the devaluation of university degrees. However, from the late 1980s on it has had to provide increased opportunities in response to the growing social demand, as well as to the needs of economic growth.

In order to better understand the heavy state presence in higher education, one needs also to understand the local political context. During the first two decades after independence, Singapore was what a local political scientist has described as an "administrative state," in which the population was systematically depoliticized, and in which the administrative and bureaucratic sectors expanded and grew in power. An elected opposition was seen by the ruling party as unnecessary for, and detrimental to, socioeconomic development. Following an unprecedented loss of votes in the 1984 general elections, the government has gradually liberalized the political climate, and has allowed more public participation in the decision-making process. However, the political leadership still firmly believes that Singapore should be a tightly run society under strong leadership (Chan, 1989).

This chapter begins by providing a profile of the higher education system in terms of historical development, enrollment rates, governance, finance, teaching, and research. The second major section deals with the links between higher education and economic development, and illustrates the various ways in which the government has sought to ensure a tight fit between the two. The final major section discusses access and equity issues such as the increasing social demand for higher education, gender and ethnic representation, and the presence of foreign students in local institutions. Two recurring themes throughout the chapter are the preeminence of the government and the predominance of economic considerations in higher education planning and policy making.

PROFILE OF THE HIGHER EDUCATION SYSTEM

Historical Development

The Universities. In 1823 Sir Stamford Raffles, who had earlier succeeded in securing Singapore as a British trading post, proposed the establishment of a native college. Raffles intended that the college should offer instruction in Chinese, Siamese, Malay, other local languages, and subjects such as history for the sons of neighboring rulers and merchants. He also envisaged that the college would provide facilities for research into the history, societies, and economies of neighboring countries (Chelliah, 1947; Lee, 1989; Wilson, 1978). Unfortunately, other colonial administrators did not share Raffles' enthusiasm for the college, and the idea failed to materialize.

It was not until 1905 that the colonial government opened a medical college in response to a petition from leading Chinese and other Asian leaders. The college, which served Singapore and Malaya, was named the King Edward VII College of Medicine in 1920. Further pressure from the local Straits Chinese British Association, as well as the threat of an American-sponsored tertiary college, spurred the government into making plans to open a college of higher education (Turnbull, 1989; Wilson, 1978). Raffles College, which began admitting students in 1928, awarded diplomas, and most of its graduates went into secondary school teaching or into junior civil service posts.

The immediate post–World War II years were marked by the acceleration of civil service localization, as well as initial moves toward self-government. As a result of the Carr-Saunders Commission's recommendations, the King Edward VII Medical College and Raffles College merged to form the degree-granting University of Malaya in 1949. The university served the needs of Singapore, Malaya, and the Borneo Territories for the next ten years. Two autonomous divisions of the university, one in Singapore and one in Kuala Lumpur, were established in 1959. Subsequently, two separate national universities were formed, and the University of Singapore came into being in 1962.

A key factor in all the above developments in higher education was that they catered only to students from English-medium schools. The British colonial authorities displayed a lack of interest in Chinese-medium education, and there was a history of antagonism between the government and the Chinese community regarding education, dating back to the early decades of the twentieth century (Wilson, 1978). In response to declining standards and enrollments in Chinese-medium schools, prominent local Chinese merchants made plans to establish a community-funded Chinese-medium university as early as 1950. Nanyang University was originally registered as a company in 1953 and was officially opened in 1956 with the help of substantial donations from the Chinese community. It had three colleges of arts, science, and commerce. The university faced many problems from its inception, including left-wing student agitation, difficulties in recruiting quality academic staff, and low academic standards (Gopinathan, 1989; Wilson, 1978). The government granted Nanyang University statutory status in 1959 but did not formally recognize Nanyang degrees until 1968.

By the early 1970s, Nanyang University's future was being threatened, not only by falling standards and difficulties with staff recruitment and retention, but also by the shrinking pool of Chinese-medium secondary school students. The situation was aggravated by the increasing numbers of students who had opted for the English-medium University of Singapore or for foreign universities from 1960 on (Lee, 1978). In 1980 the Nanyang University Council unanimously accepted the prime minister's proposal to merge the two universities to form the English-medium National University of Singapore (NUS). The prime minister's proposal was in turn based on the recommendations of a British academic, Sir Frederick Dainton, in favor of developing a single, strong comprehensive university. The decision to close Nanyang University had to be undertaken with particular caution, lest the government be accused by Chinese-medium-educated Singaporeans of killing off Chinese language and culture (Lee, 1980a). The NUS had an enrollment of 17,541 undergraduate and postgraduate students in 1992 (Department of Statistics, 1993:298) in eight faculties: architecture and building, arts and social sciences, business administration, dentistry, engineering, law, medicine, and science.

After the formation of the NUS, the English-medium Nanyang Technological Institute (NTI) was set up on the Nanyang University campus in 1981. It was intended that this institute would eventually develop into a technological university in 1992. The NTI initially offered engineering degree courses and its graduates received NUS degrees. In 1991 the government decided on the basis of a second report by Dainton to convert the NTI into a second comprehensive university, the Nanyang Technological University (NTU). With the benefit of hindsight, it was now clear that the earlier Dainton report in 1979 had seriously underestimated the social and economic demand for higher education. Besides engineering courses, the NTU offers courses in accountancy, business, applied science, and communication studies. The Institute of Education (with its origins in the Teachers' Training College established in 1950) and the College of Physical Education (established in 1984), both teacher training institutions, were also merged to form the National Institute of Education, an autonomous division of NTU. This new institute is the sole teacher training institution in Singapore. The total NTU enrollment (including the National Institute of Education) was 14,772 in 1993 (Department of Statistics, 1994:301).

As part of government moves to make higher education more accessible, especially to working adults, an Open University started functioning with about nine hundred part-time students in January 1994. The privately run Singapore Institute of Management (SIM) administers the three bachelor degree programs in English language and literature, mathematics, and computer science in conjunction with the British Open University, which, besides awarding the degrees, has also agreed to provide academic, administrative, and technical consultancy services until July 1997. Several NUS advisors are also helping the new institution develop degree programs. In addition, the government has assisted the Open University with a one-time capital and development grant of S 38 million (U.S.$1 = S 1.50), and has provided it with land. Further, the Public Service Commission has agreed to recognize the degree awarded by the Open University for the purpose of employment in the civil services.

The Polytechnics. The Singapore Polytechnic (SP), which enrolled its first students in 1958, was the first polytechnic established in Singapore, and was modeled along the lines of British polytechnics. It offered English-medium instruction leading to diplomas in engineering, accountancy, architecture and building, and nautical studies. From the late 1960s on, the SP's role has been to provide middle-level technical personnel in support of the government's industrialization program. The SP had 18,694 full- and part-time students in 1992 (Department of Statistics, 1994:302).

The Ngee Ann College was established in 1963, in much the same tradition as Nanyang University, as a private college funded by a Chinese community clan group. It initially offered degree courses, conducted mainly in Chinese, in arts, science, and commerce, and faced problems similar to those of Nanyang University. Internal reforms led to the college dropping its degree programs in favor of diploma courses in engineering and commerce. The college became a public education institution in 1968 and was renamed the Ngee Ann Technical College. It assumed its present name, the Ngee Ann Polytechnic, in 1982, by which time it had become an English-medium institution.

As part of its expansion plans for higher education, the government has opened two new polytechnics in rapid succession. The Temasek Polytechnic opened in 1990, followed two years later by the Nanyang Polytechnic. Both polytechnics offer courses similar to those of their more established counterparts, as well as starting courses not previously available in local polytechnics, for instance, design, nursing, radiography, physiotherapy, and occupational therapy.

Enrollment Rates

While higher education enrollments have grown substantially in the past three decades, access to higher education has until recently remained selective. While 92.8 percent of children in the six to seventeen age group were enrolled in educational institutions in 1992 (Department of Statistics, 1993:15), 16 percent and 29 percent of the relevant age cohort gained admission to local universities and polytechnics, respectively, that year (Cost Review Committee, 1993:77). These figures do not include students studying in privately run institutions. In addition, there were about 11,500 Singaporeans pursuing undergraduate and postgraduate courses in overseas universities in 1990 (Lau, 1992:127)—about half the total enrollment in local universities that year. The most common reasons for overseas studies include an inability to gain admission to desired courses in local institutions, the unavailability of certain courses such as veterinary science locally, and sponsorship by the government or private corporations.

Other Higher Education Institutions

A number of privately funded institutions exist outside the "mainstream," and cater to the large social demand for higher educational qualifications. The largest among these is the SIM, which was established in 1964 by a group of senior management executives from various fields in the private and public sectors to provide management training. It offers doctoral, master's, and bachelor's degree programs in finance, management, and information technology, as well as diploma and certificate courses in management. The degree courses are run in conjunction with various universities in England, Australia, and the United States. The SIM enrolled 6,454 students in 1992 (SIM, 1992:29).

There are two fine arts colleges, the Nanyang Academy of Fine Arts and the La Salle-Singapore Airlines College of the Arts, both of which offer diploma courses. These colleges have also recently made efforts to provide bachelor's degree programs conducted jointly with foreign universities in Britain and Australia. Each of these colleges enrolls less than a thousand full-time students.

Lastly, there are numerous external degree programs being run by statutory boards, professional groups, and private commercial schools. These courses are predominantly in computing, management, business, and finance, with most of the degrees being awarded by universities in Britain, Australia, and the United States. An estimated 4,500 people were enrolled in such courses in 1992 (*Straits Times*, July 26, 1993). Since the early 1990s, a growing number of private organizations have begun offering master of business administration programs conducted in the Chinese language in conjunction with leading Chinese universities such as Beijing University and Shanghai Jioa Tong University. The status of these external degrees relative to those obtained through full-time study depends in some cases on the reputation of the degree-granting institution within Singapore, and also in some instances on whether the degrees are awarded recognition by government or professional bodies such as the Public Service Commission or the Singapore Medical Council.

Government Control of Higher Education

The universities and polytechnics are under the direct charge of the Ministry of Education, which in 1992 established a University Grants Commission to advise the minister on the allocation of funds and resources for the universities. The main control mechanisms are finance and the appointment of senior academic and administrative staff. In addition, all the constitutions of the various institutions are prescribed by parliamentary acts. The government clearly plays a dominant interventionist role in controlling and directing major policy decisions concerning the higher education institutions. The former prime minister Lee Kuan Yew has on more than one occasion personally intervened in policy decisions affecting these institutions. For instance, he expressly forbade the formation of an academic staff union in the NUS in 1980 (Lee, 1980b), and played an instrumental role in the closing down of the Nanyang University and the subsequent establishment of the NUS. Given the pivotal role the higher education institutions play in human resource development, which has in turn been identified as the cornerstone of national economic survival, it is perhaps understandable to some extent that the government is unwilling to completely divest itself of any influence over these institutions.

There is a British legacy in the pattern of management in the universities.

Table 16.1
Percentage Breakdown of Government Recurrent Educational Expenditure

Year	Primary	Secondary	Vocational	Universities	Polytechnics	Teacher Training	Higher Education Total
1982/83	34.3	32.9	4.8	15.9	5.6	1.8	23.3
1984/85	31.7	30.8	5.2	18.9	7.0	1.7	27.6
1986/87	30.1	31.5	5.4	18.9	8.0	1.6	28.5
1988/89	30.6	33.3	5.0	17.7	7.7	1.4	26.8
1990/91	29.6	31.8	4.7	19.6	8.4	1.3	29.3
1992/93	27.8	30.2	4.4	20.2	9.8	1.5	31.3

Source: Department of Statistics (1994:314).

Both universities have the president of Singapore as their chancellor, along with pro-chancellors who are appointed by the chancellor to act on his behalf whenever necessary. The NUS vice chancellor and the NTU president, both of whom are appointed by the respective councils, are the chief academic and administrative officers in their institutions, and both of them are assisted by deputies. The councils, which are the executive bodies, comprise the vice chancellor or president, several lecturers, and a mixture of people appointed by the government, the council, and the chancellor. Academic matters are governed by the senates, which provide for faculty representation.

All four polytechnics have similar administrative structures, with boards of governors forming the chief governing bodies. With the exception of the principals, all board members are appointed by the minister of education. The respective senates (the board of studies in the case of the SP) take charge of academic matters and provide for faculty representation.

Finance

In line with its heavy emphasis on human resource development, education accounts for a major proportion of government operating expenditure (29 percent in 1992). The percentage of the education budget allocated to higher education has increased both in numerical terms and as a percentage of the overall education budget (31.3 percent in 1992–93) (see table 16.1). That this is a relatively large proportion is borne out by the fact that higher education enrollments accounted for only 12.2 percent of the total student enrollment in educational institutions in 1992 (Department of Statistics, 1994:291). The official justification for this disproportionately large allocation of funds is that a heavy investment in higher education is crucial to Singapore's success in the global economy (*Straits Times*, May 18, 1992).

The government has provided substantial subsidies for higher education. It finances all the development expenditures of these institutions and a substantial proportion of recurrent costs, so that the fees charged represent a minor proportion of actual recurrent costs (Asher, 1984). For instance, in the 1984–85 academic year, NUS and SP student fees represented from between 2.5 percent and 11.2 percent, and between 7.2 percent and 9.7 percent, respectively, of average recurrent costs. The issue of whether such high fee subsidies should continue was first raised in Parliament by the education minister in 1985 (*Parliamentary Debates*, 45, March 25, 1985:cols. 1418–21). It was decided that tuition fees would rise progressively, with a corresponding reduction in the government's share of recurrent costs. Several arguments have been offered in support of this decision. They include the disproportionate amount of money being spent on higher education, as well as the excessive burden on taxpayers because of increasing operating costs. Also, since graduates of higher education institutions generally earn more than nongraduates, it is only fair that they should bear a larger proportion of their tuition costs. These changes in higher education financing come amid government moves since the mid-1980s to pass a greater proportion of the operating costs of social services such as education and health to the public (Low, 1991). The object of such moves is to lessen government subsidies and to make Singapore more self-reliant (Vasil, 1992).

Since the mid-1980s, tuition fees have risen sharply in order to recover a greater proportion of recurrent costs through student fees. For instance, the annual tuition fees for local medical students in the NUS have soared from S 1,200 in 1985–86 to S 3,900 in 1988–89, S 7,200 in 1990–91, and S 12,250 in 1993–94. However, the government continues to subsidize a substantial proportion of operating costs—79 percent of university tuition cost in 1992 (Cost Review Committee, 1993:71). The prime minister has given the assurance that the government will fund all basic research in the universities so as not to pass on the costs of such research to students in the form of fee increases (*Straits Times Weekly Edition*, September 17, 1994). In another move to mobilize more community and private resources, the government launched an endowment scheme for the two universities in 1991 with three main target groups: graduates and undergraduates, the general public, and large corporations. It eventually aims to reduce the proportion of university recurrent expenditure provided by government grants to 60 percent, with the remainder coming from student fees (25 percent), endowment fund income (10 percent), and miscellaneous income (5 percent) (*Parliamentary Debates*, 58, May 7, 1991:col. 38).

In response to concerns expressed both from within and outside the government over the affordability of higher education, the government has established a S 100 million loan fund for university students, who can borrow up to 70 percent of their fees at an interest rate that is an average of the prime interest rate of the four major Singapore banks. The loans are to be repaid within twenty years, beginning two years after graduation. A S 50 million loan fund has also been established for polytechnic students. After some initial reluctance, the government finally agreed in 1989 to allow funds to be withdrawn from the Central Provident Fund, a national insurance and pension fund, to pay for tuition fees for full-time courses in local universities and polytechnics.

HIGHER EDUCATION AND ECONOMIC DEVELOPMENT

The first phase of Singapore's industrialization program, which was launched in 1960, involved the policy of import substitution. After independence in 1965, this policy was replaced with one based on export-oriented and labor-intensive industrialization. A major restructuring program was launched in 1979, involving an emphasis on skill- and technology-intensive industries, with a focus on research and development (R&D). The economic recession of 1985–86 led the government to form an Economic Committee to chart new directions for future economic growth. The committee's report outlined various strategies to attain its goal of Singapore becoming a developed nation by the 1990s. Among these was the need to upgrade the education level of the population. Particular mention was made of the fact that the proportion of the workforce with higher education compared unfavorably with that of Taiwan, Japan, and the United States. More important, the committee recommended that universities and polytechnics increase their annual intake, at both the undergraduate and postgraduate levels in the former case. In addition, heavy emphasis was laid on the development of competence in selected technologies: information technology, biotechnology, robotics and artificial intelligence, microelectronics, laser technology and optics, and communications technology (Ministry of Trade and Industry, 1986).

In the early 1990s, more economic reports were launched, including the *National Technology Plan 1991* and *The Strategic Economic Plan*. The former plan was drawn up by the newly established National Science and Technology Board (NSTB), which was formed to enhance Singapore's international competitiveness in science and technology. The NSTB stressed the need to improve R&D capability in order not to lag behind the other newly industrialized countries, the United States, and Europe. The list of selected technologies identified in the 1986 Economic Committee report was expanded to include food and agrotechnology, manufacturing technology, materials technology, and medical sciences. The NSTB also stressed the role of the universities in expanding the pool of R&D personnel. *The Strategic Economic Plan* outlined the government's goal for Singapore to have the same per capita GNP as the United States by the year 2030. Several recurrent themes were stressed: the need to upgrade the education levels of the population and to nurture a pool of skilled personnel in key technologies, along with the importance of developing innovative and creative skills.

A major theme in any discussion about higher education in Singapore is the single-minded gearing of higher education, under firm government direction, toward economic development goals. For instance, the government has stated unequivocally on numerous occasions that university education cannot be divorced from economic needs (see, for instance, *Parliamentary Debates*, 50, March 21, 1988:col. 1114). The universities and polytechnics have been assigned clearly demarcated roles. The universities are to serve three main objectives: to provide top-level professionals, managers, planners, and researchers; to raise the intellectual tone of society; and to act as a benchmark in maintaining high educational standards in Singapore (*Alumnus*, March 1992:17; *Parliamentary Debates*, 55, March 28, 1990:col. 986), while the polytechnics serve to provide middle-level technologists, supervisors, and managers (*Parliamentary Debates*, 55, March 28, 1990:col. 986). The government is also not in favor of allowing the polytechnics to offer degree courses—another clear indication of its plans for a stratified higher education system (*Straits Times*, July 24, 1991).

Government leaders constantly stress that a country such as Singapore, which does not have natural resources, has no viable alternative to relying on developing and utilizing its human resources in the service of economic development. Official discourse reveals a frank and painful awareness of the limitations imposed by the size of the country. For instance, Lee Kuan Yew has stated publicly that although the two local universities have facilities and staff on par with the best universities in the United States or the United Kingdom, he does not think that the NUS and the NTU are equal in stature to those universities. This is because the latter group of universities has a relatively much broader population base from which to draw the best students (*Straits Times Weekly Edition*, August 20, 1994:1).

In line with the gearing of higher education toward economic needs, the government established a Committee on Professional and Technical Education (CPTE) in 1979. The CPTE, which is chaired by the minister of trade and industry, projects and recommends enrollment and staffing figures in the universities, polytechnics, and vocational training institutes. As a result of CPTE recommendations, university and polytechnic enrollments increased by 168 percent and 166 percent, respectively, from 1980 to 1990 (see table 16.2). Even prior to the establishment of the CPTE, enrollment patterns and the opening of new courses, for example, in engineering, business, and biotechnology, had been clearly in response to perceived economic needs (Seah, 1983).

As part of the drive to promote R&D, the universities have established various specialized research institutes, which are funded by the NSTB. These include the Institute of Systems Science, the Institute of Molecular and Cell Biology, the Institute of Microelectronics, and the Magnetics Technology Centre in the NUS, and the GINTIC Institute of Manufacturing Technology in the NTU. Both the NUS and the NTU, as well as the polytechnics, have strengthened their links with industry by establishing industrial liaison networks to promote technology transfer, offer consultancy and training services, and embark on joint commercial projects.

The concern with economic relevance extends beyond monitoring enrollment levels to regulating access to certain fields of study. For instance, from 1979 on a quota was placed on the percentage of top-scoring university entrants who could be admitted to medicine and dentistry courses in the NUS, on the grounds that a more even spread of talent was needed in the various disciplines (*Parliamentary Debates*, 38, March 16, 1979:cols. 763–66). Replying to the criticism that the quota denied some students the right to freely pursue their career ambitions, a government spokesman said: "The Government subsidizes the cost of training in the universities not to satisfy personal ambitions but to meet the nation's economic and social needs" (*Straits Times*, May 21, 1991). In 1993, the government announced plans to restrict the growth of the legal profession. These moves included reducing the NUS law faculty intake, derecognizing external law degrees obtained in or after 1996, and restricting the number of overseas universities whose legal degrees are recognized by the government (Committee on the Supply of Lawyers, 1993). Concern was expressed that an excess of lawyers would constitute a misallocation of valuable manpower resources. In the same vein, the Singapore Medical Council decided in 1993 to reduce the number of foreign medical schools whose degrees are recognized within Singapore from 176 to 28. The council was responding to government concern that there would soon be too many doctors per capita (*Straits Times*, November 9, 1993). Another method used to influence the choice of courses is the offering of both local and overseas scholarships in fields identified as priority areas, such as engineering and teaching.

The extremely hard-headed approach toward higher education is part of a pervasive pragmatism in overall government policy. The government constantly asserts that a small country such as Singapore cannot survive otherwise. However, several academics have criticized the government for an excessive reliance on "instrumental rationality" (Chua, 1985; see also Koh, 1989). Others have expressed concern that university students are not well read and knowledgeable about current affairs, and lament the inadequate attention being paid to aesthetic education (*Straits Times*, September 13, 1990, March 22, 1993; September 11, 1993). For its part, the government has expressed concern over some of these very issues. For instance, it has acknowledged the difficulty in getting young people "interested and convinced that art is an essential part of life" (*Sunday Times*, September 26, 1993:20). However, the overwhelming tone of official discourse conveys the unapologetic message that it would be extremely unwise to jettison the "basic principles" of "realism and pragmatism" that have thus far enabled Singapore to succeed economically (*Sunday Times*, December 5, 1993).

Internationalization of Higher Education

A major prong of the national economic development strategy outlined in *The Strategic Economic Plan* is a policy of internationalization, in order to use "global resources, global technology and global talent" (p. 59). As part of this plan, Singapore is to develop into an international center of learning (*Alumnus*, March 1992:14).[2] At the institutional level, the universities and polytechnics are increasing their links with overseas institutions of higher learning. For instance, the NTU has signed a memorandum of understanding with Cornell University to initiate collaborative activities in communication education and research (*NTU News*, April 1993:1). Although the universities and polytechnics were originally modeled on British institutions,[3] there is increasing influence from the North American academic model. Both the NUS and the NTU have introduced a hybrid modular system for certain undergraduate programs, a move that combines features of the British and North American university systems. At the same time, all the polytechnics have adopted a modular academic system. Another development that will increase international linkages is the government decision to allow more foreign universities to run courses in conjunction with various local private organizations.

Staff Flows. Besides increasing institutional linkages, the flow of teaching and research personnel into and out of Singapore is growing. An increasing number of local teaching staff are being sponsored for postgraduate studies in overseas universities, while others are involved in academic staff exchange programs. At the same time, the government has openly welcomed the importation of foreign teachers and researchers from all over the world, in recognition of the difficulties of relying solely on local talent (Lee, 1980b:18–19). It is recognized that it is not possible to completely localize the recruitment of academic staff in higher education institutions (Lee, 1980b). Foreign academics also serve in various capacities such as external examiners and members of advisory panels and review boards. They are often consulted for advice and assistance in major higher education planning and policy-making decisions, such as the formation of the NUS and the establishment of the Open University. The majority of these expatriates are from the traditionally English-speaking countries. The use of the English language in higher education in Singapore has been an advantage in this regard. Since the late 1980s, the NUS has recruited an increasing number of staff from the People's Republic of China. For instance, eighteen out of forty-four lecturers in the mathematics department in 1993 were from China, as were nine out of fifty-four research fellows in the Institute of Molecular and Cell Biology (National University of Singapore, 1994:94–95, 104–5).

Despite the policy of liberal expatriate recruitment, the government hopes to have Singaporeans in charge of most departments (Lee, 1980b). There has been a history of conflict between the government and several expatriate academics who have criticized various government policies. The government has made its stand on the matter clear, as exemplified in the following statement by a former cabinet minister, who was at one point concurrently serving as vice chancellor of the University of Singapore:

Expatriates have their role to play, even in Singapore, but they become obnoxious when the adventurous and the brash exploit the politeness of Asians by venturing into the local political arena or offering gratuitous advice on how to run the government or the university. . . . However we organise the University is our business, and expatriates who come to teach must fit themselves into our system. I cannot imagine Indians, Pakistanis or Chinese expatriates in Western Universities telling their rectors, presidents or vice-chancellors how to run their universities much less how prime ministers should govern their countries. (Toh, 1973:53)

As to the problem of determining the somewhat nebulous boundary between academic freedom and interference in domestic politics, Lee Kuan Yew has said that "common sense and academic judgment can be left to mark out these bounds" (cited in Josey, 1968:158). The government's stand on this issue has been criticized by an opposition parliamentarian (*Parliamentary Debates*, 47, March 17, 1985:cols. 474–76) and a few disgruntled former expatriate academics (Puccetti, 1972; Wilkinson, 1988).

Student Flows. Two-way student flows represent another form of growing regionalization and internationalization. For instance, in 1992 the NUS launched a collaborative master's in public policy program together with Harvard University, with a specific Southeast Asian focus (*Campus News, 97,* 1992:6). That same year, the Ministry of Foreign Affairs started the Singapore Cooperation Programme, under which individuals, mostly from the Southeast Asian and Asia-Pacific regions, are sponsored for various training courses, some of which are conducted by the universities and polytechnics (Suryahti, 1993). The percentage of foreign students (the vast majority of whom are from Malaysia) in undergraduate courses in the NUS and the NTI in the 1989–90 academic year varied from 14.1 percent in engineering to 4.0 percent in arts and social sciences. The percentage of foreign students appears to have declined overall. For instance, the previous figure for engineering represents a sharp drop from 41.6 percent in 1985–86. Likewise, the percentage for medicine declined from 19.7 percent in 1985–86 to just 6.9 percent in 1989–90 (*Parliamentary Debates*, 54, February 22, 1990:cols. 1131–32). No official explanation has been offered for this decline, but it may be attributable in part to the need to cater to the growing pressure for admission from local students.

Despite the decline in the percentage of foreign students, the increasing social demand for higher education has led to concern among parliamentarians and community leaders that foreign students may be depriving Singaporeans of university places. Questions have also been raised about the cost of subsidizing foreign students' fees. The government has stated unequivocally that its first priority is to provide university places for all Singaporeans who qualify for admission. In addition, foreign students have to satisfy more stringent entry requirements than local students (*Parliamentary Debates*, 45, March 26, 1985: cols. 1444–46; 58, May 7, 1991:cols. 46, 63). Students from ASEAN (Association of Southeast Asian Nations) member nations, and those from non-ASEAN nations, pay one and a half times and twice the amount local students do, respectively. The government has also stated that a reasonable target would be for foreign students to form about 20 percent of university intakes (*Parliamentary Debates*, 45, March 26, 1985:col. 1451). Its rationale for admitting these students is characteristically pragmatic. First, all foreign students have to sign a bond to live and work in Singapore for at least three years upon their graduation, thus adding to the limited local talent pool. Admitting these students thus represents a prime investment, as Singapore is able to tap their talent without having had to pay for their education prior to university. Next, local students have the opportunity to interact with students from other societies and learn more about those societies. This interaction will not only contribute toward a better-rounded university education, but will also help local students in their future job-related contacts with foreigners. Lastly, when foreign students return to their home countries, there will eventually be a network of such students, especially in neighboring nations, occupying key positions in the public and private sectors (*Parliamentary Debates*, 45, March 26, 1985:col. 1447; 50, March 21, 1988: cols. 1103–4; 58, May 7, 1991:cols. 63–64).

The promotion of international student flows has been given further impetus with the announcement in 1994 that the Singapore and British governments were exploring strategies to forge partnerships between British companies and colleges and their Singaporean counterparts. These partnerships would then engage in marketing open university courses and other education services in China and Southeast Asia. The courses would use English as the medium of instruction (*Straits Times*, April 9, 1994).

In addition to the inflow of foreign students, the number of Singaporean students studying in foreign higher education institutions has steadily increased in the past few decades. A key point to note is that the government annually sends top-scoring school leavers to prestigious foreign universities for undergraduate programs. These students will assume key administrative positions in the civil service on their return. The former prime minister has explained in characteristically pragmatic terms the advantages of top students studying in a top university in the United States or the United Kingdom: "You have the opportunity to network, to build up friendships and lifelong relationships with their best, their future political and corporate leaders" (*Straits Times Weekly Edition*, August 20, 1994:1).

To date, Singaporean students have largely opted for studies in the traditionally English-speaking countries. The most popular destinations for overseas polytechnic and university education in 1990 were, in descending order, the United States, the United Kingdom, Australia, and Canada (Lau, 1992:127). However, a cabinet minister recently encouraged local students to study in non-English-speaking countries, such as Japan and Germany, in order to broaden economic opportunities for Singapore (*Straits Times*, November 4, 1992). Local institutions have begun sending students overseas for work stints as part of the government's globalization strategy. Furthermore, students in the two universities can now accumulate study credits for courses taken in certain overseas universities.

The Malaysian Challenge. Singapore's efforts to promote itself as a regional higher education center are now being challenged by similar efforts on the part of the Malaysian government. These plans include the building of three more universities; allowing foreign universities to establish branch campuses in Malaysia; and encouraging the private sector to establish colleges and to offer twinning programs with local and foreign universities (*Straits Times Weekly Edition*, April 30, 1994; *New Straits Times*, December 28, 1993; June 22, 1994; June 30, 1994). In addition, incentives are being offered to attract Malaysian scientists working abroad, as well as scientists from developing countries, to work in Malaysia (*New Straits Times*, June 17, 1994). The Malaysian government aims to have Malaysia become an industrialized nation by the year 2020 and has identified several key technologies—biotechnology, automated manufacturing, electronics, advanced materials and information technology—to be explored toward this end (*New Straits Times*, August 4, 1994). It should be noted that these technologies have been identified as key technologies by the Singapore government as well.

A small but growing number of Singaporean students are enrolling in external degree courses conducted by private colleges in Malaysia. These colleges have links with universities in Australia, Canada, New Zealand, the United States, and the United Kingdom. Not only do such courses represent a much cheaper alternative to studies in the latter group of countries; they also offer opportunities for students who are unable to gain admission to Singapore universities. Furthermore, admission requirements are reportedly "more flexible" (*Straits Times*, April 9, 1994:17). It will be interesting to see the extent to which the Singapore government can cope with this challenge to its plans, especially when one considers not only the geographical proximity of the two countries, but also the relatively lower cost of living in Malaysia. Also, it remains to be seen to what extent the flow of Singaporeans to universities in the traditionally English-speaking countries is diverted to Malaysia.

ACCESS AND EQUITY ISSUES

Access to higher education was relatively restricted and selective until the beginning of the 1990s. This policy of restricted access existed even while social demand for higher education, especially at the university level, was steadily increasing. Many students have had to turn to overseas institutions. The growing number of external degree courses conducted by private institutions and bodies also helps meet the rising demand for university qualifications.

There are several reasons for the high social demand. First, continued economic growth in the post-independence period (except during the 1985–86 recession) has meant a steady demand for university and polytechnic graduates in the workforce. Another key reason is that higher education qualifications provide Singaporeans with an important route to high-income employment and socio-economic status. An employment survey of 1991 NUS and NTU graduates revealed that the median gross starting monthly salary was S 1686, compared with a median gross monthly income of S 919 for all employed persons that same year (Ministry of Labour, 1993:17; National University of Singapore, 1992:68). Although university and polytechnic graduates constituted 8.1 percent and 5.3 percent, respectively, of the workforce in 1992, they constituted 44.8 percent and 9.5 percent, respectively, of those with a gross monthly income of S 3,000 or more (Ministry of Labour, 1994:74). A third reason is the rapid expansion of primary and secondary education enrollment, as well as increased percentage pass rates in various primary and secondary school leaving examinations, which have resulted in an increased pool of candidates meeting the minimum entry qualifications for higher education.

The increasing social demand for higher education has centered on access to the universities. Concern was voiced by parliamentarians over the fact that about half of all NUS applicants were unsuccessful in the mid-1980s. Several members of Parliament questioned the need to plan university admission figures in accordance with manpower projections, and asked whether NUS admission standards were unduly high (*Parliamentary Debates*, 50, March 21, 1988:cols. 1080–95). The government's main fear has been that of graduate unemployment, not only because it represents a mismatch of human resources, but also because of its attendant political and social consequences. Another fear is that failure to maintain rigorous admission standards will lead to the devaluation of university degrees (Lee, 1977:8; *Parliamentary Debates*, 50, March 21, 1988:cols. 1098–1108; 55, March 28, 1990:cols. 986–87).

At the end of the 1980s and the beginning of the 1990s, the government announced plans to increase substantially the proportion of each age cohort in higher education. These plans were a direct response not only to economic imperatives, but also to the growing social demand for higher education. Consideration also had to be taken of those who could not afford the cost of overseas studies (Goh, 1991). The target for the year 2000 is to have 40 percent and 20 percent of each age cohort in the polytechnics and the universities, respectively, compared to 20 percent and 15 percent, respectively, in 1991. The universities have also been directed to admit more polytechnic graduates to their degree programs. Another important part of these expansion plans was the decision to provide more opportunities for mature students to obtain polytechnic and university qualifications. Besides starting the Open University, the government adopted a more liberal policy toward the conducting of external degree courses by private organizations (Tan, 1991).

The overriding concern with economic relevance manifested itself in warnings by government ministers that any expansion plans had to be in line with Singapore's economic and social needs, in particular, the increasing of its productivity and economic competitiveness vis-à-vis other countries. The dangers of graduate unemployment and deterioration in academic standards were also stressed. The Ministry of Education and the Ministry of Trade and Industry will monitor the various courses offered by higher education institutions and ''take corrective action from time to time'' to ensure their economic relevance (Tan, 1991:42).

However, it is becoming increasingly more difficult for the government to influence enrollment patterns and decisions by controlling enrollments and access to various courses in local institutions. Growing affluence haš meant that more people now have the option of obtaining an overseas education, often at their own expense. For instance, despite the greater access provided to polytechnic diploma-holders in local universities, the number of diploma-holders applying for admission to the two local universities dropped substantially in 1993. The drop was attributed to the increasing number of students who chose to enroll in overseas institutions that offer faster graduation times and greater chances of access (*Straits Times*, October 28, 1993). The prime minister has pointed out that it may be increasingly difficult to attract top students to take up government scholarships due to increasing affluence and competition from scholarships offered by private companies (*Straits Times*, August 19, 1993).

Another key problem facing the Singapore government concerns the retention of local professionals, who in most cases have been educated at considerable public expense. Singapore's growing integration into the global economy means that it will have to compete in the global market in order to retain these professionals. Official concern has been expressed since the late 1980s about the disproportionately high number of highly educated and skilled people among the ranks of emigrants. It remains to be seen whether various measures, such as the provision of channels for greater political consultation and the increased attention being paid to artistic and aesthetic activities, will reduce emigration among the highly educated section of the population. While the government has now resigned itself to the fact that emigration is a worldwide phenomenon, it, in its usual pragmatic manner, now sees Singaporean emigrants as valuable network links for Singaporeans engaged in foreign business ventures (*Straits Times*, April 18, 1994).

Gender

Female participation rates in all higher education institutions have increased from 1960 to 1990 (see table 16.2). The increase in female enrollment has been so great that females now predominate overwhelmingly in various faculties and courses, such as the arts and social sciences faculty in the NUS, the school of accountancy and business in the NTU, the teacher training courses in the National Institute of Education, and the accountancy, business studies, design, and health sciences courses in the polytechnics. However, females still remain underrepresented in other courses, such as medicine, dentistry, and engineering in the universities, and engineering in the polytechnics.

Gender imbalances in certain fields have been the subject of government concern for a variety of reasons. The low proportion of females (about 10 percent) in engineering courses in the universities has been described by a govern-

Table 16.2
Higher Education Enrollments, 1960–1990

Year	Universities	Polytechnics	Teacher Training	Total
1960	3502 (23.0)	2342 (2.3)	2327 (51.7)	8171 (25.2)
1965	4996 (28.1)	3208 (9.9)	5603 (58.0)	13807 (36.0)
1970	6990 (34.8)	4692 (8.1)	2001 (69.5)	13683 (30.7)
1975	8540 (44.1)	9276 (18.8)	685 (79.4)	18501 (32.7)
1980	9078 (44.2)	11105 (22.5)	2328 (84.9)	22511 (37.7)
1985	17071 (46.6)	21610 (27.4)	1232 (78.2)	39913 (37.2)
1990	24341 (46.7)	29550 (34.8)	1781 (75.7)	55672 (41.3)

Note: Figures in parentheses denote the percentage of females.
Sources: Department of Statistics (1983:238); Department of Statistics (1994:301–2).

ment · minister as "the biggest misallocation" in higher education (*Parliamentary Debates*, 50, March 28, 1988:col. 1505). In the case of the NUS medical and dental faculties, the proportion of female students has been kept at about one-third since 1979 as a result of a deliberate government policy. The minister for health justified the decision on the grounds that not only was the attrition rate for women doctors very high; they were also very choosy about hospital postings, and were "clock-watchers" (*Parliamentary Debates*, 38, March 16, 1979:cols. 766–67). He described the high attrition rate as "a considerable loss in investment," clear evidence once again of the constant use of economic language in discussions of higher education. The validity of these assertions was recently challenged in Parliament by a female parliamentarian who is also a doctor (*Straits Times*, March 13, 1993), but to date there have been no indications that the discriminatory policy will be rescinded. Another issue that has aroused official concern is the rapid feminization of the teaching profession since the 1960s. Ministry of Education figures show that females comprised 69.5 percent of school teachers in 1993 (Ministry of Education, 1992:

5). Two official reasons cited for the concern are that women are less ambitious and therefore less willing to apply for promotion to senior positions, and that boys need male role models (*Straits Times*, March 13, 1978; November 26, 1987). However, repeated government attempts to attract men into teaching have had little success so far: Only 10.4 percent of the 1993 intake for teacher training were males, and this represented an increase over the previous year's figure of 7.4 percent (*Straits Times Weekly Edition*, March 19, 1994:4).

The issue of gender imbalance in higher education took on national significance when it became entangled in the extremely controversial "Great Marriage Debate" in 1983 (for critiques of government policy, see Blake and Blake, 1984; Henry and Davies, 1992). In mid-August of that year, Lee Kuan Yew expressed concern that Singapore faced the prospect of a declining talent pool, with disastrous consequences for the economy and society, if current marriage and procreation trends continued. First, there was an inverse relationship between the educational level of married women and the number of children they had. At the same time, Singaporean men tended to marry their educational equals or inferiors, with the result that increasing numbers of well-educated women were remaining single (Saw, 1990:appendix A).

Later that month, the NUS announced that recently imposed language proficiency entry requirements would be relaxed with immediate effect. The rationale given was that since women tended to be better than men in languages, the entry requirements had led to more women than men being admitted to the university in the past few years. If this trend were to continue, the problem of unmarried women graduates would be aggravated (*Straits Times*, November 11, 1983; November 20, 1983). This incident clearly illustrates again both the ability and the determination of the government to steer higher education policies in desired directions in order to meet prescribed social and economic goals.

Over a decade after the "Great Marriage Debate" began, official concern persists over marriage trends among university graduates as well as disparities in child-bearing patterns between highly educated and less educated women. There has been an increase in the percentage of male university graduates marrying female university graduates. However, despite the introduction since the mid-1980s of child-bearing incentives for better educated women and, conversely, incentives for less educated women to bear fewer children, there are currently still no signs that the "fertility gap" is being bridged. Government leaders repeatedly warn of the dire demographic and economic consequences if these trends continue (*Straits Times*, June 14, 1993; July 30, 1994).

Ethnicity

Both government and community leaders have expressed increasing concern since the 1980s over the problem of minority educational underachievement, with most of the focus being on the two numerically largest communities, the Malays and Indians (see, for instance, Action Committee on Indian Education,

1991; Tan, 1993). The available figures show evidence of minority underrepresentation in higher education enrollments in 1990. The ethnic breakdown of local students in local universities was as follows: 90.7 percent Chinese, 3.5 percent Malays, 5.0 percent Indians, and 0.8 percent from other minorities. Chinese students comprised 90.9 percent of the local students in the polytechnics, Malays 6.3 percent, Indians 2.5 percent, and other minorities 0.4 percent (Lau, 1993a:168–69). The 1990 population census figures revealed that Malay university and polytechnic graduates are underrepresented in all fields of study, constituting only 1.8 percent of all university degree-holders and 3.3 percent of all polytechnic graduates. The Indians are overrepresented in certain fields such as law (accounting for 19.4 percent of all law degree-holders), but are underrepresented in fields such as engineering, computer studies and statistics, management, accountancy, commerce, architecture, and building science. They comprise 6.6 percent of all university degree-holders and 2.5 percent of all polytechnic diploma-holders (Lau, 1993a:204, 213). In fact, the proportional underrepresentation in the case of both the Malay and Indian communities begins earlier at the secondary level of schooling (ibid.:168–69). The ethnic disparities in educational attainment are reflected in income disparities as well. Average monthly incomes for Chinese, Malays, and Indians in 1990 were S 1,497, S 1,049, and S 1,195, respectively. Of these three ethnic groups, the Chinese had the smallest proportion of wage earners earning below S 1,000 and the highest proportion earning S 3,000 or more (Lau, 1993b:16, 17).

The government has explicitly rejected the use of admission quotas as a means of redressing ethnic disparities in educational achievement. Instead, it has encouraged the formation of, and provides financial and intrastructural assistance to, several ethnically based self-help organizations. These groups leave the specific mission of improving socioeconomic and educational achievement to the respective ethnic communities. The bulk of these organizations' efforts at improving educational achievement involves tuition classes for primary and secondary school students, the provision of financial aid, family counseling and referral services, and parent outreach programs. The first of these organizations, Mendaki, was formed in 1982. This was followed by the setting up of three organizations—the Singapore Indian Development Association, the Chinese Development Assistance Council, and the Association of Muslim Professionals—in 1991. It may seem strange that the Chinese community, which does not face the problem of underrepresentation in higher education, should need to form such an organization. The formation of the Chinese-based group may be seen in part as a government move in response to the perception on the part of some sections of the Chinese community that the government was paying insufficient attention to their concerns. The swing of votes away from the ruling party during the 1991 general elections was attributed in part to this discontent (Singh, 1992). It is still too early to tell if these efforts will eventually result in more proportional ethnic representation in higher education institutions.

A particularly contentious issue in the case of the Malay community was the proposal, first raised by then First Deputy Prime Minister Goh Chok Tong in 1989, to do away with the thirty-year-old practice of granting free tuition to all Malay students in local higher education institutions. The government would instead hand over the sum it spent annually on Malay fee subsidies to Mendaki, a Malay self-help group. Malays who could afford to pay tuition fees should do so. The money saved would then be available for Mendaki to use for educational development programs for Malays in general. A key argument put forward in favor of the idea was that while the original practice of free higher education was initiated to help the Malays improve themselves educationally, it needed to be reexamined now that there were more affluent Malays. The proposal was extremely controversial, but was eventually accepted by Mendaki the following year. The new means-tested fee subsidy scheme started in 1991 with the help of an initial S 17 million government grant (Tan, 1993).

CONCLUSION

Higher education in Singapore has undergone rapid expansion and structural reorganization in the past three and a half decades. Throughout this period a prime concern has been the gearing of higher education toward meeting the needs of the economy. This has been manifested in such areas as curricular changes, enrollment policies, and research priorities. The most recent trend in this respect is on meshing higher education into the process of internationalization in the context of a global economy.

Another feature of Singapore higher education is the dominant interventionist role played by the government in directing higher education policy and planning toward prescribed social and economic goals. It is perhaps understandable that in a newly independent nation lacking in natural resources, the government has been reluctant to leave the development of higher education entirely in the hands of academics and administrators in the universities and polytechnics. The Singapore case clearly illustrates that a heavy state presence in higher education need not impede the successful functioning of higher education. In fact, it has led to swift and flexible responses to perceived changes in both national and global economic circumstances. At the same time, however, this heavy state presence has its shortcomings. For instance, some individuals have had to subordinate their career choices to government-dictated enrollment policies motivated by economic considerations.

After a period of relatively selective access to higher education, there are now plans to enroll 60 percent of each age cohort in universities and polytechnics by the year 2000. These plans have been formulated in response to both economic needs and increasing social demand for higher educational qualifications, especially university degrees. In addition, greater opportunities are being provided for older students to obtain university and polytechnic qualifications.

The Singapore higher education system holds several key lessons for other countries, both within and outside of Asia, that are concerned with problems of quality and quantity in higher education. The government has adopted a well-coordinated approach to policy planning and implementation. Also, it is quick to identify potential niches for Singapore within the wider global economy and to then marshal resources within the higher education system toward the filling of those niches. Next, the higher education system has been generously funded and resourced, even as the government attempts to broaden the revenue base. The clear message is that higher education is a prime national investment worthy of government as well as nongovernment support. Another useful lesson concerns the way in which student and staff flows into and out of the country are encouraged. There is the prudent recognition that fostering international links is vital to ensuring that Singapore is able to keep up with the latest developments and advances in teaching, research, and technology. At the same time, the almost exclusive use of English as the medium of instruction has facilitated the fostering of such links.

The prospects for Singapore higher education as it approaches the twenty-first century are extremely bright. The entire system is well regarded internationally in terms of academic standards and general efficiency. The major funding problems that are plaguing many other systems are noticeably absent, and enrollment expansion plans are currently underway. Four major trends can be forecast for higher education.

First, it is clear that the overriding concern with economic relevance will continue. Course curricula and enrollment patterns, as well as the growth in research and development, will be monitored closely to ensure that they are consonant with government-perceived social and economic needs. At the same time, the links between the higher education institutions and industry will intensify.

Second, the policy of internationalization will be maintained, as manifested in student, staff, and technology flows into and out of Singapore. Recent advances in information technology will further increase these international links. For instance, videoconferencing is now being used for some course lectures in the NUS. At the same time, however, the spread of information technology also means that with the growing worldwide access to knowledge, it will be more difficult for Singaporean higher education to maintain its edge over other national systems of higher education amid the increasingly competitive global economic environment. The concurrent Malaysian bid to be the regional higher education center is one example of the increasingly competitive stakes involved.

Third, there is a need to meet increasing social demands for higher education qualifications, especially university degrees. The government has committed itself to providing greater opportunities for working adults to acquire such qualifications. In particular, the number of private organizations offering distance learning programs will increase. Nevertheless, the characteristic concern with economic competitiveness will mean government monitoring of course enrollments, curricula, and standards. The dilemma facing students who have to subordinate their personal career ambitions to economically driven enrollment policies will continue as well. However, there are already signs that a greater proportion of students are now able to circumvent official restrictions on access to various courses in local institutions by pursuing an overseas education. The viability of state regulation of enrollment patterns is therefore being increasingly challenged. Two further challenges face the government as access continues to broaden: achieving a more balanced gender representation in enrollment in certain fields, and redressing the current underrepresentation of the Malay and Indian minorities.

Fourth, an increasing share of the costs of financing of higher education will be borne by private individuals and the corporate sector. The decision to allow the private sector to run the Open University, as well as the more liberal policy toward commercially run external degree courses, reflect this trend. The pegging of tuition fees at a constant percentage of recurrent costs will mean steady annual fee increases. A major challenge will be to ensure that existing loan schemes are adequate, so as not to deny low-income students the chance for higher education.

What all these trends have in common is that with higher education playing such a key role in Singapore's development, it is likely that the large government influence that has been a feature over the past three decades will continue. However, as pointed out earlier in this chapter, it is becoming increasingly difficult for the government to exert its influence in certain domains such as individual enrollment decisions and career choices. Also, with the increasing participation of the private sector in financing and conducting higher education, as well as in institutional research, the government may find it necessary to reexamine the degree of control it needs to exercise over higher education.

NOTES

1. The former prime minister Lee Kuan Yew described the problem facing the University of Singapore in the immediate postindependence period: "One of our problems is how to transform a colonial institution originally designed for training subordinate staff for the schools, medical service, and administration of this country, into a centre of higher learning where our youths are trained and imbued and inspired with the ideals of building our new nation" (cited in Toh, 1973:49).

2. The plan to turn Singapore into a regional and international center of learning dates back to 1981 (*Parliamentary Debates*, 40, March 6, 1981:col. 492).

3. For instance, Lee Kuan Yew has said that the NUS should have as a yardstick for academic standards a good university in Britain, such as the University of London (Lee, 1980b.:20).

REFERENCES

Action Committee on Indian Education. 1991. *At the Crossroads: Report of the Action Committee on Indian Education*. Singapore: Author.

Alumnus. 1992.

Asher, M. G. 1984. *Financing the Development of Higher Education in Singapore*. Singapore: Regional Institute of Higher Education and Development.

Blake, M., and A. Blake. 1984. May–August. "Intelligence, Achievement and Opportunity: Some Questions." *Social Dimension*, 5–8.

Campus News. 1992.

Chan, H. C. 1989. "The PAP and the Restructuring of the Political System." In Kernial Singh Sandhu and Paul Wheatley, eds., *Management of Success: The Moulding of Modern Singapore*. Singapore: Institute of Southeast Asian Studies.

Chelliah, D. D. 1947. *A Short History of the Educational Policy of the Straits Settlements*. Kuala Lumpur: Acting Government Printer.

Chua, B. H. 1985. "Pragmatism of the People's Action Party Government in Singapore: A Critical Assessment." *Southeast Asian Journal of Social Science, 13*, 29–46.

Committee on the Supply of Lawyers. 1993. *Report on the Legal Profession*. Singapore: Ministry of Law.

Cost Review Committee. 1993. *Report of the Cost Review Committee*. Singapore: Singapore National Printers.

Department of Statistics. 1983. *Economic & Social Statistics Singapore 1960–1982*. Singapore: Author.

———. 1993. *Yearbook of Statistics Singapore 1992*. Singapore: Author.

Goh, C. T. 1991. "Tertiary Education: Where Do We Go from Here?" *Speeches, 15* (3), 8–11.

Gopinathan, S. 1989. "University Education in Singapore: The Making of a National University." In P. G. Altbach and V. Selvaratnam, eds., *From Dependence to Autonomy: The Development of Asian Universities*. Dordrecht: Kluwer Academic.

Heng, G., and J. Devan. 1992. "State Fatherhood: The Politics of Nationalism, Sexuality, and Race in Singapore." In A. Parker, M. Russo, D. Sommer, and P. Yaeger, eds., *Nationalisms and Sexualities*. New York: Routledge.

Josey, A. 1968. *Lee Kuan Yew*. Singapore: Donald Moore.

Koh, T. A. 1989. "Culture and the Arts." In K. S. Sandhu and P. Wheatley, eds., *Management of Success: The Moulding of Modern Singapore*. Singapore: Institute of Southeast Asian Studies.

Lau, K. E. 1992. *Singapore Census of Population 1990 Statistical Release 1: Demographic Characteristics*. Singapore: Department of Statistics.

———. 1993a. *Singapore Census of Population 1990 Statistical Release 3: Literacy, Languages Spoken and Education*. Singapore: Department of Statistics.

———. 1993b. *Singapore Census of Population 1990 Statistical Release 4: Economic Characteristics*. Singapore: Department of Statistics.

Lee, E. 1989. "The Colonial Legacy." In Kernial Singh Sandhu and Paul Wheatley, eds., *Management of Success: The Moulding of Modern Singapore*. Singapore: Institute of Southeast Asian Studies.

Lee, K. Y. 1977. "Higher Education: Abiding Commitment Essential." *Speeches, 1* (7), 7–37.

———. 1978. "Bilingualism and Higher Education in Singapore." *Speeches, 1* (9), 1–14.

———. 1980a. "Three Options for Nanyang University." *Speeches, 3* (10), 1–24.

———. 1980b. "NUS Must Be Innovative and Outward-looking." *Speeches, 3* (12), 10–29.

Low, L. 1991. *The Political Economy of Privatization in Singapore: Analysis, Interpretation and Evaluation*. Singapore: McGraw-Hill.

Ministry of Education. 1992. *Education Statistics Digest 1992*. Singapore: Author.

Ministry of Labour. 1993. *Report on the Labour Force Survey of Singapore*. Singapore: Author.

———. 1994a. *Report on the Labour Force Survey of Singapore 1992*. Singapore: Author.

———. 1994b. *Report on the Labour Force Survey of Singapore 1993*. Singapore: Author.

Ministry of Trade and Industry. 1986. *The Singapore Economy: New Directions*. Singapore: Author.

———. 1991. *The Strategic Economic Plan: Towards a Developed Nation*. Singapore: Author.

National Science and Technology Board. 1991. *National Technology Plan 1991*. Singapore: Author.

National University of Singapore. 1992. *1991 NUS and NTU Graduate Employment Survey*. Singapore: Author.

———. 1993. *1993–94 General Information*. Singapore: Author.

New Straits Times. Various dates.

NTU News. 1993.

Parliamentary Debates, Singapore: Official Report. Various issues.

Puccetti, R. 1972. "Authoritarian Government and Academic Subservience: The University of Singapore." *Minerva, 10,* 223–41.

Saw, S. H. 1990. *Changes in the Fertility Policy of Singapore*. Singapore: Times Academic.

Seah, C. M. 1983. *Student Admission to Higher Education in Singapore*. Singapore: Regional Institute of Higher Education and Development.

Singapore Institute of Management (SIM). 1992. *Annual Report 1992*. Singapore: Author.

Singh, B. 1992. *Whither PAP's Dominance? An Analysis of Singapore's 1991 General Elections*. Petaling Jaya, Malaysia: Pelanduk.

Straits Times. Various dates.

Straits Times Weekly Edition. Various dates.

Sunday Times. Various dates.

Suryahti, A. L. 1993, May–June. "Contributing to the Global Society." *Singapore,* 16–17.

Tan, E. T. J. 1993. *Educational Underachievement of the Malay Minority in Singapore 1981–1992: Problems and Policies*. Unpublished master's diss., University of Hong Kong.

Tan, T. K. Y. 1991. "The Outlook for Tertiary Education." *Speeches, 15* (4), 37–41.

Toh, C. C. 1973. "Intellectual Decolonization of the University of Singapore." In *Towards Tomorrow: Essays on Development and Social Transformation in Singapore*. Singapore: National Trades Union Congress.

Turnbull, C. M. 1989. *A History of Singapore 1819–1988*. 2nd ed. Singapore: Oxford University Press.

Vasil, R. 1992. *Governing Singapore*. Singapore: Mandarin.

Wilkinson, B. 1988. "Social Engineering in Singapore." *Journal of Contemporary Asia, 18,* 165–88.

Wilson, H. E. 1978. *Social Engineering in Singapore: Educational Policies and Social Change 1819–1972*. Singapore: Singapore University Press.

17

SOUTH KOREA

Sungho H. Lee

The development of higher education in Korea is the product of many influences and factors. On the one hand, it has been molded and influenced by a variety of Western forces. On the other hand, traditional Korean values and systems have had an extraordinary resistance and persistence.

For its long history of over 4,300 years, Korea has had well-developed ideas and practices related to providing people with higher education. However, in the premodern age, namely, prior to the latter part of the nineteenth century, there was no well-articulated system of higher education in Korea. Educational institutions were strictly divided into two types: state-run and private institutions. The state-run institutions were mostly those of higher learning, which opened their doors only to the selected youth of the privileged upper class. The private institutions of education were for the primary and middle levels of education.

During the past one hundred years, the higher education system in Korea has been subjected to critical review on at least four occasions. The outcome of the first of these reviews, after the Western missionary arrivals in the 1880s, was the establishment of higher education institutions based on an American system of higher education. These successful institutions had the support of the indigenous people, and were crucial to shaping contemporary Korean higher education.

By the turn of the century, however, such Western influences were suspended when the Korean Kingdom was subjected to Japanese aggression and was ultimately annexed to Japan in 1910. The early institutions of higher education established by the American missionaries lost their college status. The development of higher education in Korea during the thirty-six years of Japanese occupation (1910–45) was extremely retarded. Koreans were given very few opportunities to receive a higher education.

With the end of World War II in 1945, Korea was liberated from Japanese colonialism but was administered by the U.S. Military Government for three years (1945–48). The United States continued to influence Korean education during their participation in the reconstruction of Korea after the Korean War, from 1953 to the mid-1960s.

During the past three decades, through a succession of five-year economic development plans first initiated in 1962, Korea experienced dramatic economic growth and became one of the newly industrializing countries in Asia, successfully developing its economic, social, and political spheres. In a country like Korea, where very few natural resources are available, a well-educated workforce is a key to socioeconomic development. The rapid expansion of higher education in Korea was matched by a societal demand for highly skilled human resources. In this vein, higher education in Korea deserves recognition for contributing to national achievement by virtue of its own indigenous modernization system and, partly, the accumulated Western influences. What is certain is that in a relatively short period, Korean higher education developed a reasonably clear educational philosophy, curricular system, and quantitative expansion and that it became a source of national development and welfare. The progress made during the past half century is reassuring.

DEVELOPMENT OF THE HIGHER EDUCATION SYSTEM

Pre-Independence Developments

Western Missionary Movements and Their Impact. The basic strategy of Western missionaries in Korea was to initially establish secondary schools, then to upgrade these schools to junior colleges, and eventually to turn them into Western-style four-year institutions of higher education. These missionary efforts were very successful, not only in proselytizing on behalf of the Christian faith but also in introducing the structure and content of Western higher education. This influenced the development of a democratic ideology of freedom and independence and spread the idea that education was for everyone. The early American missionaries brought more than just establishment of the institutions of higher learning and a concern for curriculum and instruction for young Koreans. For example, they introduced modern scientific curriculum and educational methods to Korean higher education. Nevertheless, the early American missionaries had to confront Korean nationalism and reform movements. Due to the fact that American missionaries were foreigners, outsiders, and representatives of Western culture, they were seemingly rejected by the indigenous group. However, both sides shared a number of common beliefs and practices. They both advocated for the independence and self-determination of the Korean people. They were against government authoritarianism, which in later years was strengthened by the Japanese aggressors. Between 1885 and 1910, a total of 796 schools from elementary to college levels were established and maintained by the Western missionaries. This is a significant number as it comprised about 35 percent of the entire number of formal schools in Korea (Sohn, 1987: 548–63).

Japanese interruption of the indigenous developments. Declaring Korea to be a part of Japan, the Japanese government enacted various regulations and ordinances to control and restrict every aspect of the political, social, cultural, and economic movements of the Koreans. The colonial regime allowed the Koreans extremely few opportunities to chart their own destiny. Any effort on the part of the Koreans to establish a close relationship with Western powers was crushed. The colonial policy forced the Koreans to remain in isolation and to stop developing and maintaining their own educational system. The major goal of Japanese educational policy was to assimilate Koreans by means of education. Education was used for obliterating the Korean nationality in terms of language, family name, religion, and almost every other area of life.

For the thirty-six years of Japanese occupation, highly concerted efforts were made by the Western missionaries and indigenous forces to resist the Japanese educational policy and to preserve the national essence in education. A new and broader sense of unity emerged, and nationalism became one of the principal manifestations of the process of education. More Koreans went to the United States for study and returned home to work for Korean independence. Some were active in education and played the role of a vanguard in adopting Western styles and ideas. The indigenous forces, however, were not necessarily united. Much dispute arose over Western influences. The indigenous intellectuals, trained in the United States or in the domestic mission schools, preferred a new education and strongly advocated the adoption of Western ideas. Some of them insisted on accepting even the Western influence transmitted by Japan. Sung-Hwa Lee pointed out this indirect Western influence through Japan as follows: "It is important to keep in mind that . . . the greatest influence was brought from Japan. Therefore, it is natural to assume that whatever had influenced Japan from the outside world would also be brought to education in Korea, in thought and in organization, during the thirty-six years of Japanese occupation" (Lee, 1958:195–96). It must be noted, however, that the Western impact transmitted by Japan was a degenerated one that the Japanese brought for the purpose of oppressing and controlling the Koreans.

Post-Independence Developments

After Korea was liberated from Japanese colonial rule in 1945, the next most important foreign influence on the development of Korean higher education was the close relationship to the United States. The first U.S. presence in Korea began with a trusteeship managed by the U.S. Military from 1945 through 1948. However, the new Republic was set back by the disastrous consequences of the Korean War (1950–53). The U.S. presence was more significant this second time during its participation in the reconstruction of the country for the decade starting in 1953.

It is understandable that, when all levels of education were ruined, the primary and secondary levels were given top priority. More concern and finance were invested into those two levels of education. But significant progress was also made in the development of higher education by the U.S. Military Government. For instance, the curriculum and its organization of higher education were implanted according to the American style. In particular, the American philosophy of higher education for a large number of capable students was strongly advocated, and it made a meaningful impact on the expansion of educational opportunity in higher education by region, level, and social class. However, it should also be noted that some have criticized the U.S. Military Government's policy on education and the U.S. aid program to Korean higher education during 1953–63. Some reasons include the lack of preparation or preplanning on the part of the United States and its ignorance of traditional Korean modes of thought and behavior.

Contemporary Developments

The higher education system in Korea includes four categories of institutions: (1) two- to three-year junior vocational colleges, (2) four- to six-year universities or colleges (bachelor's degrees), (3) graduate schools (master's and doctoral degrees), and (4) nondegree-granting institutions at the postsecondary level.

When Korea was liberated from Japanese colonial rule in 1945, there were only 19 institutions of higher education to accommodate 7,819 students and 753 faculty members. During the past half century, however, the Korean higher education system has experienced rapid growth. The wave of quantitative growth crested in the 1980s. The total number of institutions of higher education increased to 295 by 1994, a fifteenfold increase. The enrollment of higher education reached about 1.8 million, an increase of more than 228 times since independence, while the number of faculty members increased only about 49 times (see tables 17.1 and 17.2).

According to 1993 statistics, the enrollment in elementary schools of Korea was more than 100 percent; in middle schools, 96.3 percent; in high schools, 90.0 percent; and in various types of higher education, 44.8 percent of each relevant age group of the population. The enrollment in higher education institutions per 1,000 population in Korea was about 47.7 in 1993. On the other hand, 99.7 percent of all elementary school graduates advance to middle schools, 95.3 percent of all middle school graduates go on to high schools, and 69.8 percent of high school graduates continue their studies in various institutions of higher education (Korean Educational Development Institute, 1993:42–44, 70–71).

Table 17.1
Quantitative Growth of Korean Higher Education

Year	Institutions		Faculty members				Students	
	Number	Growth rate	Number	Growth rate	Number	Growth rate	A*	B**
1945	19	1.0	1,490	1.0	7,819	1.0	-	0.5
1955	74	3.9	2,626	1.8	84,996	8.4	-	4.0
1965	162	8.6	6,801	4.6	141,636	18.2	7.1	4.9
1975	204	10.7	13,981	9.4	296,219	38.0	8.8	6.9
1985	255	13.4	33,483	22.5	1,209,647	154.7	37.1	31.1
1994	295	15.5	52,010	34.9	1,781,786	227.9	49.3	49.4

*A: Percent of the enrollment of the population aged eighteen to twenty-one years old.
**B: Number of students per 1,000 population.
Source: Ministry of Education, Statistical Yearbook of Education (each pertinent year).

CHANGING FUNCTIONS AND PATTERNS OF HIGHER EDUCATION

Governance and Finance

One of the long-held basic tenets of higher education has been that the individual institution must be autonomous. Definitions of autonomy are usually understood within the context of the latitude required for administrative action by executives, and includes both the freedom of the faculty as a body to set institutional goals and make decisions that determine the essential character of the individual institutions, and the freedom of individual faculty members to decide academic matters for which they have responsibility. Yet no institution of higher education in Korea has enjoyed such autonomy. A salient feature of Korean higher education has been direct government involvement in the academic administration of higher education. In this highly centralized system, the government holds the power to decide on the establishment of new institutions, enrollment quotas, admission procedures, academic programs, financial allocation, and so on.

Since the early 1980s, however, there has been an urgent and increasing demand for a new strategy of development to rejuvenate the institutions of higher education by mobilizing academic expertise. This need collectively culminated in 1982, when a nongovernment and collective body of four-year institutions of higher education, known as the Korean Council for University Education, came into being. The primary function of the council is to insure a

Table 17.2
Number of Higher Education Institutions, Students, and Faculty Members, 1994

Type		Institution	Student	Faculty Member
2-3 year Jr. Vocational College	Public	9 (6.7)	20,376 (4.2)	551 (5.9)
	Private	126 (93.3)	486,430 (95.8)	8,824 (94.1)
	Subtotal	135 (100.0)	506,806 (100.0)	9,375 (100.0)
4-year College & University	Public	37 (26.1)	303,706 (26.4)	13,085 (30.9)
	Private	105 (73.9)	847,022 (73.6)	29,236 (69.1)
	Subtotal	142 (100.0)	1,150,728 (100.0)	42,321 (100.0)
Graduate School	Public	85 (23.1)	33,644 (30.6)	–
	Private	283 (76.9)	76,339 (69.4)	–
	Subtotal	368 (100.0)	109,983 (100.0)	–
Miscellaneous School	Public	0 (0.0)	0 (0.0)	0 (0.0)
	Private	18 (100.0)	14,269 (100.0)	314 (100.0)
	Subtotal	18 (100.0)	14,269 (100.0)	314 (100.0)
Total	Public	46 (15.6)	357,726 (20.1)	13,636 (26.2)
	Private	249 (84.4)	1,424,060 (79.9)	38,374 (73.8)
	Subtotal	295 (100.0)	1,781,786 (100.0)	52,010 (100.0)

Notes: 1. The numbers in parentheses denote the percentage distributions between public and private.
2. The Air & Correspondence college and the fourteen open colleges are excluded. In 1994, 310,955 students were enrolled in the Air & Correspondence College and 101,412 students were enrolled in the fourteen open colleges.
3. The number of faculty members excludes assistants, part-time lecturers, guest professors, and honorary professors.
4. The number of graduate schools is not usually included in the total number of higher education institutions because they are established in attachment to the four-year institutions.

Source: National Institute of Educational Evaluation, *Statistical Yearbook of Education, 1994* (Seoul: Ministry of Education, 1994).

basic level of quality and considerable independence and autonomy through the practice of professional evaluation of higher education institutions and programs.

In addition, the election of president in each institution by direct vote of faculty members, and the organization of a faculty council, have demonstrated that there is a symbolic shift away from central control and toward internal governance of Korean higher education. The late 1980s and early 1990s in Korean higher education was a time when traditional state authority was externally diffused. At the same time, the administrative executives in institutions of higher education were also relatively diffused and the power of constituencies of the institution so loosely related to each other as to make purposeful cooperation very difficult. This worked against resolving problems and bringing about further development in higher education as a whole as well as individual institutional development.

In terms of the government budget, 3.8 percent of the GNP in 1993 was apportioned to the Ministry of Education, which accounted for 23.4 percent of the total national budget (Korean Educational Development Institute, 1993:291). In Korean higher education, there are three major sources of income: the national government, tuition and fees, and private endowments and gifts. Within the public and private sectors, the distribution of income by sources is quite different. According to the analysis by the Ministry of Education in 1992, the national government share accounted for 71.7 percent of the income of public institutions, compared with only 1.7 percent of the income of private institutions. On the other hand, the share of students' tuition and fees accounted for 28.3 percent of the income of public institutions, while it was 80.3 percent of the income of private institutions. The increased reliance on students' tuition and fees in private institutions means that many private institutions today are faced with very serious financial constraints. The students in the state-run public four-year institutions of higher education pay about 30 percent less tuition than those in private institutions. But the public institutions spend more money on educating students than the private ones. In 1993, the average education expenditure per student was U.S.$4,414 per year in public institutions but U.S.$3,983 in private institutions (Korean Educational Development Institute, 1993:317). And it should also be noted that endowments by foundations to private institutions are minimal except in the case of a few select private institutions.

Curriculum and Instruction

The curriculum in many departments of Korean colleges and universities has been based on the American model. Even though some native Korean conditions have affected and modified curriculum development, the content selection and organization are mainly shaped by American-educated faculty members.

The school year begins on March 1 and is divided into two equal terms: first semester (March through June) and second semester (September through December). Each semester must include at least sixteen class-weeks. From 1984, a summer session was adopted at every four-year institution to increase the time, space, and academic options available to students. In obedience to the national education law, all the baccalaureate degrees in any four-year institution of higher education require at least 140 credit hours, in which 30 percent should be devoted to general education. The idea of the major, however, dominates Korean higher education so completely that it has all but eliminated any genuine program of general education. The ideal goal of general education is formulated but its actual objectives are not clearly defined. General education is always advocated as an important element of undergraduate education in theory but regarded as peripheral in practice. Moreover, the Korean undergraduate curriculum is departmentally fragmented and overspecialized. There is a tendency to offer specialized courses on the grounds that a valid major must contain a high degree of specialization or that students need such specialization to prepare for graduate school. In practice, a major in Korean colleges and universities may be simply a collection of courses in a certain specialty area lacking balance or cohesion. The students spend a large portion of their time on the required and elective major courses (Lee, 1992a:181–98; 1987:67–150). At the undergraduate level in 1992, there were 558 different kinds of major departments but only 25 baccalaureate degrees in terms of their legal nomenclature. Fragmentation in majors is much stronger in natural sciences and engineering, humanities, arts, and physical education than in other fields. On the average, the same major department is established in only seven to eight colleges and universities.

To increase the learning opportunities of students and their responsibility for planning their own programs, some innovative ideas have been employed. For example, the major-minor and the double-major systems were adopted in addition to an advanced program for superior students in some general education subjects. Also, though the medium of instruction in Korean institutions of higher education is the native language, a few institutions have begun to adopt English as the medium of instruction in a limited number of courses.

Another notable feature of Korean higher education during the past half century has been transfer of emphasis in undergraduate education from the humanities and social sciences to the natural sciences and engineering. In Korea's traditional Confucian society, the autocratic class valued teaching and learning above natural and/or technical sciences. However, by the 1960s, Koreans adopted an innovative policy emphasizing higher education in the natural sciences and engineering fields, which has continued to the present. In putting into practice such a policy, the government has moderately increased the enrollment quota in the science and engineering fields every year, while limiting the increases in the humanities and social science fields. In 1993, enrollment in the natural science and engineering fields in four-year institutions accounted for 43 percent of the total student population, compared with 14 percent in the humanities and 26 percent in the social sciences (Korean Education Development Institute, 1993:46).

Graduate Education and Research

Korean graduate education was influenced by the Japanese system, which in turn was modeled on the German system. Graduate education following the American model began to develop when Yonsei University opened a new American-style doctoral degree program in 1961. During the next three decades, graduate education in Korea grew rapidly in size, structure, and function. Korean's graduate schools of today are divided into two types: academic graduate schools, which are research-oriented, and professional graduate schools, which emphasize practical experience or professional knowledge.

The current graduate education system in Korea has several salient characteristics. First, both American and Japanese characteristics coexist. For example, education in academic graduate schools is patterned after the American system in its outward appearance. The procedure of conferring degrees is quite similar to that of American graduate schools. Course requirements, qualifying examinations, requiring two foreign languages, thesis writing, and oral defenses are all standard practice in Korean graduate education. However, evidence of the Japanese system is still present in such curricular features as the apprentice mode.

Second, many critics have raised the concern that the current academic graduate education does not allow for either specialization or breadth. The number of credits required is quite small: only twenty-four credits for a master's degree and thirty-six additional credits for a doctoral degree. It may be true that with this small number of course requirements, neither narrow specialization nor emphasis on breadth is possible. Another problem raised by the critics is that, in Korea, many graduate schools are established as a decoration to enhance the image of the undergraduate program or to increase the revenue from tuition and fees. In Korean higher education, role differentiation among the institutions is not well achieved but each and every institution tries to develop itself as a full-service university.

Third, Korean graduate education also faces the problem of disproportion. There has been a severely disproportionate production of doctoral degrees in a few major fields. The majority of domestically earned doctoral degrees were in the medical sciences. The situation has greatly improved but even a decade ago, the number of domestic doctoral degree-holders in the humanities, social sciences, natural sciences, and engineering fields was easily countable. Traditionally, Korean faculty members have highly regarded apprenticeship, which encouraged them to hold their students for long periods of time before conferring doctoral degrees. This is one of the reasons why so many bright young students have sought their degrees in foreign countries, particularly the United States. The disproportion of doctoral degree production by fields is still conspicuous.

Fourth, another disproportion is found in the faculty organization based on undergraduate departments. In Korea, few graduate schools have their own full-time cadre of faculty of sufficient scholarly stature and experience. Their teaching and advising of graduate students is often viewed as an additional load or an extra source of income to their normal undergraduate teaching.

Finally, graduate schools in Korea have been identified with the "research" mission of higher education. Teaching and learning in the graduate schools are highly dependent on the research achievements of the faculty members. Research has been regarded as the link between professors and graduate students as well as among the professors themselves. The graduate schools in Korea, as in other countries, have been the most productive system for providing research personnel to society. Korean higher education, particularly graduate education, is being asked to accommodate the expected change in the industrial structure for the coming years and to employ innovation and invention so as to generate endogenous technology within a national research system. The primary role of the academic system in Korea will be to expand the endogenous source of scientific and technological creations through the promotion of production, assessment, and validation of ideas through research.

Academic Nationalism

The Western, especially American, influence on Korean higher education is unmistakable and perpetuated by the American-educated faculty members in colleges and universities. Their influence on Korean higher education ranges from classroom teaching methods, curricular content, university administration, and governance to the models of thought on teaching and research. In the 1970s, conflicts began to arise in various forms, such as between the Korean-educated younger faculty and the older members without doctoral degrees, and between Korean-educated doctoral degree-holders and American-educated doctoral degree-holders. Conflicts between these groups arose as an expression of neo-nationalism within the academic community. Neo-nationalism was more fully embraced by the emerging new generation, which had been educated only with "Hangul," the Korean native language, in their primary and secondary schools. However, dependence on Western theories and practices is being overcome not only by Korean-educated scholars but also by their American-educated colleagues. Both are attempting a Koreanization of teaching and research within their colleges and universities.

CHANGING STUDENTS AND FACULTY

Profile of Korean Students

With the traditionally strong zeal for higher education but with limited access due to government-controlled enrollment quotas, a social problem began to emerge in the early 1970s. That problem manifested itself as an accumulated increase in the so-called reexaminers for the annual college entrance examination. Among the new enrollment into four-year colleges and universities in 1994, 26 percent were reexaminers (Ministry of Education 1994:672).

In terms of gender, about 37 percent of students in the junior colleges and about 32 percent of those in four-year institutions of higher education are women (Ministry of Education, 1994:562). Graduates from the junior colleges have better job market opportunities than those from four-year institutions. In 1994, about 74 percent of the graduates from junior colleges were employed, whereas only 61 percent of those from four-year institutions were employed. Nevertheless, the employment rate of female graduates is much lower than that of male graduates: Sixty-seven percent of female graduates from junior colleges and 48 percent of those from four-year colleges and universities found work after graduation.

The employment rate of graduate (master's and doctoral degrees) degree-holders was about 86 percent, much higher than that of bachelor's degree-holders. In terms of academic discipline, there was little difference in employment rates among the junior colleges. However, in the case of four-year institutions, the employment rate of graduates from the natural science and engineering fields was quite high (65 percent) compared to that from the humanities (54 percent) and the social sciences (59 percent) (Ministry of Education 1994:578–83).

During the period from 1977 to 1993, the Korean government sent a total of 1,353 students with full scholarships for graduate study to foreign countries, and invited a total of 293 foreign students, providing full scholarships, for advanced study to Korea (Ministry of Education, 1994:774). The total number of students studying abroad in 1990 amounted to 53,875 in 44 countries, of which 57 percent were studying in North American countries and about 42 percent in the natural science and engineering fields. The total number of foreign students studying in Korea, including those studying at their own expense, was 2,237 in 1990, of which 31 percent came from Taiwan, 30 percent from Japan, and 23 percent from the United States (Presidential Council on Education, 1991:32–35).

Student Activism

In Korea, student governments operate at all institutions, and some of them have a large degree of collective power and independence. The Korean Union of College Students (KUCS) consists of student associations at each and every higher education institution in all provinces. The KUCS has become increasingly active in seeking greater student participation in university governance. Although not affiliated with any political party, it has strong radical leanings. However, since Kim Young Sam took office as president of the Republic of Korea in February 1993, crowning a transition to democracy that broke a thirty-year tradition of military rule, some student associations of leading universities began to break away from the KUCS.

The proportion of all students who are actively or radically involved in campus disorders and who are members of the student activist organizations that lead to these disorders has gradually decreased. The consensus is that radical student activism is now obsolete, but it is also clear that on particular issues, the small minority of activists could mobilize substantial student support. Instead of political or ideological concerns, students have a growing concern about their right to learn as a sort of consumerism movement. It is reflected in their advocacy for student evaluation of instruction or measures of faculty teaching effectiveness, and in their demand for more participation in university governance. It is likely that students will continue to expect a larger role in the making of decisions that affect them.

Profile of Korean Professoriate

In Korean higher education, men dominate the professoriate at four-year institutions. Only 12 percent of the faculty are female. In terms of age, about 86 percent are in the prime ages of 36 to 65, with the mean age in 1991 being 40.1 years old (Lee, 1992b:13).

In Korea, the percentage of all faculty with doctorates has risen substantially over the years from 10 percent in 1967 to 74 percent in 1990. A doctoral degree is now a prerequisite for initial employment as a faculty member in most four-year institutions. The percentage of faculty members who earned their highest degrees from domestic institutions has risen to 77 percent, whereas only 23 percent earned their highest degrees abroad (Lee, 1992b:14–15). The full-time faculty in institutions of higher education invariably consists of four academic ranks: instructor, assistant professor, associate professor, and (full) professor. There is no restriction in the rank distribution in the department just as in the university or college. Looking into the distribution of faculty members by their rank in 1991, 34 percent were professors, 31 percent associate professors, 25 percent assistant professors, and 10 percent instructors. Thus, the faculties in Korea have become top-heavy.

The Korean faculty members are largely autonomous in the use of their time in their professional work: instruction, research, public service, and administration. In most institutions of higher education in Korea the minimum legal teaching load of a full-time faculty member is 9 credit hours per week. In 1991, Korean faculty members worked 52.5 hours on average per week when classes were in session and 51.4 hours per week during the vacation periods. When classes are in session, for the average faculty member, 22.9 hours are devoted to instruction, 16.9 hours to research, 4.5 hours to public service, 4.8 hours to administration, and 3.4 hours to other professional activities. In terms of income, about 40 percent of faculty members earn between U.S. $10,000 and U.S. $24,999 and about 47 percent earn between U.S. $25,000 and U.S. $39,999 for an academic year. Korean faculty earn about 80 percent of their income from their academic institution and 20 percent from academic activities outside their institution (Lee, 1992b:25–28).

On the average, Korean faculty members spend 14.4 hours per week in the classroom, which means that many faculty members suffer from heavy teaching loads. A majority of the Korean faculty members teach by the lecture method. The professors who teach undergraduate courses are most likely to require their students to attend class regularly, to write several short papers, and to take two or more examinations for successful completion of their courses. In 1991, the Korean professors were equally distributed into two groups: one whose interests lie primarily in teaching and the other whose interests lie primarily in research (Lee, 1992b:39).

In the Korean academic community, a great proportion of research is achieved by a small proportion of faculty members. About three-quarters of Korean professors have neither authored nor edited scholarly books in the past three years. On average, each Korean faculty member authors 0.15 books, edits 0.10 books, and writes 1.59 articles per year. However, a very large majority of faculty members, 83 percent, are currently engaged in research projects (ibid.:43–44).

On the whole, Korean professors perceive their institutional governance as relatively centralized. They do not believe that they have reasonable involvement in the decision-making process at the institutional level, though they do exert considerable influence in the decision-making process at the department level. Nevertheless, Korean professors perceive their institutions as supporting academic freedom. As to student involvement in university governance, many professors oppose it, even in determining policy affecting the students.

The university–government relationship in Korea has been a critical issue. Professors often criticize government interference in their institutional governance, while the government has insisted on using its authority to protect the quality of higher education. However, Korean higher education is undergoing a paradigmatic shift, from government hegemony to university autonomy, and from autocratic external governance to democratic internal governance.

International affiliation of college and university professors is essential to success in their responsibilities, particularly for research. Yet, a majority of Korean professors have had no international affiliation. In one ten-year period (1981–90), 76 percent of the faculty had no opportunity to work collaboratively with a professor from another country on a research project (ibid.: 57). In similar fashion, international activities conducted by their own institutions have been quite minimal.

FUTURE DEVELOPMENTS

As already discussed, most of the private institutions of higher education in Korea have depended chiefly on students' tuition and fees for their financial survival. However, looking ten or twenty years into the future, the decrease of the eighteen- to twenty-two-year-old age group, and thus the decline in the number seeking higher education, may determine whether these institutions can remain financially independent. In addition to increased demand for government support to the private institutions, there is a need to develop alternative sources of income. In addition, there is increasing pressure to manage the investment to education more efficiently and effectively. In this respect, there will be a growing demand on all the Korean private institutions of higher education.

Another major problem facing Korean higher education will be the effects of uniformity of institutions of higher education. This uniformity has been brought about, in part, by the rigidity of government higher education policy, but it is also caused by the inertia within institutions. Entering the twenty-first century, only idiosyncratic institutions can survive. Investment will favor an institution that shows its superiority in a certain field or program rather than a full-fledged institution that furnishes all kinds of academic sundry goods of low quality. In the past, it was possible for an institution of higher education to exist because of the great demand by potential students. But in the future, the quality of an institution will be the prime criterion of choice by consumer-minded students.

The major factor affecting the future of higher education in Korea is the government's decision to shift its power to the institutions. Many observers of higher education in Korea have come to realize that the government interferes far too much in academic policies and that its involvement in higher education should be limited to the establishment of overall purposes and policies. Thus, direct intervention by the government will decrease and the breadth and depth of institutional autonomy will be expanded, but only on the condition that they assume social responsibility and academic accountability.

Finally, one more observation must be noted about the political life of Korean professors in the future. Faculty activism appears to be the most important of the new intramural issues for the Korean colleges and universities. The professors in many institutions have begun to organize their own councils and to raise their voices against their governing boards. Such interest in quasi-unionism among academics will continue to grow. Yet divisions are also beginning to appear among professors within campuses along the lines of self-interest. These trends suggest that administration in the future should involve faculty in institutional governance and decision making.

REFERENCES

Korean Educational Development Institute. 1993. *Educational Indicators in Korea*. Seoul: Author.

Lee, Sungho H. 1987. *Curriculum Development in Korean Universities and Colleges* (in Korean). Seoul: Yonsei University Press.

———. 1992a. *Conflicts in Korean Higher Education* (in Korean). Seoul: Neutinamu.

———. 1992b. "The Academic Professor in Korea." Paper presented at the 8th World Congress of Comparative Education, Prague, Czechoslovakia.

Lee, Sung-Hwa. 1958. "The Social and Political Factors Affecting Korean Education, 1885–1950." Unpublished Ph.D. Diss., University of Pittsburgh.

Ministry of Education. 1994. *Statistical Yearbook of Education*. Seoul: Author.

Presidential Council on Education. 1991. *Educational Policy for Globalization Era* (in Korean). Seoul: Author.

Sohn, Insoo. 1987. *History of Korean Education* (in Korean). Seoul: Muneumsa.

18

SRI LANKA

Swarna Jayaweera

For over two thousand years of recorded history the island of Sri Lanka, situated south of the Indian subcontinent, had its own identity, in spite of periodic invasions from India, an economy based on agriculture and irrigation, and a culture and education system largely influenced by Buddhism interacting with Hinduism. In the sixteenth century, the first Western colonizers reached the island, resulting in the control of the coastal areas successively by the Portuguese and the Dutch until the end of that century but with little impact on higher education. The British gained control of the whole island in the early nineteenth century, and Western legal, economic, and education systems and social norms and practices were superimposed on the indigenous society for over a century.

The colony's economy was structured to meet imperial needs for raw materials, markets, and opportunities for investment of capital accumulated in industrializing Britain, resulting in the development of a plantation sector exporting first coffee and, after its collapse, tea and rubber from the late nineteenth century, to the detriment of domestic agriculture and industry. Uneven socioeconomic development, however, created regional disparities in the provision of health, education, and other services. The process of political socialization and acculturation through the English language, Christianity, and Western-oriented educational institutions created a dual society comprising a small English-educated elite from secondary and subsequently higher education institutions, and the majority of the population who were restricted to elementary education in the local languages, Sinhala and Tamil. These two societies lived in almost culturally disparate worlds.

In 1931, a period of political transition commenced with the introduction of universal franchise and semirepresentative government, culminating in political independence in 1948. Local policy makers were strongly motivated to reduce the socioeconomic inequalities created partly by colonial rule, and in this context, implemented in the 1940s a package of social policies providing free primary, secondary, and higher education, free health services, and subsidized staple food (rice) that accounts for the relatively high physical quality of life in a low-income country.

However, the decline in the prices of plantation exports in the world market from the late 1950s, deterioration in the terms of trade and the balance of payments, slow economic growth, diminishing resources, and a burgeoning population plagued socioeconomic development. The economy was not able to absorb the increasing labor force, resulting in the rise of unemployment from 7.3 percent at the census in 1963 to 13.4 percent in 1969–70. Unemployment has been around 14 percent in the 1980s and 1990s. The most vulnerable group in the past twenty-five years has been youth, particularly products of secondary and higher educational institutions who find it difficult to obtain employment in a shrinking services sector as in the past.

Since the late 1970s the liberalizing of the economy has led to higher economic growth rates. But the reduction in public expenditure resulting from the imposition of IMF–World Bank Structural Adjustment Programmes has affected adversely the quantitative and qualitative development of education. Massive unemployment still persists, poverty and undernutrition are reported to have increased, and income disparities have widened, affecting the utilization of educational facilities. The political environment has been volatile for over a decade. The ethnic conflict has escalated since 1983 in the north and east, and youth insurgency fueled by economic and social disparities and political unrest has led to violence in the south, including in the universities.

UNIVERSITIES IN SRI LANKA—INSTITUTIONAL DEVELOPMENT

In ancient and medieval Sri Lanka, Buddhist religious institutions (*pirivenas*) and Brahmin household education imparted higher learning while professional skills were acquired through nonformal modes of apprenticeship. Under colonial rule, such modalities survived, but were overshadowed by structures modeled on Western institutions that were introduced chiefly to produce Western-trained personnel for the administration and delivery of services.

Only two institutions provided higher education to those aspiring to the professions—the Medical College established by the colonial government in 1870 and the institution started by the Council of Legal Education in 1876. The Normal School that functioned for a brief period in the mid-nineteenth century, the teacher training institutions established from 1880, the Agricultural School (1880–1901) and its successor opened in 1917, and the Technical School started in 1893 did not achieve the status of higher education institutions.

Although universities were opened in India in the mid-nineteenth century and there was pressure in Sri Lanka from local leaders and the products of the

English secondary schools for a local university, the colonial administration displayed overt reluctance until eventually a University College was opened in 1921 to prepare for the external arts and science degrees of the University of London. By the end of colonial rule, therefore, the British tradition of a selective higher education was reflected in the access to higher education of a small elite in Sri Lanka.

Efforts to change this tradition to meet the socioeconomic needs that surfaced in the postcolonial decades were hampered by three main factors: (1) the absence of an overall higher education policy; (2) the dominance of universities in higher education; and (3) limited financial and institutional provisions by the state for higher education. Developments, in fact, were often the result of ad hoc measures that were responses to immediate sociocultural pressures.

Sri Lanka has, currently, nine universities—eight conventional universities and an open university. Their evolution took place over five decades at a much slower pace than the expansion of the school system.

The first university in Sri Lanka was established in 1942 as the University of Ceylon by amalgamating the University College and the Medical College. The university was originally an autonomous, unitary, and residential university in the Oxbridge tradition but without its college structure, and was not planned to enroll more than one thousand students who were expected to be the intellectual elite in the country. Social pressures, however, overwhelmed the university and transformed its character. It expanded until it was divided into two institutions in 1967: the Universities of Peradeniya and Colombo. Meanwhile, two *pirivenas*, or centers of Buddhist learning, in the suburbs of Colombo were elevated to university status in 1959—Vidyodaya University (now the University of Jayawardenapura) and Vidyalankara University (now the University of Kelaniya)—to meet the demand from the products of the expanding secondary schools for higher education in Sinhala.

Four more universities on the same model were established in the 1970s and 1980s. The College of Technology on the outskirts of Colombo was given university status at the beginning of the 1970s and became the University of Moratuwa. At the same time a university was opened in Jaffna in the north to satisfy Tamil aspirations. Two University Colleges started in the south and east in the early 1980s that became the University of Ruhuna (1984) and the Eastern University (1986). The External Services Agency that conducted examinations for external degrees and diplomas from 1971 was absorbed into the Open University, established in 1980 in a suburb of Colombo to extend opportunities for higher education through the distance education mode.

Three of the older universities, the technology-based university, and the Open University are located in or near the capital city of Colombo; the University of Peradeniya and the three new universities are situated in the more developed central, northern, and southern provinces and in the eastern provinces, leaving the interior of the island without higher education facilities. A large proportion of students in the eight universities are nonresidential. All nine universities function under the supervision of the University Grants Commission, which works with the government in the direction and coordination of universities but is expected to protect the academic autonomy of the universities.

These universities have, in all, thirteen academic streams ranging from medical-related and engineering courses to management, law, social sciences, and humanities. The University of Peradeniya is the largest higher education institution with six faculties—medical and dental, veterinary science, engineering, agriculture, science, and arts—while the University of Moratuwa offers only engineering and architecture. These institutions have three-year general degree and four-year special or professionally oriented courses, and in the case of the medical faculties, a five-year course (UGC, 1990). Curricula and methodologies have not changed radically over the years. Efforts in the 1970s to meet perceived employment needs by introducing job-oriented courses in the arts faculties of two universities were unsuccessful. The Open University has linkages with the labor market as the majority of students enrolled in education and technology courses are already employed. The nine universities have a staff of 2,020, of whom 31.9 percent are women. Staff development for university teaching and research is in the form of postgraduate education in foreign universities, chiefly in the United Kingdom and the United States.

The development of postgraduate institutes since the early 1970s has been an outcome of the desire to promote centers of excellence and specialization within the country. The Postgraduate Institute of Medicine of the University of Colombo (1974), the Postgraduate Institute of Agriculture of the University of Peradeniya (1974), the Postgraduate Institutes of Pali and Buddhist Studies (1977) and of Archaeology (1976) of the University of Kelaniya, the Postgraduate Institute of Management of the Sri Jayawardenepura University (1986), and the Institute of Computer Technology of the University of Colombo (1987) cater to the needs of advanced education and specialization. The Faculty of Graduate Studies established in the University of Colombo in the 1990s offers interdisciplinary postgraduate courses in fields such as labor studies, women's studies, and regional studies. Three undergraduate institutes also cater to interests that are not included in mainstream degree courses—the Institute of Aesthetic Studies of the University of Kelaniya and the Institute of Indigenous Medicine and the Institute of Workers' Education of the University of Colombo.

Efforts have been made also to expand opportunities for higher education by opening institutions that offer two-year professionally oriented diploma courses with expectations of acquiring a subsequent university degree. Six such junior universities were established in the late 1960s, but were closed in two years after a change of government because they were unsuccessful in catering to the needs of employment or to the demand for higher education. In 1991–93, eleven affiliated university colleges (AUCs) were opened by the University Grants Commission, one each in seven of the nine provinces and two each in two provinces. AUCs are affiliated to different universities for administrative and academic supervision. They offer two-year diploma courses in areas such as accounting and finance, food technology, travel and tourism, entrepreneurship, science, home economics, agriculture, and English. They have not met student aspirations as the avenue to university degrees remains unclear (UGC, 1993).

ENROLLMENT IN UNIVERSITIES

Admission to universities is after twelve or thirteen years of school education, on the basis of performance at the General Certificate of Education (GCE) Advanced Level Examination. Students qualify for admission if they score an aggregate of 180 marks with passes in three of the four subjects they offer in the science, arts, or commerce streams. Entry from this pool of eligible students is determined (since 1972) by competitive performance to fill a merit quota of 30 percent of the admissions, allocation of district quotas on a population basis to fill 65 percent of the places, and allocation of a special quota of 5 percent places for educationally disadvantaged districts. A very small quota is admitted on special criteria such as performance in sports.

Only around 2 percent to 3 percent of the twenty- to twenty-four-year-old age group receive a university education, in contrast to 88 percent of the five- to fourteen-year-old age group receiving primary and junior secondary education, and around 40 percent of the fifteen- to nineteen-year-old age group receiving senior secondary education. This sharp decline in participation is partly the result of a lack of adequate places in the universities for students who reach minimum entry levels in performance.

Expansion in student enrollment has been affected by changes in policy perspectives at different times. As seen in table 18.1, the University of Ceylon began in 1942 with an enrollment of 904 students. Enrollment increased slowly to 2,950 in 1958 despite the introduction of free education in 1945 and the perceptions of parents and students that higher education was a major agent of socioeconomic mobility. The medium of instruction in senior secondary education changed from English to Sinhala and Tamil only in 1958–59. The explosion in university enrollment that followed this change led to a threefold increase in the student population from 4,039 in 1959 to 14,210 in 1965. However, university admissions were frozen to 3,500 per year from 1967 to 1976 in an effort to contain graduate unemployment, thus limiting the student population to around 12,000 for a decade. A more liberal policy of university admissions since then to meet demand pressures led to an increase in student numbers to 18,913 in 1985–86.

Since 1987, frequent closure of universities and the consequent accumulation of students deprived of the opportunity to complete their courses and admission of "backlogs" since 1990 resulted in a student enrollment of 31,447 in 1990–91. The actual figures corresponding to pre-1987 statistics would be an annual undergraduate student population of 20,000 a year in the eight conventional universities. Postgraduate students are around 2,000 in number. The proportion of arts students increased from around 40 percent in the 1940s to 76 percent in

Table 18.1
Student Enrollment in Universities

Year	Total	Male	Female	Percent Female
1942	904	813	91	10.1
1945	1,065	932	133	12.5
1950	2,036	1,655	381	18.7
1955	2,431	1,781	650	26.7
1960	4,723	3,587	1,136	24.1
1965	14,210	9,631	4,579	32.2
1970	11,813	6,570	5,243	44.4
1975	12,648	7,496	5,152	40.7
1980	17,494	10,544	6,950	39.7
1985	18,913	10,753	8,160	43.1
1990	31,447	17,926	13,521	42.9

Source: University Council Reports, Reports of the Vidyodaya and Vidyalankara Universities, Reports of the NCHE, University of Sri Lanka and University Grants Commission.

1965 as the expansion in senior secondary education was largely in the arts streams and declined to around 46 percent in 1990 as numbers admitted to arts courses were reduced and commerce became a popular avenue for nonscience students.

The Open University began with 3,654 students in 1980. The total enrollment increased to 13,127 in 1985–86, declined to 7,469 in 1986–87, and increased again to 15,459 in 1990–91. The five postgraduate institutes are small in size and had an enrollment of 1,300 in 1990. The three undergraduate institutes had 874 students in the same year (UGC, 1990). The affiliated university colleges had 1,127 students in their second year of existence in 1992.

The percentage of women students in universities increased gradually from 10.1 percent at the inception of the University of Ceylon in 1942 to 24.1 percent in 1960 and 44.4 percent in the four universities in 1970. Since then the percentage has fluctuated between 40 percent and 44 percent and was 42.9 percent in 1990–91 as women students are underrepresented in the Engineering Institution, which became a university in the early 1970s. Around 35 percent to 40 percent of the Open University students are women, and they are underrepresented likewise in technology-related courses. Female enrollment is relatively low in postgraduate institutes—40 percent in the Postgraduate Institute of Medicine, but between 5 percent and 20 percent in the Postgraduate Institute of Agriculture, Management, and Archaeology. Over half the students (56.4 percent) in the affiliated university colleges are women. It appears that women are disadvantaged only in participation in technology-related courses (table 18.2).

Around 70 percent of all students were from the rural sector or from small towns by the mid-1960s. Table 18.3 presents the changes in the social composition of the universities, reflecting a more egalitarian distribution of opportunities. The percentage of students from professional and white-collar families declined from 81 percent in 1950 to 34 percent in 1967, and those from urban and rural nonaffluent families increased from 11 percent to 60 percent (Strauss, 1951; Uswatte-Aratch, 1974); this distribution has not changed significantly in subsequent years (Jayaweera, 1984; UGC 1990).

It was inevitable, however, that the unequal distribution of senior secondary school facilities in science education should widen regional disparities in university admissions and enrollment and that around 70 percent of entrants to science courses should come from districts with the best-equipped schools—Colombo, the metropolitan and relatively affluent district, and Tamil Jaffna in the north—thereby reinforcing socioeconomic and ethnic disparities (table 18.4).

In a population in which over 70 percent are Sinhalese, 18 percent are indigenous Tamils and descendants of immigrant South Indian plantation labor, 7 percent are Moors and Malays, and one percent are Burghers and other groups, the student distribution in universities in 1946 was 61.7 percent Sinhalese, 29.4 percent Tamils, 4.0 percent Moors and Malays, and 4.9 percent Burghers (table 18.4). This ethnic imbalance, a legacy of the colonial administration and increasingly assailed by the resurgent Sinhala Buddhist majority who had obtained access in 1956 to the political power structure, was removed by 1969 in the arts faculties as a consequence of the expansion of senior secondary schools teaching arts subjects. Disparities continued to be wide in entry to science-based courses; almost equal proportions of Sinhalese and Tamils were enrolled in the medical and engineering faculties in the 1960s and tensions ran high on the issue of unequal access to these economically rewarding and prestigious courses as a consequence of better educational facilities in Tamil Jaffna since colonial rule.

From the early 1970s regional and ethnic disparities were artificially adjusted by quotas to conform better to population distribution. The social class composition, however, remained virtually unchanged as quotas continued for two decades without commensurate efforts to reduce inequalities in the provision of senior secondary education facilities, particularly in science education, although the percentage of students receiving state scholarships increased from 8.7 percent in 1981–82 to 56.3 percent in 1985–86. Hence, both interdistrict and intradistrict disparities have persisted and students from professional and middle-class families are still privileged in access to professional science-based courses.

The adverse effects of the imposition of quotas on the educationally developed

Table 18.2
Distribution of University Students by Faculty

Faculty	1975			1990		
	Total	Female	Percent Female	Total	Female	Percent Female
Medicine	1,239	584	47.1	3,615	1,523	42.1
Dentistry	193	108	55.9	398	192	48.2
Veterinary Science	108	53	49.1	261	118	45.2
Agriculture	390	100	25.6	1,502	624	41.5
Engineering	1,210	126	10.4	3,054	365	11.9
Architecture	73	21	28.8	281	100	35.6
Science	1,797	660	36.7	5,795	2,410	41.6
Management Studies	889	263	29.6	5,905	2,626	44.5
Law	144	61	42.4	967	512	52.9
Social Sciences/Humanities	5,634	2,563	45.5	9,666	5,051	52.3
Education	971	613	63.1			
Total	12,648	5,152	40.7	31,447	13,521	42.9
Total & Prof. science-based courses	3,213	992	30.9	9,111	2,922	32.1
Total science courses	1,797	660	36.7	5,795	2,410	41.6
Total arts-based courses	7,638	3,500	45.8	16,538	8,189	49.5

Source: University of Sri Lanka Reports (1975); University Grants Commission Statistical Handbook (1990).

Table 18.3
University Entrants by Parents' Occupation

	1950		1967	1977	
	Male	Female	Total	Male	Female
Professional and Management	55.5	69.5	12.0	8.9	11.3
Teaching	12.6	7.2	8.0	9.8	10.5
Middle-level (e.g., electrical)	20.3	20.3	16.0	15.3	14.3
Small Farmers and Rural Workers	6.3	1.4	31.0	31.5	27.9
Urban Workers	4.2	1.4	11.0	15.2	15.0
Unemployed	—	—	8.0	8.3	8.5
Unspecified	—	—	14.0	10.0	10.2
Total	100.0	100.0	100.0	100.0	100.0

Sources: Strauss (1951); Uswatte-Aratch (1974); Jayaweera (1984).

Colombo and Jaffna districts have had far-reaching consequences. Alienated and radicalized Tamil youth who are concentrated in schools in these districts have taken up arms in the ethnic conflict that escalated in the mid-1980s into a traumatic war. There has been an exodus of Sinhalese professionals overseas in search of higher education facilities for their children, who tend to be excluded by unconscionably high cutoff marks for quotas in the Colombo district. At the same time, competition for entry creates frustration and distorts the education process by giving priority to examination-oriented role learning in schools (table 18.5).

OTHER TERTIARY EDUCATION INSTITUTIONS

In Sri Lanka, universities have been almost synonymous with higher education in the absence of a pluralistic tertiary education structure. Other than in-service professional training by state and private sector establishments, alternative higher education opportunities are offered in degree-granting institutions and professional institutions.

A handful of institutions have been recognized as degree-granting institutions under the Universities Act as amended in 1985. The North Medical College, established in 1981 as a private institution, was recognized in 1988 for the award of the medical degree of the University of Colombo, but student and public agitation through the 1980s against a private institution that appeared to receive state patronage and cater to the privileged led to its incorporation into the State University of Kelaniya in 1989. The Institute of Technological Studies, established as a private higher education institution affiliated with the U.S. University of Houston in Texas, was granted degree-awarding status in 1989, and the State Institute of Surveying and Mapping was granted the same in 1990. The students

Table 18.4

Percentage Distribution of University Students and Population in Census Year by Ethnic Origin

	Sinhalese	Sri Lanka Tamil	Indian Tamil	Moor	Burgher	Malay & other	Total	Total Number
1946								
Population Percent	69.4	10.0	11.7	5.6	0.6	1.7	100.0	6,657,339
University Students	61.7	29.4	—	2.8	4.9	1.2	100.0	1,302
1953								
Population Percent	69.3	11.0	12.0	6.0	0.6	1.0	100.0	8,097,845
University Students	60.2	33.7	—	1.7	3.2	1.2	100.0	2,392
1963								
Population Percent	71.0	11.1	10.6	6.7	0.4	0.2	100.0	10,582,064
University Students	81.8	16.2	—	1.2	0.3	0.5	100.0	7,816
1971								
Population Percent	72.0	11.0	9.4	7.1	0.3	0.1	100.0	12,689,897
University Students	79.0	18.2	—	2.4	0.2	0.2	100.0	12,074
1981								
Population Percent	73.9	12.6	5.6	7.4	0.6	0.2	100.0	14,848,346
University Entrants	76.4	19.2		3.9		0.5	100.0	5,057
1991								
University Entrants	76.5	16.7		6.5		0.3	100.0	7,140

* The few Indian Tamils in the university have not been counted separately.

Source: Census of Ceylon, Report of the University of Ceylon University of Sri Lanka and University Grants Commission.

Table 18.5
University Education, Demand, and Supply, 1943–84

Year	Gr. 12 Enrollment	No. of Candidates CGE A/L Exam Applicants	No. admitted to University	Percent entered University	Enrollment in University	Percent Females	% Arts-based Courses
1943	n.a.	350	197	56.3	904	11.5	37.2
1946	n.a.	1,171	372	31.7	1,302	13.7	39.7
1950	n.a.	1,443	438	30.3	2,036	18.7	38.5
1955	2,900	2,096	658	31.3	2,431	26.7	40.8
1959	6,173	3,938	1,189	30.0	4,039	24.4	55.0
1965	26,250	31,199	6,359	20.3	14,422	32.2	76.1
1970	23,075	30,973	3,457	10.9	11,813	44.4	71.2
1975	41,054	48,432	3.482	8.4	12,648	40.7	60.4
1979	82,973	101,015	5,255	5.2	16,032	39.9	62.8
1985	67,722	105,500	5,630	5.3	18,217	42.8	55.6
1990	105,239	120,471	8,970	7.4	31,447	42.9	49.6

Source: Ministry of Education, University of Sri Lanka, and University Grants Commission.

in the Sir John Kotelawala Defence Academy take the arts degree examinations of the University of Colombo. The National Institute of Education, the academic arm of the Ministry of Education, has powers under its own act to grant degrees and has recently introduced a course leading to the bachelor of education degree. Enrollments in all these institutions are minuscule in comparison with enrollment in universities.

Tertiary education institutions that provide professional training are also limited in number. The technical colleges, which have increased in number from the first college in 1893 to 29 in 1983, offer courses at 3 levels (craft, technician, and professional [Higher National Diploma in Commerce or Technology]), but the amount of students taking tertiary-level courses was less than 5 percent of 18,000 students enrolled in these institutions in the 1980s and 1990s. The Law College has 900 students and the 8 colleges of education have around 3,000 students. Other small institutions that offer opportunities for higher education are the Institute of Engineering, Institute of Chemistry, and School of Social Work. Higher agriculture education is not offered outside universities. CINTEC (Computer and Information Technology Course of Sri Lanka) has conducted a national examination in computer studies since 1991 for students enrolled in computer courses in private institutions. A hundred students appeared for the first examination. Professional courses that attract the largest number of students are those conducted by the Institute of Chartered Accountants (around 10,000) and the Chartered Institute of Management Associations (CIMA) (around 4,000). The numbers that complete the final examinations of these institutions are, however, very small.

Access to other higher education institutions such as the Law College and accountancy and management-related courses, which are fee-levying and concentrated in Colombo, is limited to aspirants from families with resources. Technical colleges are located in many districts, but those offering tertiary-level courses are found in Colombo and in other provincial capitals. Hence, regional and socioeconomic disparities are even stronger barriers to higher education outside the universities.

DEVELOPMENT IN HIGHER EDUCATION IN THE INTERNATIONAL CONTEXT

The earliest higher education institutions—the medical and university colleges and the first University of Ceylon (1942)—were modeled closely on British institutions. The university replicated the structures, the curricula, the English medium, and the patterns of staff recruitment and development within the framework of university autonomy, academic freedom, and the Western humanistic tradition. Unfortunately, rigidity in the adoption of the model tended to alienate the university from the society in the perception of its critics (Needham Report, 1959).

Over the years, some of the elements of the model changed, such as the concept of autonomy and the medium of instruction in arts and nonprofessional science courses and curricula, but the vestige of academic orientation and perceptions of higher education as an upward social mobility route survived. The first university was also a structural model to the seven other universities. New models were also sought from the West for new institutions—the single university with a number of campuses (1971–77) from California (United States), the Open University from the United Kingdom, and the junior colleges and affiliated university colleges from the United States. The delay in developing the faculty of graduate studies of the University of Colombo, an American model grafted onto a British model, illustrated the problems caused by the interface of institutions with different underlying social philosophies. The dichotomy between universities and other tertiary-level institutions was also a legacy of British colonial rule—a legacy of dominance of universities that appears to impede the development of a pluralistic tertiary education structure.

The most visible manifestations of the influence of the changing external environment operated through macroeconomic developments. The polarization of countries into developed and developing countries after the Second World War, the overarching objectives of policy makers in developing countries to reduce the gap as early as possible, and the dependency structures created by unequal center-periphery relations influenced the course of higher education.

First, the adoption of exogenous concepts and norms entrenched in modernization and human capital theories (Schultz, 1963; Becker, 1964; Denison, 1967) obfuscated educational thinking within the country. In a situation in which a stagnant economy could not absorb the labor force, theories of mismatch between university education and employment and the assumptions of dysfunctionalism of university education (ILO, 1971; Dore, 1976) in an environment with few job opportunities and overall unemployment led to policies to freeze university admissions between 1967 and 1977, to undervalue the arts and social sciences, and to introduce job-oriented university courses for arts graduates which, in the absence of employment opportunities, aggravated problems in the labor market. Manpower projections, which are largely academic exercises in an unstable economy, continue to influence plans for expansion (UGC Corporate Plans, 1984–92).

Second, unequal international economic relations as in the case of trade have stymied economic growth and constrained expenditure on higher education. While overall public expenditure on education declined from 4.5 percent of the GNP and 16 percent to 20 percent of the national budget in the 1960s to 2.3 percent and 8 percent, respectively, by 1985, expenditure on higher education has been less than 0.5 percent of GNP for several decades, declining from 10 percent to 6 percent to 8 percent of the education budget (Indraratne, 1992). The reduction in educational expenditure as a component of IMF–World Bank structural adjustment policies has exacerbated economic constraints and limited the development of tertiary educational institutions. Both universities and other institutes have not been able to meet the demand for admission generated by an expanding secondary school system.

A major consequence of economic constraints has been the dependence on donor aid. Such dependence affects the development of institutions. It also affects research priorities, which tend to be influenced by donor priorities rather than by national needs in a context in which only 0.25 percent of the expenditure on higher education is allocated for research.

HIGHER EDUCATION, THE LABOR MARKET, AND SOCIAL STABILITY

One of the goals of the first university in 1942 was to develop an academic elite who would occupy with ease their role as national leaders, administrators, and professionals. The universities have continued to fulfill this role in the public sector but private sector establishments have been less positive in their attitude to university graduates and have tended to rely on private institutions or on in-service training.

With declining economic growth and an expanding university population and labor force in the 1960s, the products of the universities, particularly arts graduates, have been vulnerable to unemployment in a shrinking labor market. There is, however, a dual relationship between higher education and the labor market. A university degree is required for entry to a high-level profession, but a degree, even a professional one, does not guarantee employment.

Policies to cope with this problem were determined often by immediate pressures and by perceptions based on human capital theory transplanted in economically developing countries. From the 1970s, vocationalization obtruded into the university sector (ILO, 1971), while the tertiary education sector outside the universities and its potential linkages with the labor market were ignored. Job-oriented courses in development studies, public finance and taxation, and estate management were introduced after consultation with the national planning authorities, and 51 percent of arts students were enrolled in these courses in 1971. These courses had to be abandoned in 1976, however, when their products could not be absorbed into employment (Bastianpillai, 1983). Graduate unemployment studies found that graduates of these courses were even more unsuccessful in finding jobs than the graduates of conventional arts subjects who at least had access to teaching jobs (SLFUW, 1980; Marga, 1983). The limited absorptive capacity of the labor market continued to be the major cause of unemployment (Alailima, 1992).

In fact, graduate unemployment had to be contained in politically volatile contexts by special state interventions to absorb unemployed graduates into the services sector: the Graduate Training Programme in the public sector in 1972; the appointment of thousands of arts graduates as teachers in 1976 on the eve of a general election; the appointment under the Graduate Placement Programme of 94.2 percent of the arts graduates from 1976–84 as teachers; the appointment of around seven thousand arts graduates as teachers in 1990 after the private sector failed to employ them despite pressure from the government; and the current proposal on the eve of another election to absorb the eight thousand unemployed arts graduates into the public sector as development assistants attached to administrative divisions. Graduate unemployment hovered around 10 percent annually in the 1980s and is susceptible to vicissitudes in the macroeconomic environment.

Attempts in the corporate plans for universities (UGC, 1982–92) to project admissions according to manpower projections of the national planners have not achieved their expected outcomes in a society that is in the throes of economic restructuring, privatization, and political changes. The most positive developments have been the diversification of courses to meet demands from a few areas of potential economic growth such as food technology and the attempts that are being made to bring the universities closer to employers, particularly the Federation of Chambers of Commerce and Industry. The Open University already has such links. The affiliated university colleges are still in their infancy and their relationship with employment is still nebulous.

Outside the universities, the accountancy, management, law, and education courses are structured to meet the needs of specific professions for trained personnel. The technical colleges, however, do not appear to have a placement program or any links with employers in formulating their courses. There is a large vacuum in this sector in relation to the changing needs of the labor market in a country that aspires to be a newly industrializing country.

The relationship between higher education and social stability has been a negative indicator of external efficiency in the past two decades. Sporadic student agitation and strikes have been a feature of university life since the 1960s. Unemployment and perceptions of deprivation and alienation among youth from economically disadvantaged families vis-à-vis the establishment, however, led to a short-lived youth insurgency in 1971 under a revolutionary group, the Janatha Vimukthi Peramuna (Future Freedom Front), and university graduates and students were among the leaders in the conflict.

In 1987, the political instability engendered by the ethnic conflict in the north was exacerbated by the resurgence of the JVP, and the violence that engulfed the country and the universities resulted in the closure of universities from 1987 to 1989. Student activism, interstudent political rivalry, conflict with the state, and reprisals by the state filled these years and their legacy has been intermittent disruption of academic schedules. As the Youth Commission reported, economic disparities and the anger of youth who have received a higher education in the national languages but are excluded by their lack of proficiency in English from the commanding heights of the economy and society continuously fuel unrest and destabilize society (Youth Commission Report, 1990).

THE GOVERNANCE OF HIGHER EDUCATION

While nonuniversity institutions in the tertiary education sector are either under direct state control and management (technical colleges, colleges of education) or are private institutions (Law College, the Chartered Institute of Management Associates [CIMA], the Institute of Technological Studies [ITS]), universities have had a checkered experience in governance with respect to university autonomy and academic freedom.

Until 1966 the University of Ceylon was an autonomous institution with a high degree of academic freedom despite its total dependence on government funds. The university selected its staff and students, its court elected its vice chancellor, and it made its own decisions regarding councils, teaching methods, examinations, research, and development plans. The erosion of this concept of autonomy was the outcome of social pressures on the universities and the concern of the state to ensure that universities supported by it were responsive to national needs. This concern was strengthened by the perception that the University of Ceylon was isolated from its environment and alienated from emerging social needs (Needham Commission, 1959). It is an index also of the politicization of education that each change of government, as in 1965, 1970, and 1977, was followed by change in the governance of universities.

The inroads of the state into university autonomy were first made through the Higher Education Act No. 20 of 1966, which gave the minister of education responsibility for issuing general directives to the new structure created for co-ordinating and supervising university education—the National Council of Higher Education (NCHE). The council had powers to disburse and control the expenditure for higher education allocated by the state, to maintain academic standards, to be in charge of the administration of all state higher education institutions, and to coordinate higher education with national needs. The NCHE became the central agency responsible for admissions according to the directives of the state, and vice chancellors were appointed by the council, thus taking over two important responsibilities of universities.

The University Act No. 1 of 1972 went further and restructured the six university institutions as a single university with a centralized, monolithic administration. Admissions, the medium of instruction, and development plans were under the control of the minister of education. Vice chancellors and registrars were appointed by the minister from three names submitted by the boards of regents, and deans were appointed by vice chancellors. Further, the single university administration controlled the development of the campuses by ''rationalizing'' and restructuring courses.

Act No. 16 of 1978 was formulated reportedly to restore university autonomy. The instrument introduced for this purpose was the University Grants Commission (UGC), modeled on the University Grants Committee in Britain. The UGC was given wide powers to plan and coordinate universities in conformity with national policies, to allocate state funds to universities, to maintain academic standards, to regulate admissions to universities, and to recommend to the executive president of Sri Lanka three names for the appointment of vice chancellors. The president and cabinet have responsibility for deciding the number of university places for admissions, the medium of instruction, and financial provision. In addition, the new Ministry of Higher Education, created in 1978 to supervise all higher education institutions including universities, and the Ministry of University Affairs, created in 1989, added new layers of state intervention. At present, therefore, universities are supervised by the UGC, which works with the government.

Increasing state intervention has also affected some aspects of the academic freedom enjoyed by members of universities. Student admissions and allocation to courses are regulated by mechanisms introduced to meet social needs. Student unions have been active since the early decades and universities have been virtual microcosms of national politics, with student elections having the flavor of mini-general elections. Student participation in university bodies was introduced in the 1970s. However, student unions were banned in 1983, abolished in 1985, and restored only in 1990. Student unrest and conflict escalated during these years as the violence in the political environment spilled over to universities. Student violence and counterstate violence emanating from emergency regulations imposed to cope with civil strife and terrorism threatened human rights, including even the right to life of students, staff, and administrators. In the north, the "Tigers," who have taken up arms against the state, control universities and intellectual life (Thiranagama et al., 1990). The tempo of unrest in the political environment and in the universities declined in the 1990s with the collapse of the JVP, and universities appear to have returned to their pre-1985 social climate.

Despite this erosion of academic freedom, some of the basic freedoms, such as the right of universities to appoint staff to develop their curricula, teach, examine, and carry out research without external control, have survived. University staff (except key personnel) have always enjoyed prestige and independence from political interference. They still have more freedom of expression and association than members of the public service.

FUTURE DEVELOPMENTS

In the Sri Lankan context, the major issues that confront policy makers in higher education are the need to meet both social demand and development needs and to create a diversified tertiary education structure to meet these demands and needs. There is considerable ongoing public discussion and task force activity on these critical issues.

The trends that may unfold as the country moves into the twenty-first century are likely to be determined by three imperatives: the demand for equality of opportunity, the need to make graduates of higher education employable, and the necessity of incorporating equity, intellectual excellence, academic freedom, and social responsibility in a framework of holistic human development.

Five decades of free education and concomitant social gains have created an ethos in which public resistance to IMF–World Bank proposals for cost recovery and user fees in the higher education sector will continue, making it politically unwise to implement such policies. The state will be under pressure to expand opportunities in order to increase the current unconscionably low percentage of the relevant age group with access to higher education. It is likely that such provision will be made in the university subsector through the reorganization of the affiliated university colleges as viable higher education institutions. It can be anticipated that the path is unlikely to be smooth in view of persistent efforts to replicate such institutions to meet parochial political needs. Expansion is also likely to take place in the nonuniversity tertiary sector by revamping some of the technical colleges and encouraging private enterprise.

The low level of public expenditure on higher education has been a cause for concern and efforts are likely to be made to increase allocation of public funds and to mobilize other resources. Resource allocation for expansion as well as quality improvement and, in particular, adequate remuneration of staff to prevent an exodus to management and professional positions in the private sector will be major concerns.

Policy makers and higher education institutions will be increasingly preoccupied with strategies to enhance the employability of the graduates of these institutions. As the private sector has preferred in the past to train secondary school leavers on the job rather than recruit university graduates, measures such as establishing linkages between employers and higher education institutions and providing courses in English and personality development to meet the demands of this sector will receive priority. Diversification of courses, particularly in growth areas in the economy, will be accelerated. It is also likely that the Indian Institute of Technology (IIT) will become a model for some new higher education institutions in view of the state's objective of reaching the status of a newly industrializing country in the early twenty-first century. The shift from arts to sciences in university admissions may be modified by the emergence of the commercial sector as a source of increasing employment.

Structural changes in the higher education sector may include the evolution of new modes of administration, supervision, coordination, and communication within and outside the country through computer networks. It is unlikely that the state will cease to intervene in higher education. But universities are already restive under the supervision of the UGC and the latter may divest itself of some of its administrative tasks and concentrate on planning and coordination. The proposal to create a National Agency for Academic Awards to regulate academic standards outside the universities while promoting diversification may assist in developing tertiary education institutions that will promote alternative paths to aspirants to higher education. Liaison with the Tertiary and Vocational Education Commission will facilitate coordination.

Student unrest will continue to reflect pressures in the external environment but the traumatic years of closures and violence in the late 1980s have focused attention on the need for modalities of conflict resolution, at least within institutions. The current concern with human rights and national harmony and the introduction of courses in human rights education may promote more informed and broader perceptions that will help reconcile the demands of equity, freedom, efficiency, and effectiveness in higher education and promote greater cohesion within institutions and in society.

REFERENCES

Alailima, Patricia J. 1992. "Education-Employment Linkages: The Macro Profile." *Sri Lanka Journal of Social Sciences, 15*, 1–46.

Bastianpillai, B. 1983. "The Job-oriented Courses in the Universities of Sri Lanka." In *University Education and Graduate Employment in Sri Lanka*. Colombo: Marga Institute.

Becker, G. 1964. *Human Capital*. New York: Columbia University Press.

Denison, F. 1967. *Why Growth Rates Differ*. Washington: The Brookings Institution.

De Silva, C. R. 1978. "The Politics of University Admissions: A Review of Some Aspects of the Admission Policy in Sri Lanka, 1971–1978." *Sri Lanka Journal of Social Sciences, 1* (2), 88–123.

Dore, R. P. 1976. *The Diploma Disease: Education Qualification and Development*. London: Allen and Unwin.

Indraratne, A. V. de S. 1992. *Economics of Higher Education in Sri Lanka*. New Delhi: Navrang.

International Labour Organization. 1971. *Matching Employment Opportunities and Expectations*. Geneva: Author.

Jayaweera, Swarna. 1984. "Access to Higher Education—The Social Composition of University Entrants." *University of Colombo Review, 1,* (4), 6–40.

Marga Institute. 1983. "University Education and Graduate Employment in Sri Lanka." Columbo.

Needham Report. 1959. Sessional Paper 23. 1959. Report of the Ceylon University Commission. Government Press.

Sessional Paper 1. 1990. Report of the Presidential Commission on Youth. Government Press.

Sessional Paper 23. 1959. Report of the Ceylon University Commission (Needham Report). Government Press.

Schultz, T. W. 1963. *The Economic Value of Education*. New York: Columbia University Press.

SLFUW. 1980. "Sri Lanka Federation of University Women, Study of Unemployment Among University Graduates." Columbo.

Strauss, M. 1951. "Family Characteristics and Occupational Choice of University Entrants." *University of Ceylon Review, 1*(2), 125–35.

Thiranagama, Rajini, et al. 1990. *The Broken Palmyrah*. Claremont, Calif.: SLSI (Sri Lanka Studies Institute).

University Grants Commission (UGC). Various dates. Corporate Plan for University Education. 1990, Statistical Handbook.

———. 1993. Report on the Affiliated University Colleges.

Uswatte-Aratch, G. 1974. "University Admissions in Ceylon: Their Economic and Social Background and Employment Expectations." *Modern Asia Studies, 1*(4), 6–40.

Youth Commission Report. 1990. Sessional Paper 1. 1990. Report of the Presidential Commission on Youth. Government Press.

19

TAIWAN

Shun-fen Chen

Taiwan, an island off the southeast coast of mainland China, is a province of the Republic of China. It is one of the most densely populated areas in the world, 35,873 square kilometers in size with over 20 million inhabitants.

Taiwan's earliest immigrants were from Southeast Asia. The number of their descendants, the aborigines of Taiwan, is about 300,000, comprising 1.6 percent of the current total population of Taiwan. Large-scale immigration from southeast China began in the seventeenth century. The island came under the control of China after a short period of Dutch rule (1620–62). It was in 1895 that Taiwan was ceded to Japan after China was defeated in the Sino-Japanese War. A Western-style system of education was established in Taiwan for the first time during the Japanese occupation period. The medium of instruction was Japanese.

Taiwan was restored to China at the end of World War II after forty-one years of colonization. Four years later, in 1949, the central government of the Republic of China moved to Taiwan after being defeated by the Communists in a civil war. Over 1.5 million Kuomingtang (Nationalists) supporters fled to the island during that time. The Chinese mainland, taken by the Communists, has been under the rule of the People's Republic of China since then. Those postwar immigrants from China and their offspring, the so-called mainlanders, make up less than 14 percent of the total population of Taiwan.

There are scores of dialects in China. The official language, Mandarin Chinese, has been the only medium of instruction allowed in Taiwan's primary and secondary schools since 1943. The government language policy was enforced so thoroughly that the younger generations today speak Mandarin fluently while the aboriginal, dialects seldom spoken, are even facing the danger of extinction. Whether the dialects or language of the aborigines should be taught in school has become a controversial issue in recent years.

Forty years after Taiwan was transformed from a traditional agricultural society into a newly industrialized society, the country became the seat of the
Republic of China. In 1992, Taiwan's GNP per capita reached U.S.$10,202,
with an annual economic growth rate of over 6 percent. Education has also
expanded considerably over the past four decades. The total number of schools
and colleges has increased four times, from 1,504 in 1950 to 6,819 in 1992
(Ministry of Education, 1993a:x). Although many people believe that education
contributes to Taiwan's "economic miracle," the relationship between educational expansion and economic growth needs to be further explored (Young,
1994:35–36).

Compared to its economic growth, Taiwan's political development has been
much slower. Opposed to the mainland China military, the government imposed
martial law in 1940, which deprived people of certain rights assured in the
Constitution. It was not until 1986 that the first opposition party, the Democratic
Progressive Party (DPP), declared its establishment. In 1987 martial law was
lifted after thirty-eight years of imposition. The government subsequently
adopted a series of liberalization measures, such as the restoration of the right
to form political parties, the removal of controls on newspapers, loosening the
restrictions on foreign exchange, and permitting people to visit their relatives
on the Chinese mainland.

Higher education in Taiwan has long been criticized for too much government
intervention. Along with political reforms, many college professors and students
have strongly urged more academic freedom and institutional autonomy in recent years. In response to such requests, the government has revised the University Act. Although the Enforcement Rules of the University Act, to be
enacted by the Ministry of Education and then approved by the Executive Yuan,
has yet to be implemented, university reform in the direction of autonomy is
already on the way. This chapter focuses on recent issues related to university
autonomy.

PROFILE OF THE HIGHER EDUCATION SYSTEM

Historical Development

Taiwan's higher education system was established during the period of Japanese occupation. At the end of World War II it consisted of one university,
one higher school, and a few colleges (equivalent to junior colleges today). Since
the main purposes of higher education were to provide research material and
high-level manpower for Japan's colonial policy, all of these institutions emphasized research, and the size of their enrollment was very small (Wu, Chen,
and Wu, 1989:123, 333).

In 1945, Taiwan was restored to China. The island's education system was
soon replaced by the one adopted on the mainland since 1922, which mainly
follows the American prototype. As a result, colonial influences on Taiwan's

education are not as significant as those in other Third World countries that have recently proclaimed independence (ibid.: 123). After the central government of the Republic of China moved to Taiwan, Chinese educational policy was enforced on the island more thoroughly than before. Japanese influence thus diminished further (ibid.).

Between 1954 and 1972, higher education expanded rapidly. The number of tertiary institutions increased from nine to ninety-nine. During this period, especially after 1963, scores of junior colleges were established in order to train the mid-level manpower needed for the nation's economic development.

Beginning in 1973, the expansion of higher education was suddenly continued. This was due to a policy that stopped approving applications for the establishment of new private institutions. At the same time, the manpower development plan adopted by the government suggested that the annual growth rate of tertiary enrollment be lowered to 5 percent or less (Chang, 1993:230). Such a restrictive policy lasted for more than a decade and was lifted in 1985.

In 1992, there were 124 institutions of higher learning, including 50 universities and independent colleges and 74 junior colleges. The ratio of the number of public institutions to that of private ones was 1:2. Total enrollment at tertiary institutions was 653,162 (540,454, when students in the first three years of five-year junior college programs were excluded). Among them, about 70 percent were enrolled in private institutions.

Colonial and Postcolonial Legacies

As mentioned previously, Taiwan's higher education system was established during the Japanese occupation period. Immediately after World War II, higher education institutions established in the colonial period were renamed and reorganized based on the Chinese model, except for one that was disbanded. Most of these institutions continued to function and still enjoy prestige due to their well-developed administrative structure and research facilities.

Nevertheless, the Chinese government wanted to lessen Japanese influences on Taiwan's education. The Japanese educational system was replaced with a Chinese system immediately after Taiwan was restored. The only university founded by the Japanese, Taihoku Imperial University, was renamed National Taiwan University. The chair system was replaced by departments and most Japanese professors were replaced by Chinese professors. An American credit system was adopted. Students took courses for which credits were counted.

At the same time, classroom sessions were conducted in Mandarin Chinese in place of Japanese. Freshmen at the National Taiwan University, being unfamiliar with Mandarin and Chinese literature, had to take Mandarin language courses in order to understand the classroom instruction.

After the Nationalist government moved to the island, the tendency toward centralization became obvious. College curricula was mostly determined by the Ministry of Education. The organization of institutions of higher learning was unified with little flexibility. Almost every policy regarding higher education was made by the government. Centralization has since been a characteristic of Taiwan's higher education.

In summary, Taiwan's higher education system was established during the period of Japanese rule; however, the system did not follow the model of its colonial master after Taiwan was restored to China. It now reflects both Chinese and American features.

The Definition of What Constitutes Higher Education

It is difficult to give a clear definition of higher education due to the complexity of institutions. The term "higher education" usually refers to education provided by junior colleges, independent colleges, and universities. In spite of its frequent appearance in official documents, such a usage is misleading in some cases. The problem mainly comes from one type of institution, junior colleges. There are three kinds of programs offered by the junior colleges (to be illustrated in the following section), among them a five-year program that admits junior high school graduates and should not be treated as a postsecondary program. Therefore, it would be more accurate to say that higher education in Taiwan refers to postsecondary education provided by universities, independent colleges, and junior colleges. Such a definition can be found in an official publication, *Education Statistical Indicators Republic of China* (Ministry of Education, 1993b:iv), where higher education refers to education at colleges and universities excluding the first three years of the five-year junior college program.

Types of Institutions of Higher Education

There are three types of higher education institutions: (1) universities, (2) independent colleges, and (3) junior colleges. Universities consist of at least three colleges. Those with only one or two colleges are called independent colleges. Both universities and independent colleges offer four-year programs leading to a bachelor's degree. Many of them also offer master-level programs, and some offer doctoral-level programs depending on the academic performance of the departments concerned. Junior colleges provide two-, three-, or five-year programs leading to a diploma. Two-year programs are designed for vocational high school graduates, three-year programs for academic high school graduates, and five-year programs for junior high school graduates. It should be noted that students in the first three years of a five-year junior college program are the same age as those in high school. Therefore, it would be reasonable to exclude them when counting students of higher education. Yet faculty members offer courses for these students with the same academic structure as college courses, and they may also offer courses for senior students at the same junior college. It would be inappropriate to exclude them from the statistics as faculty members of higher education.

Enrollment Rates

According to the Ministry of Education (1993a:33), in 1991 about 37.9 percent of the age group from eighteen to twenty-one attended higher education institutions, including those in degree programs at independent colleges and universities and those in diploma programs at junior colleges. The figure would drop to 20 percent for degree programs only. The enrollment rate in primary education for the same academic year was 98.7 percent, and that in secondary education was 86.2 percent.

THE CHANGING FUNCTIONS AND PATTERNS OF HIGHER EDUCATION

Policy and Planning

According to the Constitution of the Republic of China, the state has power to supervise educational institutions at all levels. In practice, educational policy and planning are conducted by the Ministry of Education in cooperation with other government units. For instance, many important education policies originated from the nation's economic development planning (Young, 1994:44–48). This was especially obvious after 1965, when manpower development became an integrated part of the country's economic planning. The annual growth rate of college enrollments in general as well as the speed of expansion in different fields was specifically designed at different phases of the manpower plan (Lao, 1994:25–30). By adjusting the number of college openings in different fields, Taiwan's government successfully increased the proportion of enrollment in science and technology in the past twenty years. For example, the ratio of college students majoring in natural sciences and technology to those in humanities and social science was 47:53 in 1976; it was 58:42 in 1992 (Ministry of Education, 1993b:45).

In addition to the government's economic sector that affects the development of higher education, the Department of Defense also exerts influence over educational policies. One example is the requirement of military training for all college and high school students. The issue of abolishing military training is controversial and will be discussed later.

Governance and Finance

Centralization has been an important feature of Taiwan's higher education. The Ministry of Education not only approves the establishment of new institutions and departments, but also controls the size of enrollment, tuition rates, required courses, minimum graduation credits, and so on at all institutions, both public and private. Presidents of public institutions are chosen and appointed by the Ministry. Those of private ones are appointed by their board of trustees with the approval of the Ministry.

Public institutions receive their annual budgets from the government, with specified amounts for different categories; tuition collected from students has to be submitted to the government. The major income of private colleges and universities comes from tuition. Government subsidies to the private sector are limited.

Being tightly controlled by the government, higher education is politicized to a great extent just as are other levels of education (Young, 1990:228). In response to the recent liberalization trend, the Ministry of Education announced that it would grant institutions more autonomy in various areas. At the same time, the Ministry urged public institutions to make efforts to raise funds and find resources from the society at large rather than being solely dependent on the government. If the budget of a public university were to come from diversified sources, there would be a greater chance for institutional autonomy.

The principle of university autonomy was confirmed by lawmakers in the first article of the newly revised University Act, which reads, "the university is protected by academic freedom and is entitled to institutional autonomy with the sole limit of laws." In other words, government intervention at colleges and universities is bound to be altered substantially. However, it should be noted that this institutional autonomy does not apply to junior colleges.

Stratification within the System

In general, four-year colleges and universities emphasize both teaching and research, while junior colleges that offer diploma programs emphasize teaching. Among the four-year institutions, public rather than private institutions are preferred by most students because faculty qualifications of the former are usually better than those of the latter. In addition, tuition rates in the public sector are two-thirds less than those in the private sector.

Recently the Department of Higher Education of the Ministry of Education (1993:2) proposed that private universities with limited resources concentrate their efforts on the teaching of undergraduate students. This can be interpreted as a government intention to develop a policy of stratification with public institutions emphasizing both graduate programs and research activities, and private institutions emphasizing undergraduate teaching.

Another proposal contributing to stratification was raised by the president of the Academia Sinica during the Seventh National Education Conference held by the Ministry of Education in June 1994. Under the proposal, public institutions would be categorized into three groups: research-oriented universities, teaching-oriented universities, and community colleges (*United Daily*, 1994:6). Government funds for research universities would likely be much higher than for the institution. Whether the above proposals for stratification can be accepted by academia remains to be seen.

Curriculum

College curriculum includes the following three components: (1) general required courses, (2) departmental required courses, and (3) electives. Subjects in the first two components are stipulated by the Ministry of Education in the "List of College Required Courses," while electives are offered by the individual departments, with the approval of the institution.

Before 1992, in addition to physical education and military training, every college student, irrespective of major, had to take twenty-eight credits of general required courses, plus four to six credits of "general education courses" (i.e., certain courses outside a student's major field, for the purpose of broadening knowledge). The general required courses include Chinese (8 credits), English (8 credits), general history of China (4 credits), and one of the following alternatives (2 credits): the Constitution of the Republic of China, international relationships, introduction to philosophy, or introduction to law.

Two of these required courses, the doctrine of Dr. Sun Yat-sen and military training, were included due to the country's special situation in the early 1950s when the central government had just moved to Taiwan. They have been viewed as political courses serving as an ideological control over students (Young, 1990: 228). As political reforms began in the mid-1980s, college students and professors overtly attacked the appropriateness of these two subjects as college required courses. In 1987 the Union for Advancing the Reform of the University Act, the first intercampus student organization in postwar Taiwan, was established. Abolishing the military education requirement on campus was one of its major requests (Deng, 1993:147). In the spring of 1989 the university council for the National Taiwan University, the most prestigious university on the island, suggested to the Ministry of Education that the doctrine of Dr. Sun Yat-sen be offered as an elective (Young, 1994:326).

In response to requests for curriculum reform, the Ministry of Education substantially revised the "List of College Required Courses" in its periodical review of college curriculum, and planned to enforce the new list in September 1990. It was proposed in the revised list that for general required courses, "areas" instead of "subjects" be stipulated. Colleges might offer several course requirements. The proposed areas include Chinese (6 credits), foreign language (6 credits), history (4 credits), the Constitution and national spirit of the ROC (4 credits), and general education courses (8 credits).

It should be noted that the area "the Constitution and national spirit of the ROC" is much broader than the formerly required subject, the doctrine of Dr. Sun Yat-sen. This means that colleges may choose to offer, or students may choose to take, a subject other than the doctrine course. As expected, strong resistance to this reform sprang from certain faculty members who had been teaching the doctrine course. Unable to solve the problem, the Ministry of Education postponed enforcing the new general course requirement. In other words, only the revised departmental required courses were implemented in September

1990. The Ministry's concession angered those who advocated curriculum reform. In 1991, more than five hundred college professors jointly issued a statement requesting the Ministry of Education to abolish the "List of College Required Courses." They alleged that the list was unconstitutional since the government, according to the Constitution, has only the power of supervising colleges rather than telling them exactly which subjects to teach (University Reform Union, 1993:172).

The general required courses part of the revised list was finally brought into effect in September 1993, with some colleges having a one-year grace period.

The college curriculum became an issue again when the University Act was promulgated in January 1994. Since university autonomy granted by the act without doubt applies to curriculum, it would be illegal for the Ministry of Education to enforce the "List of College Required Courses." In other words, each individual university has the right and responsibility to design its own curriculum.

In spite of the new situation, the Ministry of Education intends to maintain certain general required courses, especially military training. Therefore, the Ministry proposed, in the Enforcement Rules of the University Act, an article that requests all universities to collectively decide and implement a set of general required courses. However, a number of professors, including professors of law, pointed out that the article would contradict the act. The National Taiwan University has decided to design its own curriculum without following the general required courses collectively decided by universities. Whether other institutions will observe the article is uncertain.

Language Medium of Instruction

Mandarin Chinese, the official language, is the only medium of instruction permitted in Taiwan's primary and secondary schools. It is also used for instruction in college classrooms (except in foreign language courses). English may be used, although it rarely is, for instruction by college professors, who may not be able to speak Mandarin fluently. Recently a law professor reported that the dialect can also be used for academic purposes, not only for daily life (Liu, 1993:193–99). This unusual practice could also be a reaction or even a protest of the fact that the mother tongue of the majority had long been overlooked, intentionally, by the government.

The issue of academic dependency merits attention here. Although Mandarin Chinese is used for instruction, instructors often refer to English terms in classroom teaching since the content of lectures usually comes from Western textbooks, except for a few subjects such as Chinese literature. At the graduate level, the major reading materials are publications from industrialized countries, mostly in English. In addition, research topics and methods applied by college professors show a similar trend. A psychologist pointed out that this academic dependency has created a crisis in Taiwan's social sciences (Hwang, 1994:280–84).

Current Reforms in the College Admission System

For the past forty years high school graduates in Taiwan have been admitted to institutions of higher learning based solely on their scores on the entrance examination. Institutions of the same type usually hold a joint entrance examination, with member institutions taking turns to be in charge of the major examination affairs each year. Among these examinations the most competitive is the Joint College Entrance Examination (JCEE), first held in 1954 with over a hundred thousand applicants each year over the past decade. In spite of its advantages, such as providing fair competition and avoiding duplicated admissions, the JCEE has been blamed for distorting education at high schools and hampering university autonomy in undergraduate admissions.

In order to improve the admission system, a task force—the College Entrance Examination Center (CEEC)—was set up in 1989 by the joint efforts of all four-year institutions of higher learning under the sponsorship of the Ministry of Education. Three years later, in 1992, the CEEC submitted to the Ministry of Education a reform proposal as its work report. The proposed admission system is basically a two-step, triple-channel device. To be specific, in this "Diversified System of College Admissions (DSCA)" all applicants need to take a first-stage common examination in five basic subjects (Chinese, English, math, natural sciences, and social studies) and then go through any one of the following channels for the second stage (College Entrance Examination Center, 1992:20–22):

1. The Improved Joint College Entrance Examination (IJCEE). This is applicable to the majority of high school graduates. Students take CEEC examinations in certain subjects relevant to their interests. Those with satisfactory results will be offered a place via CEEC based on their preferences.

2. The Recommendation and Selection Program (RSP). This is applicable to high school students with special talents/abilities and motivations. Universities conduct their own assessment and admit the students who are recommended by high schools, based on their qualifications.

3. The Access Learning Program (ALP). This is applicable to students who have graduated from high school over one year previously and have taken college foundation courses in the extension division of colleges or universities. Those who pass the examination held by the CEEC in relevant subjects will be admitted as matriculated students.

The DSCA proposal has so far been partially accepted by the Ministry of Education. The RSP was first implemented on a small scale for the college freshmen of 1994, with 7,404 candidates competing for 1,410 openings (Newsletter of Education, 1994:2). It was extended on a larger scale the following year due to satisfactory effects achieved.

In view of the imperative of reform to the current college admission system, the CEEC Foundation was formally established at the beginning of 1993 with the government as its biggest donor. The CEEC, formerly a task force, thus turned into a formal organization under the sponsorship of the CEEC Foundation. The reform it proposes is already on its way, but its effectiveness needs to be assessed.

RESPONSES TO INTERNAL DEMANDS

General Description of College Students

In 1992, enrollment at higher education institutions was 653,162. Among those, 46 percent were female. When students in the first three years of the five-year junior college programs were subtracted, the figure of higher education enrollment drops to 540,454. As previously stated, degree programs are offered only in the four-year colleges and universities. If only such programs are considered, the number of college students in 1992 was 304,359, of which 10.3 percent were graduate students (Ministry of Education, 1993a:21).

Student Movements

College students in Taiwan were widely considered tame compared with their counterparts in Japanese, Korean, and Western universities. Prior to 1986, when Taiwan was still under martial law, there had been virtually no student movements. Student newspapers were controlled by the university administration through severe censorship. Intercampus student organizations were not allowed to form. In the early 1980s student activists appeared mainly at the National Taiwan University. They struggled to establish a student government by direct vote of all the students and to abolish censorship of student publications (Dent, 1993:9–12). Neither goal was achieved at that time.

Campus movements pursuing liberalization have become widespread since 1986. In addition to the National Taiwan University, student activists at other universities also urged freedom of expression and strongly challenged the censorship. Many of them were warned or even punished by the university administration. Protesting the administration's repression, student activists formed "underground groups," organizations without administration approval, on individual campuses. They successfully published "underground newspapers" to motivate the university hierarchy to loosen control on student publications. The fact that students who anonymously attacked university administrative officers and their policies through those newspapers incurred no punishment revealed the inefficiency of the censorship.

In March 1987 members of an underground student group at the National

Taiwan University petitioned the Legislative Yuan to amend the University Act. This was the first time that organized college students requested reforms outside their own campus (ibid.:86–89). Dissident student groups on different campuses further exchanged ideas and experiences through an intercampus network. In July 1987 an intercampus student organization, the Union for Advancing the Reform of the University Act, emerged as soon as martial law was lifted. By holding panel discussions, dispensing flyers, and initiating campus demonstrations, the union urged reformation of the University Act in the following directions: granting universities autonomy, upholding students' civil rights, and abolishing military training (ibid.: 145–47). The union was reorganized seven months later to include other social movement themes as its reform targets.

The student group was the pioneer in initiating the revision of the University Act in the 1980s. It was not until 1989 that professors from different universities tried to exert influence on the legislature to amend the University act.

General Description of Faculty

Status. The social status of college faculty is very high. A large-scale survey of the reputation of forty different occupations revealed that college professors possess the highest reputation (Lin, 1992:65), comparable to that of college presidents, ministers of the central government, or justices. Further linked to previous surveys, the reputation of college faculty has remained high over the past twenty years (ibid.:31)

Gender. In 1992 the total number of full-time faculty members teaching at tertiary institutions was 31,430 (Ministry of Education 1993a:9). Among them 32 percent were female. The proportion of female teachers at primary and secondary levels in the same year were 61 percent and 53 percent, respectively (Ministry of Education 1993b:34).

Rank. There have been four ranks for college faculty: teaching assistant, instructor, associate professor, and professor. In 1992, 15 percent of the tertiary faculty were professors, 27 percent associate professors, 39 percent instructors, and 18 percent teaching assistants (Ministry of Education, 1993a:103, 106). In the newly revised University Act, a new rank, assistant professor, is being added while the rank of teaching assistant is being cancelled. A brand-new Ph.D., if appointed by the university based on the new act, will be given the rank of assistant professor rather than associate professor as before. In other words, he or she will be formally evaluated twice before reaching the highest rank. According to the Ministry of Education, such a change would raise the productivity of junior faculty.

Faculty Struggle for Autonomy in Presidential Selection

As previously stated, public universities have been under the direct control of the Ministry of Education. It is the minister who has the power to select and appoint the president of a public university, with the consent of the premier. Even in the private sector the appointment of a president, which is supposed to be a legal right of the board of trustees, has to have the approval of the minister. As a result, most of Taiwan's college presidents are closely connected with the ruling party; many of them were former government officials (University Reform Union, 1993:77–84). Since a president has the legitimate power to appoint the dean of academic affairs, the dean of student affairs, the dean of general affairs, college deans, and department chairpersons, government control of the presidency usually results in politicization on campus.

As the political climate changed, especially after martial law was lifted in 1987, more and more academics have joined the struggle for more academic freedom and institutional autonomy. The so-called government-appointed presidents were cited as complements in government intervention, and thus became a target of campus reform.

To cope with the changing society, the government was forced to amend the University Act. In the government's version of the draft amendment to the act it was suggested that the government seek advice formally before appointing a college president, which was too small a reform step. A more radical article in another draft amendment proposed by lawmakers suggested that the presidents be elected by all members of the university council. Deliberation on these two draft amendments in the Legislative Yuan began in early 1989. After ardent debate during the first reading, which was completed in June 1992, the article was substantially revised.

According to the revised article, presidents of public universities would be appointed by the Ministry of Education through a two-stage search process. The first-stage presidential search committee, formed by the university, would choose two or three candidates for the university president. The second-stage committee, formed by the Ministry of Education, would select one from the list as the president.

In reaction to the many years of government repression, faculty members at two prestigious universities (National Taiwan University and National Taiwan Normal University) announced in the fall of 1992 that they would not accept any "government-appointed presidents" and planned to search for new presidents based on the article that had just passed its first reading. On the other hand, the minister of education openly expressed his opposition to the article, and sought to revise it during the second reading. At the same time he asserted that until the amendment was finally passed by the Legislative Yuan, he still had the power to choose university presidents (Chen, 1994:133).

The antagonism between the two sides was obvious and it appeared that neither side would yield. Both academics and the public were waiting to see the final result. Perhaps by chance, the minister of education was assigned to another post in a cabinet reshuffle. The new minister of education later announced that he would respect institutional autonomy in deciding on presidential candidates and would select the new president from the list of candidates submitted by the two universities (ibid.:2).

It was clear that the two universities had finally won the battle. The candidate screened by the National Taiwan University presidential search committee and selected by the university council by the highest vote was finally appointed as the new president of the university in mid-1993. The same situation occurred at NTNU shortly after.

The third reading of the University Act was completed at the end of 1993 and the article regarding presidential selection remained unchanged from the first reading. Besides the new act being promulgated in January 1994, colleges and universities in Taiwan will have to ponder how to search for and select a suitable candidate instead of fighting with the so-called government-appointed presidents. This leads to a new challenge for all the universities.

FUTURE DEVELOPMENTS

Along with the political reform beginning in 1986, Taiwan's higher education system has been gradually transformed. The promulgation of the newly revised University Act in early 1994 was further laid a legal foundation for decentralization and depoliticization. However, one can hardly expect any fundamental change in the higher education system in the foreseeable future. The conservative attitude of the government is a lingering obstacle to change. Certain articles of the proposed Enforcement Rules of the University Act have revealed that the Ministry of Education intends to hold its influence and stifle autonomy. The traditional academic climate is another obstacle. Institutions of higher learning are accustomed to following the government; most will continue to be so inclined.

In general, government control over four-year college education will be loosened to a limited extent. Universities will play a decisive role in choosing their presidents. Students will have more say in their education. There will be no more nationwide departmental required courses. General required courses might exist for a period of time, but in more flexible forms. Public institutions will be less financially dependent on the government, although reluctantly.

Some aspects of higher education will still be under the government's control. For example, the establishment of new instructions or departments will have to be approved by the Ministry of Education. Neither the enrollment for each department nor tuition rates are expected to be determined solely by the institutions.

Another trend that may shape the future development of higher education is financial retrenchment. The proportion of public funds allocated to higher education is bound to shrink. All the institutions need to cope with the new situation.

REFERENCES

Chang, Pi-chi. 1993. "The Role and Function of Education in the Six-Year National Development Plan." In Adult Education Center, ed., *Cultural Change and Edu-*

cational Development. National Chung Cheng University, Chayi: Adult Education Center, National Chung Cheng University.

Chen, Shun-fen. 1991. "Taiwan." In P. G. Altbach, ed., *International Higher Education: An Encyclopedia*. Vol. 1. New York: Garland.

———. 1994. *Selection of the College President* (in Chinese). Taipei: Lucky Books.

College Entrance Examination Center, ROC. 1992. *A Diversified System of College Admissions: A Proposal for Reforming College Admissions* (in Chinese). Unpublished monograph.

Deng, Pi-yuing. 1993. *Taiwan's Student Movement in the 1980s* (in Chinese). Taipei: Frontier.

Department of Higher Education, Ministry of Education. 1993. *Policy of the Ministry of Education Regarding Medium-Range Development of Private Institutions* (in Chinese). Taipei: Department of Higher Education, Ministry of Education.

Hwang, Kwang-Kuo. 1994. "In Search of the Primacy of Knowledge: On the Direction of Local Identity of the Social Sciences." In Oscar Jiaw Ouyang and Jenq-jye Hwang, eds., *The Idea of College Education* (in Chinese). Taipei: Lucky Books.

Lao, Wen-chi. 1994. "Retrospect on the Development of Taiwan's Higher Education in the Past Forty Years." In Oscar Jiaw Ouyang and Jenq-jye Hwang, eds., *The Idea of College Education* (in Chinese). Taipei: Lucky Books.

Lin, Ching-chung. 1992. "A 3rd Survey on the Occupation Reputation and Professional Image of Teachers in ROC." In Chinese Comparative Education Association, ed., *A Comparison of Education on Both Sides of the Strait* (in Chinese). Taipei: Lucky Books.

Liu, Hsing-yi. 1993. "The Reason for Lecturing in *Hokkien* in My Class." In Yen-sheng Chang, ed., *Creating Taiwan's New Culture*. Taipei: Frontier.

Ministry of Education. 1993a. *Education Statistics of the Republic of China*.

———. 1993b. *Education Statistical Indicators*. Republic of China.

Newsletter of Higher Education. 1994. No. 35.

University Reform Union, ed. 1993. *A White Paper on Taiwan's Higher Education* (in Chinese). Taipei: China Times.

Wu, Wen-hsing, Shun-fen Chen, and Chen-tsou Wu. 1989. "The Development of Higher Education in Taiwan." *Higher Education, 18*, 117–36.

Young, Yi-rong. 1990. "Development through Education: Myth or Reality?" *International Journal of Educational Development, 10* (2/3), 227–30.

Young, Yi-rong. 1994. *Education and National Development: Experience of Taiwan* (in Chinese). Taipei: Laureate.

20

VIETNAM

Dang Ba Lam

Vietnam is located on the eastern side of the Indo-China peninsula. The South China Sea runs the length of the eastern side of the country.

According to scholars, the first Vietnamese state was that of the "Hung" kings, established around 2000 B.C. This was followed late in the third century B.C. by the state of Au Lac, established by King An Duong. Then, in 179 B.C., Zhao Tou occupied Au Lac. He was king of Nan Yue, a southern state of China.

Vietnam then found itself under Chinese domination for eleven centuries. However, the Vietnamese endeavored throughout this time to maintain their own culture, language, and habits. They were to rise up many times to attempt to regain their political independence; in A.D. 938 Ngo Quyen succeeded in bringing the one-thousand-year period of Chinese control to an end.

This independence was to last ten centuries, with accompanying cultural and economic development. Buddhism greatly influenced the culture. However, Confucianism also developed and gradually became the orthodox ideological system.

In the middle of the nineteenth century, Western nations already occupied numerous Asian states. In 1857, the French army launched attacks on Vietnam and by 1887 the whole of Vietnamese territory was under French domination. From this point on, France attempted to impose its Western culture through education and religion.

Following the Second World War and the surrender of the Japanese forces in Asia, the Vietnamese people rose up successfully in the 1945 August Revolution. On September 2, 1945, the establishment of the Democratic Republic of Vietnam was proclaimed. However, the French colonists immediately staged a comeback to Vietnam, obliging the Vietnamese people to wage a further war of resistance to once again gain their independence.

The Dien Bien Phu military defeat for France in 1954 led to a French withdrawal from the north of Vietnam. A Geneva Agreement divided Vietnam into two zones, with the Democratic Republic in the north and a U.S.-backed administration in the south, in Saigon. A further war of resistance against U.S. military forces in particular was to last another twenty years.

The reunification of Vietnam, with Hanoi as the capital, came after April 30, 1975, the day of the collapse of the Saigon administration. Eleven years later, in 1986, the Vietnamese leadership decided to regenerate its socioeconomic management and introduce a multisector economy, with an innovative planning process and effective exploitation of the levers of the economy. The year 1990 was considered the year when the economy moved into a new stage of development, and a strategy for socioeconomic development for 1991–2000 was adopted.

After reunification in 1975, Vietnam first pursued development as a planned economy. In 1987, Vietnam began to transfer to a market economy approach with a socialist orientation. The aim, as stated in the "Strategy for Socio-Economic Stabilization and Development to the Year 2000," is "to continue with the abolition of a system based on bureaucratic centralism and state subsidies, to establish harmoniously and conduct efficiently the state-controlled market system."

In place of detailed planning targets and controls, production decisions for state enterprises are being developed with the requirement that those enterprises be profitable in the open market. The private sector and foreign investment are being actively encouraged. The new economic policy seeks to mobilize the potential of all sectors of the economy. Emerging from these changes is the realization that Vietnam needs an educated and trained workforce, capable of handling modern technology.

According to the 1989 census sample results, 74.2 percent of the population aged 13 years and above was economically active; the estimated labor force was 28.7 million. Scientific and technical personnel numbered 3.4 million, or 12 percent of the workforce. In 1990, the state sector employed 12.8 percent of the total workforce; however, this represented 86 percent of the professionally trained labor force. The nonstate sector accounted for 86.5 percent of the total labor force, while employing only 2 percent of professionally trained labor. Professionally trained people mostly work in industry, construction, and services. Agriculture, forestry, and fisheries, engaging over 70 percent of the national labor force, employed only 7 percent of those with professional training.

Vietnam has fifty-four ethnic groups. The largest proportion of the population belongs to the "Kinh" group (87.1 percent). After the Kinh, the largest ethnic groups are Tay, Thai, Hoa, Khmer, and Muong. They range in size from 1.4 percent to 1.8 percent of the population. The Socialist Republic of Vietnam is a state made up of all the groups living in Vietnam. Vietnamese people have the right to speak and write in their own languages, continuing and developing cultural traditions and habits.

The Vietnamese political system is comprised of the following organizations:

- The Communist Party of Vietnam, which is the ruling party governing the country.

- The National Assembly at a nationwide level and the People's Committees at the provincial and district levels, being the highest bodies of state and local power, respectively. Members are elected universally and equally by ballot.

- The National Front, which is a mass organization bringing together all citizens. Its tasks are to provide national unity; to participate in establishing and consolidating the people's power; to care for the people's welfare; to help people observe the Constitution and its laws; and to control the activities of state bodies.

- The Vietnamese Labour Union, which is a sociopolitical organization for working people. It also cares for people's welfare, participates in government and social management, and supervises and controls the activities of state bodies and enterprises.

- Other organizations such as the Women's Association and the Youth Communist Union.

In Vietnam, women and men have equal status, with women contributing enormously to political, economic, social, and cultural activities. Among academic staff, female teaching staff represent 71 percent in primary education, 45 percent in secondary education, and 32 percent in higher education.

At present, the Vietnamese government is implementing a policy of openness, cooperating with countries both within the Southeast Asia region and worldwide. Vietnam is located in the Pacific Zone, which is expected to be a hub of dynamic development in the twenty-first century. Many newly industrializing countries (NICs) of the region have been investing in Vietnam, creating favorable conditions for further socioeconomic development.

It is in these circumstances that the system of higher education in Vietnam must be reconstructed to respond to the changing demands of society and to overcome its own weaknesses.

PROFILE OF THE HIGHER EDUCATION SYSTEM

Higher education in Vietnam began with the building of Quoc Tu Giam in 1076—the first Royal College in Vietnam—at the time of King Ly. The Vietnamese feudal education system was greatly influenced by Chinese feudal education for ten centuries.

The Vietnamese feudal education system included public and private schools, with private schools contributing much to the dissemination of knowledge. There were three course areas: Buddhist studies, military studies, and Confucianism and literature.

The number of students learning Confucianism and literature was the largest. The learning materials were the classical texts on Confucianism. The learning methods were mainly scholastic and dogmatic, with the materials and exercises in Chinese. Vietnamese could be used for lectures. A consequence of this teaching-learning method was that the students often did not formulate an independent approach to thinking.

In 1919, the Imperial Court, on orders from the French, announced the abolition of Vietnamese feudal education. The French style of education was then introduced more fully. A number of universities and colleges were established in Indochina to train colonial administrators and professionals. By 1945, all such institutions had been located in Hanoi.

Between 1900 and 1924, the institutions called universities or colleges in Hanoi were in fact often specialized professional schools, sometimes only at a secondary level. In particular, there was a School of Medicine and Pharmacy, the Indochina Veterinary School, a School of Law and Administration, a Teacher Training College, a School of Agriculture, and a School of Trade.

In the 1924–25 academic year, France implemented educational reform that changed the status of such establishments into real colleges. This included increasing enrollment requirements, lengthening the duration of courses, and making curriculum improvements. Between 1939 and 1945, France established the Indochinese University, based on various colleges of Hanoi. At that time, the status of all colleges in Indochina was considered to be that of modern higher education. However, the colleges were small. The maximum number of students in the Indochinese University was 1,000, of which the School of Medicine and Pharmacy had the largest number with 300 to 350 students.

Following the August 1945 Revolution, the Democratic Republic of Vietnam carried out educational reform on the basis of nationalization, scientific principles, and popularization. Two immediate tasks were identified: to substitute Vietnamese teachers for the French teachers and to encourage and expand the use of Vietnamese as the medium of instruction in higher education.

In 1946, when France launched war on the Democratic Republic of Vietnam, the colleges were evacuated from Hanoi into the rural areas and the mountains. Some colleges had to stop teaching and, by 1949, only the Medical College, the Engineering College, and the College of Art were operating. However, from 1951 to 1954, the College of Science, a Teacher Training College, and tertiary-level preparatory courses were also established.

The curriculum was designed according to the needs of a state at war. Training courses focused mainly on medicine, agriculture, weapons, and diplomacy. Instructional methods combined practice with theory in the active war setting. The Dien Bien Phu military defeat of the French then brought peace in 1954, but Vietnam was divided into two zones.

From 1956 to 1975, a higher education system was built up in North Vietnam, including universities, polytechnic colleges, and various other specialized colleges. In 1975, in North Vietnam, there were 30 higher education institutions with 8,400 teachers and 56,000 students. In South Vietnam, there were 7 public universities and 7 private universities and colleges, with 166,000 students. Reunification of the North and South in 1975 saw the establishment of one socialist higher education system in the country. All universities and colleges were re-organized into the public sector while private colleges were abolished.

Influenced by the example of the Soviet Union and other socialist countries, Vietnam established polytechnic institutes teaching industrial, construction, and transportation courses. Courses related to heavy industry actually dominated in these institutes, leading to an eventual separation into a civil engineering college and a college of communication and transport. Universities were developed according to the same socialist example, concentrating on fundamental natural and social science.

Today, the country has 102 universities, colleges/junior colleges, and institutes. These are sometimes multidisciplinary, but more often are specialized. The figures are as follows: multidisciplinary (9); industrial engineering (13); agro-forestry-fishery (6); economics (6); medical and sports (8); art colleges (7); teacher training institutions (47), including national teacher training colleges (9), national junior teacher training colleges (8), and provincial teacher training colleges (30); and other colleges (6). Annually, 125,000 students in the various specializations necessary for the country's socioeconomic development are trained in the universities and colleges. The position of higher education within Vietnam's comprehensive education system can be seen in figure 20.1.

Vietnamese is the only language of instruction in the universities and colleges. This leads to modernization of the Vietnamese language with the constant addition of new technical terms. However, graduates of the universities and colleges may not be strong in foreign languages, restricting international communication.

THE CHANGING FUNCTIONS AND PATTERNS OF HIGHER EDUCATION

In Vietnam, responsibility for the higher education system lies with the following bodies and groups. The Ministry of Education and Training is responsible for policy making, guidance, and supervision in connection with all the education programs and the administration of the higher education institutions. Some provinces administer junior colleges to meet particular needs.

Funding of the higher education system is the responsibility of the central and provincial levels of government, although the central government provides most of the funds for salaries, scholarships, and other expenditures (e.g., maintenance and repair of buildings, furniture and equipment, teaching materials and books). Thirty-nine higher education institutions are responsible to the Ministry of Education and Training. The remainder are responsible to other Ministries, such as Health, Culture, Finance, and Law.

Within the Ministry of Education and Training, five departments are directly higher education linked: Higher Education; Postgraduate Education; Continuing Education; Teacher Education; and Political Education.

Rectors of universities or colleges are nominated by the minister of the Min-

Figure 20.1
The National Education System of Vietnam

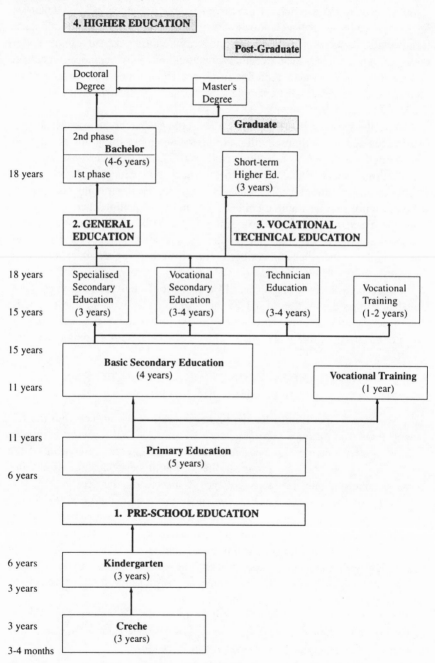

istry to which a particular university or college is responsible. The number of vice rectors depends on the size of the institution. Faculties are organized into disciplinary groups and subject units. The institutions also have consultative committees, such as the Rector's Consultative Committee, which includes deans, division chiefs, and some prestigious teachers, or a Dean's Consultative Committee, which would include subject heads and also some prestigious teachers.

A system of laws, statutes, and regulations has been developed over the past few years to consolidate the legal basis for the management of institutions. This task has not yet been completed, and indeed has lagged behind the drive for "renovation." This is especially the case regarding the field of management relations between the central government (the various ministries) and the institutions themselves, not least in the area of regulations for the self-government of institutions.

The regulations that have been developed currently provide that the Ministry of Education and Training will fund institutions through fixed expenses, to include salaries and scholarships. Regarding personnel, the Ministry of Education and Training determines the staffing of institutions, controlling salary levels and the employment of teachers. With regard to course organization, the Ministry of Education and Training approves new courses and the education programs, develops the examination statutes, and confers degrees.

In addition, the Commission for Education, Culture, and Children's Affairs of the National Assembly and the Commission for Science and Education of the Party Central Committee are also responsible for policy making in higher education. The institution that assists the Ministry of Education and Training in researching strategy, policy, and the master plan and management of the development of higher education is the National Institute for Educational Development.

Higher education qualification programs range from 3 years (associate bachelor) to 8 years (doctorate) of required training (see figure 20.1). Long higher education programs are offered in most institutions: medical and dental sciences (6 years); industrial engineering (5 years); and 4 years for most other degree level qualifications. In general, most programs consist of 1.5 to 2 years of general education, followed by specialization.

Short diploma programs are also offered in junior colleges, with a duration of about three years. Most higher education is government-sponsored, but private education is now encouraged and a few such programs can be found.

Short-term training in higher education is aimed at covering the need for a large workforce with the advanced scientific, technical, and professional knowledge required chiefly by localities. Many courses have been jointly opened by the needy work units and local colleges on a contract basis. Some short-term courses have been opened especially for ethnic minorities living in highland and remote areas, as well as on offshore islands.

In-service training and correspondence courses are offered in the universities and colleges. Such courses were established in 1960 and are funded both by the government and the learner's own organization. Provincial in-service training centers were set up to facilitate the provision of university and college in-service training courses at different localities. Currently, there are thirty-one provincial training centers, of which twenty-two are independent and nine are attached to a related university or college located in the province.

In the past thirty years, this "in-service training" provision has contributed greatly to the improvement of the qualifications of working people, thus helping meet the requirements for socioeconomic development. From 1960 to 1990, 140,000 people graduated from universities and colleges by this method, constituting 11 percent of the total number of graduates nationally.

In 1993, two open universities were set up: one in Hanoi and one in Ho Chi Minh City. These two universities will act as coordinators for the turning of the local in-service training centers into an open training network, using the mass media for educational purposes. Eleven other higher education institutions also run distance education courses.

Most institutions operate two semesters of fifteen teaching weeks, with two weeks of examinations in each academic year (an academic year runs from September to June). Since 1988–89, many universities have adopted a credit point system, allowing students greater choice of subjects in approved combinations. In 1991, forty-three out of sixty universities had adopted the two-phase degree program: phase I consists of two years of foundation knowledge and techniques; phase II covers two years of specialized knowledge and techniques. Most degree courses are of four years' duration, with medical and dental science lasting six years and industrial engineering five years. Teaching depends heavily on lectures. With nearly thirty formal contact periods scheduled weekly, little time is available for independent study.

Training at the master's level is undertaken as per the decision of the Council of Ministers, issued on March 9, 1991. Such students are trained for two years in the full-time format or for three years in the in-service format.

Since 1987, higher education has been seeking its "renewal," with a wish to develop a flexible higher education system appropriate to the policy of openness in the economy.

Following this open policy of the Vietnamese government, higher education authorities have, step by step, been expanding international cooperation through the participation of education officials, researchers, and teachers in international workshops, study tours, and training. Vietnam has also invited numerous international organizations like the UN, UNESCO, and UNDP to assist and participate in the implementation of educational development projects in Vietnam.

International cooperation and experience exchanges have contributed to improved curricula for some courses, making them appropriate for market economy conditions. Vietnam has especially expanded its cooperation within the Southeast Asia region: rejoining SEAMEO; helping the Asian Institute of Technology set up an AIT center in Hanoi; and sending students for training in Southeast Asian countries.

Vietnamese higher education has always attempted to combine theory with practice and to integrate instruction with research and production. Before 1990, universities and colleges had the major task of training cadres for the country's socioeconomic development. The activity of scientific research was only one part of the teaching-learning process. Since 1990, the scientific research activities in universities and colleges have been clearly identified and defined as part of the national scientific research system. The results of many scientific research projects carried out by universities and colleges have been used in practice, and have contributed greatly to socioeconomic development.

In 1989, the Ministry of Education and Training allowed universities and colleges to establish scientific research-production units. By 1990, there were 111 units of scientific research and social service. Thirteen units belong to the Ministry of Education and Training, with a further 98 units belonging to 23 universities and colleges.

To improve the relevance of education and training to the needs of social and economic development, Vietnam has now begun to review its higher education system, curricula, and courses. A variety of institution types now exist, including public, semiprivate, and private institutions. They offer long and short, full-time and part-time courses, distance learning, contract, and in-service courses.

To overcome the weaknesses in the system and to respond to the demands of a changing society, Vietnam has embraced new concepts and introduced a number of measures to develop the higher education system. This can be demonstrated in table 20.1.

Innovation measures have already brought some improvements to higher education.

The number of new full-time enrollments increased from 22,786 in 1990–91 to 27,551 in 1992–93 (state budget provided for 15,855 students), and subsequently to 38,930 in 1994–95 (state budget provided for 17,440).

The modes of delivery have been diversified. In 1991–92, the number of in-service students reached 38,000; in the following year, 52,960. Thirty thousand students participated in various short-term programs.

The first step in reconstruction of the higher education network has already taken place. In 1993, the government decided to combine three major Hanoi universities into one national-level multidisciplinary institution. Further multidisciplinary universities were established in Ho Chi Minh City, Thainguyen, and Hue through amalgamation of a number of specialized universities and colleges.

The research and development activities of universities and colleges are becoming more active. The MOET is now implementing 3 national research programs, 80 national projects, and 640 ministerial-level projects. Funding for R&D in the state budget accounted for VND 11.5 billion; R&D activities funded by contracts reached VND 100 billion.

International relations for Vietnamese higher education have also expanded. Presently, there is registered contact with 19 countries, 10 international organizations, 34 NGOs, and 60 universities and colleges. Vietnamese and foreign

Table 20.1
Concepts and Measures Introduced into Vietnam's Higher Education System

In the past	At present
* Objectives of higher education:	
- Training of scientific and technical manpower for state organizations and enterprises.	- Training of specialists for all sectors of the national economy and social activities. - To meet the needs of the people in knowledge and culture.
* Planning and management of higher education:	
- Centralised planning of admissions and training.	Decentralised planning at provincial and sector level with central co-ordination. - Training according to contracts. - To meet students' individual requests.
- Almost all education activities funded by state central budget.	- Funding provided by state central budget, provincial and sectorial budgets. - By contracts with employers. - By tuition fees. - By R & D and service activities of universities and colleges.
- Distribution of jobs - employment after graduation.	- By planning. - By contracts. - Employment arrangements by students themselves.
* Organisation of teaching - learning process:	
- Admission of students by only one national examination; all students admitted would have a Government financial "fellowships"; and almost all would graduate as per planned. - Narrow specialisation from the beginning. - Single curriculum. - No possibility of individual learning programme.	- Universities and colleges organise their entrance examinations with different dates, 1/3 of admitted students will have "fellowships"; selection and competition during the learning process. - Wide profile of training; 2 cycles of undergraduate training. - Modular programme with credit system. - Acceptance of individual learning programme.
* Organisation of R & D and social service activities:	
- By state planning, with state funding. - Voluntary non-profit activities.	- By state planning & funding. - By contracts. - Social service, non-profit. - By contract. - Contribution to universities & colleges budget, supplementary salaries for staff.
* Institutional administration:	
- Passive participation of staff members and students in the decision making and administration activities.	- Larger and more active participation. - Promotion of leading cadres in universities and colleges based on vote by staff members and with participation of students.

higher education institutions are implementing 21 projects jointly, at a funding level of U.S.$25 million.

RESPONSES TO INTERNAL DEMANDS

The current development of the country now requires three things of higher education: that it raise the people's intellectual level; that it train talented people; and that it meet the changing demand for manpower. Increasing the number of students is therefore one of the main thrusts of the strategic direction of higher education.

In general, enrollment over the past decade of all types of higher education students remained relatively stable. Enrollment did fall between 1980 and 1985 from 120,800 to 85,700 students. However, it had recovered to 126,000 by 1989, and indeed has continued to increase further over the past two years. There are presently around 20 students per 10,000 inhabitants, representing approximately 3 percent of the total population in the eighteen- to twenty-four-year-old age group.

University graduates represent only 1.5 percent of the total population: 2.1 percent of the males, 1.1 percent of the females, 4.5 percent of the urban population, and 0.7 percent of the rural population. Ethnic minority students represent 8.7 percent of higher education students. However, even at these low rates, absorption of graduates by the labor market is becoming problematic.

Formerly, university and college graduates were placed in employment positions by the government. Now they must find jobs themselves in all the economic sectors. The transition to a market economy has created new demands for employees with new specializations. Vietnam has seen increased demand for specialists in the following areas: construction; business management; marketing; foreign trade; law; information technology and computing; and the English language.

This situation has influenced the professional orientation of students. For example, in 1987, 21.6 percent of students were registered in teacher training colleges, 17.2 percent in the economics universities, 15 percent in universities of agriculture, forestry, and fishery, and 8 percent in the civil engineering universities. In 1992, the figures had risen to 24.2 percent in the economics universities and 14.7 percent in the civil engineering universities, while the figures had fallen to 11.1 percent for the teacher training colleges and 6.8 percent for agriculture, forestry, and fishery universities. This has been the result of natural regulation of the job market. Administrators and educational research agencies have been studying this to help organize and assist learners' admissions into the various universities and colleges.

As well as education at home, the Vietnamese government has often sent students abroad to study. In the 1951–54 period, 593 students went abroad. Then, from 1955 to 1975, 30,775 people went abroad to study. Such study outside Vietnam has been in the former countries of the Soviet Union, the

German Democratic Republic, and Czechoslovakia, and China, Hungary, Bulgaria, Poland, and Cuba. Fifty-five percent of such students were trained in the former Soviet Union. In recent years, many teachers, researchers, specialists, and students have been sent to Australia, Belgium, Britain, France, India, Japan, and the United States. The AIT in Bangkok has been a place of benefit for many too.

Vietnam has also trained students from other countries in a variety of subjects, including the Vietnamese language. In particular, students from Laos and Cambodia have attended Vietnam's institutions.

The Vietnamese government has always paid attention to the training and upgrading of its higher education teaching staff. By 1993, Vietnamese higher education had 20,456 teachers, with 31.3 percent being female, 3 percent being from ethnic minorities, and 45 percent being over the age of 40. Of those staff, 12 percent are doctors and 5 percent are associate professors or professors. The salaries of teachers (and other education staff) are very low, and are not keeping pace with increases in the cost of living. A serious consequence of low salaries is that many teachers often seek income from work outside their normal jobs. This results in a reduction of the quality of their work, their dedication to it, and the time they have available for the extra assistance that many students need outside normal university hours. Available 1991 data indicate that approximately 67 percent of teachers work overtime, with 50 percent involved in jobs that do not relate to their profession.

There are many difficulties attached to the professional development of higher education teachers. Vietnam has no institution that specializes in upgrading the teachers of universities and colleges. It can be considered that scientific research in universities and colleges, in connection with one's subject, is a form of development for staff. However, it has not really been paid adequate attention, with only 6 percent of the country's research budget allocated for such work. In past years though, approximately 30 percent of higher education teachers did experience some form of formal upgrading training.

FUTURE DEVELOPMENTS

In 1993, the Vietnamese government decided to continue with a policy of "renovation" of education and training. The Party Central Committee has decided that by the year 2005, the higher education system has to overcome the following weaknesses: general low quality and efficiency; weak teaching; irrationality in the structure of the higher education system and its management; and poor equipment levels.

The trends for higher education in Vietnam over the next decade are likely to be as follows:

1. Improvement of the higher education structure with an expansion in student numbers; modernization of the curriculum and teaching methods; and a strengthening of the

linkage between research and industry. Educational quality will be differentiated with the establishment of institutions to educate students in small numbers to high-quality levels and institutions to educate large numbers of students to meet the demands and requirements of the nation's socioeconomic development.

2. Reform of the objectives, curriculum, and methods for education and training, with a strengthening of the linkages between education and training and the nation's socio-economic development. Such a reform will take account of developments within education and training worldwide.

3. Upgrading and strengthening of teaching staff, through new approaches to appointments, transfers, promotion, and remuneration. This is to be assisted by the development of new education laws and regulations, especially reviewing the relationship between the central and institutional levels for the organization and management of higher education.

4. Provision of continuing education options, which will allow all people to learn by an appropriate method to the level of their ability.

REFERENCES

Constitution of the Vietnam Socialist Republic. 1992.

Dang Ba Lam. 1994. *Development Papers, No. 16.* Bangkok: UNESCAP.

Le Van Giang. 1985. *History of Vietnam Higher Education and Vocational Training.* Hanoi: National Institute for Higher Education and Vocational Training.

National Project: Education Sector Review and Human Resources Sector Analysis Final Report. 1992. Hanoi.

Nguyen Khac Vien. 1993. *A Long History.* Hanoi: Gioi.

State Planning Committee. 1990. Report on Vietnam Economy.

Vietnam Population Census of 1989. Samples Results. 1992. Hanoi.

SELECTED
BIBLIOGRAPHY

Agarwal, B. L. 1985. "Nexus between Jobs and Degrees." In J. V. Raghavan, ed., *Higher Education in the Eighties*. New Delhi: Lancer International.

Ahmad, Ibrahim. 1972. "Higher Education in Malaysia." *Bulletin of the UNESCO Regional Office for Education in Asia, 7* (1), 99–113.

Ahmad, M. 1992. "Bangladesh." In B. R. Clark and Guy R. Neave, eds., *The Encyclopedia of Higher Education: National Systems of Higher Education*. Vol. 1. Oxford: Pergamon.

Ahmed, G. 1992. "Bangladesh." In W. Wickremasinghe, ed., *Handbook of World Education: A Comparative Guide to Higher Education and Educational Systems of the World*. Houston: American Collegiate Service.

Alailima, Patricia J. 1992. "Education-Employment Linkages: The Macro Profile." *Sri Lanka Journal of Social Sciences, 15*, 1–46.

Aldana, B. 1949. *The Educational System of the Philippines*. Manila: University Publishing.

Algar, Hamid, trans. 1980. *Constitution of the Islamic Republic of Iran*. Berkeley: Mizan.

———. 1981. *Islam and Revolution: Writings and Declarations of Imam Khomeini*. Berkeley: Mizan.

Altbach, Philip G. 1982. *Higher Education in the Third World: Themes and Variations*. Singapore: Maruzen Asia.

———. 1989. "Higher Education and Scientific Development: The Promise of Newly Industrialized Countries." In Philip G. Altbach et al., eds., *Scientific Development and Higher Education: The Case of Newly Industrializing Nations*. New York: Praeger.

———. 1993. "The Dilemma of Change in Indian Higher Education." In Suma Chitnis and Philip G. Altbach, eds., *Higher Education Reform in India: Experience and Perspectives*. New Delhi: Sage.

———. 1997. *The Academic Profession in Higher Education: A Study of Fourteen Countries*. Princeton: The Carnegie Foundation for the Advancement of Teaching.

Altbach, Philip G., and Suma Chitnis, eds. 1993. *Higher Education Reform in India: Experience and Perspectives*. New Delhi: Sage.

Altbach, Philip G., and S. Gopinathan. 1982. "The Dilemma of Success: Higher Education in Advanced Developing Countries." In Philip G. Altbach, ed., *Higher Education in the Third World: Themes and Variations*. Singapore: Maruzen Asia.

Altbach, Philip G., and Viswanathan Selvaratnam. 1989. *From Dependence to Autonomy: The Development of Asian Universities*. Amsterdam: Kluwer Academic.

Amano, Ikuo. 1986. "Educational Crisis in Japan." In William K. Cummings et al., eds., *Educational Policies in Crisis*. New York: Praeger.

———. 1989. "The Dilemma of Japanese Education Today." In James J. Shields Jr., ed., *Japanese Schooling—Patterns of Socialization, Equality, and Political Control*. University Park: Pennsylvania State University Press.

Amarshi, Azeem, Kenneth Good, and Rex Mortimer. 1979. *Development and Dependency: The Political Economy of Papua New Guinea*. Melbourne: Oxford University Press.

American Council on Education. 1976. *An Analysis of U.S.-Iranian Cooperation in Higher Education*. Washington, D.C.: Overseas Liaison Committee.

Anderson, C. Arnold, and M. Bowman, eds. 1963. *Education and Economic Development*. Chicago: Aldine.

Arasteh, Reza. 1962. *Education and Social Awakening in Iran*. Leiden: E. J. Brill.

———. 1963. "The Growth of Higher Institutions in Iran." *International Review of Education, 7,* 327–34.

Arcelo, A., and R. C. Sanyal. 1983. *Employment and Higher Education in the Philippines* (HELMS II Report). Manila: Ministry of Education, Culture and Sports; Fund for Assistance to Private Education; International Institute of Educational Planning.

Asher, M. G. 1984. *Financing the Development of Higher Education in Singapore*. Singapore: Regional Institute of Higher Education and Development.

Asian Development Bank. 1989a. *Lao People's Democratic Republic Education Sector Study*. Vol. 4: *Teachers and Their Training*. Manila, Philippines: Author.

———. 1989b. *Lao People's Democratic Republic Education Sector Study*. Vol. 5: *Technical, Vocational, and Higher Education*. Manila, Philippines: Author.

———. 1992. *Lao People's Democratic Republic*. Education and Development in Asia and the Pacific Series. Vol. 1. Manila, Philippines: Author.

Association of Commonwealth Universities. 1993. *Commonwealth Universities Yearbook*. 69th ed. Vol. 2. London: Author.

Association of Indian Universities. 1992. *Universities Handbook*. 25th ed. New Delhi: Author.

Ayman, Iraj. 1974. *Educational Innovation in Iran*. Paris: UNESCO.

Bacchus, M. K. 1980. *Education for Development or Underdevelopment?* Ontario: Wilfrid Laurier University Press.

———. 1981. "Education for Development in Underdeveloped Countries." *Comparative Education, 17* (2), 215–27.

Barani, Amin. 1961. *The Modernization of Iran, 1921–41*. Palo Alto, Calif.: Stanford University Press.

Barron, P., and A. Paul. 1977. *Peace with Horror*. London: Hodder & Stoughton.

Bastianpillai, B. 1983. "The Job-Oriented Courses in the Universities of Sri Lanka." In *University Education and Graduate Employment in Sri Lanka*. Colombo: The Marga Institute.

Bazaco, Evergisto. 1953. *History of Education in the Philippines*. Manila: University of Santo Tomas.

Becker, E. 1986. *When the War Was Over: Cambodia's Revolution and the Voices of Its People*. New York: Simon and Schuster.

Becker, G. 1964. *Human Capital*. New York: Columbia University Press.

Beheshti, H. S. N.d. *System of Education in the Islamic Republic of Iran*. Tehran: Ministry of Culture and Higher Education.

Bilodeau, C. 1955. "Compulsory Education in Cambodia." In C. Bilodeau, S. Pathammavong, and Q. H. Lê, eds., *Compulsory Education in Cambodia, Laos and Viet-Nam*. Paris: UNESCO.

Blaug, M., ed. 1969. *Economics of Education*. Vol. 2. Harmondsworth: Penguin.

Blaug, M., et al. 1969. *The Causes of Graduate Unemployment in India*. London: Penguin.

————. 1970. *An Introduction to the Economics of Education*. Harmondsworth: Penguin.

Borzeix, Jacques. 1991. "A French University in the South Pacific." In David R. Jones, V. Lynn Meek, and John Weeks, eds., *Explorations in Higher Education: A South Pacific Critique*. Melbourne: Centre for the Study of Higher Education, University of Melbourne.

Bourhis, R. Y. 1982. "Language Policies and Language Attitudes: Le monde de la francophonie." In E. B. Ryan and H. Giles, eds., *Attitudes towards Language Variation: Social and Applied Contexts*. London: Edward Arnold.

Bowman, M. H. 1966. "Review of F. Harbison and C. A. Myers, *Education, Manpower, and Economic Growth*." Reprinted in *Economics of Education*, vol. 2, ed. M. Blaug.

Boyer, Ernest, Philip Altbach, and Mary Jean Whitelaw. 1994. *The Academic Profession in International Perspective*. Princeton: The Carnegie Foundation for the Advancement of Teaching.

Bray, Mark. 1993. "Education and the Vestiges of Colonialism: Self-determination, Neocolonialism and Dependency in the South Pacific." *Comparative Education, 29* (3), 333–48.

Bray, Mark, Surengiin Davaa, Seth Spaulding, and John C. Weidman. 1994. "Transition from Socialism and the Financing of Higher Education: The Case of Mongolia." *Higher Education Policy, 7* (4), 36–42.

Bray, Mark, and Steve Packer. 1993. *Education in Small States: Concepts, Challenges and Strategies*. Oxford: Pergamon.

Bunge, Frederica M. 1981. *North Korea: A Country Study*. U.S. Secretary of the Army.

Burgler, R. A. 1990. *The Eyes of the Pineapple: Revolutionary Intellectuals and Terror in Democratic Kampuchea*. Saarbrücken, Germany: Verlag Breitenbach.

Can, Le Thac. 1991. "Higher Education Reform in Vietnam, Laos, and Cambodia." *Comparative Education Review, 35* (1), 170–76.

Carnoy, M. 1974. *Education as Cultural Imperialism*. New York: David Mckay.

Carnoy, Martin, and Henry Levin. 1985. *Schooling and Work in the Democratic State*. Stanford: Stanford University Press.

Center for Applied Linguistics. 1978. *Teaching English to Cambodian Students*. Arlington, Va.: Author.

Chan, H. C. 1989. "The PAP and the Restructuring of the Political System." In Kernial Singh Sandhu and Paul Wheatley, eds., *Management of Success: The Moulding of Modern Singapore*. Singapore: Institute of Southeast Asian Studies.

Chanda, N. 1986. *Brother Enemy: The War after the War.* San Diego: Harcourt Brace Jovanovich.

Chandler, D. P. 1993. *A History of Cambodia.* 2nd ed. Boulder, Colo.: Westview.

Chang, Pi-chi. 1993. "The Role and Function of Education in the Six-Year National Development Plan." In Adult Education Center, National Chung Cheng University, ed., *Cultural Change and Educational Development.* Cha-yi: Adult Education Center, National Chung Cheng University.

Chelliah, D. D. 1947. *A Short History of the Educational Policy of the Straits Settlements.* Kuala Lumpur: Acting Government Printer.

Chen, Shun-fen. 1991. "Taiwan." In P. G. Altbach, ed., *International Higher Education: An Encyclopedia.* Vol. 1. New York: Garland.

———. 1994. *Selection of the College President* (in Chinese). Taipei: Lucky Books.

Cheong Siew Yoong. 1989. "Research and Productivity in the Malaysian University: A Case Study of the Department of Botany, University of Malaya." In Philip G. Altbach et al., eds., *Scientific Development and Higher Education: The Case of Newly Industrialized Nations.* New York: Praeger.

Chitnis, Suma. 1993. "Gearing a Colonial System of Education to Take Independent India Towards Development." In Suma Chitnis and Philip G. Altbach, eds., *Higher Education Reform in India: Experience and Perspectives.* New Delhi: Sage.

Choi, P. K. 1995. "Women and Education in Hong Kong." In V. Pearson and B. K. P. Leung, eds., *Women in Hong Kong.* Hong Kong: Oxford University Press.

Chowdhury, Kowsar P. 1983. "Educational Development in Bangladesh with Special Emphasis on Universalization of Primary Education." Unpublished M.Ed. thesis, Faculty of Graduate Studies and Research, The University of Alberta.

Chua, B. H. 1985. "Pragmatism of the People's Action Party Government in Singapore: A Critical Assessment." *Southeast Asian Journal of Social Science, 13,* 29–46.

Chung, Sung Jin. 1984. *Fostering the Huge Corps of Intellectuals in the Democratic People's Republic of Korea.* Pyongyang: Social Science.

Chung, Young-soo. 1990. "Pukhan ui kyoyuk yinyum" (Education Ideology of North Korea). In Chung Kyu, Hwang, Huh Suk, Chung Young-soo, Lee Sung-ho, and Lee Chung-gak, eds., *Pukhan kyoyuk ui chomyong (Spotlight on North Korean Education).* Seoul: Pommunsa.

Clark, Burton R. 1992. "Comparative Higher Education." In Marvin C. Alkin, ed., *Encyclopedia of Educational Research.* New York: Macmillan.

Clayton, T. 1995. *Education and Language-in-Education in Relation to External Intervention in Cambodia, 1620–1989.* Ann Arbor, Mich.: University Microfilms.

———. In press. *Restriction or Resistance? Educational Development in French Colonial Cambodia.* Educational Policy Analysis Archives.

Colletta, Nat J. 1980. *American Schools for the Natives of Ponape: A Study of Education and Cultural Change in Micronesia.* Hawaii: University Press of Hawaii.

Collins, Randall. 1979. *The Credential Society: An Historical Sociology of Education and Stratification.* New York: Academic.

Committee on the Supply of Lawyers. 1993. *Report on the Legal Profession.* Singapore: Ministry of Law.

Craft, A., ed. 1992. *Quality Assurance in Higher Education.* London: Falmer.

Crocombe, Ron. 1987. *The South Pacific: An Introduction.* 4th ed. Auckland: Longman Paul.

Crocombe, Ron, Tupeni Baba, and Malama Meleisea 1988. "The Development of Higher Education in the Pacific Islands." In Ron Crocombe and Malama Meleisea, eds., *Pacific Universities: Achievements, Problems and Prospects.* Suva: Institute of Pacific Studies, University of the South Pacific.

Crocombe, Ron, and Marjorie Tuainekore Crocombe. 1994. *Post-Secondary Education in the South Pacific: Present Patterns and Future Options.* London: The Commonwealth Secretariat.

Crocombe, Ron, and Malama Meleisea. 1988. "Achievements, Problems and Prospects: The Future of University Education in the South Pacific." In Ron Crocombe and Malama Meleisea, eds., *Pacific Universities: Achievements, Problems and Prospects.* Suva: Institute of Pacific Studies, University of the South Pacific.

Cumings, Bruce. 1990. *The Two Koreas: On the Road to Unification?* Headline Series. New York: The Foreign Policy Association.

Cummings, William K. 1981. "Notes on Higher Education and Indonesian Society." *Prisma: The Indonesian Indicator No. 21.* The Institute for Economic and Social Research, Education and Information, Jakarta, Indonesia.

Cummings, William K., and Salman Kasenda. 1989. "The Origin of Modern Indonesian Higher Education." In P. G. Altbach and V. Selvaratnam, eds., *From Dependence to Autonomy.* Dordrecht, The Netherlands: Kluwer Academic.

Cummins, J. 1986. "Empowering Minority Students: A Framework for Intervention." *Harvard Educational Review, 56,* 18–36.

Curtin, Timothy. 1989. "The Evaluation of Human Capital: A Comment on Recent Literature Relating to Papua New Guinea." *Papua New Guinea Journal of Education, 25* (2), 51–55.

Curtis, G. 1989. *Cambodia: A Country Profile.* Stockholm: Swedish International Development Authority.

Dahal, M. K. 1992. "Population and Development: Issues in Nepalese Perspectives." In B. K. Karki Chhetri, ed., *Population and Development in Nepal.* Central Department of Population Studies.

Dahl, R. A. 1956. *A Preface to Democratic Theory.* Chicago: University of Chicago Press.

Daroesman, I. P., and Ruth Daroesman. 1992. *Degrees of Success: A Tracer Study of Australian Government Sponsored Indonesian Fellowships 1970–1989.* Australian International Development Assistance Bureau and The International Development Program of Australian Universities and Colleges.

Davis, D., and E. Vogel, eds. 1990. *Chinese Society on the Eve of Tiananmen: The Impact of Reform.* Cambridge, Mass.: Harvard University Press.

De Silva, C. R. 1978. "The Politics of University Admissions: A Review of Some Aspects of the Admission Policy in Sri Lanka, 1971–1978." *Sri Lanka Journal of Social Sciences, 1* (2), 88–123.

Delvert, J. 1956. "L'æuvre française d'enseignement au Cambodge." *France-Asie,* 125–27, 309–20.

Deng, Pi-yuing. 1993. *Taiwan's Student Movement in the 1980s* (in Chinese). Taipei: Frontier.

Denison, F. 1967. *Why Growth Rates Differ.* Washington: The Brookings Institution.

Djitæ, P. G. 1993. "Francophonie: Gain d'humanitæ ou perte d'identitæ?" *Language Problems and Language Planning, 17,* 254–64.

Djojonegoro,-Ing Wardiman. 1993. "Human Resources and Education Policy." Paper presented at the Second Economist Conferences' Roundtable with the Government of the Republic of Indonesia, Jakarta, Ministry of Education and Culture, Republic of Indonesia.

Doeriat, Winoto. 1990. *Does Management Education Make a Difference? A Case Study of IPPM 10–Month Management Training Program Graduate's Career Progress Five Years after Graduation.* Unpublished Ph.D. diss., Harvard University.

Dore, R. P. 1976. *The Diploma Disease: Education Qualification and Development.* London: Allen and Unwin.

Dorney, Sean. 1991. *Papua New Guinea.* Sydney: Random House.

Douglas, Norman, and Ngaire Douglas. 1989. *Pacific Islands Yearbook.* 16th ed. Sydney: Angus & Robertson.

Dove, Linda. 1983. "Political Context of Education in Bangladesh 1971–80." In P. Broadfoot et al., eds., *Politics and Change: An International Survey.* London: Croom Helm.

Duvieusart, B., and R. Ughetto. 1973. *République Khmère: Project de Restructuration du système d'éducation.* Paris. UNESCO.

Education in the Islamic Republic of Iran. 1993. Tehran: Ministry of Education.

Ek Sam Ol. 1991. "The Situation of Higher and Technical Education in the State of Cambodia since January 7th 1979." Paper presented at the Cambodian Workshop on Reconstruction and Development, Penang, Malaysia.

Epstein, E. H. 1992. "Editorial." *Comparative Education Review, 36,* 409–16.

Faaland, J., and J. R. Perkinson. 1976. *Bangladesh: The Test Case of Development.* London: C. Hurst.

Falgout, Suzanne, and Paula Levin, eds. 1992. *Socialization and Schooling Research in Pacific Societies.* Special issue of *Anthropology and Education Quarterly 23* (1).

Farmarfarmayan, Hafez. 1968. "The Forces of Modernization in Nineteenth Century Iran: A Historical Survey." In W. R. Polk and R. L. Chambers, eds., *Beginnings of Modernization in the Middle East.* Chicago: Chicago University Press.

Fatimah Hamid Don, Jasbir Sarjit Singh, Mogana Dhamotharan, and Moses Samuel. 1985. *Higher Education and Employment in Malaysia: The Experiences of Graduates.* Kuala Lumpur: Institute of Advanced Studies, University of Malaya.

Fischer, Michael M. J. 1980. *Iran: From Religious Dispute to Revolution.* Cambridge, Mass.: Harvard University Press.

Forest, A. 1980. *Le Cambodge et la colonisation française: Histoire d'une colonisation sans heurts (1897–1920).* Paris: Editions L'Harmattan.

Fujimura-Fanselow, Kumiko. 1985. "Women's Participation in Japanese Higher Education." *Comparative Education Review, 29* (4), 471–89.

———. 1989. "Japan." In Gail P. Kelly, ed., *International Handbook of Women's Education.* New York: Greenwood.

Fujita, Hidenori. 1989. "A Crisis of Legitimacy in Japanese Education—Meritocracy and Cohesiveness." In James J. Shields, Jr., ed., *Japanese Schooling—Patterns of Socialization, Equality, and Political Control.* University Park: Pennsylvania State University Press.

Gannicott, K. G., ed. 1990. *Education for Economic Development in the South Pacific.* Pacific Policy Paper 6. Canberra: National Centre for Development Studies, The Australian National University.

Gilley, J. W. 1991. *Thinking about American Higher Education.* New York: Macmillan.

Goh, C. T. 1991. "Tertiary Education: Where Do We Go from Here?" *Speeches, 15* (3), 8–11.

Goldman, M. 1992. "The Intellectuals in the Deng Xiaoping Era." in A. L. Rosenbaum, ed., *State and Society in Chinese: The Consequences of Reform.* Boulder, Colo.: Westview.

Goldman, M., T. Cheek, and C. L. Hamrin, eds. 1987. *China's Intellectuals and the State: In Search of a New Relationship.* Cambridge, Mass.: Harvard University Press.

Gonzalez, Andrew. 1989. "The Western Impact on Philippine Higher Education." In Philip G. Altbach and V. Selvaratnam, eds., *From Dependence to Autonomy: The Development of Asian Universities.* Dordrecht, The Netherlands: Kluwer Academic.

———. 1992. "Higher Education, Brain Drain and Overseas Employment in the Philippines: Towards a Differentiated Set of Solutions." *Higher Education, 23,* 21–31.

———. 1993a. "The Apostolate of the Mind in the Asian Setting: The Culture of Higher Education and Personnel." *Perspective, 13* (3) 12–17 and *Perspective 13* (4) 12–16. Philippines.

———. 1993b. "Identifying Research Priorities in the Philippines." *Tanglaw, 2* (1) 7–9.

Goodman, Roger. 1993. *Japan's "International Youth."* Oxford: Clarendon.

Gopinathan, S. 1989. "University Education in Singapore: The Making of a National University." In P. G. Altbach and V. Selvaratnam, eds., *From Dependence to Autonomy: The Development of Asian Universities.* Dordrecht: Kluwer Academic.

Griffin, K., and A. R. Khan, eds. 1972. *Growth and Inequality in Pakistan.* London: Macmillan.

Gyallay-Pap, P. 1989. "Reclaiming a Shattered Past: Education for the Displaced Khmer in Thailand." *Journal of Refugee Studies, 2,* 257–75.

Haas, M. 1991. *Genocide by Proxy: Cambodian Pawn on a Superpower Chessboard.* New York: Praeger.

Habir, Ahmad D. 1991. "The Development of Business Education in Indonesia." In Hill, Hall ed., *Indonesian Assessment 1991.* Canberra: Australian National University.

Habu, Mostyn. 1985. "The Impact of Scale, Isolation and Dependence on Educational Development: Solomon Islands." Paper presented at the Pan-Commonwealth Experts' Meeting on Educational Development for the Small States of the Commonwealth, Mauritius.

Haing Ngor. 1987. *A Cambodian Odyssey.* New York: Macmillan.

Hale, E. 1965. *The Financing of Universities in Hong Kong.* Hong Kong: Government Printer.

Hara, Kazuo. 1992. "Jugyo keikaku to jugyo hyoka" (Class Planning and Evaluation). *IDE, 332,* 5–13.

Harbison, G. H. 1973. *Human Resources as the Wealth of Nations.* London: Oxford University Press.

Harbison, G. H., and C. A. Myers. 1964. *Education, Manpower, and Economic Growth.* New York: McGraw-Hill.

———. 1969. "Strategies of Human Resource Development." In M. Blaug, ed., *Economics of Education.* Vol. 2. Harmondsworth: Penguin.

Haris, G. T. 1985. "Constraints on Research in Malaysian Universities." *Southeast Asian Journal of Social Science, 13* (2), 80–92.

Harrison, B. 1962. *University of Hong Kong: The First 50 Years.* Hong Kong: Hong Kong University Press.

Hayden, H. 1967. *Higher Education and Development in South-East Asia: Country Profiles.* Paris: UNESCO.

Hayes, A. C. 1993. "The Changing Demand for Children and Socio Economic Development in Nepal." Paper presented at the National Seminar on "Population and Sustainable Development in Nepal," March 22–26, Central Department of Population Studies, Tribhuvan University.

Hayhoe, Ruth. 1989. *China's Universities and the Open Door.* New York: M. E. Sharpe.

Helu, Futa. 1988. " 'Atenisi Institute and University." In Ron Crocombe and Malama Meleisea, eds., *Pacific Universities: Achievements, Problems and Prospects.* Suva: Institute of Pacific Studies, University of the South Pacific.

Heng, G., and J. Devan. 1992. "State Fatherhood: The Politics of Nationalism, Sexuality, and Race in Singapore." In A. Parker, M. Russo, D. Sommer, and P. Yaeger, eds., *Nationalisms and Sexualities.* New York: Routledge.

Hindson, Colin. 1987. "Educational Aid in the South Pacific: A Look at Priorities." *Directions, 9* (1), 26–41.

Hirschhorn, N., L. Haviland, and J. Salvo. 1991. *Critical Needs Assessment in Cambodia: The Humanitarian Issues.* Washington, D.C.: USAID.

Hong Kong Financial Times. 1994. July 20.

Huq, M. S., et al. 1980. *Higher Education and Employment in Bangladesh.* Paris: IIEP (International Institute for Educational Planning).

Hurtado, S. 1992. "Tribhuvan University: Challenges and Remedies." *Education and Development 1991–92.* Kathmandu: Centre for Educational Research Innovation and Development.

Husen, Torsten. 1991. "The Idea of the University: Changing Roles, Current Crisis, and Future Challenges." *Prospects, 21* (2), 171–88.

Hwang, Chung Kyu, et al. 1990. *Spotlight on North Korean Education.* Seoul: Bobmunsa.

Hwang, Kwang-Kuo. 1994. "In Search for the Primacy of Knowledge: On the Direction of Local Identity of the Social Sciences." In Oscar Jiaw Ouyang and Jenq-jye Hwang, eds., *The Idea of College Education* (in Chinese). Taipei: Lucky Books.

Indraratne, A. V. de S. 1992. *Economics of Higher Education in Sri Lanka.* New Delhi: Navrang.

International Labour Organization. 1971. *Matching Employment Opportunities and Expectations.* Geneva: Author.

International Monetary Fund. 1995. *World Economic Outlook.*

Ishida, Hiroshi. 1993. *Social Mobility in Contemporary Japan.* Stanford: Stanford University Press.

Islam, T. 1975. *An Analysis of Public Recurring Expenditure of Higher Education.* Dhaka: Government of Bangladesh, University Grants Commission.

The Japan–United States Educational Commission, Educational Information Service. 1992. *EIS Annual Report.*

Jasbir Sarjit Singh. 1989. "Scientific Personnel, Research Environment, and Higher Education in Malaysia." In Philip G. Altbach, ed., *Scientific Development and Higher Education.* New York: Praeger.

Jayaram, N. 1990. *Sociology of Education in India.* Jaipur: Rawat.

———. 1991. "Higher Education in India: State Policy and Social Constraints." *Higher Education Policy, 4,* 36–40.

———. 1992. "India." In Bruce S. Cooper, ed., *Labor Relations in Education: An International Perspective.* Westport, Conn.: Greenwood.

———. 1993a. "The Education-Employment Mismatch: A Sociological Appraisal of the Indian Experience." *International Perspectives on Education and Society, 3,* 123–43.

———. 1993b. "The Language Question in Higher Education: Trends and Issues." In Suma Chitnis and Philip G. Altbach, eds., *Higher Education Reform in India: Experience and Perspectives.* New Delhi: Sage.

Jayaweera, Swarna. 1984. "Access to Higher Education—The Social Composition of University Entrants." *University of Colombo Review, 1* (4), 6–40.

Jikhad-e Daneshgahi (University Crusade). 1990. *Daneshgah-e Enquelab* (The University of Revolution). Tehran: Ettela'at Foundation.

Johnson, Jean M. 1993. *Human Resources for Science and Technology: The Asian Region.* Surveys of Science Resources Series, Special Report, National Science Foundation, NSF 93–303, Washington, D.C.

Jones, David R., V. Lynn Meek, and John Weeks, eds. 1991. *Explorations in Higher Education: A South Pacific Critique.* Melbourne: Centre for the Study of Higher Education, University of Melbourne.

Josey, A. 1968. *Lee Kuan Yew.* Singapore: Donald Moore.

Joshi, R. K. 1990. "Education and Polity: A Historical Perspective." *Education and Development 1989–90.* Kathmandu: Centre for Educational Research Innovation and Development.

Kacimaiwai, Pamela. 1988. "Reaching the Off-Campus Majority." In Ron Crocombe and Malama Meleisea, eds., *Pacific Universities: Achievements, Problems and Prospects.* Suva: Institute of Pacific Studies, University of the South Pacific.

Kamal, Salih. 1992. "Economic Growth and Education Reform: Some Fundamental Issues of Education Policy." Paper presented at the "Seminar on Educational Restructuring and Economic Growth: Role of the Private Sector," November 3–4, Malaysian Institute of Economic Research, Kuala Lumpur, Malaysia.

Kamat, A. R. 1985. *Education and Social Change.* Bombay: Somaiya.

Kamishiro, Kazuyoshi. 1993. "Daigakusotsu no rodoichiba—genjo to tembo" (The Labor Market for University Graduates—Present Situation and Future Outlook). *IDE, 345,* 5–11.

Kansakar, T. R. 1993. "Setting Priorities for Budha Nilkantha School." *Rising Nepal,* September 26.

Karim, A. H. M. 1993. *Education in Bangladesh: A Status Report, March 1993.* Dhaka: World Bank, General Education Project.

Karthigesu, R. 1986. "Distribution of Opportunities in Tertiary Education in Malaysia: A Review of the Fifth Malaysia Plan." *Pendidik dan Pendidikan, 8,* 34–47.

Keyfitz, Nathan, and Mayling Oey Gardiner. 1988. *Autonomy for Indonesian Universities.* Mimeo.

Khan, Tajul Islam. 1988. "Financing Higher Education in Bangladesh." Regional Seminar on Mobilization of Additional Funding for Higher Education, Bangkok, August 22–27, UNESCO Principal Regional Office for Asia and the Pacific, Bangkok.

SELECTED BIBLIOGRAPHY

Khandker, Shahidur R., Mahmudul Alam, and Vincent Greaney. 1995. *The Determinants and Impact of Basic Skill Attainment: The Role of School and Targeted Credit Programs in Bangladesh.* Education and Social Policy Department, the World Bank and Bangladesh Institute of Development Studies.

Kiernan, B. 1985. *How Pol Pot Came to Power: A History of Communism in Kampuchea, 1930–1975.* London: Verso.

Kiljunen, K., ed. 1984. *Kampuchea: Decade of the Genocide.* London: Zed.

Kim, Chang Ho. 1990. *History of North Korean Education.* Pyongyang: Social Science Publishing.

Kim, Dong Kyu. 1990. *Pedagogy of North Korea.* Seoul: Mun Maek Sa.

Kim, Hyong Chan. 1990. *North Korean Education.* Seoul: Ulyoumunhwasa.

Kim, Il Sung. 1977. *Theses on Socialist Education.* Pyongyang, Korea: Foreign Languages Press.

Kim, Ransoo, and Yong Sop Ahn. 1993. "Higher Education in South and North Korea." *Higher Education Policy, 6,* (2), 29–36.

Kim, Sun-ho. 1990. "Kodung Kyoyuk" (Higher Education). In Kim Hyong-chan, ed., *Pukhan ui kyoyuk (North Korean Education).* Seoul: Uryu Munhwasa.

Kim, Tong-gyu. 1990a. "Kyoyuksa" (Educational History). In Kim Hyong-chan, ed., *Pukhan ui kyoyuk (North Korean Education).* Seoul: Ulyoumunhwasa.

———. 1990b. *Pukhan kyoyukhak (Pedagogy of North Korea).* Seoul: Munmaeksa.

Kingdom of Cambodia. 1993. *Phnom Penh University.* Phnom Penh: Author.

Kitamura, Kazuyuki. 1986. "The Decline and Reform of Education in Japan: A Comparative Perspective." In William K. Cummings et al., eds., *Educational Policies in Crisis.* New York: Praeger.

———. 1991. "The Future of Japanese Higher Education." In Edward R. Beauchamp, ed., *Windows on Japanese Education.* New York: Greenwood.

———. 1992. "Gakusei ni yoru jugyo hyoka" (Class Evaluation by Students). *IDE, 332,* 18–26.

Klitgaard, Robert. 1986. *Elitism and Meritocracy in Developing Countries: Selection Policies for Higher Education.* Baltimore: Johns Hopkins University Press.

Kobayashi, Shinichi. 1993. "Maker banare wa tomattaka" (Has the Trend Away from Manufacturing and Production Ceased?). *IDE, 345,* 46–51.

Koh, T. A. 1989. "Culture and the Arts." In K. S. Sandhu and P. Wheatley, eds., *Management of Success: The Moulding of Modern Singapore.* Singapore: Institute of Southeast Asian Studies.

Kokuritsu Fujin Kyoiku Kaikan. March 1991. *Heisei ninendo koto kyoiku kikan ni okeru joseigaku kanrenkoza kaisetsu jokyo chosa kekka hokoku* (Survey of Courses on Women's Studies and Related Subjects in Institutions of Higher Education in Japan [fiscal 1990]). Saitama-ken: Kokuritsu Fujin Kyoiku Kaikan (National Women's Education Centre).

Kosugi, Reiko. 1993. "Daisotsusha no ritenshoku" (Job-Changing among University Graduates). *IDE, 345,* 58–62.

Kumar, Krishna. 1987. "Reproduction or Change? Education and Elites in India." In Ratna Ghosh and Matthew Zachariah, eds., *Education and the Process of Change.* New Delhi: Sage.

Kwon, Hyuk Kie. 1991, Summer–Fall. *North Korea Quarterly* (61–62). Hamburg, Germany: Institute for Asian Affairs.

————. 1992. *President Kim Il Sung and Development of Education in Korea.* Pyong-yang: Kyowon Sinmun.

————. 1993. *Developments in North Korea.* Seoul: Naewon.

Lao, Wen-chi. 1994. "Retrospect on the Development of Taiwan's Higher Education in the Past Forty Years." In Oscar Jiaw Ouyang and Jenq-jye Hwang, eds., *The Idea of College Education* (in Chinese). Taipei: Lucky Books.

Laracy, Hugh, ed. 1989. *Ples Bilong Iumi: Solomon Islands, The Past Four Thousand Years.* Suva: Institute of Pacific Studies, University of the South Pacific.

Law, Wing Wah. 1995. "The Impact of Socio-Political Transition on Higher Education: Taiwan." Paper presented at the International Symposium on Education and Socio-Political Transition in Asia, May 29–31, University of Hong Kong.

Le, T. C. 1991. "Higher Education Reform in Vietnam, Laos, and Cambodia." *Comparative Education Review, 35,* 170–76.

Lee, Chung-gak. 1990. Pukhan ui kyoyuk chungchaek gwa hengchung mit kodung kyoyuk (Educational Policy, Administration and Higher Education of North Korea). In Chung Kyu Hwang, Chung Young-soo, Huh Suk, Lee Sung-ho, and Lee Chung-gak, eds., *Pukhan kyoyuk ui chomyong (Spotlight on North Korean Education).* Seoul: Pommunsa.

Lee, E. 1989. "The Colonial Legacy." In Kernial Singh Sandhu and Paul Wheatley, eds., *Management of Success: The Moulding of Modern Singapore.* Singapore: Institute of Southeast Asian Studies.

Lee, K. Y. 1977. "Higher Education: Abiding Commitment Essential." *Speeches, 1* (7), 7–37.

————. 1978. "Bilingualism and Higher Education in Singapore." *Speeches, 1* (9), 1–14.

————. 1980a. "Three Options for Nanyang University." *Speeches, 3* (10), 1–24.

————. 1980b. "NUS Must Be Innovative and Outward-looking." *Speeches, 3* (12), 10–29.

Lee, Molly N. N. 1994. "Private Education in Malaysia: Social Implications." *Education Journal, 21* (2) / 22 (1), 157–67.

Lee, Sung-Hwa. 1958. *The Social and Political Factors Affecting Korean Education, 1885–1950.* Unpublished Ph.D. diss., University of Pittsburgh.

Lee, Sungho H. 1987. *Curriculum Development in Korean Universities and Colleges* (in Korean). Seoul: Yonsei University Press.

————. 1992a. *Conflicts in Korean Higher Education* (in Korean). Seoul: Neutinamu.

————. 1992b. "The Academic Professor in Korea." Paper presented at the 8th World Congress of Comparative Education, Prague, Czechoslovakia.

Lin, Ching-chung. 1992. "A 3rd Survey on the Occupation Reputation and Professional Image of Teachers in ROC." In Chinese Comparative Education Association, ed., *A Comparison of Education on Both Sides of the Strait* (in Chinese). Taipei: Lucky Books.

Liu, Hsing-yi. 1993. "The Reason for Lecturing in *Hokkien* in My Class." In Yen-sheng Chang, ed., *Creating Taiwan's New Culture.* Taipei: Frontier.

Locard, H. 1993. *Social Sciences at the University of Phnom Penh.* Phnom Penh: Author.

Low, L. 1991. *The Political Economy of Privatization in Singapore: Analysis, Interpretation and Evaluation.* Singapore: McGraw-Hill.

Luciolli, E. 1988. *Le mur de bambou.* Paris: Médecins Sans Frontieres.

Luteru, Pa'o H. 1993. "Aid and Education in Small Systems: A South Pacific Perspective." In Kevin Lillis, ed., *Policy, Planning and Management of Education in Small States*. Paris: International Institute for Educational Planning.

Madsen, R. 1990. "The Spiritual Crisis of China's Intellectuals." In D. Davis and E. Vogel, eds., *Chinese Society on the Eve of Tiananmen: The Impact of Reform*. Cambridge, Mass.: Harvard University Press.

Maenu'u, Leonard. 1988. "Solomon Islands." In Ron Crocombe and Malama Meleisea, eds., *Pacific Universities: Achievements, Problems and Prospects*. Suva: Institute of Pacific Studies, University of the South Pacific.

Mak, G. C. L. 1991. "The Schooling of Girls in Hong Kong: Progress and Contradictions in the Transition." In Gerard A. Postiglione and Julian Y. M. Leung, eds., *Education and Society in Hong Kong: Toward One Country and Two Systems*. New York: M. E. Sharpe.

Mauch, J. E., and P. L. W. Sabloff, eds. 1995. *Reform and Change in Higher Education: International Perspectives*. New York: Garland.

McCall, Grant. 1984. "The University of the South Pacific: Context, Purpose and Prospect." *Vestes, 27* (2), 55–64.

Mehmet, Ozay, and Yip Yat Hoong. 1985. "An Empirical Evaluation of Government Scholarship Policy in Malaysia." *Higher Education, 14*, 197–210.

Mehran, Golnar. 1990. "Ideology and Education in the Islamic Republic of Iran." *Compare, 20*, 53–65.

———. 1991. "The Creation of the New Muslim Women: Female Education in the Islamic Republic of Iran." *Convergence, 24*, 42–52.

———. 1992. "Iran." In Peter W. Cookson, Alan R. Sadovnik, and Susan F. Semel, eds., *International Handbook of Education Reform*. Westport, Conn.: Greenwood.

Meyer, John W. 1980. "The World Polity and the Authority of the Nation-State." In A. Bergesen, ed., *Studies of the Modern World-System*. New York: Academic.

Monsell-Davis, Michael, and Som Naidu. 1989. "Reaching Out: Distance Teaching and Higher Education in the South Pacific." *International Journal of Educational Development, 9* (3), 183–94.

Morizon, R. 1931. *Monographie du Cambodge*. Hanoi: Imprimerie d'Extrême-Orient.

Murphy, Penelope. 1985. "UPNG as an Agent of Social Stratification: An Analysis of Output by Sex." In Mark Bray and Peter Smith, eds., *Education and Social Stratification in Papua New Guinea*. Melbourne: Longman Cheshire.

———. 1989. "Universities, Government Intervention and the Commission for Higher Education in Papua New Guinea." *International Journal of Educational Development, 9* (3), 175–82.

Murugasu, V. 1993. *Encouraging Private Sector Education Study (TA No. 1776–LAO)*. Manila, Philippines: Asian Development Bank.

Mysliwiec, E. 1988. *Punishing the Poor: The International Isolation of Kampuchea*. Oxford: Oxfam.

Nagai, Michio. 1971. *Higher Education in Japan: Its Take-off and Crash*. Tokyo: University of Tokyo Press.

Naik, J. P. 1982. *The Education Commission and After*. New Delhi: Allied.

Nakamura, Mitsuo, and Setsou Nishino. 1993. "Islamic Higher Education in Indonesia." *Higher Education Policy, 6* (2), 92–101.

Nakosteen, Mehdi. 1964. *History of Islamic Origins of Western Education, A.D. 800–1350*. Boulder, Colo.: University of Colorado Press.

Nash, Madeleine J. 1994. "Tigers in the Lab: Asian Born, U.S. Trained Researchers Are

Headed Home to Challenge the Technological Supremacy of the West." *Time* (International Edition), November 21, pp. 48–49.

Nasr, Seyyed Hossein. 1987. *Traditional Islam in the Modern World.* London: KPI, Ltd.

National University of Singapore. 1992. *1991 NUS and NTU Graduate Employment Survey.* Singapore: Author.

———. 1993. *1993–94 General Information.* Singapore: Author.

Neilsen, Dean. 1990. *A Review of Teacher Education Issues in Indonesia.* Improving the Efficiency of Educational Systems Project.

Nguyen Khac Vien. 1993. *A Long History.* Hanoi: Gioi.

Nguyen-vo, T. H. 1992. *Khmer-Viet Relations and the Third Indochina Conflict.* Jefferson, N.C.: McFarland.

Nishizawa, Yoshiyuki. 1992. "Ryugakusei gyosei no gendankai" (The Current Stage in Foreign Student Administration). *IDE, 335,* 54–60.

Népote, J. 1979. "Education et développement dans le Cambodge moderne." *Mondes en Développement, 28,* 767–92.

Osborne, M. E. 1969. *The French Presence in Cochinchina and Cambodia: Rule and Response (1859–1905).* Ithaca, N.Y.: Cornell University Press.

Ozaki, Hitoshi. 1992. "Gakujutsu kokusai koryu no hoko" (The Direction of International Exchange in Arts and Sciences). *IDE, 335,* 19–26.

Passin, Herbert. 1965. *Society and Education in Japan.* New York: Teachers College Press.

Pautler, Albert J., ed. 1994. *High School to Employment Transition: Comtemporary Issues.* Ann Arbor, Mich.: Prakken.

Pazargadi, Alaedin, trans. 1986. *Educational Revolution as Regarded by Imam Khomeini.* Tehran: Bonyad-e Be'that.

Pike, D. 1987. *Vietnam and the Soviet Union: Anatomy of an Alliance.* Boulder, Colo.: Westview.

Pin Yathay. 1987. *Stay Alive, My Son.* New York: Touchstone.

Pinto, Marina. 1984. *Federalism and Higher Education: The Indian Experience.* Bombay: Orient Longman.

Planning Commission, Government of India. 1992. *Eighth Five Year Plan, 1992–97.* Delhi: The Controller of Publications.

Ponchaud, F. 1978. *Cambodia Year Zero.* New York: Holt, Rinehart and Winston.

Postiglione, G. A. 1996. "Hong Kong's Academic Profession in a Period of Profound Change." In Philip Altbach, ed., *The Academic Profession in Higher Education: A Study of Fourteen Countries.* Princeton: The Carnegie Foundation for the Advancement of Teaching.

Postiglione, G. A., and J. Y. M. Leung. 1991. *Education and Society in Hong Kong: Toward One Country and Two Systems.* Armonk, N.Y.: M. E. Sharpe.

Postiglione, G. A., and T. H. Tang, eds. Forthcoming. *Hong Kong in the World Community: Internationalization at Risk?* Armonk, N.Y.: M. E. Sharpe.

Pradhan, G. S. 1992. *Universal Literacy—Challenges for the 1990s.* Kathmandu: CERID.

Pradhan, R. M. 1992. "Population and Education in Nepal." In Karki Chhetri Bal Kumar, ed., *Population and Development in Nepal.* CDPS, Tribhuvan University.

Puccetti, R. 1972. "Authoritarian Government and Academic Subservience: The University of Singapore." *Minerva, 10,* 223–41.

Quinlan, A. 1992. *Education Reform in Cambodia*. Master's thesis, University of London.

Ramirez, Francisco O., and Molly N. N. Lee. 1995. "Education, Science and Development." in Gerard A. Postiglione and W. O. Lee, eds., *Social Change and Educational Development: Mainland China, Taiwan and Hong Kong*. Hong Kong: Center of Asian Studies, University of Hong Kong.

Ramsey, G. 1991. "The Need for National Policies in Education." *Unicorn, 17* (1), 34–41.

Raza, Moonis, and Y. P. Aggalwal. 1991. "Higher Education in Contemporary India." In Moonis Raza, ed., *Higher Education in India*. New Delhi: Association of Indian Universities.

Raza, Moonis, et al. 1985. "Higher Education in India: An Assessment." In J. V. Raghavan, ed., *Higher Education in the Eighties*. New Delhi: Lancer International.

Regmi, M. P. 1987. "Historical Development of Psychology in Nepal." In G. H. Blowers and A. M. Turtle, eds. *Psychology Moving East. A Westview Special Study*. Boulder, Colo.: Westview Press.

Rhee, Dong Gun, and Su Il Choi. 1979. *Juche Ideology in the Ideological and Methodological Foundation of Socialist Education*. Pyongyang: Science Encyclopedia.

Rhee, Yong Bok. 1984. *Education in the Democratic People's Republic of Korea*. Pyongyang: Social Science Publishing.

Robie, David. 1989. *Blood on Their Banner: Nationalist Struggles in the South Pacific*. London: Zed.

Rosenbaum, A. L., ed. 1992. *State and Society in China: The Consequences of Reform*. Boulder, Colo.: Westview.

Saliq, 'Isa. 1975. *Tarikh-e Farhang-e Iran* (History of Iranian Culture). Tehran: Tehran University Press.

Salmi, Jamil. 1991. "The Higher Education Crisis in Developing Countries." Background Series. No. PHREE/91/37. Washington, D.C.: World Bank.

Sanyal, Bikas. 1990. *Changes in Higher Educational Management* (Notes). Paris: International Institute of Educational Planning, UNESCO.

Saw, S. H. 1990. *Changes in the Fertility Policy of Singapore*. Singapore: Times Academic.

Scalapino, Robert, ed. 1963. *North Korea Today*. New York: Praeger.

Scalapino, Robert, and Lee Chong-sik. 1972. *Communism in Korea*: Part 2, *The Society*. Berkeley: University of California Press.

Schattschneider, E. E. 1960. *The Semisovereign People: A Realist's View of Democracy in America*. New York: Holt, Rinehart, and Winston.

Schultz, T. W. 1960. "Capital Formation by Education." *Journal of Political Economy*, June.

———. 1963. *The Economic Value of Education*. New York: Columbia University Press.

Seah, C. M. 1983. *Student Admission to Higher Education in Singapore*. Singapore: Regional Institute of Higher Education and Development.

Selvaratnam, V. 1986. "Dependency, Change and Continuity in a Western University Model: The Malaysian Case." *Southeast Asian Journal of Social Science, 14* (2), 29–51.

———. 1988. "Ethnicity, Inequality, and Higher Education in Malaysia." *Comparative Education Review, 32* (2), 173–96.

Selvaratnam, V., and S. Gopinathan. 1984. "Higher Education in ASEAN Towards the Year 2000." *Higher Education, 13*, 67–83.

Sen, A. K. 1966. "Economic Approaches to Education and Manpower Planning." In *Indian Economic Review*, vol. 1. Reprinted in *Economics of Education*, vol. 2, ed. M. Blaug.

Shadan Hojin Nihon Shiritsu Daigaku Renmei. 1991. *Daigaku Kasseika e no Teigen* (Proposal for Activating Universities). Tokyo.

Sharifah Maimunah bt Syed Zin and Keith M. Lewin, eds. 1993. *Insights into Science Education: Planning and Policy Priorities in Malaysia*. Paris: IIEP (International Institute for Educational Planning).

Sharom, Ahmat. 1980. "Nation Building and the Universities in Developing Countries: The Case of Malaysia." *Higher Education, 9*, 721–41.

———. 1985. "The Relevance of the American Higher Education Model for Malaysia." In Philip G. Altbach, ed., *An Asean-American Dialogue: The Relevance of American Higher Education to Southeast Asia*. Singapore: RIHED.

Sherlock, Philip, and Rex Nettleford. 1990. *The University of the West Indies: A Caribbean Response to the Challenge of Change*. London: Macmillan.

Shiritsu Daigaku Renmei. 1991. *Daigaku kasseika e no teigen—kyoin jinji seido no kaizen ni mukete* (Proposals for Activating Universities—Toward an Improvement of the Faculty Personnel System). Tokyo: Shadan Hojin Shiritsu Daigaku Renmei.

Shirk, Susan. 1982. *Competitive Comrades: Career Incentives and Student Strategies in China*. Berkeley: University of California Press.

Singh, Amrik. 1988. "Introduction." In Amrik Singh and G. D. Sharma, eds., *Higher Education in India: The Social Context*. Delhi: Konark.

Singh, B. 1992. *Whither PAP's Dominance? An Analysis of Singapore's 1991 General Elections*. Petaling Jaya, Malaysia: Pelanduk.

Smith, R. M. 1965. *Cambodia's Foreign Policy*. Ithaca, N.Y.: Cornell University Press.

Snodgrass, Donald. 1991. "Indonesia." Mimeo. Harvard Institute of International Development.

Sobhe, Khosrow. 1982. "Education in Revolution: Is Iran Duplicating the Chinese Cultural Revolution?" *Comparative Education, 18*, 271–80.

Sohn, Insoo. 1987. *History of Korean Education* (in Korean). Seoul: Muneumsa.

Soltanzadeh, Hossein. 1985. *Tarikh-e Madares-e Iran* (History of Iranian Schools). Tehran: Agah.

Spaulding, Seth. 1990. "Educational Development and Reform on the Soviet Periphery: Mongolian People's Republic and Lao People's Democratic Republic." *Journal of Asian and African Affairs, 2* (1), 109–24.

Strauss, M. 1951. "Family Characteristics and Occupational Choice of University Entrants." *University of Ceylon Review, 1* (2), 125–35.

Strudwick, Jerry. 1991. *A Reverse Tracer Study of Graduates from the Faculties of Economics, Engineering, and Mathematics and Basic Sciences from the HEDS Project Institutions*. Vol. 1: *Tracer Study Report*. Arlington, Va.: Institution for International Research.

Sunarto, Kamanto. 1992. *Penyusunan Strategi Program Hibah Bersaing: Bidang Ilmu-Ilmu Sosial*. Jakarta: Universitas Indonesia.

Sunarto, Kamanto, et al. 1990. *Final Report: Study on the Impact Evaluation Study in Indonesia*. University of Indonesia Inter-University Center for Social Science.

Suryahti, A. L. 1993, May–June. "Contributing to the Global Society." *Singapore*.

Szyliowicz, Joseph S. 1973. *Education and Modernization in the Middle East*. London: Cornell University Press.

Takei, Kazuyoshi. 1992. "Nihon ryugaku fair" (Japan's Study Abroad Fair). *IDE, 335*, 31–36.

———. 1993. "Tokushu kurasu settchi de daigaku shingakusha ga kyuzo." *Asahi Shimbun*, September 20, p. 9.

Tan Jee-Peng, and Alain Mingat. 1992. *Education in Asia: A Comparative Perspective of Cost and Financing*. World Bank Regional and Sectoral Studies. Washington, D.C.: World Bank.

Tan Mui Hong. 1994. *Education Guide Malaysia*. Kuala Lumpur: Challenger Concept.

Tan, E. T. J. 1993. *Educational Underachievement of the Malay Minority in Singapore 1981–1992: Problems and Policies*. Unpublished master's diss., University of Hong Kong.

Teasdale, Robert. 1993. "Higher Education in Small Systems: A Pacific Island Perspective." In Kevin Lillis, ed., *Policy, Planning and Management of Education in Small States*. Paris: International Institute for Educational Planning.

Thapa, K. B. 1992. "Feudalism in Nepal: A Perspective of Socioeconomic History." *Tribhuvan University Journal*, June, 67–73.

Thomas, Murray. 1988. "The Islamic Revival and Indonesian Education." *Asian Survey, 28* (9).

Thomas, R. Murray. 1981. "Universal Eleven-Year Compulsory Education." *Indo-Korean Friendship, 12* (8–9).

———. 1983. "The Democratic People's Republic of Korea (North Korea)." In R. Murray Thomas and T. Neville Postlethwaite, eds., *Schooling in East Asia: Forces of Change*. New York: Pergamon.

Thomson, R. S. 1945. "The Establishment of the French Protectorate over Cambodia." *Far Eastern Quarterly, 4*, 313–40.

Throsby, C. D., ed. 1987. *Human Resources Development in the Pacific*. Pacific Policy Paper 3. Canberra: National Centre for Development Studies, The Australian National University.

Tickoo, Champa. 1980. *Indian Universities*. Madras: Orient Longman.

Todaro, M. P. 1977. *Economic Development in the Third World*. London: Longman.

Toh, C. C. 1973. "Intellectual Decolonization of the University of Singapore." In *Towards Tomorrow: Essays on Development and Social Transformation in Singapore*. Singapore: National Trades Union Congress.

Torhorst, M. 1966. "The Development of the Educational System in the Kingdom of Cambodia." In *Educational Systems of Some Developing Countries in Africa and Asia*. Dresden: Verlag Zeit Im Bild.

Treffgarne, C. 1986. "Language Policy in Francophone Africa: Scapegoat or Panacea?" In *Language in Education in Africa: Proceedings of a Seminar Held in the Centre of African Studies*. Edinburgh: Centre of African Studies.

Turnbull, C. M. 1989. *A History of Singapore 1819–1988*. 2nd ed. Singapore: Oxford University Press.

Uili, Tau'ili'ili. 1988. "Le Iunivesite Aoao O Samoa (Le IAOS)" (The National University of Samoa). In Ron Crocombe and Malama Meleisea, eds., *Pacific Universities: Achievements, Problems and Prospects*. Suva: Institute of Pacific Studies, University of the South Pacific.

UNESCO. 1988. *Higher Education and National Development in Four Countries: India,*

Bangladesh, Thailand and the Philippines. Bangkok: UNESCO Principal Regional Office for Asia and the Pacific.

————. 1991. *Inter-sectoral Basic Needs Assessment Mission to Cambodia.* Bangkok: Author.

————. 1994. *Rebuilding Quality Education and Training in Cambodia.* Phnom Penh: Author.

————. Various dates. *The Statistical Yearbook.* Paris: Author.

UNICEF. 1989. *Cambodia: The Situation of Women and Children.* Phnom Penh: Author.

Universiti Sains Malaysia. 1994. *Malaysia: Fact Sheets.* Penang: Woman and Human Resources Studies Unit, School of Social Sciences.

University Grants Commission. Various dates. Corporate Plan for University Education.

————. 1990. Statistical Handbook.

University of Indonesia. 1993. *Universitas Indonesia.* Jakarta: University of Indonesia.

U.S. Agency of International Development (USAID). 1993. *Executive Summary; Baseline Overview Report of Mathematics and Basic Sciences in the HEDS Level One Universities. Higher Education Development Support.* Jakarta, Indonesia.

————. 1995. "Cambodia." Gopher Document: U.S. Agency for International Development/Regional-Country Focus/Asia and the Near East/Cambodia/Congressional Presentation FY96/Cambodia.

Ushiogi, Morikazu. 1986. "Transition from School to Work: The Japanese Case." In William K. Cummings et al., eds., *Educational Policies in Crisis.* New York: Praeger.

Uswatte-Aratch, G. 1974. "University Admissions in Ceylon: Their Economic and Social Background and Employment Expectations." *Modern Asia Studies, 8* (3), 289–318.

Van Den Berg, Ewe, ed. 1991. *Science and Mathematics Education in Indonesia: An Introduction with Specific Recommendations for a Project to Support Science and Mathematics Programs at Selected Universities in Sumatra.* Washington, D.C.: Academy for Educational Development.

Van Den Bor, Wout, and James C. M. Shute. 1991. "Higher Education in the Third World: Status Symbol or Instrument for Development?" *Higher Education, 22,* 1–15.

Van Trease, Howard. 1990–91. "Distance Education at the University of Papua New Guinea: Issues and Developments." *Papua New Guinea Journal of Education 26* (2); 27 (1), 111–28.

Vasil, R. 1992. *Governing Singapore.* Singapore: Mandarin.

Vickery, M. 1984. *Cambodia: 1975–1982.* Boston: South End.

————. 1986. *Kampuchea: Politics, Economics and Society.* London: Pinter.

————. 1991. "Cambodia." In D. Allen and N. V. Long, eds., *Coming to Terms: Indochina, the United States, and the War.* Boulder, Colo.: Westview.

Vreeland, Nena. 1976. *Area Handbook for North Korea.* Washington, D.C.: Foreign Area Studies of American University.

Wang, Gungwu. 1970. "Malaysia: Contending Elites." In Wang Gungwu, ed., *Community and Nation: Essays on Southeast Asia and the Chinese.* Kuala Lumpur: Heinemann Educational Books (Asia).

————. 1992. "Universities in Transition." *Oxford Review of Education, 24,* 17–27.

Wasuka, Moffatt. 1989. "Education." In Hugh Laracy, ed., *Ples Bilong Iumi: Solomon*

Islands, The Past Four Thousand Years. Suva: Institute of Pacific Studies, University of the South Pacific.

Watts, K., C., Draper, D. Elder, J., Harrison, Y. Higaki, and J. C. Salle. 1989. *Kampuchea Needs Assessment Study.* United Nations Development Program.

Webster, Justin. 1994. "Success in Hong Kong: Universities Attract Top International Scholars Despite Concern about Colony's Future after 1997." *The Chronicle of Higher Education.*

Weidman, John C. 1995. "Diversifying Finance of Higher Education Systems in the Third World: The Cases of Kenya and Mongolia." *Education Policy Analysis Archives 3* (5).

Weinstein, B. 1976. "Francophonie: A Language-Based Movement in World Politics." *International Organization, 30,* 485–507.

———. 1980. "Language Planning in Francophone Africa." *Language Problems and Language Planning, 4,* 56–75.

———. 1985. "Francophonie: Purism at the International Level." Paper presented at the conference, "The Politics of Language Purism: A Rhetoric of Authentication," East-West Center, University of Hawaii, Honolulu.

Wendt, Albert. 1989. "Personal Reflections on the University of the South Pacific." *Papua New Guinea Journal of Education, 25* (2), 91–94.

Whitaker, D. P., J. M. Heimann, J. E. MacDonald, K. W. Martindale, R.-S. Shinn, and C. Townsend. 1973. *Area Handbook for the Khmer Republic (Cambodia).* Washington, D.C.: U.S. Government Printing Office.

Wilkinson, B. 1988. "Social Engineering in Singapore." *Journal of Contemporary Asia, 18,* 165–88.

Williams, P. 1992. "The UK Academic Audit Unit." in A. Craft, ed. 1992. *Quality Assurance in Higher Education.* London: Falmer.

Wilson, H. E. 1978. *Social Engineering in Singapore: Educational Policies and Social Change 1819–1972.* Singapore: Singapore University Press.

Wong, Suk-Ying, and Molly N. N. Lee. 1992. "Bridging the Formal and Non-Formal Mode: A Comparative Study of Distance Higher Education in Asia." Paper presented at the VIIIth World Congress of Comparative Education, July 8–14, Prague, Czechoslovakia.

World Bank. 1986. *Financing Education in Developing Countries: An Exploration of Policy Options.* Washington, D.C.: Author.

———. 1989. *Bangladesh Public Expenditure Review: Public Resources Management During the Fourth Five-Year Plan.* Washington, D.C.: Author.

———. 1991. *World Development Report, 1991.* New York: Oxford University Press.

———. 1992a. *Cambodia: Agenda for Rehabilitation and Reconstruction.* Washington, D.C.: Author.

———. 1992b. *Pacific Regional Post Secondary Education Study.* Washington, D.C.: Population and Human Resources Division, Author.

———. 1993a. *Policy Options for Higher Education Reform.* Washington, D.C.: Author.

———. 1993b. *The World Development Report.* Washington, D.C.: Author.

———. 1994a. *Lao People's Democratic Republic Country Economic Memorandum.* Report No. 12554–LA. Washington, D.C.: World Bank, Country Operations Division, Country Department I, East Asia and Pacific Region.

———. 1994b. *World Development Report 1994: Infrastructure for Development.* New York: Oxford University Press.

————. 1995a. *Bangladesh: Recent Economic Development and Priority Reform Agenda for Rapid Growth.* Washington, D.C.: Author.

————. 1995b. *Priorities and Strategies for Education: A World Bank Review*, Washington, D.C.: Author.

Wu, K. B. 1992. *Higher Education in Hong Kong.* Washington, D.C.: World Bank.

Wu, Wen-hsing, Shun-fen Chen, and Chen-tsou Wu. 1989. "The Development of Higher Education in Taiwan." *Higher Education, 18*, 117–36.

Yang, Key P., and Chang-boh Chee. 1963. "The North Korean Educational System: 1945 to Present." In Robert Scalapino, ed., *North Korea Today.* New York: Praeger.

Yeung, K. W. 1994. "The Need for International Cooperation in Vocational Training." Paper presented at the 21st General Meeting and ASAIHL (Association of Southeast Asian Institutions of Higher Learning) Seminar, December 2–4, Hong Kong.

Young, Mei Ling, and Ng Siew Kiat. 1992. "Balancing the Roles of Public and Private Sectors in Education and Training." Paper presented at the "Seminar on Educational Restructuring and Economic Growth: Role of the Private Sector," November 3–4, Malaysian Institute of Economic Research, Kuala Lumpur, Malaysia.

Young, Yi-rong. 1990. "Development through Education: Myth or Reality?" *International Journal of Educational Development, 10* (2–3), 227–30.

————. 1994. *Education and National Development: Experience of Taiwan* (in Chinese). Taipei: Laureate.

Zagoria, D. S. 1988. "The Soviet-Vietnamese Alliance." In J. J. Zasloff, ed., *Postwar Indochina: Old Enemies and New Allies.* Washington, D.C.: Foreign Service Institute, U.S. Department of State.

INDEX

Asian Development Bank, 102, 168, 169, 170, 171

Asian higher education: access and equity in, 176; colonial heritage in, xv-xvi; cultural traditions in, xv-xvi, xix; economic development role of, xvi, xviii, 1, 13; English language usage in, x; enrollment rates, xvi; finance, xvii-xviii; institutionalization of, 174; internationalization of, x, xvii; private initiatives in, x; rapid growth of, ix; research function of, ix; science and technology in, 10, 15, 174; socioeconomic context of, xviii-xix; state roles in, xix; Western models in, x-xi. *See also specific country*

Bangladeshi higher education, 1–17; admissions policy, 10; collaborative universities in, 15; curriculum and language of instruction in, 10–11; demographic and socioeconomic context in, 2–4; elitism in, 2, 4, 9–10; faculty, 14; finance, 6–10; governance and structure, 4, 8–9; and graduate unemployment, 12–13, 16–17; institutional typology in, 4–5; policy and planning, 5–8; private-sector in, 7–8, 15–16; re-

search function in, 14; student activism in, 11–12, 15; student enrollment and selection in, 5, 11; system hierarchy in, 10

Cambodian higher education, 21–32; access in, 30; communist dogma in, 27–28, 29; contemporary problems in, 30; French colonial system in, 22–23; geographic and demographic context of, 21–22; institutes, 24, 26–27, 29, 30, 31–32; Khmer Rouge destruction of, 25; language of instruction in, 24–25, 27, 29, 30; postoccupation developments in, 28–32; during Sihanouk regime, 23–25; tuition in, 30; during Vietnamese occupation, 25–28

Caston, Geoffrey, 257

Chinese higher education, 37–54; composition of, 39–40; Cultural Revolution policies of, 39, 50; curriculum, 45; decentralization trend in, 47–48; "Educational Revolution" of Great Leap Forward in, 38–39; enrollment and admissions policy, 40, 48–50; faculty, 50–54; finance and governance, 42–45; graduate prospects in, 50; historical development of, 38–50; institutional ty-

ABOUT THE EDITORS
AND CONTRIBUTORS

D. BADARCH is President of the Technical University of Mongolia. He holds a Ph.D. in Technical Science/Engineering.

REGESURIIN BAT-ERDENE is a graduate student at the University of Pittsburgh. He has worked as a Deputy Director for Higher Education in the Mongolian Ministry of Science and Education, and as a specialist on both the State Committee of Science, Technology and Higher Education and the State Committee of Higher and Specialized Secondary Education.

MARK BRAY is a Reader in the Department of Education of the University of Hong Kong. He is the author of many articles on educational finance, a specialist on education in small societies, and a consultant to several development agencies.

SHUN-FEN CHEN is Professor with the Center for Teacher Education, National Tsing-Hwa University. She is author of *Selection of University Presidents* (in Chinese). Before August 1996, she had taught at National Taiwan Normal University for seven years. During 1990–91, she was Visiting Scholar at the School of Education, University of Reading, England.

KOWSAR P. CHOWDHURY is a specialist on education, women, and development. She has been working with the World Bank as a consultant since 1991. She was Research Officer for the Second Primary Education Project conducted by the Ministry of Education, Bangladesh. Her areas of specialization are women's education, literacy, and alternative school systems.

BONG GUN CHUNG received his master's degree in political science from the University at Wisconsin-Madison. He is presently on leave from the Ministry of Education of Korea and is doing doctoral work in the Department of Educational Foundations at the University of Hawaii. His current research is on educational reform in South Korea.

THOMAS CLAYTON is on the faculty of the Department of Administrative and Policy Studies, School of Education, at the University of Pittsburgh. He established the State University of New York at Buffalo English Language Training Center in Phnom Penh, Cambodia, in 1991.

WILLIAM K. CUMMINGS is Director for the Center for Comparative and Global Studies in Education of the State University of New York at Buffalo. He has worked for many years in Indonesia on educational issues both with the Ford Foundation and as a consultant. Professor Cummings, who holds a Ph.D. from Harvard University, is interested in the academic profession, knowledge production, and the links between universities and clients.

DANG BA LAM is Professor and Director of the National Institute of Higher Education and Vocational Education in Hanoi, Vietnam.

KUMIKO FUJIMURA-FANSELOW received a Ph.D. in comparative education from Columbia University and is currently Professor of Education and Women's Studies at Toyo Eiwa Women's University in Tokyo. She is the coeditor of *Japanese Women: New Feminist Perspectives on the Past, Present, and Future* (1995). Her articles on Japanese higher education and women's education have appeared in such journals as *Comparative Education Review, Gender and History*, and *Gender and Education*. She has also contributed chapters to *International Handbook of Women's Education; Japanese Education; Patterns of Socialization, Equality, and Political Control; Windows on Japanese Education*; and *Women of Japan and Korea*.

OCHIR GEREL is Professor and Chair of the Department of Geology at the Technical University of Mongolia. He holds a D.Sci. degree in Technical Science/Geology.

ANDREW GONZALEZ is Professor of Languages and Literature at De La Salle University, Manila, Philippines. He was Executive Secretary of the Linguistics Society of the Philippines and editor of the *Philippine Journal of Linguistics* from 1971 to 1995 and has published extensively on Philippine sociolinguistics and national language development.

N. JAYARAM is Professor of Sociology at Bangalore University, India. Presently he is on deputation as Visiting Professor of Indian Studies at the Department of Sociology, University of the West Indies, St. Augustine, Trinidad. He is on the Steering Committee of the International Network on the Role of Universities in the Developing Areas (INRUDA). He has published widely on education in India, and his publications include *Higher Education and Status Retention* (1987) and *Sociology of Education in India* (1990).

SWARNA JAYAWEERA received her master's and doctoral degrees from the University of London and was a Postdoctoral Fellow at Columbia University, New York. She was Professor of Education and Head of the Department of Social Science Education at the University of Colombo. She was in turn UNESCO Advisor and UNICEF Consultant on the Access of Women to Education in Nepal and has been a consultant to UN agencies and bilateral agencies in Sri Lanka and in the Asian Region on education and on women's issues. She is a co-founder and currently Joint Coordinator of the Center for Women's Research in Sri Lanka. She has published extensively on women and on education.

SUNGHO H. LEE is Professor of Education at Yonsei University, Seoul, South Korea. He has worked in various capacities which included Dean of Students at Yonsei University, Vice-Chairman of the Presidential Commission on the 21st Century, and Assistant Minister of Education in the Ministry of Education, South Korea. He has published many books and articles largely on Korean higher education, and curriculum and instruction for school education, which include *Curriculum Development in Korean Universities and Colleges* (1987), *Conflict in Korean Higher Education* (1992), and *Korean Academic Professoriate* (1992).

MOLLY N. N. LEE is Associate Professor of Education at University of Sciences, Penang, Malaysia. She teaches sociology of education and science teaching methods courses. Her research interests are science education, teacher education, and comparative education. She has written a number of articles on education in Malaysia concerning higher education, private education, science education, teacher education, school curriculum, and language policies.

GRACE C. L. MAK is Associate Professor in the Department of Educational Administration and Policy of the Chinese University of Hong Kong. She has published on education and development in China and Hong Kong, and is editor of *Women, Education, and Development in Asia* (1996). She is also the Vice-President of the Comparative Education Society of Hong Kong.

MANASSE MALO is Director of the Inter-University Center for the Social Sciences at the University of Indonesia. Professor Malo, who holds a Ph.D. from the University of Wisconsin, works on educational issues and urban problems. He is also Vice-President of the Indonesian Sociological Association.

GOLNAR MEHRAN is Assistant Professor of education at Al-Zahra University, Tehran, Iran. Her main research interests are education in the Middle East, female education, and literacy training in the Third World. She is the author of various articles on postrevolutionary educational transformation in Iran, including "Socialization of School Children in the Islamic Republic of Iran," *Iranian Studies* 22:35–50; "The Creation of the New Muslim Woman: Female Education in the Islamic Republic of Iran," *Convergence* 24:42–52; and "Social Implications of Literacy in Iran," *Comparative Education Review* 36:194–211.

WEIFANG MIN is Vice President of Peking University and Director of its Institute of Higher Education. He earned his doctorate from Stanford University and has published many articles on economics of education. He is a regular consultant for the World Bank's educational projects.

YUOK NGOY is Vice Dean of the Faculty of Law and Economics Sciences in Phnom Penh, Cambodia. Before assuming his current duties, he held positions in the Ministry of Education's Department of Higher and Technical Education and at the Institute of Economics.

GERARD A. POSTIGLIONE is Associate Professor in the Department of Education of the University of Hong Kong and Director of its Advanced Studies in Education and National Development program. His last book, co-edited with Lee Wing On, is entitled *Social Change and Educational Development: Mainland China, Taiwan, and Hong Kong*. Dr. Postiglione, who holds a Ph.D. from the State University of New York at Albany, is ex-President of the Comparative Education Society of Hong Kong.

GAY GARLAND REED received her M.Ed. and Ph.D. from the University of Virginia and is an Assistant Professor in the Department of Educational Foundations at the University of Hawaii. Most of her research has focused on moral/political education in the People's Republic of China and on issues related to cultural values and education.

MURARI PRASAD REGMI was born in Nepal. He earned a Ph.D. in psychology from the University of Saugar, India, in 1982, and received advanced training in psychology in Free University, Berlin, Germany. He is Reader and Head of the Department of Psychology at the Tribhuvan University in Kathmandu, Nepal. He is the author of *The Gurungs: Thunder of Himal* and is co-author of *Psychology Moving East* (1987). He has published articles in international journals, and nine books in psychology and four in literature. His research focused on moral reasoning, learning process, and self-esteem of university students in Nepal.

KAMANTO SUNARTO is Associate Director of Graduate Studies at the University of Indonesia. Professor Sunarto, who holds a Ph.D. from the University of Wisconsin, has written extensively on Indonesian higher education.

ENG THYE JASON TAN is Lecturer in the Division of Policy and Management Studies, National Institute of Education, Singapore. He has published several articles on school privatization initiatives in Singapore and minority educational achievement in Singapore.

JOHN C. WEIDMAN is Professor and former Chairman of the Department of Administrative and Policy Studies in the School of Education at the University of Pittsburgh, where he is also a Senior Associate in the Institute of International Studies in Education. He has held the UNESCO Chair of Higher Education Research in the Institute of Research and Postgraduate Studies at Manseno University College in Kenya (Fall 1993); has been a Fulbright Scholar and Visiting Professor of Sociology of Education on the Philosophical Faculty I of Augsburg University in Germany (Winter Semester, 1986–87); and has worked on Asian Development Bank projects in Mongolia (1993) and Laos (1994–95).

ISBN 0-313-28901-8

HARDCOVER BAR CODE